PROGRAMMING
LANGUAGES
DESIGN
AND IMPLEMENTATION

TERRENCE W. PRATT

Department of Computer Sciences
Computation Center
University of Texas at Austin

PRENTICE-HALL, INC.
Englewood Cliffs, N. J.

Library of Congress Cataloging in Publication Data

PRATT, TERRENCE W.
  Programming languages: design and implementation.

  Bibliography
  1. Programming languages (Electronic computers)
I. Title.
QA76.7.P7   001.6'424   74-16114
ISBN 0-13-730432-3

For

Kirsten, Randy, and Laurie

15 14 13 12 11

Printed in the United States of America.

PRENTICE-HALL INTERNATIONAL, INC., London
PRENTICE-HALL OF AUSTRALIA, PTY. LTD., Sydney
PRENTICE-HALL OF CANADA, LTD., Toronto
PRENTICE-HALL OF INDIA PRIVATE LIMITED, New Delhi
PRENTICE-HALL OF JAPAN, INC., Tokyo

CONTENTS

3   Data   *40*

4   Operations   *98*

5   Sequence Control   *122*

15 SNOBOL4   *443*

16 APL   *475*

17 Epilogue: The Turing Language and Language Universality   *500*

PREFACE

Computer programming language design and the interplay between language design and implementation are the two central concerns of this book. The design and implementation of programming languages, during the relatively brief span since the first version of FORTRAN in the mid-1950's, has been more art than science. The underlying principles have always been vague at best, and the accumulation of accepted design alternatives has been far slower than one might expect considering the hundreds of programming languages that have come into existence during the period. The central goal of this book is to bring together the various facets of language design and implementation within a single conceptual framework. The most difficult problem has been to find a framework with both the breadth to encompass the concepts in a wide variety of languages and the depth to allow the relationships among variants of the same concept in different languages to be clearly seen. The result of this endeavor is found in Part I of this book, in which many of the concepts in programming languages are identified, discussed, and implementation techniques presented. In Part II seven of the most widely used programming languages are described individually in terms of the concepts developed in Part I. The book is intended both as a text for an undergraduate or beginning graduate survey course on programming languages and as a useful reference to concepts, terminology and languages for practicing programmers.

Part I is organized in the following manner. Chapter 1 develops some of the motivation for the study of programming language design and implementation. Chapter 2 outlines the basic approaches to language implementation. Chapters 3 through 7 form the core of the book, developing the key concepts in the four areas of *data*, *operations*, *control structures*, and *storage management*. Chapter 8 fills out the treatment with a brief discussion of the *operating environment* of a language. *Syntax*, which often makes up a major part of discussions about programming languages, plays a lesser role here. Chapters 3 through 8 are concerned primarily with *semantic structures* and *run-time representations* in languages. Syntax enters only occasionally as a topic of interest, although many examples of various syntactic constructs in languages are found in these chapters. Chapter 9 considers directly the topic of syntax and its effect on language structure and translator design.

Topic selection has been a major problem throughout Part I. What are the key concepts in programming languages? Those selected here have seemed most central, but inevitably some topics have been slighted, and some have been altogether omitted. Doubtless few readers will find the selection entirely to their liking. In an area where there is so little agreement on general principles this cannot be helped. Nevertheless perhaps the overall breadth and balance of the treatment may serve to outweigh somewhat its deficiencies in particular topic areas.

The choice of languages to include in Part II has been even more difficult. Two major criteria have guided the selection: widespread use and diversity of concept. On the one hand, inclusion of the most widely used languages has seemed a necessity if the book is to have value as a text and reference; on this basis I have been guided toward the older, more well established languages: ALGOL 60, FORTRAN and COBOL. On the other hand, variety of language design concept is also to be desired if the languages are to exemplify as many of the concepts of Part I as possible. On this basis I have included the list processing language LISP, the string processing language SNOBOL4, and the interactive language APL. PL/I was chosen both because of the new concepts it contains, and because it is the most widely used general purpose language. Many other languages besides these seven were considered for inclusion, but ultimately restrictions of space and time narrowed the choice. In actual fact the choice of languages should not be too significant, for the intent in Part I is to build a framework for the analysis of languages which is applicable by the reader to whatever language he is using or may later encounter. Part II shows how the analysis might be done in seven specific cases, but hopefully the reader will attempt the same sort of analysis to further his understanding of other languages.

As a text

The book is intended as an upper division undergraduate text for a one semester course in programming languages and data structures (such as the course I2 in the ACM Curriculum 68). It is suitable as a beginning graduate text with some supplementary material from the literature. Since it presumes only an elementary background —knowledge of at least one high-level language and a basic knowledge of machine organization and assembly language programming—it could also be used as a lower division undergraduate text by suitable choice of topics.

A survey course on programming languages and data structures is difficult to teach because of the multiplicity of language and implementation concepts which might be treated. There are dozens of languages in fairly wide use, each with its own set of concepts and implementation techniques. How is one to survey this diversity without the result being simply a hodge-podge of unrelated detail? The answer provided by this book is found in the conceptual framework of Part I. The study of a language is organized around the central areas of data, operations, sequence control, data control, storage management, operating environment, and syntax. Part II provides example analyses of seven of the most widely used programming languages. Each chapter provides references for further reading and problems involving, for the most part, application of the concepts to new situations.

There are two different approaches that might be used in a course organized around this material. The simplest approach is to take Part I more or less sequentially, with the instructor providing examples from particular languages to illustrate the material more fully as appropriate. I have found this approach successful with more mature students in a beginning graduate course. At this level the text was supplemented with readings in the literature, and class discussion concentrated on the more complex concepts in the text. The course involved no programming problems—the emphasis was entirely on design questions.

The alternative approach, which I have used at the junior level with students having only two previous computer science courses, is to work back from the languages to the concepts. The instructor chooses three to five of the languages in Part II, including at least one that the entering students have already used. The text is supplemented by the usual manuals for these languages, and the students write elementary programs in each language as the course progresses. The appropriate chapters in Part II, beginning with the chapter on the known language, are taken up after an initial quick pass through Part I. As the concepts in each of the chosen languages are developed and contrasted, the relevant sections of Part I are brought in to provide the necessary depth to support the discussion. By staying close to particular languages, which the student is at the same time applying in practical programming exercises, proper motivation is provided for the study of the general concepts of Part I. The choice of exactly which languages to study in depth is dependent on three factors: the background of the students entering, the languages available on the computer at hand, and the interests of the instructor. It has been my experience that for the undergraduate student a detailed study of a language loses its interest and effectiveness unless coupled with the opportunity to write and run programs in the language at the same time. The organization of the text should allow considerable flexibility in the choice of languages to meet local situations. At the end of the course, if time permits, a particularly useful larger project is to have the student learn and analyze a locally available language that is not described in Part II.

Acknowledgements

This book is based largely on experience in teaching programming language concepts at the University of Texas at Austin. A number of people have contributed to the book through their thoughtful reviews of the manuscript: Jeffery Ullman, Ralph Griswold, Saul Rosen and Daniel Friedman. The students in my classes who suffered through early versions of these notes and provided numerous suggestions also contributed. Ann Patterson was responsible for the typing of much of the manuscript. My wife, Ruthie, typed a number of the remaining chapters and endured many evenings and weekends while the book was in preparation. My thanks to all of these people, and to the Department of Computer Sciences and the Computation Center of the University of Texas for their support during this work.

T.W.P.

Austin, Texas

PART **|** CONCEPTS

1 THE STUDY OF PROGRAMMING LANGUAGES

Any notation for the description of algorithms and data structures may be termed a *programming language*, although we usually also require that a programming language be implemented on a computer. The sense in which a programming language may be "implemented" on a computer is considered in the next chapter. In the remainder of Part I the design and implementation of the various components of a language are considered in detail. Part II illustrates the application of the concepts in the design of seven major programming languages: FORTRAN, ALGOL 60, COBOL, PL/I, LISP 1.5, SNOBOL4, and APL. However, before approaching the general study of programming languages, it is worth considering the possible value of such a study to a computer programmer.

1-1. WHY STUDY PROGRAMMING LANGUAGES?

Hundreds of different programming languages have been designed and implemented. Sammet [1969] lists 120 which have been fairly widely used, and almost every computer installation of any size has others which are unique to that center. This plethora of languages stands in confusing contradiction to the fact that most programmers never venture to use more than a few languages, and many confine their programming entirely to one or two languages. In fact many practicing programmers work at computer installations where use of a particular language such as PL/I, COBOL, or FORTRAN is required. What is to be gained by study of a variety of different languages if it is unlikely that one will ever have occasion to use them?

2

In fact there are excellent reasons for such a study, provided that you go beneath the superficial consideration of the "features" of languages and delve into the underlying design concepts and their effect on language implementation. Five primary reasons come immediately to mind:

1. *To improve your understanding of the language you are using.* Many languages provide an often bewildering myriad of features which when used properly are of benefit to the programmer but which when used improperly may eat up large amounts of computer time unnecessarily or lead the programmer into tedious and time-consuming logical errors. Even a programmer who has used a language for years may never use some features and may only poorly understand others, a situation that is often aggravated by confusing language manuals which necessitate trial-and-error prc-gramming to discover exactly how a particular feature works. A typical example is found in the use of recursion. Recursion is a handy programming feature available in many languages, but it is usually expensive in execution time. When properly used it may allow the direct implementation of elegant and efficient algorithms, but in other cases it may cause an astronomical increase in execution time for a simple algorithm. Moreover, the cost of recursion varies depending on the language implementation. The programmer who knows nothing of the design questions and implementation difficulties which recursion implies is likely to shy away from this somewhat mysterious construct. However, a basic knowledge of the principles and implementation techniques behind recursion allows the programmer to understand the relative cost of the construct in a particular language and from this understanding to determine whether the extra cost of recursion is warranted in a particular programming situation. Alternatively, if you are using a language such as FORTRAN or COBOL in which recursion is not allowed, an understanding of the design and implementation difficulties of recursion may clarify what otherwise appears as a rather arbitrary language restriction.

2. *To increase your vocabulary of useful programming constructs.* It has often been noted in studies of human thinking that language serves both as an aid to thinking and a constraint. Properly, a person uses a language to express what he is thinking, but it is equally true that language serves to structure how one thinks, to the extent that it is difficult to think in ways which allow no direct expression in words. Familiarity with a single programming language tends to have a similar constraining effect. In searching for data and program structures suitable to the solution of a problem, one tends

to think only of structures which are immediately expressible in the languages with which one is familiar. By studying the constructs provided by a wide range of languages, and the manner in which these constructs are implemented, a programmer increases his programming "vocabulary." The understanding of implementation techniques is particularly important, because in order to use a construct while programming in a language that does not provide it directly, the programmer necessarily must provide his own implementation of the new construct in terms of the primitive elements actually provided by the language. For example, the subprogram control structure known as *coroutines* is useful in many programs, but few languages provide a coroutine feature directly. A FORTRAN programmer, however, may readily simulate a coroutine structure in a set of FORTRAN programs if he is familiar with the coroutine concept and its implementation, and in so doing may be able to provide just the right control structure for a large program.

3. *To allow a better choice of programming language.* Of course, when the situation arises, a knowledge of a variety of languages may allow choice of just the right language for a particular project, thereby reducing the required coding effort enormously. For example, FORTRAN or COBOL programmers are often faced with the need to write a program to do some minor string processing, e.g., reformatting some improperly formatted input data. Such a program may be used only once or a few times. Coded in FORTRAN or COBOL the program might be tedious and time-consuming to write, but written in the string-processing language SNOBOL4 it might require only a few minutes and a dozen lines to code. The programmer with a knowledge of SNOBOL4 is at a decided advantage.

4. *To make it easier to learn a new language.* A linguist, through a deep understanding of the underlying structure of natural languages, is often able to learn a new foreign language quickly and relatively easily compared to the struggling novice who understands little of the structure even of his native tongue. Similarly, a thorough knowledge of a variety of programming language constructs and implementation techniques allows the programmer to more easily learn a new programming language when the need arises. Moreover, because of his greater depth of understanding, the programmer is likely to immediately see more clearly how the language is *properly* used—which constructs are costly to use and which are relatively cheap.

5. *To make it easier to design a new language.* Few programmers ever think of themselves as language designers, yet all are. The input data formats for any program in fact define a programming language (an idea explored in greater depth in the next chapter). Although for most programs this *input data language* is relatively trivial, it is characteristic of larger programming projects that the input data language increasingly takes on the character of a true programming language, containing declarations, statements, expressions, etc. The programmer who is aware of the concepts and pitfalls in programming language design and of the techniques for language implementation has a better foundation for the proper design of input data languages, even if he never in fact designs what is ordinarily termed a programming language. For example, the design and implementation of a computer operating system usually also involves the design and implementation of a *job control language* which is used to communicate with the operating system routines. Many of the same constructs and design criteria which apply to ordinary programming languages also apply to the design of a job control language.

From this discussion it should be apparent that there is much more to the study of programming languages than simply a cursory look at the features provided by a variety of languages. In fact, many similarities in features among languages are deceiving—the same feature in two different languages may be implemented in two very different ways, and thus the two versions may differ greatly in the cost of use. For example, almost every language provides an addition operation as a primitive, but the cost of performing an addition in, e.g., FORTRAN and SNOBOL4 may vary by an order of magnitude. The study of programming languages must necessarily include the study of implementation techniques, particularly techniques for the run-time representation of different constructs, as well as the study of the interplay between the binding times of various program and data elements and the run-time structures required. It is the run-time structures which largely determine the cost of using a given language construct. The run-time structures are also those which a programmer needs to know in order to program a construct into a language which does not contain it.

The emphasis on implementation structures in this book is somewhat in conflict with a much more prevalent view that language descriptions should be *implementation-independent*; i.e., the programmer should be unaware of the underlying run-time structures used in the language implementation. The latter view is characteristic of most language manuals and texts in which a language is described as a collection of features—data types, operators, statement types, etc.—which the programmer may combine into programs according to certain specified rules. Implementation-independent descriptions are of value to the beginner or the occasional user of a programming language, but a serious programmer who intends to make more than casual use of a language needs the depth provided by an understanding of the language implementation.

In Parts I and II of this book numerous language constructs are discussed, accompanied in almost every case by a design for the implementation of the construct on a conventional computer. Where the implementation techniques are fairly standard, only a single technique may be mentioned. In more complex cases more than one technique may be suggested, and often the problems suggest further alternatives. However, no attempt has been made to be comprehensive in covering possible implementation methods. The same language or construct, if implemented on the reader's local computer, may differ radically in cost or detail of structure when different implementation techniques have been used or when the underlying computer hardware differs from the simple conventional structure assumed here.

1-2. WHAT MAKES A GOOD LANGUAGE?

The design of high-level programming languages has yet to be perfected. Each of the languages in Part II has many shortcomings. The programmer, faced with the task of choosing a language appropriate to a given problem solution, needs to be able to evaluate the strengths and weaknesses of a language. What should he look for? In part the answer depends on the type of problem, the expected size of the program, its likely uses, and the number of people involved. However, some general guidelines are apparent.

Of the seven languages described in Part II, FORTRAN, LISP, ALGOL 60, and COBOL have been in wide use since the early 1960s; APL, SNOBOL4, and PL/I are more recently designed but have quickly attracted a substantial group of users. Each of these languages might be classified as "successful," yet the reasons for the success of each seem different. During the same time period, many tens or hundreds of other languages have been designed, implemented, and used for some period of time and then have fallen into disuse. One may equally question the reasons for their demise.

In part the reasons for the success or failure of a language tend to be external to the language itself. For example, part of the reason for the success of COBOL in the United States may be laid to governmental regulations for its use in certain areas of programming directed by government agencies. Likewise, part of the reason for the success of FORTRAN and PL/I may be attributed to the strong support of various computer manufacturers who have expended large amounts of money and manpower in providing sophisticated implementations and extensive documentation for these languages. The success of SNOBOL4 may be due in part to an excellent early text describing the language (Griswold et al. [1971]).

ALGOL 60 and LISP have benefited from their use as objects of theoretical study by students of language design as well as from actual practical use.

The task of implementing a language on a given computer is almost always a major one. Preparation, testing, documentation, and maintenance of a language implementation require man-years of labor for any language of substantial complexity. Reimplementation of a language on a new computer may tax the resources of any computing center, and thus languages often fall into disuse as computer installations move to new machines.

In spite of the major influence of some of these external reasons for a language's success, or lack of it, it is the programmer who ultimately, if sometimes indirectly, determines which languages live and die. Many reasons might be suggested to explain why programmers prefer one language over another. Let us consider some of these.

1. *Clarity, simplicity, and unity of language concept.* A programming language provides both a conceptual framework for thinking about algorithms and a means of expressing those algorithms for machine execution. The language should be an aid to the programmer long before he reaches the actual coding stage in programming. It should provide him with a clear, simple, and unified set of concepts that he can use as primitives in developing algorithms. To this end it is desirable to have a minimum number of different concepts, with the rules for their combination being as simple and regular as possible. Subtle and capricious language constraints should be avoided, and of course the language must be unambiguous. It is this semantic clarity, this clarity of concept, which seems the most significant determiner of the value of a language.

2. *Clarity of program structure.* Closely related to but quite different from the idea of semantic clarity of a language is the concept of syntactic clarity of programs written in the language. The syntax of a language greatly affects the ease with which a program

may be written, tested, and later understood and modified. Many languages contain syntactic constructions which are likely to lead to programmer errors. At best such constructions lead to trivial syntax errors caught during translation, e.g., the use of a comma after the statement number in a FORTRAN DO statement. At worst they generate statements which are correct syntactically but mean something radically different. For example, in SNOBOL4 the presence or absence of a single blank character in a statement often radically changes the meaning. A language should have the property that constructs which *mean* very different things *look* different; i.e., semantic differences should be mirrored syntactically. Additionally, it is extremely useful to allow minor but obvious variations in the way a statement is written, as is done to a large extent in COBOL.

More important to the programmer than a syntax which is simply not misleading or error-prone is a syntax which when properly used allows the program structure to reflect the underlying logical structure of the algorithm. In the approach to good program design known as *structured programming*, programs are designed hierarchically from the top down (main program to lowest-level subprograms) using only a restricted set of control structures at each level—simple statement sequences, iterations, and certain kinds of conditional branching. When properly done the resulting algorithm structures are easy to understand, debug, and modify. Ideally it should be possible to translate such a program design directly into appropriate program statements which reflect the structure of the algorithm. Often, however, the language syntax does not allow such a direct encoding. For example, FORTRAN relies heavily on statement labels and GOTO statements as control structures and provides few alternatives. As a result the form of a FORTRAN program cannot ordinarily be made to reflect very clearly the control structure of the underlying algorithm, and much of the effort expended in developing a properly structured algorithm is likely to be lost in the translation into FORTRAN code. This is part of the basis for the "GOTO controversy" (see Section 5-3). One of the major arguments favoring ALGOL over FORTRAN in the teaching of introductory programming, in spite of the much wider practical use of FORTRAN, is that ALGOL encourages elegant program design far more than FORTRAN.

Clarity of program structure provides many benefits for the programmer. When the structure of the program reflects the structure of the underlying algorithm then the program immediately becomes easier to write, debug, modify, and understand. A nicely designed algorithm may be completely obscured if the syntax of the programming language forces it into an unnatural mold.

3. *Naturalness for the application.* The language should provide appropriate data structures, operations, control structures, and a natural syntax for the problem to be solved. One of the major reasons for the proliferation of languages is just this need for naturalness. A language particularly suited (in both syntax and semantics) to a certain class of applications may greatly simplify the creation of individual programs in that area. Often if a major amount of programming in a particular area is contemplated, it may be an extremely useful first step to design and implement a programming language just for that class of applications. COBOL, for business applications involving file handling, and SNOBOL4, for string processing, are two languages in Part II with an obvious slant toward particular (although very large) classes of applications.

4. *Ease of extension.* A substantial part of the programmer's task in constructing any large set of programs may be viewed as *language extension.* Having decided on the data structures, operations, etc., needed for the problem solution he must then decide how to simulate these structures using the more primitive features provided by the actual programming language, thus conceptually extending the original language to include the simulated structures. In this regard the properties of the base language may substantially aid or hinder these extensions. The language should allow extension through simple, natural, and elegant mechanisms. Almost all languages provide subprogram definition mechanisms for this purpose, but most languages are otherwise rather notably weak in this area.

5. *External support.* The technical structure of a programming language and its implementation is only one aspect affecting its utility. A long list of other external factors determine whether a particular language may be effectively utilized in a particular application. The activity of constructing a large set of interrelated programs involves more than just designing and coding; programs must also be stored, tested, modified, and ultimately made available for use. Such facilities are seldom part of the language itself (but see Chapter 16 on APL). More commonly they are provided by the operating system if supported by the computer system at all. If supported by a strong array of facilities for program testing, editing, storage, and the like, a technically weak language may be easier to work with than a stronger language without the external support. The presence of complete and usable documentation and a tested and error-free implementation are also strong determinants of the utility of a language.

An important question in many large programming tasks is that of the *transportability* of the resultant set of programs. A language which is widely available and whose definition is independent of the features of a particular machine forms a useful base for the production of transportable programs. SNOBOL4 and COBOL are two languages whose success in part has been based on an appeal to transportability.

6. *Efficiency.* The tricky criterion of efficiency has been left for last. Efficiency is certainly a major element in the evaluation of any programming language, yet there is a variety of different measures of efficiency:

a. *Efficiency of program execution.* In the earlier years of computing, questions of efficiency were almost exclusively directed toward efficiency of program execution. Research on the design of optimizing compilers, efficient register allocation, and the design of efficient run-time support mechanisms was important. Efficiency of program execution, although always of some importance in language design, is of primary importance for large production programs which will be executed many times.

b. *Efficiency of program translation.* When a language like FORTRAN or ALGOL 60 is used in teaching, the question of efficient translation (compilation) rather than efficient execution may be paramount. Typically, student programs are compiled many times while being debugged but are executed only a few times. In such a case it is important to have a fast and efficient compiler rather than a compiler which produces optimized executable code.

c. *Efficiency of program creation, testing, and use.* Yet a third aspect of efficiency in a programming language is exemplified by the language APL. For a certain class of problems a solution may be designed, coded, tested, modified, and used in APL with a minimum waste of programmer's time and energy. In a very real sense APL may be said to be efficient in that the overall time and effort expended in solving a problem on the computer is minimized. It is probably fair to say that this sort of overall efficiency in use of a language has come to be as important a concern in many cases as the more traditional concern with efficient program execution or compilation.

1-3. A NOTE ON TERMINOLOGY

Many technical terms related to programming languages and language implementations lack a generally accepted definition. Often the same term has been used by different writers to name a variety of concepts, e.g., the term *interpreter*, or alternatively, the same concept has been denoted by a variety of different terms, e.g., the data structure termed a *stack* here, which has been also called a *pushdown list* and *LIFO* (last-in-first-out) *list*. In this book standard terminology has been adopted wherever possible. For example, the term *stack* now seems the most generally accepted term for that type of data structure. In cases where there seems to be little agreement on a standard definition, however, as, for example, with the term *interpreter*, a precise definition is adopted for the purposes of this text (see, for example, the definition of *interpreter* in Chapter 2), maintaining what seems to be the major denotation of the term insofar as possible. The reader should exercise due caution with terms for which he approaches the text with a preconceived definition.

A more difficult problem concerns concepts for which there is no generally accepted terminology at all. In these relatively few cases an appropriate terminology has been introduced in the text. Two prominent examples are the introduction of the term *data control structure* (Chapter 6) for those aspects of a language concerned with identifiers, scope rules, referencing environments, and parameter transmission, and the distinction between the operations of *referencing* and *accessing* in data structures. Here an attempt has been made to avoid conflict with other occasional uses of these terms but perhaps has not always been successful. Again the reader is cautioned.

1-4. REFERENCES AND SUGGESTIONS FOR
FURTHER READING

Numerous texts exist which discuss programming at an introductory level, often in the context of a particular programming language. More general texts on programming language structure, design, and implementation are relatively few. Sammet [1969] provides the most complete survey of existing languages; see also Sammet [1972]. Harrison [1973], Elson [1973], Wegner [1968], Higman [1967], and Galler and Perlis [1970] provide alternative approaches to some of the same topics treated here. Ledgard [1971], Cheatham [1971], and Rosen [1972] provide useful short surveys of various issues in language design and implementation.

The literature on *structured programming* is particularly relevant as background for the study of language design because of the general emphasis in this work on the overall structure of program design and construction. The book by Dahl et al. [1972] is particularly good. See also Dijkstra's ACM Turing Award Lecture [1972b], Wirth [1971a, 1973], and the volume edited by Hetzel [1973].

2 PROGRAMMING LANGUAGE PROCESSORS

A *computer* is an integrated set of algorithms and data structures capable of storing and executing programs. A computer may be constructed as an actual physical device using wires, transistors, magnetic cores, and the like, in which case it is termed an *actual computer* or *hardware computer*, but it may equally be constructed using software, by programs running on some other computer, in which case it is a *software-simulated computer*. A programming language is implemented by constructing a *translator* which translates programs in the language into *machine language programs* capable of being directly executed by some computer. The computer that executes the translated programs may occasionally be a hardware computer, but ordinarily it is a *virtual computer* composed partially of hardware and partially of software. An understanding of these concepts provides the necessary foundation for understanding the more specialized topics in the following chapters.

2-1. THE STRUCTURE AND OPERATION OF A COMPUTER

For our purposes it is convenient to divide the discussion of a computer's structure into six major aspects, which correspond closely to the major aspects of a programming language:

1. *Data*. A computer must provide various kinds of elementary data items and data structures to be manipulated.

2. *Primitive operations.* A computer must provide a set of primitive operations useful for manipulating the data.

3. *Sequence control.* A computer must provide mechanisms for controlling the sequence in which the primitive operations are to be executed.

4. *Data control.* A computer must provide mechanisms for controlling the data supplied to each execution of an operation.

5. *Storage management.* A computer must provide mechanisms to control the allocation of storage for programs and data.

6. *Operating environment.* A computer must provide mechanisms for communication with an external environment containing programs and data to be processed.

These six topics form the subject matter for the six main chapters in this part of the book. They also form the basis for the analysis and comparison of the languages described in Part II. However, before looking at these topics in the rather complex context of high-level programming languages, it is instructive to view them within the simple context of an actual hardware computer.

Hardware computer organizations vary widely, but Fig. 2-1 illustrates a fairly typical conventional organization. A *main memory* contains programs and data to be processed. Processing is performed by an *interpreter* which takes each machine language instruction in turn, decodes it, and calls the designated *primitive operation* with the designated operands as input. The primitives manipulate the data in main memory and in high-speed registers and also may transmit programs or data between memory and the *external operating environment.* Only a small part of the structure of the computer is brought out by such a schematic. Let us consider the six major parts of the computer in more detail.

Data. The schematic of Fig. 2-1 shows three major data storage components: main memory, high-speed registers, and external files. Each of these has an assumed internal organization. Main memory is usually organized as a linear sequence of bits subdivided into fixed-length words or bytes. The high-speed registers consist of short word or address-length bit sequences and may have special subfields which are directly accessible. External files are usually subdivided into records, each of which is a sequence of bits or bytes.

An actual computer also has certain built-in data types which can be manipulated directly by hardware primitive operations. A

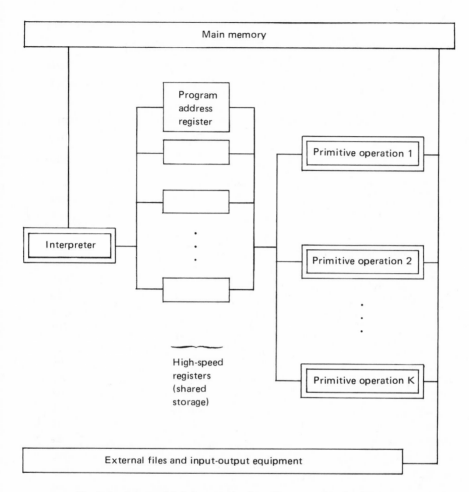

Fig. 2-1. Schematic of the organization of a conventional computer.

common set might include integers (fixed-point numbers), single-precision reals (floating-point numbers), fixed-length character strings, and fixed-length bit strings (where the length is equal to the number of bits or characters that fit into a single word of storage).

Besides these obvious hardware data elements we must also consider programs as a form of data. As with the other built-in data types there must be a built-in representation for programs, termed the *machine language representation* of the computer. Typically a machine language program would be structured as a sequence of memory locations, each containing one or more instructions. Each instruction in turn is composed of an operation code and a set of operand designators.

Operations. A hardware computer must contain a set of built-in primitive operations, usually paired one to one with the operation codes that may appear in machine language instructions. A typical set would include primitives for arithmetic on each built-in number data type—e.g., real and integer addition, subtraction, multiplication, and division—primitives for testing various properties of data items—e.g., test for zero, positive, and negative numbers—primitives for accessing and modifying various parts of a data item—e.g., retrieve or store a character in a word and retrieve or store an operand address in an instruction—primitives for controlling input-output devices, and primitives for sequence control—e.g., unconditional and return jumps.

Sequence Control. The next instruction to be executed at any point during execution of a machine language program is usually determined by the contents of a special *program address register*, which always contains the memory address of the next instruction. Certain primitive operations are allowed to modify the program address register in order to transfer control to another part of the program, but it is the *interpreter* that actually uses the program address register and guides the sequence of operations.

The interpreter is so central to the operation of a computer that its operation deserves more detailed study. Typically the interpreter executes the simple cyclic algorithm shown in Fig. 2-2. During each cycle the interpreter gets the address of the next instruction from the program address register (and increments the register value by 1), fetches the designated instruction from memory, decodes the instruction into an operation code and a set of operand designators, fetches the designated operands (if necessary), and calls the designated operation with the designated operands as arguments. The primitive operation may modify data in memory or registers, access input-output devices, or change the execution sequence by modifying the contents of the program address register. After execution of the primitive the interpreter simply repeats the above cycle.

Data Control. Besides an operation code, each machine language instruction must specify the operands that the designated operation is to use. Typically an operand might be in main memory or in a working register. An actual computer must incorporate a means of designating operands and a mechanism for retrieving operands from a given operand designator. Likewise the result of a primitive operation must be stored in some designated location. We term these facilities the *data control* of the computer. The conventional scheme is to simply associate integer *addresses* with memory locations and

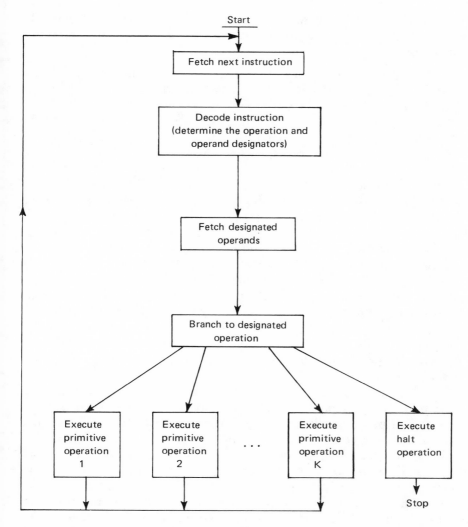

Fig. 2-2. Basic procedure for program interpretation and execution.

provide operations for retrieving the contents of a location given its address (or alternatively for storing a new value in a location whose address is given). Similarly, registers are also often designated by simple integer addresses.

Storage Management. Hardware storage management mechanisms are often essentially nonexistent. In the simplest design no storage management facilities are built into the hardware; programs and data reside in one fixed place in memory throughout program execution.

In more sophisticated computer designs it is now common to include facilities for *paging* or *dynamic program relocation* directly in the hardware.

Operating Environment. The operating environment of an actual computer ordinarily consists of a set of peripheral storage and input-output devices. These devices represent the "outside world" to the computer, and any communication with the computer must be by way of the operating environment. Often there are hardware distinctions between various classes of devices in the environment, based on differences in use or in speed of access, e.g., high-speed storage (magnetic drums, extended core), medium-speed storage (magnetic disks), low-speed storage (tapes), and input-output devices (readers, printers, user terminals, operator console).

An understanding of the *static organization* of a computer in terms of data, operations, control structures, and the like provides only part of the picture. Full understanding requires that we also see clearly the *dynamic operation* of the computer during program execution: What are the contents of the various storage components at the start of execution, what operations are executed in what sequence, how are the various data components modified as execution proceeds, and what is the final result of program execution?

A convenient means of viewing the dynamic behavior of a computer is through the concept of *computer state.* Consider the process of program execution by the computer to proceed through a series of states, each defined by the contents of memory, registers, and external storage at some point during execution. The initial contents of these storage areas define the *initial state* of the computer. Each step in program execution transforms the existing state into a new state through modification of the contents of one or more of these storage areas. This transformation of state is termed a *state transition.* When program execution is complete, the *final state* is defined by the final contents of these storage areas. Program execution may be seen in terms of the sequence of state transitions made by the computer. We understand the dynamic operation of the computer if we can predict the sequence of state transitions which execution of any given program will cause.

2-2. HARDWARE AND FIRMWARE COMPUTERS

At the beginning of this chapter a computer was defined as an integrated set of algorithms and data structures capable of storing and executing programs. The programs executed by a computer are, of course, written in the machine language of the computer. Ordinarily we think of computers as operating on a rather low-level machine language, with simple instruction formats and operations such as "add two numbers" and "load a register with the contents of a memory location." However, machine languages are not restricted to be low-level. Choose any programming language—FORTRAN, PL/I, APL, etc.—and specify precisely a set of data structures and algorithms which define the rules for execution of any program written in the language. In so doing you are necessarily defining a computer, a computer whose "machine language" is the programming language you chose. Each program defines an initial state for the computer, and the rules for program execution define the sequence of state transitions that the computer will make during program execution. The result of execution of the program is determined by the final state of the computer when program execution is complete (if ever).

Given a precise definition of a computer, it is always possible to *realize the computer in hardware*, that is, to construct a hardware device whose machine language is precisely that of the defined computer. This is true even if the machine language is FORTRAN, APL, or some other high-level language. In suggesting this possibility we are appealing to an important basic principle behind computer design: *Any precisely defined algorithm or data structure may be realized in hardware.* Because a computer is simply a collection of algorithms and data structures, we may assume that its hardware realization is a possibility, regardless of the complexity of the computer or its associated machine language.

Actual hardware computers usually have a rather low-level machine language only because of practical considerations—a computer with FORTRAN or APL as its machine language is likely to be considerably more complex (and hence more costly) and considerably less flexible in a variety of computing tasks than a computer with a low-level machine language. A hardware computer with a low-level general-purpose instruction set and a simple, unstructured main memory and register set may be programmed to "look like" any of a broad range of computers relatively efficiently, as we shall see in the following sections. Computers with high-level machine languages have occasionally been constructed (see, e.g., Chesley and Smith [1971]), but other techniques for implementation of high-level languages are usually preferable to hardware realization.

An increasingly common alternative to the strict hardware realization of a computer is the *firmware computer*, simulated by a *microprogram* running on a special *microprogrammable hardware computer.* The machine language of this computer consists of an extremely low-level set of *microinstructions,* which usually specify simple transfers of data between main memory and high-speed registers, between the registers themselves, and from registers through processors such as adders and multipliers to other registers. A special microprogram is coded, using this simple instruction set, that defines the interpretation cycle and the various primitive operations of the desired computer. The microprogram *simulates* the operation of the desired computer on the microprogrammable *host* computer. Ordinarily the microprogram itself resides in a special read-only memory in the host computer and is executed at high speed by the host computer hardware. This microprogram simulation of a computer is essentially the same, in concept, as the software simulation technique discussed in the next section, except that the host computer in this case is especially designed for microprogramming and provides execution speeds for the simulated computer comparable to those obtained by direct hardware realization. Microprogram simulation of a computer is sometimes termed *emulation.*

The implementation through microprogram simulation of firmware computers with high-level machine languages is likely to become an increasingly attractive alternative for programming language implementation. Microprogrammed implementations of a number of languages have already been proposed or constructed, including implementations of APL (Hassit et al. [1973]) and EULER (Weber [1967]). Unfortunately, there is not space here to pursue this interesting topic. Suggestions for further reading in this area are found at the end of this chapter.

2-3. TRANSLATORS AND SOFTWARE-SIMULATED COMPUTERS

In theory it may be possible to construct a hardware or firmware computer to execute directly programs written in any particular programming language, and thus to construct a LISP, APL, or PL/I computer, but it is not ordinarily economical to construct such a machine. Practical considerations tend to favor actual computers with rather low-level machine languages, on the basis of speed, flexibility, and cost. Programming, of course, is most often done in a high-level language far removed from the hardware machine language itself. The question that actually faces the language implementor, then, is how to get programs in the high-level language executed on the actual computer at hand, regardless of its machine language.

There are two basic solutions to this implementation question:

1. *Translation* *(compilation)*. A translator could be designed to translate programs in the high-level language into equivalent programs in the machine language of the actual computer. Translated programs could then be executed directly by the interpreter and primitive operations built into the hardware. The general term *translator* denotes any language processor that accepts programs in some *source language* (which may be high- or low-level) as input and produces functionally equivalent programs in another *object language* (which may also be high- or low-level) as output. A *compiler* is a translator whose source language is a high-level language and whose object language is close to the machine language of an actual computer, either being an assembly language or some variety of machine language (relocatable or absolute). Two other terms for specialized types of translators are commonly used:

a. An *assembler* is a translator whose object language is the machine language of some actual computer (or some similar form such as relocatable machine code) and whose source language, an assembly language, represents for the most part a simple transliteration of the object machine code. Instructions in the source language are translated one for one into object language instructions.

b. A *loader* (or *linking loader*) is a translator whose object language is actual machine code and whose source language is almost identical, usually consisting of machine language programs in *relocatable* form together with tables of data specifying points where the relocatable code must be modified to become truly executable.

Translation of a high-level source language into executable machine language programs often involves more than one translation step. For example, it is not uncommon to have FORTRAN programs first compiled into assembly language, then assembled to produce relocatable machine code, and finally loaded and linked to produce executable machine code. Moreover, the compilation step itself may involve a number of *passes* which progressively translate the program into various intermediate forms before producing the final object program.

2. *Software simulation (software interpretation)*. Rather than translating the high-level language programs into equivalent machine

language programs, we might instead *simulate*, through programs running on another host computer, *a computer whose machine language is the high-level language*. To do this we construct a set of programs in the machine language of the host computer that represents the algorithms (and data structures) necessary for the execution of programs in the high-level language. In other words, we construct with software running on the host computer the high-level language computer which we might otherwise have constructed in hardware. This is termed a *software simulation* (or *software interpretation*) of the high-level language computer on the host computer. The simulated computer accepts as input data a program in the high-level language. The main simulator program performs an interpretation algorithm similar to that of Fig. 2-2, decoding and executing (with the aid of other programs representing the primitive operations of the language) each statement of the input program in the appropriate sequence and producing (with the aid of other programs representing the output operations of the high-level language) the specified output from the program.

Note the difference between software simulation and translation. Both translator and simulator accept programs in the high-level language as input. However, the translator simply produces an equivalent program in its object language, which must then be executed by the hardware interpreter. The simulator executes the input program directly. If we were to follow the processing of the input program by both translator and simulator, we would observe the translator processing the program statements in their physical input sequence and the simulator following the logical flow of control through the program. The translator would ordinarily process each program statement exactly once, while the simulator might process some statements repeatedly (if they were part of a loop) and might ignore others completely (if control never reached them).

Pure translation and pure simulation form two extremes. In practice pure translation is seldom used except in cases where the input language is in fact quite similar to the machine language, as in the case of assembly languages. Pure simulation is also relatively rare except in the case of operating system control languages or interactive languages. More commonly a language is implemented on a computer by a combination of translation and simulation. A program is first translated from its original form into a form which is more easily executable, and then this executable form of the program is decoded and executed by simulation. In Part II of this book we shall have occasion to study a number of different varieties of translation-simulation trade-offs.

Translation and simulation provide different advantages in a programming language implementation. Some aspects of program structure are best translated into simpler forms before execution; other aspects are best left in their original form and processed only as needed during execution. The basic advantages of translation are seen by considering statements in the original source language program which are executed repeatedly, e.g., statements within program loops or statements in subprograms that are called more than once. Execution of such a statement typically requires a fairly complicated decoding process to determine the operations to be executed and their operands. Often most or all of this process is identical each time the statement is executed. Thus if the statement is executed 1000 times, the identical decoding must be performed 1000 times. If instead the statement is translated into a form which is very simple to decode, for example, as a sequence of machine language instructions, then the complex decoding process need be executed only once by the translator, and only a simple decoding of the translated statement is needed during each of the 1000 repetitions during execution. The total savings in processing time may be substantial. The disadvantage of translation is connected with storage. Typically a single source language statement may expand during translation into hundreds of machine language instructions. Although execution of these machine language instructions is more efficient, they may take up a great deal more storage than the original statement. For example, execution of a single PRINT statement might require hundreds or even thousands of machine language instructions, because of the need to format the output, check the status of the output device, manipulate buffers, etc. Moreover, *each* PRINT statement requires a similar expansion.

Simulation provides almost an inverted set of advantages. By leaving statements in their original form until they need to be executed, no space is wasted storing long code sequences because the basic code need be stored only once in the simulation routine, but the total cost of decoding must be paid each time the statement is to be executed. As a general rule translation is used when a source language construct has some rather direct representation in the machine language, for then the code expansion is likely not too severe and the advantage of efficient execution outweighs the loss in storage. In other cases simulation is likely the rule.

The key question overall in a language implementation tends to be whether the base representation of the program during execution is that of the machine language of the actual computer being used. This provides the basis for the common division of languages (more precisely, language implementations) into those which are *compiled* and those which are *interpreted*:

1. *Compiled languages.* FORTRAN, ALGOL 60, PL/I, and COBOL are commonly thought of as languages which are compiled. This means that programs in these languages are usually translated into the machine language of the actual computer being used before execution begins, with simulation being confined to a set of *run-time support routines* which simulate primitive operations in the source language which have no close analogue in the machine language. The advantage of utilizing a machine language representation for programs during execution is that the hardware interpreter may be utilized to decode and initiate execution of primitive operations. By using the hardware interpreter, very fast program execution is often realized. It is important to understand, however, that extensive software simulation may be used in implementing parts of the language processor other than the interpreter; for example, data control structures and storage management, as well as many primitive operations, may be software-simulated in a compiled language. Typically, the translator for a compiled language is relatively large and complex, and the emphasis in translation is on the production of a translated program that executes as efficiently as possible.

2. *Interpreted languages.* LISP, SNOBOL4, and APL are languages often implemented by use of a software interpreter. In such a language implementation, the translator does not produce machine code for the computer being used. Instead the translator produces some intermediate form of the program that is more easily executable than the original program form yet that is different from machine code. The interpretation procedure for execution of this translated program form must be represented by software because the hardware interpreter cannot be used directly. Use of a software interpreter ordinarily results in relatively slow program execution. In addition, languages which are software-interpreted also tend to require extensive software simulation of primitive operations, storage management, and other language features. Translators for interpreted languages tend to be rather simple, with most of the complexity of the implementation coming in the simulation software.

2-4. TRANSLATION AND SIMULATION IN TWO LANGUAGES: FORTRAN AND SNOBOL4

Consideration of implementations of a typical compiled language and a typical interpreted language clarifies the interplay between translation and simulation that is typical of programming language implementations in general. FORTRAN is the simplest of the compiled languages considered in Part II, and it allows the maximum of translation when implemented on a conventional computer. SNOBOL4 is an excellent example of an interpreted language. Note carefully, however, that the terms *compiled* and *interpreted* really refer to *language implementations* rather than languages. It is not inherent in the design of FORTRAN that its implementation must be based on a compiler. Athough FORTRAN is usually implemented using a compiler, it could equally be implemented using a software interpreter; it simply is rather impractical to do so in most cases. Similarly, SNOBOL4 can be (and has been) implemented by compilation, although most SNOBOL4 implementations are interpretive.

FORTRAN, a Compiled Language

In the usual FORTRAN implementation, programs go through an extensive translation process that produces output code which is directly executable by the hardware interpreter of the underlying actual computer. Software simulation is used for various primitive operations: input-output, exponentiation, square root, sine, cosine, etc. Thus the simulated computer for FORTRAN is partially hardware and partially software. Ordinarily every effort is made to use hardware features directly and minimize software simulation so as to minimize execution time for FORTRAN programs. A complete description of FORTRAN and its implementation is given in Chapter 10. However, let us view some selected aspects to get a picture of the relation between translation and simulation in a FORTRAN implementation.

Data. Hardware representations for data items are used wherever possible. The hardware representation for integers and reals is used directly. Arrays are translated into simple blocks of storage, the basic hardware data structure.

Operations. Hardware operations are used directly for most operations, including arithmetic, linear array accessing, and testing. Where appropriate hardware operations are not available, as in complex arithmetic or multidimensional array accessing, there is usually a simple *in-line* simulation of the operations by code sequences. In only a few cases, most notably in input-output operations, is software simulation by run-time routines necessary.

Sequence Control. Most FORTRAN sequence control features are replaced during translation by equivalent constructs in machine language. For example, arithmetic expressions are replaced by simple machine code sequences, and DO loops are translated into machine code increment, test, and loop structures.

Data Control. The data control structure of FORTRAN programs is translated directly into an equivalent machine language data control structure. This is accomplished by use of a strict static storage allocation scheme, in which each identifier in the original FORTRAN program may be translated into a single fixed memory address at execution time. Thus the hardware data control structures may be used directly.

Storage Management. Basically, FORTRAN programs require no storage management during execution, which reflects the fact that hardware storage management is seldom available and thus any storage management would have to be software-simulated.

Environment. The language input-output (I/O) structure is based on a relatively simple external environment of I/O devices, with powerful I/O operations for reading and writing blocks of data from these devices in various formats. This is the major area where the FORTRAN language structure cannot be easily translated into equivalent hardware constructs. The I/O facilities provided by the hardware ordinarily are substantially more complex in structure and provide few, if any, facilities for automatic data formatting. Since translation of FORTRAN I/O statements into equivalent sequences of hardware operations would be extremely complex and result in many hundreds or thousands of machine code instructions for each original FORTRAN I/O statement, it is natural to use software simulation. For this purpose a sizable package of run-time support routines which simulate the desired I/O operations is necessary. An I/O statement is translated into a relatively simple machine code sequence which represents basically a call of the appropriate I/O routine.

Many features of the FORTRAN language are understandable only when one understands the underlying goal of allowing direct translation of FORTRAN programs into equivalent hardware machine code programs, with software simulation restricted to input-output and a few other minor operations such as standard functions. As a result of this design emphasis, FORTRAN programs may be translated into machine code programs which are extremely fast to execute and yet which also require only relatively small amounts of memory for program storage. To enforce this design criterion, however, major restrictions on FORTRAN program structures are required, with a corresponding loss in language flexibility for the programmer. The most obvious case results from the desire to utilize directly the hardware data control features and to enforce the assumed lack of hardware storage management facilities. This forces data structures to be of fixed size and requires all data structures and variables to be allocated storage statically, before execution of a program begins.

SNOBOL4, an Interpreted Language

The design and implementation of SNOBOL4 illustrate a quite different set of goals, typical of interpreted languages. In the usual SNOBOL4 implementation, programs are translated into a prefix code form which represents a simple decoding of the original program statements and expressions into a sequence of function calls. The functions represent the primitive operations in the simulated computer and corrrespond closely to the basic operators in the language: concatenation, pattern matching, assignment, etc. The form of the prefix code bears no resemblance to the hardware machine language. Instead it is chosen simply to be a convenient input form for the software interpreter which controls execution of programs. There is little direct use of hardware features during execution; software simulation is the rule. Again a complete description of SNOBOL4 is left to a later chapter, but a description of some representative features will clarify the differences from the FORTRAN approach.

Data. There is some use of hardware representations for partial representation of data. In representing character strings, for example, the hardware representation is used for the characters, although the string data element itself includes a descriptor which is software-simulated. Numbers also require a software-simulated descriptor, but the actual value is represented using the underlying hardware representation. Data structures are almost entirely software-simulated except that the underlying hardware storage structure may be utilized in part for the storage of array elements.

Operations. Usually all SNOBOL4 operations must be software-simulated. Even arithmetic operations such as + cannot be translated directly into equivalent machine instructions because the SNOBOL4 + requires that the descriptors of the operand numbers be checked for type during execution before an actual addition is performed. Thus while a SNOBOL4 addition operator will ultimately utilize the hardware addition operation to add two numbers, a substantial amount of software simulation is also required. Many of the primitive operations, such as concatenation and pattern matching, are so different from the usual hardware operations that translation into equivalent machine code sequences would entail hundreds or thousands of machine code operations. Software simulation is the appropriate choice in such cases.

Sequence Control. Statements are constructed using the usual expression syntax, with infix operators, parentheses, and precedence rules determining the sequence of operations. As in FORTRAN this control structure is translated into a simple sequence of primitive operation designators before execution. Between statements a simple test and GOTO structure is utilized which is retained in the translated program. Although these control structures are superficially similar to those in the usual hardware, the flexibility of SNOBOL4 in allowing computed labels, statement "failure," and termination at arbitrary points, etc., makes any direct translation into equivalent hardware control structures difficult. Software simulation of all sequence control mechanisms is the rule.

Data Control. SNOBOL4 data control structures have little in common with hardware data control structures. For example, any of the uses of identifiers in the original program as variables names, statement labels, subprogram names, etc., may be modified during execution. It is extremely difficult to associate identifiers with particular memory addresses during translation as is done in FORTRAN because changes in the denotation of the identifier during execution may invalidate the association. Instead of direct use of the hardware data control structure, a more flexible data control structure is software-simulated, utilizing a table of identifiers and their current associations during execution.

Storage Management. Many of the features of SNOBOL4 require storage allocation during execution, e.g., recursion, pattern matching, and data structure creation. Because appropriate hardware storage management features are ordinarily not available, a complex storage management system must be software-simulated.

Operating Environment. The operating environment of a SNOBOL4 program includes only very simple external data storage devices for input and output of strings, together, possibly, with external programs which may be loaded and unloaded during execution. As in FORTRAN the manner of accessing this assumed operating environment is largely at odds with what is actually provided by the hardware or operating system, and thus substantial software simulation is necessary to simulate the desired interface with the operating environment. It is interesting to note that the FORTRAN package of simulation routines used for input-output is often used in SNOBOL4 implementations for simulation of input-output as well.

The differences between the SNOBOL4 implementation based almost entirely on software simulation and the FORTRAN implementation based almost entirely on direct use of the hardware are apparent. Whereas FORTRAN is designed so that language restrictions allow direct program translation into machine code, SNOBOL4 is designed expressly to allow great language flexibility with few constraints, resulting in the need for extensive software simulation during execution. FORTRAN programs have the advantage of extremely fast execution (except when input-output is involved). SNOBOL4 programs execute rather slowly, but the great flexibility of the language may allow use of more appropriate algorithms than with the much more restricted FORTRAN language.

2-5. VIRTUAL COMPUTERS

At the beginning of this chapter a computer was defined to be an integrated set of algorithms and data structures capable of storing and executing programs. In the preceding sections we have considered a variety of ways in which a given computer might actually be constructed:

1. Through a *hardware realization*, representing the data structures and algorithms directly with physical devices.

2. Through a *firmware realization*, representing the data structures and algorithms by microprogramming a suitable hardware computer.

3. Through *software simulation*, representing the data structures and algorithms by programs and data structures in some other programming language.

4. Through some *combination* of these techniques, representing various parts of the computer directly in hardware, in microprograms, or by software simulation as appropriate.

A hardware computer is termed an *actual computer*. A computer that is partially or wholly simulated by software or microprograms is properly termed a *virtual computer*. When a programming language is implemented the run-time data structures and algorithms used in program execution define a computer. Because this computer is almost always at least partially software-simulated, we speak of this as the *virtual computer defined by the language implementation*. The machine language of this virtual computer is the executable program form produced by the translator for the language, which may take the form of actual machine code if the language is compiled, or, alternatively, may be some arbitrary data structure if the language is interpreted. The data structures of this virtual computer are the run-time data structures that are used during program execution. The primitive operations are those operations that are actually executable at run time and that have not been reduced during translation to sequences of simpler operations. Sequence control, data control, and storage management structures are those used at run time, regardless of representation by software or hardware (or microprograms).

The virtual computer associated with a language implementation is clearly distinct from the language itself. Different implementations of the same language may have quite different virtual computers. A program written in a language serves only to define the desired initial state of the virtual computer simulated by the language implementation, specifying what data structures should initially exist, what sequences of primitives are to be executed, etc. The language implementor, however, has wide latitude in determining the virtual computer structures actually used and the details of their simulation on the underlying actual computer.

A programmer who intends to make serious use of a programming language needs to have a clear picture of what is happening during program execution in terms of the structure and operation of the virtual computer defined by the language implementation: How are the programs and data represented, what are the primitive operations and sequence control and data control structures that are being simulated, and what sort of storage management is occurring? Moreover, it is important that he understand which parts of this virtual computer are represented directly in hardware and which are software-simulated, because the cost of programming an algorithm in a particular way may be heavily dependent on the cost of simulating the underlying operations and structures on which it is based.

In this text emphasis is placed on structures that exist during program execution. The translation step is of rather secondary importance here, for two reasons. While knowledge of the details of translator construction is of great importance to language implementors, such knowledge is of lesser importance to the language user. For example, while it is rather critical for the serious user of FORTRAN to understand in some depth the FORTRAN virtual computer and the manner in which it is simulated on his actual computer, it is of lesser value to know the details of exactly how the FORTRAN compiler converts his FORTRAN program as input into the machine language program which the compiler outputs and which is actually executed, e.g., the details of symbol table structures, parsing algorithms, lexical scans, and code generation and optimization. The second reason for deemphasizing the translation process is simply one of space. The study of translation techniques is important, but it should be taken up *after* a study of languages and virtual computers. There is not space in a single text to cover both aspects adequately. In Chapter 9 the outlines of the subject of syntax and translation are sketched in basic form, and references for further study are provided.

2-6. HIERARCHIES OF COMPUTERS

The virtual computer that a programmer uses when he programs in some high-level language is in fact formed from a *hierarchy of virtual computers*. At the bottom there must, of course, lie an actual hardware computer. However, the ordinary programmer seldom has any direct dealing with this computer. Instead this hardware computer is successively transformed by layers of software (or microprograms) into a virtual computer which may be radically different. The second level of virtual computer (or the third if a microprogram forms the second level) is usually defined by the complex collection of routines known as the *operating system*. Typically the operating system provides simulations for a number of new primitives and data structures that are not directly provided by the hardware, e.g., external file structures and file management primitives, and also deletes certain hardware primitives from the operating-system-defined virtual computer so that they are not accessible to the operating system user, e.g., hardware primitives for input-output, error monitoring, multiprogramming, and multiprocessing. The operating-system-defined virtual computer is usually that which is available to the implementor of a high-level language. The language implementor provides a new layer of software that runs on the operating-system-defined computer and simulates the operation of the virtual computer for the high-level language. He also provides a translator for translating user programs into the machine language of the language-defined virtual computer.

Occasionally there may be yet another layer of software between the programmer and the actual hardware: A language like SNOBOL4 is sometimes implemented by coding the translator and simulation routines in another high-level language such as FORTRAN. It would be appropriate to say in such a case that the SNOBOL4 virtual computer is being simulated on the FORTRAN virtual computer, which in turn is being simulated on the operating-system-defined virtual computer, which is itself being simulated on the actual hardware computer (or on the firmware computer that is being simulated by microprograms on the hardware computer).

The hierarchy in fact does not end with the high-level language implementation. The programs that a programmer runs add yet another level to the hierarchy. What is the machine language of this programmer-defined, software-simulated virtual computer? The machine language is composed of the *input data* for these programs. Once the programmer has his programs running, he "writes a program" to operate the virtual computer defined by these programs by choosing an appropriate set of input data. If this view seems far-fetched it is because for many programs the input data formats are so simple as to constitute only a most trivial programming language. However, it is apparent that every programmer constructing the lower levels in our hierarchy must have held exactly that view, because at each level the programs and data structures constructed in fact represented a simulation of a virtual computer that programmers at the next level programmed.

Implicit in the above discussion is a central concept that deserves explicit mention: *the equivalence of programs and data*. We are accustomed to considering certain kinds of objects in programming as "program" and others as "data." This is often a useful intuitive distinction, but, as the above discussion makes clear, it is a distinction that is more apparent than real. That which is program in one context is likely to become data in another. For example you may write an ALGOL program, but to the ALGOL compiler that program is input data which it is to process. The output data produced by the compiler is, to you, a program in machine language. You may request execution of this program, but a closer look at the manner of program execution might convince you that in fact the program is just data to the interpreter used by the executing computer. In the same vein we may always consider the inputs to any program equivalently as data to be processed or as program to be executed.

2.7. BINDING AND BINDING TIME

In the preceding sections the *translator/virtual computer* structure common to all programming language implementations has been described. We have stressed the importance of understanding the gross structure of a language implementation if one is to use the language properly in programming. In this section we shall view the same question in a somewhat different light. We may encompass much of the discussion in terms of the central concepts of *binding* and *binding time*.

Binding is not a concept that allows a single precise definition, nor is binding time. There are many different varieties of bindings in programming languages, as well as a variety of binding times. Without attempting to be too precise, we may speak of the *binding* of a program element to a particular characteristic or property as simply the choice of the property from a set of possible properties. The time during program formulation or processing when this choice is made is termed the *binding time* of that property for that element. In addition we wish to include within the concepts of binding and binding time the properties of program elements that are fixed either by the definition of the language or by its implementation.

Classes of Binding Times

While there is no simple categorization of the various types of bindings, there are a few main binding times that may be distinguished if we recall our basic assumption that the processing of a program, regardless of the language, always involves a translation step followed by execution of the translated program.

1. *Execution time (run time).* The most common bindings are performed during program execution. These include bindings of variables to their values, as well as in many languages the binding of data structures and variables to particular storage locations. Two important subcategories may be distinguished:

a. *On entry to a subprogram or block.* In many languages important classes of bindings are restricted to occur only at the time of entry to a subprogram or block during execution. For example, in ALGOL the binding of formal to actual parameters and the binding of arrays and variables to particular storage locations may occur only on entry to subprograms or blocks.

b. *At arbitrary points during execution.* Other important classes of bindings may occur at any point during execution of a program. The most important example here is the basic binding of variables to values through assignment.

2. *Translation time (compile time).* In many languages, especially those that are compiled, important classes of bindings are performed during translation. These translation-time bindings may include the specification of types for variables, type and size of data structures, and often the detailed structure of data, e.g., in the record descriptions of COBOL. Occasionally, e.g., in FORTRAN, bindings of variables and data structures to particular storage locations are also performed at translation time, often at *load time*, the last stage of translation when translated programs are linked and loaded into memory in their final executable form.

3. *Language definition time.* Most of the structure of a programming language is, of course, fixed at the time the language is defined, most often in the sense of specifying the sets of alternatives from which a programmer is allowed to choose in writing his programs. Commonly the possible alternative statement forms, data structure types, program structures, etc., are all fixed at language definition time.

4. *Language implementation time.* In every language there are elements whose definitions are left unspecified in the language definition and which must be filled in when the language is implemented on a particular actual computer. The definitions of arithmetic operations and number representations are the most obvious examples. In most languages an attempt is made to minimize such implementation-dependent aspects. A program written in the language that uses a feature of the language whose definition has been fixed at implementation time will not necessarily run on another implementation of the same language, or, even more troublesome, may run and give different results.

To illustrate the variety of bindings and binding times, consider the simple assignment statement

$$Y := X + 10$$

Suppose that this statement appeared within some program written in language L. We might inquire into the bindings and binding times of at least the following elements of this statement:

1. *Value of the variable X.* We assume that there is a set of possible values for the variable X, i.e., one of the properties associated with the variable X is its value. When is the particular current value of X fixed, and how is the binding of X to its value accomplished? The answer for most programming languages is that the value associated with X is fixed (i.e., bound) at execution time and that this binding is accomplished by execution of an assignment statement with X on the left-hand side of the assignment operator.

2. *Type of the variable X.* A second property of the variable X is its *type*, e.g., **real** or **integer**. When and how is the type of X determined? Commonly, if the language L is a compiled language such as FORTRAN, ALGOL, or PL/I, the type of X must be specified when the program is written. The usual mechanism is a *declaration* such as the ALGOL declaration

real X

Conceptually, there is a set of possible types for the variable X from which one must be chosen by the programmer. We speak of the type of a variable being bound at *compile time* or *translation time* in this case. Of course, the choice of the type of X fixes the set of possible values that X may take on at execution time and may also fix the amount of storage allocated for the value of X.

3. *Set of possible types for the variable X.* While the type of X may be fixed at compile time, when and how is the set of possible variable types fixed? In most languages the set of possible data types is fixed at *language definition time*, e.g., only types **real, integer, Boolean, complex,** and **string** might be allowed. This need not be the case, however. For example, in SNOBOL4 the set of types may be extended by the programmer at execution time.

4. *Representation of the constant 10.* The integer ten has both a representation as a constant in programs, using the string 10, and a representation at execution time, commonly as a sequence of bits. The choice of decimal represenation in the program (i.e., using 10 for ten) is usually made at *language definition time*, while the choice of a particular sequence of bits to represent ten at execution time is usually made at *language implementation time*.

5. *Properties of the operator +.* Let us consider the binding times of the various properties of the operator + in the statement. The choice of the symbol + to represent the addition operation is made at *language definition time*. However, it is common to allow the same

symbol + to represent *real addition, integer addition, complex addition*, etc., depending on the context. In a compiled language it is common to make the determination of which operation is represented by + at *compile time*. The mechanism for specifying the binding desired is usually the typing mechanism for variables: If X is type **integer**, then the + in $X + 10$ represents integer addition; if X is type **real**, then the + represents real addition; etc.

Another property of the operation represented by + is its value for any given pair of operands. Thus, in our example, if X has the value 12, then what is the value of $X + 10$? Or if X has the value 2^{49}, then what is the value of $X + 10$? In other words, when is the meaning of *addition* defined? The meaning is usually fixed at *language implementation time* and is drawn from the definition of addition used in the underlying hardware computer.

In summary, for a language like ALGOL the symbol + is bound to a set of *addition operations* at language definition time, the addition operations are defined at language implementation time, each particular use of the symbol + in a program is bound to a particular addition operation at translation time, and the particular value of each particular addition operation for its operands is determined only at execution time. This set of bindings represents one choice of possible bindings and binding times typical of a variety of programming languages. Note, however, that many other bindings and binding times are also possible.

Importance of Binding Times

In the analysis and comparison of programming languages in the following chapters many distinctions are based on differences in binding times. We shall be continuously in the process of asking the question: Is this done at translation time or at execution time? Many of the most important and subtle differences among languages involve differences in binding times. For example, almost every language allows numbers as data and allows arithmetic operations on these numbers. Yet not all languages are equally suited for programming problems involving a great deal of arithmetic. Thus, for example, while both SNOBOL4 and FORTRAN allow one to set up and manipulate arrays of numbers, a problem requiring large arrays and large amounts of arithmetic would probably be most inappropriately solved in SNOBOL4 if it could also be done in FORTRAN. If we were to try to trace the reason for this by comparing the features of SNOBOL4 and FORTRAN, we ultimately would be led to conclude that the superiority of FORTRAN in this case is due to the fact that in SNOBOL4 most of the bindings required in the program will be set up at execution time while in FORTRAN most will be set up at translation time. Thus a SNOBOL4 version of the program would spend most of its execution time creating and destroying bindings, while in the FORTRAN version most of the same bindings would be set up once during translation, leaving only a few to be handled during execution. As a result the FORTRAN version would execute much more efficiently. On the other hand, we might turn around and ask a related question: Why is FORTRAN so inflexible in its handling of arrays, numbers, and arithmetic, as compared to SNOBOL4? Again the answer turns on binding times. Because most bindings in FORTRAN are performed at translation time, before the input data are known, it is extremely difficult in FORTRAN to write programs that can adapt to a variety of different data-dependent situations at execution time. For example, the size of arrays and the type of variables must be fixed at translation time in FORTRAN. In SNOBOL4 bindings may be delayed during execution until the input data have been examined and the appropriate bindings for the particular input data determined.

The advantages and disadvantages of translation-time versus execution-time bindings revolve around this conflict between efficiency and flexibility. In languages where execution efficiency is a prime consideration, such as FORTRAN, ALGOL, and COBOL, it is common to design the language so that as many bindings as possible may be performed during translation. Where flexibility is the prime determiner, as in SNOBOL4 and LISP, most bindings are delayed until execution time so that they may be made data-dependent. In a language designed for both efficient execution and flexibility, such as PL/I, one notes that often multiple options are available that allow choices of binding times. The PL/I storage management options provide an excellent example. In the discussions of concepts and languages in the succeeding chapters, binding times will be a prime focus of interest. Wherever possible we shall try to illustrate how differences in binding times affect the structure of the language implementation.

Binding Times and Language Implementations

Language definitions are usually permissive in specifying binding times. A language is designed so that a particular binding *may* be performed at, e.g., translation time, but the actual time at which the binding is performed is in fact defined only by the implementation of the language. For example, ALGOL is designed to permit the type of variables to be determined at compile time, but a particular ALGOL implementation might instead do type checking at execution time. Thus while the definition of ALGOL permits compile-time-type checking, it does not require it. In general a language design specifies the earliest time during program processing at which a particular binding is possible, but any implementation of the language may in fact delay the binding to a later time. However, usually most implementations of the same language will perform most bindings at the same time. If the language is designed to permit compile-time bindings, then to delay these bindings until execution time will probably lead to less efficient execution at no gain in flexibility. It ordinarily is expedient to perform the bindings at the earliest possible moment.

One additional caution is needed, however. Often seemingly minor changes in a language may lead to major changes in binding times. For example, in FORTRAN the change to allow recursion and computed array dimensions, two rather simple changes in the language, would modify many of the binding times of important FORTRAN features. It is because binding times are implementation-dependent to this extent that we place emphasis on knowing your language implementation. In Part II a number of languages are analyzed. In each case a "typical" implementation of the language is assumed and the binding times of the various language elements in the context of this implementation are discussed. When approaching your own local implementation of the same language it is important to ask about the binding times in that implementation. Are they the usual ones, or have local modifications to the language caused the usual binding times to be modified?

2-8. REFERENCES AND SUGGESTIONS FOR FURTHER READING

Software simulation, translation, virtual computers, and binding times are central topics in the following chapters. Bell and Newell [1971] provide a comprehensive overview of hardware organizations. For further information on microprogramming and firmware, see the text by Husson [1970] and the two excellent survey articles by Davies [1972] and Rosin [1969]. Assemblers and loaders, two important specialized types of translators, are treated by Barron [1969] and Presser and White [1972].

2-9. PROBLEMS

2-1. Analyze the implementation of a programming language with which you are familiar. What is the executable form of a program (i.e., what is the output of the translator)? What sorts of translations are made in translating the various statements and expressions into executable form? What software simulation is necessary during program execution? Is the interpreter software-simulated? Which of the primitive operations require software simulation?

2-2. Analyze the structure of your local actual (hardware) computer. Determine the data elements, primitive operations, sequence and data control structures, storage management facilities, and operating environment which are built into the hardware.

2-3. If your local computer has an operating system, determine the structure of the virtual computer defined by the operating system. How does this virtual computer differ from the actual hardware computer? Are there features of the hardware which are restricted by the operating system, e.g., hardware instructions which are not allowed in user programs in the operating-system-defined virtual computer? What new features are provided directly in the operating system virtual computer which could be simulated only by complex software on the basic hardware computer, e.g., input-output?

2-4. The use of an operating system to provide the programmer with a virtual computer different from the basic hardware computer has three advantages. It allows the user to work with a simpler computer than is provided directly by the hardware, for example, by providing simpler and more powerful input-output facilities. It also protects the computer system from the user, in that each user may be effectively "sealed off" in his own virtual computer, so that any errors he makes will hurt only his virtual computer and not bring down the whole system and its other users as well. It also allows the operating system to allocate the resources of the system more appropriately to different users. Analyze your local operating system and the virtual computer it provides the programmer. How well does it satisfy these goals?

3 DATA

Any program, regardless of the language used, may be viewed as specifying a set of operations that are to be applied to certain data in a certain sequence. Basic differences among languages exist in the types of data allowed, in the types of operations available, and in the mechanisms provided for controlling the sequence in which the operations are applied to the data. These three areas—data, operations, and control—form the basis for the next four chapters and also the basis for much of the discussion and comparison of languages in Part II. The topic of data comes first because the concepts underlie much of the later discussion of other aspects of languages.

3-1. PROGRAMMER- AND SYSTEM-DEFINED DATA

The data that exist during execution of a program fall roughly into two categories: *programmer-defined data* and *system-defined data.* Programmer-defined data consist of the data items, e.g., numbers, arrays, and input-output files, that the programmer explicitly defines and manipulates in his program. System-defined data consist of those data items that the language implementation sets up for "housekeeping" during execution, e.g., stacks of subprogram return points, data structure descriptors, referencing environments, free space lists, input-output buffers, and garbage collection bits. System-defined data are ordinarily generated automatically as needed during program execution without explicit specification (or often even awareness) by the programmer.

Discussion of system-defined data arises naturally during consideration of the run-time simulation of various program constructs. For example, when discussing recursive subprogram calls as a control structure it is natural to consider the simulation of recursive calls using a stack of return points—the conventional simulation for recursive calls on an actual computer. For this reason system-defined data are a topic of importance in each of the chapters that follow. This chapter considers primarily programmer-defined data and their representation (i.e., simulation) in a conventional computer. However, system-defined data, in the form of run-time *data descriptors*, are a central issue in the representation of programmer-defined data. Thus this particular kind of system-defined data is taken up here. In addition many of the types of data structures discussed here (e.g., stacks and linked lists) are used both as system-defined data structures and as programmer-defined data structures in various languages.

Programmer-defined data are found in a great variety of forms in programming languages. Although most languages contain some kind of number data and some form of linear array, there is little uniformity otherwise. This tremendous variety is not surprising because one of the strong motives for the development of a new programming language is often a desire to allow direct use of a type of data structure not provided by an existing language, but it makes both impractical and pointless any attempt to survey all the different types of data in use in programming languages. Even if the discussion were fairly comprehensive in terms of existing languages, there would always be another language appearing with different data types and structures. It is the concepts underlying the design and simulation of data structures that are most important to the programmer when he undertakes the study or use of a new language. These concepts are emphasized in this chapter and exemplified by a representative set of the most common programming language data types.

3-2. LOGICAL ORGANIZATION, STORAGE STRUCTURE, AND SYNTACTIC REPRESENTATION

Chapter 2 distinguished three important concepts: programming language, the virtual computer defined by a language, and simulation of a virtual computer on an actual computer. Specialized to the particular aspect of data, the virtual computer for a language defines the *logical organization* of data items (sometimes called the *data structure*, a term reserved here to designate a structured set of data items), the simulation of that virtual computer on an actual computer defines the *storage representation* or *storage structure* for the data, and the programming language provides whatever *syntactic representation* for data is necessary. For example, consider a two-dimensional array (matrix) of integers. Commonly the programmer working with such arrays in a language like ALGOL or APL may view the logical organization of this data structure to be as in mathematics: a rectangular grid of integers laid out in the plane. The storage representation for the array would be quite different: a linear sequence of memory locations containing bit strings representing integers, together with a *dope vector* descriptor specifying type, number of dimensions, and subscript ranges for the array. Often the language provides no syntactic representation for arrays at all. The programmer may set up arrays only indirectly through execution of primitive operations that create arrays—there is no syntax provided for "writing down" a particular array of integers.

The logical organization and storage representation of data structures are the primary concerns of this chapter. Syntactic representation is a minor aspect, particularly since few languages provide direct syntactic representations for other than elementary data items such as numbers (LISP is a major exception in providing a syntactic representation for every list structure).

3-3. STORAGE STRUCTURES: DESCRIPTORS, LOCATIONS, AND BIT STRINGS

When a programmer uses a language to solve a problem he must first decide on a way to represent or encode the problem data in terms of the data structures provided by the programming language. Similarly, when a programming language is implemented on a particular computer the implementor must determine the execution-time memory representation (storage structure) for the language data structures. Unfortunately conventional computer memories provide little structure on which to develop these representations. Memories in general are structured simply as one long sequence of bits, broken at fixed intervals into addressable words or bytes. To represent a data item there is little choice but to use a consecutive sequence of bits. For example, a number might be represented by one sequence of bits, a pointer by a shorter sequence, and an array of numbers by a longer sequence. Clearly such representations are ambiguous—a given bit string might represent any of a number of different data items or collections of items, depending on the representation (encoding) being used. As a result of this ambiguity we ordinarily consider the storage representation for a given data item to be composed of (1) a *location* in memory containing (2) a *bit string* (on a binary computer), representing the encoded data, and (3) a *descriptor* (or *dope vector*), specifying the additional information necessary to decode the bit string.

A *descriptor* always includes a *data type designator*, which specifies the general class of data items to which the encoded data belong—fixed-point number, floating-point number, character string, array, list, pointer, etc. Occasionally, as in the case of number representations, the data type designator alone suffices to allow decoding of the bit string representing the data, but more generally the descriptor also contains additional items of information necessary to completely decode the bit string. Some representative descriptors for various data types are illustrated in Fig. 3-1, and numerous more detailed examples are given in later sections.

The *bit string* encoding a data item may exist in a contiguous block in memory. In this case we speak of the data as stored *sequentially*. Alternatively the string may be broken into a number of noncontiguous pieces stored in separate areas of memory and linked together by pointers. In this case the data are said to be *linked* or *chained*. Sequential and linked storage are the most common, but other techniques are applicable to special classes of data (e.g., the technique of *hash coding* for storage of sets; see Section 3-11).

The *location* of a data item is not to be confused with a memory word. A data item may be located in part of a memory word, in a group of sequential memory words, or in a group of separate words. In general a location may be designated by a memory address that specifies the word in memory where the data item bit string *begins*. To completely describe the location it may also be necessary to include a length indicator (number of words, bits, or bytes) and possibly also a designator of the position of the beginning and ending bits of the string within these memory words.

3-4. DECLARATIONS

A *declaration* is a program statement that serves to communicate to the language translator information about the properties of data

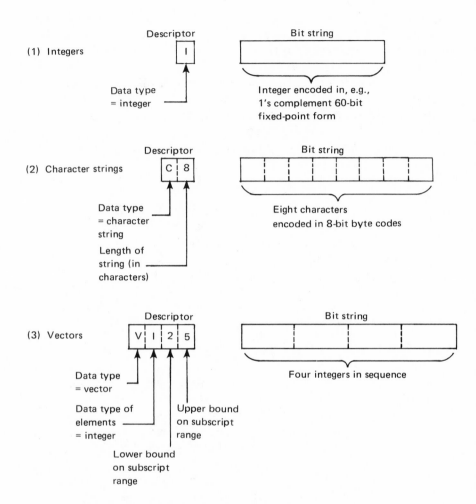

Fig. 3-1. Typical storage structures for three types of data.

during execution. A declaration may specify a variety of facts about a data item: data type, size, name, point of creation, point of destruction, subscripts for accessing, etc. Take, for example, the ALGOL declaration

integer array $A[2:10]$

This declaration specifies a point during execution where an array is to be created (on entry to the block in which the declaration occurs), a point where it is to be destroyed (on exit from the same block), its data type (one-dimensional array), the number of its elements (9), the subscripts to be used to access them (the integers 2—10), the data type of each element (**integer**), and the name by which the array may be referenced (*A*). Given this information, the ALGOL compiler may then optimize the storage and processing of the array during execution, using the techniques discussed in Section 3-8.

Declarations in programming languages serve three main purposes:

1. *More efficient storage and accessing of data structures.* The most obvious purpose of declarations is to specify properties of data structures that are invariant during program execution, such as the size, shape, and type of elements of an array. With this information provided by a declaration the language translator can optimize the storage representation and accessing computations for the structures, with a consequent reduction in storage requirements and execution time for the program being translated. The effect of declarations on storage structures and accessing computations is one of the central questions taken up in this chapter.

2. *Better storage management.* Information provided by declarations about the size, point of creation, and point of destruction of data structures serves to allow more efficient storage management during program execution. For example, ALGOL implementations may utilize a simple stack-based run-time storage management technique (see Chapter 7) in part because ALGOL declarations are designed to provide complete information about the point of creation and destruction of each ALGOL array. APL, on the other hand, uses no declarations for arrays, and this is part of the reason that APL must be implemented with a more complex and less efficient heap storage management technique.

3. *Static type checking.* An operation in a programming language is called a *type-specific operation* if its operands and results are of invariant type and a *generic operation* if the type of its operands and results may vary. For example, in a language with **real** and **integer** data types for numbers, two type-specific addition operations would be required, a *real addition* that added numbers of **real** type and produced a **real** result and an *integer addition* that added numbers of **integer** type and produced an **integer** result. A generic addition operation, on the other hand, would accept numbers in either **real** or **integer** form (or a mixture) and produce a **real** or **integer** result depending on the type of its operands.

Most high-level languages allow the programmer to use generic operations. For example, the programmer may write $X + Y$ for the addition of the values of X and Y regardless of the types of X and Y. In a language without declarations for X and Y such an expression must invoke a generic addition operation during execution that would check the type of the values for X and Y and then

1. Perform an integer addition and tag the resulting value as **integer** if both the operands were type **integer**, or

2. Perform a real addition and tag the resulting value as **real** if both the operands were type **real**, or

3. Convert the integer to a real, perform a real addition, and tag the result as type **real** if the operands were of mixed type **real** and **integer**, or

4. Output an appropriate error message and halt or attempt a recovery if one of the operands were not of type **real** or **integer**.

Obviously the generic addition operation is slow to execute because of the necessity for testing the type of the operands each time it is invoked. Also, more space is needed for data storage because each data item must include a data type descriptor. Yet a third difficulty is that conventional computer hardware typically provides built-in type-specific arithmetic operations but not generic ones, so that software simulation of the generic addition operation is necessary.

It is desirable to allow the programmer to use generic operations in programming because he then is freed from concern with data type constraints and need not provide explicit type conversion operations in his programming. However, in languages concerned with execution speed for programs, the use of generic operations at run time is too costly. Declarations of data type provide the solution to this conflict: The programmer may use generic operations in his coding but the translator may translate such operations into type-specific forms in the executable code. Consider again the sum X + Y. With a declaration of data type for X and Y such as

$$\text{real } X, Y$$

the translator may compile the + into a single real addition in the executable program form. The translator performs all the type checking during translation. Should the declaration for X and Y instead be

$$\text{real } X; \text{ integer } Y$$

then the translator may insert the proper code for conversion of the value of Y to type **real** before the addition. Alternatively a declaration

real X; Boolean Y

would allow the translator to detect an illegal type and output an appropriate error message. Basically the type declarations allow all of the generic addition operation except the actual type-specific addition itself to be performed during translation, with a consequent substantial increase in the execution speed of the translated program.

A language is said to allow *static type checking* when it requires program type declarations that allow the language translator to check data types during translation and translate generic operations in the program into type-specific operations in the executable program. The alternative is *dynamic type checking* by generic operations during program execution.

A central problem in programming language design is to find the proper balance between the added execution efficiency obtainable through declarations and the added flexibility possible without them. LISP, APL, and SNOBOL4 use no declarations at all. This omission simplifies programming in these languages and allows great flexibility in creating and manipulating data structures, but the cost is paid in dynamic type checking, less efficient data representations, and more complex storage management, all of which slow program execution. FORTRAN, ALGOL, COBOL, and PL/I require extensive declarations for all data structures and also introduce many related restrictions on the manner in which data may be created, destroyed, and modified. These requirements make programming considerably more complex, but program execution speeds are greatly enhanced.

Languages such as ALGOL and PL/I loosen the requirements for full data declarations when a slight loss in execution efficiency may be matched by a substantial gain in flexibility. Consider the case of array declarations. The most efficient storage and processing of arrays comes from requiring complete specification of type, number of dimensions, and subscript range for each dimension in a program declaration, as is done in FORTRAN. However, fixing entirely the structure of an array in this manner is quite inflexible. For example, the FORTRAN programmer is often forced to set up arrays for the worst-case input data, reserving far more storage than might actually be needed. At the opposite extreme, APL arrays need no declarations at all; they are created dynamically as needed and may be reshaped at any time. This arrangement is very flexible, but execution is slowed because the array descriptor must be checked continuously during execution. The ALGOL design hits a typical happy medium between the two. An ALGOL programmer must declare the type and the number of dimensions of an array when the program is written but need not specify the size or subscript ranges for the array. Knowing the type and number of dimensions, the ALGOL compiler is able to compile fairly efficient code for array processing during execution. A partial run-time descriptor for arrays which specifies the subscript range for each dimension must be carried during execution, and this descriptor must be checked and processed at times during array processing. However, the result is only a slight loss in execution speed, and the programmer gains the important feature of arrays whose size and subscript ranges may be determined dynamically during program execution. The PL/I language, in particular, contains numerous examples of features designed to balance in a reasonable manner the conflicting demands of flexibility and efficient execution.

Declarations play a key role in programming language design and implementation. They appear in many forms in the following chapters. Note that a declaration need not appear as an actual program statement. Many languages include declarations that are *implicit*, often taking the form of *default declarations*: declarations that hold when no other declaration is given. An example is found in the FORTRAN naming convention for simple variables: A variable that is used but not declared in a program is type **integer** by default if its name begins with one of the letters I—N, and type **real** otherwise. It is not a question of whether declarations are explicit or implicit but a question of what *information* is available to the translator that is critical. The general term *declaration* is used here to refer to any means of making information available to the translator, whether explicit or implicit.

3-5. THE RELATION BETWEEN DATA AND OPERATIONS

Almost every aspect of the subject of data is closely tied to the operations that process the data. For example, even in the representation of integers, a storage representation as a fixed-point binary number might be appropriate where integers are mainly used in arithmetic computations, while a representation as a character string of digits might be more appropriate if the most common operations were input-output transfers. Throughout this chapter the assumptions about operations that guide certain choices of storage representations are discussed, but a detailed discussion of operations is delayed until the next chapter. This organization allows a more appropriate emphasis on the common concepts that tie together operations on different types of data.

One particular type of operation, however, is so closely tied to the storage representation of data that it cannot logically be treated separately: the operation of *accessing* elements of a structure. For example, the methods for accessing elements of an array almost necessarily must be discussed at the same time as the storage representation for an array. Certain types of data may be accessed only as a whole, e.g., numbers, Boolean values, and pointers. We informally term these data *elementary data items*. With other types of data, access to subparts of a data item is allowed, e.g., arrays, lists, stacks, and input files. These are termed *structured data items*. The distinction between elementary and structured data items obviously is dependent on the language and the type of accessing operations allowed; for example, character strings in some languages (e.g., ALGOL) appear as elementary data items that can be accessed only as units for input-output and transmission to subprograms, while in other languages (e.g., SNOBOL4) each substring within a character string is individually accessible, and thus a character string serves as a structured data item.

If A is a linear array, then access to A[2], the second element of A, may be required to (1) retrieve the data item stored there or (2) retrieve the location of the element so that a new data item may be stored there. We term the former operation *value accessing* and the latter *location accessing*. Location accessing is the more basic operation, because given the location of an element it ordinarily is trivial to retrieve the value stored there. In most programming languages both types of accessing operation have the same syntax, e.g., $A[2]$ in $X := A[2] + Y$ represents a value-accessing operation, while $A[2]$ in $A[2] := X + Y$ represents a location-accessing operation. In our discussion of accessing in data structures we shall consider mainly location accessing, except where explicitly indicated to the contrary.

One further distinction is important: the distinction between *referencing* and *accessing* a data structure. Unfortunately the two terms are often used interchangeably in the literature, leading to substantial confusion. Ordinarily a data structure is given a name, e.g., the array above was named A. When we write $A[2]$ in most programming languages we actually invoke a two-step sequence, composed of first a *referencing operation* followed by a *location-* (or value-) *accessing operation*. The referencing operation determines the current referent of the identifier A, returning as its result a pointer to the location of the entire array designated by the name A. The accessing operation takes the pointer to the location of the array, together with the subscript 2 of the designated element in the array, and returns a pointer to the location of that element within the array. Only the accessing operation is of concern in this chapter. Discussion of the referencing operation (which may be far more complex and time-consuming than the accessing operation) must await a detailed consideration of the problems of identifier associations, scope rules, and referencing environments in Chapter 6.

3-6. SIMPLE VARIABLES

An identifier that is associated at each point during execution with a single elementary data item, e.g., a number, is termed a *simple variable*. At a given point during execution the *value of the simple variable* is the data item with which the identifier is currently associated; the *location of the variable* is the location of the data item. Assignment of a new value to the variable changes the data item with which the variable is associated and may also change the location of the variable. With simple variables the operations of value and location accessing are usually trivial; on the other hand, the referencing operation that determines the current location of the value associated with the identifier may be quite complex. The major issues in the storage and accessing of simple variables are brought out in the discussion of elementary data items in the next section.

3-7. ELEMENTARY DATA ITEMS

An elementary data item is one that ordinarily is accessed and modified as a unit. As mentioned above this is not an absolute distinction but may vary among languages. Numbers, character strings, Boolean values, bit strings, symbols, and pointers are the basic types taken up in this section.

Numbers

Some form of number data is basic in almost every programming language. The various classes of numbers are relatively familiar, and while the details of their treatment vary from language to language (and from computer to computer) the variations seldom make major differences in the languages. It is not our intent here to treat in detail the various number representation systems in use; instead attention is focused on the relation between number representations and descriptors.

Logical Organization. In most programming languages a single number has no internal structure beyond a sign (except in the case of complex or rational numbers, which are composed of pairs of reals or integers). It is not the internal organization of a number that matters, but the structure of the entire set of numbers available in a language: the fact that they are ordered, the extent of their finite range, and their density over this range. A wide variety of number types has been used in languages; integers, reals, double precision reals, complex numbers, and rationals are perhaps the most common.

Storage Structure. Direct use of a number representation provided by the hardware is the usual choice for a storage representation for numbers. Integers, reals, and occasionally double-precision reals and character string representations for reals are hardware-supported on most conventional computers. Where a hardware representation is used directly the logical properties of the numbers represented reflect the properties of the underlying hardware representation. In a direct hardware representation no descriptors are provided ordinarily; the number is represented as a simple (ambiguous) bit string.

Direct hardware representation for complex numbers is uncommon because they may be easily represented as pairs of reals stored in consecutive memory locations. Rationals (quotients of integers) present more of a problem. The usual reason for a rational number data type in a language is to avoid the problems of roundoff and truncation encountered in the floating-point representations of reals. As a result it is desirable to represent rationals as pairs of integers of *unbounded length*, and to accomplish this a substantial amount of software simulation is required. Some typical representations for numbers are illustrated in Fig. 3-2.

When a run-time type descriptor for numbers is required during execution, as in LISP and SNOBOL4, a different representation is required because the hardware representation provides no descriptor. In LISP a real number must be stored as a bit string together with a data type designator specifying that the bit string is an encoded real number. It is desirable to use the hardware-provided arithmetic operations because software simulation of arithmetic is usually

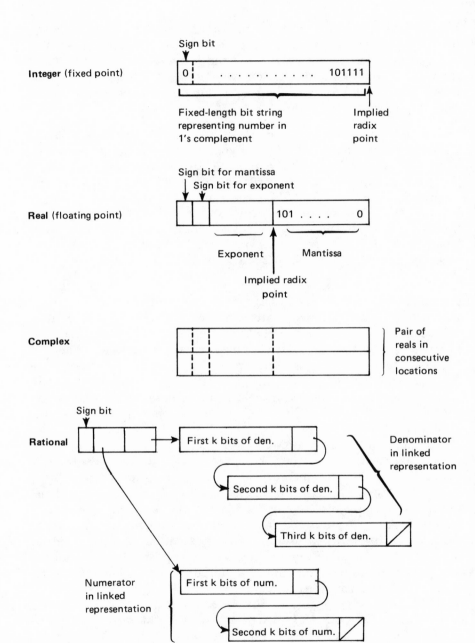

Fig. 3-2. Some storage representations for numbers (without descriptors).

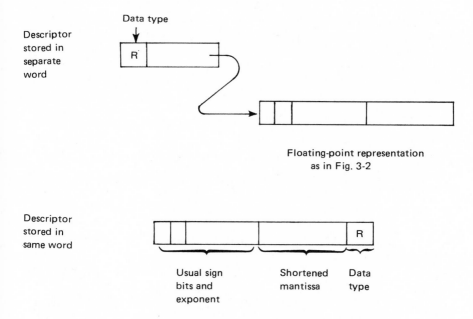

Fig. 3-3. Real number storage representations with type descriptors.

extremely costly. A typical solution might be to utilize the hardware representation in the bit string for the number and, since this bit string probably occupies a complete memory word, store the descriptor in a separate word elsewhere in memory with a pointer to the word containing the bit string. An alternative would be to use the hardware bit string number representation but drop as many of the least significant bits of the mantissa as necessary to allow the type descriptor to be stored in the same word. Using this representation the descriptor must be cleared and the number extended to full word length before the hardware arithmetic operations may be applied. Figure 3-3 illustrates these two techniques.

Characters and Character Strings

Single characters occasionally form a separate data type, as, for example, in APL character arrays. More commonly the data type is a *character string*, a sequence of individual characters.

Logical Organization. At least three different treatments of character strings may be identified:

1. *Fixed declared length.* Character strings may have a fixed declared length. Operations are restricted to those which do not change the length of the string, e.g., character substitutions. Assignment of a string value to a variable of type **character string** results in a length adjustment of the new string through truncation or addition of blank characters to the fixed length. This is the basic technique used in COBOL.

2. *Variable length to a declared bound.* A maximum string length must be declared. The string is allowed to vary in length but is truncated if it exceeds the bound. This technique is used in PL/I.

3. *Unbounded length.* Strings may vary arbitrarily in length, and no declaration of a bound is required. Storage is allocated for strings as required. This is the basic technique used in SNOBOL4.

An ordering is also often imposed on character strings based on an ordering of the characters known as a *collating sequence.* A collating sequence simply extends the usual alphabetic ordering of letters to include all other characters in the character set, thus allowing the usual alphabetization procedure to be applied to any character string.

Storage Structure. Conventional computer hardware provides a direct hardware representation for character strings. Each character is represented by a 6- or 8-bit *character code*, and a character string is represented by a sequence of such codes stored in consecutive bytes or packed into consecutive words of memory. Descriptors, as usual, are not hardware-supported. Where strings have a fixed declared length it is usually possible to use the hardware storage representation directly without a descriptor. The variable-length cases require run-time descriptors specifying the length of the string (and the bound in the fixed bound case). A common representation is to store the length as the first character in the bit string and represent the remainder of the string in the usual hardware representation. An alternative, where strings are of unbounded length, is to utilize a linked storage representation. These structures are illustrated in Fig. 3-4.

Boolean (Logical) Values and Bit Strings

Most languages support some form of binary data, either as a simple binary-valued data type (**true-false**) or in the form of a **bit string** data type. The single-bit form is usually termed a **Boolean** data type. Such binary data have an obvious storage representation in most computers as hardware bits or bit strings. In fact one of the

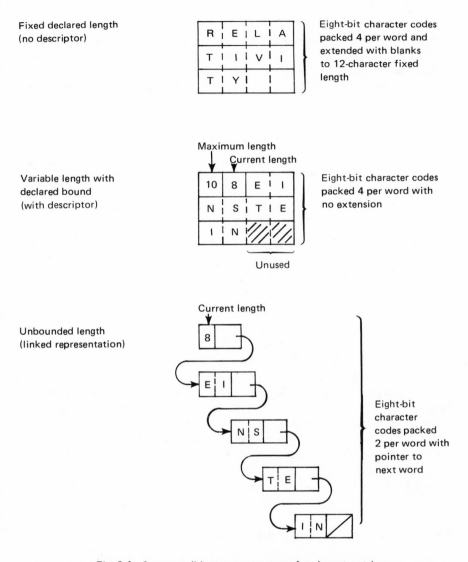

Fig. 3-4. Some possible storage structures for character strings.

primary arguments for the inclusion of the bit string data type is the direct access to the hardware bit strings that results. Bit string data are almost always declared as having fixed or bounded length. The natural operations on bit strings are the bit-by-bit logical operations: logical sum (inclusive **or**), logical product (**and**), and complement (**not**), which are commonly directly available in the hardware.

The difficulty with a bit string data type is the hardware dependence that is implied: The bit string must be directly translatable into a hardware bit string with the appropriate operations or it tends to be useless because software simulation of bit string operations is usually too inefficient. A more machine-independent approach to the bit string data type is found in the *small-set* structure discussed in Section 3-11.

Symbols (Atoms)

In many applications there is a need for data items which are simply abstract symbols. For example, in the problem of computing the permutations of a set of n objects, the elements of the set might be considered as simply a set of n symbols. The basic operation on symbols is the identity comparison: Are these two symbols the same? Syntactically symbols are usually represented by character strings.

Storage Structure. Symbols differ from character strings in that no operations other than the identity test (and input-output) apply to them. For this reason it is common to store the character string representation of symbols in a *symbol table* and represent the symbol by a pointer to this storage location. The identity test then becomes a simple comparison for identity of pointers. When needed for input-output the string form may be retrieved from the symbol table using the pointer.

The pure symbol data type is often "corrupted" by allowing the symbol table entry for a given symbol to contain other information associated with the symbol. In LISP, a typical case, symbols (called *atoms*) are represented by pointers at run time as is common, but the pointer points to a *property list* which contains not only the character string representation of the symbol (called the *print name* or PNAME) but also an arbitrary list of other properties associated with the symbol.

Pointers (References, Locations, Addresses)

Closely related to the symbol data type is the *pointer* data type, also called *reference*, *location*, or *address* in various languages. Ordinarily pointers are not directly available as data items in languages, although they may be used in the storage representations for other data items. However, in PL/I a variable may be of type **pointer** and various operations return pointers as their values. Similar structures are found in other languages, e.g., ALGOL 68. The major utility of making pointers available as a language data type is that the programmer may then create and manipulate his own data structures in a flexible manner. Pointers differ from symbols in that pointers "point to" other data items while symbols "stand for themselves." In addition, pointers are usually dynamically generated and have no external character string representation. Both symbols and pointers have a storage representation as pointers.

The use of pointers in data structure construction is discussed in more detail in Section 3-14. The inclusion of a pointer data type in languages like PL/I and ALGOL 68 has led to much controversy because of the difficulty of avoiding the creation of *dangling pointers*, pointers which point to data structures that have been destroyed (see Section 4-5).

3-8. HOMOGENEOUS FIXED-SIZE ARRAYS

In this and the following two sections the basic *linear array* data structure and its multidimensional extensions are taken up. In this discussion we shall encounter those data structures that make up the great majority of data structures found in programming languages: *vectors, arrays, lists, stacks, queues, records, property lists,* and *trees,* to name a few. Despite the variety of these structures, there are only a few basic representation principles involved. Linear arrays may be *homogeneous* (elements all with the same data descriptor) or *heterogeneous* (elements with varying data descriptors); the descriptors may be specified when the program is written (*declared descriptors*) or be left unspecified until execution (*run-time descriptors*); and the number of elements in the array may be fixed throughout its existence during execution (*fixed-size*) or may vary dynamically through insertion or deletion of elements (*variable-size*).

Extension of linear arrays to more complex multidimensional structures yields *matrices and higher-dimensional arrays, trees, records,* and *list structures* depending on the details of the extension, yet only a single underlying basic concept is involved: *Allow an element of a linear array to itself be a linear array.* We shall take up linear arrays and their multidimensional extensions roughly in order of increasing complexity, beginning with the common homogeneous fixed-size arrays found in FORTRAN, ALGOL, and many other languages.

Homogeneous fixed-size arrays are perhaps the most common data structures encountered in programming. Most languages provide such arrays as a basic built-in data structure type. Storage representation and accessing of such arrays are usually at least partially hardware-supported on conventional computers (e.g., through provision of hardware index registers and indexing operations), and this makes processing of arrays of this type fairly efficient. Applications of such arrays to the representation of problem data are so common as to merit little discussion. Vectors and matrices arise in almost every programming area.

Vectors

Logical Organization. A homogeneous fixed-size linear array is termed a *vector*. The logical organization of a vector is that of a sequence of data items, each of which may be individually accessed by its position within the sequence using an integer *subscript*. The individual data items within the sequence may be replaced by new ones through assignment, but the number of items may not be modified. Moreover, all the data items have the same descriptor, including data type, length, and any other attributes. Ordinarily the term *vector* is used only when the individual data items are elementary, rather than structured. Thus, for example, a vector might be composed of a sequence of integers, or a sequence of reals (but not a mixture of the two), or a sequence of characters or Boolean values (giving it the appearance of a character or bit string in which each character or bit is individually accessible by subscript). Occasionally one might also encounter a vector of statement labels or pointers.

Storage Structure. The homogeneity and fixed size of a vector make storage and accessing of individual elements straightforward and efficient. Homogeneity implies that the length and format of the bit string storage representation for each data item in the vector is the same, and fixed size implies that the number of such bit strings is constant throughout the lifetime of the vector. In addition homogeneity implies that the descriptors for individual data items may be replaced by a single common descriptor, which may be merged with the descriptor for the vector itself. A straightforward sequential representation of a vector, storing the bit strings representing individual elements in sequence in memory, is appropriate. The descriptor for a vector must specify (1) *vector* data type (or "array of one dimension"), (2) number of elements, or subscript range, and (3) descriptor for the elements. Figure 3-5 illustrates this storage representation.

Accessing. Accessing in vectors is controlled by subscripts whose values may be computed during execution. For example, if A is the name of a vector, then $A[I]$ designates an element of A whose position is given by the value of I, computed during execution. The situation is made more complex by the possibility of an arbitrary

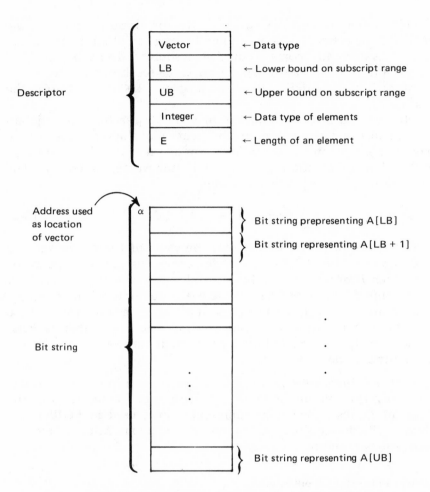

Fig. 3-5. Storage structure for a vector A with full descriptor.

lower bound on the subscript range. For example, a vector A of ten elements might be defined with a subscript range of 0 to 9 or -4 to 5, in which case $A[3]$ designates the fourth or eighth elements, respectively, of the vector.

Homogeneity and sequential storage for vector elements allow the location of the Ith vector element to be computed using the simple *accessing formula*

$$locn \ A[I] = \alpha + (I - LB) \times E$$

where I is the subscript of the desired element, α is the location of the beginning of the bit string representing the vector, LB (lower bound) is the subscript of the first vector element, and E is the length of the element. In computing the location of $A[I]$ the various data items necessary come from diverse sources: The subscript I is a direct input to the accessing operation, α is a result of the referencing operation on A, and E and LB come from the descriptor for the vector.

Observe that in the calculation of *locn* $A[I]$ each of the variables α, LB, and E is fixed at the time of creation of the vector. Accessing may be speeded considerably if the term $\alpha' = \alpha - LB \times E$ is computed at the time of creation and stored in the vector descriptor. The calculation of *locn* $A[I]$ then becomes

$$locn\ A[I] = \alpha' + I \times E \tag{3-1}$$

The above formula assumes that the value of I is known to be a valid subscript for A. If checking for erroneous values of I is to be done, then I must be tested for $LB \leqslant I \leqslant UB$, and the values of LB and UB must be present at run time in the descriptor. If no checking is to be done, then only the values of α' and E need be stored. Note that the exact variation of the acessing calculation that is most efficient is often dependent on the particular hardware configuration and hardware operations available.

Declared Descriptors. The storage representation for vectors is not dependent on the presence of declarations for vectors in the program. Basically the same representation is used in FORTRAN, where full declarations are provided, and in APL, where no declarations are given.

Matrices and Homogeneous Arrays
of Higher Dimension

The extension of vector concepts to the representation of arrays of higher dimensions is straightforward.

Logical Organization. Ordinarily a two-dimensional homogeneous array or *matrix* is organized as a rectangular grid of elements in the plane; a three-dimensional array is viewed as a three-dimensional parallelepiped; etc. Homogeneity implies that each element of the array has the same descriptor, e.g., a matrix of integers, or a matrix of reals, but not a mixture of the two representations. While this concept of logical organization is often entirely satisfactory, a slightly different view illuminates more clearly the principles on which the storage representation is based. Consider a matrix as a vector whose elements are in turn vectors; a three-dimensional array as a vector whose elements are vectors of vectors, etc. Here we have a direct application of the principle that linear arrays may be extended to higher dimensions by allowing an element of a vector to be itself a vector. Figure 3-6 illustrates these two views. Note that homogeneity requires that in a matrix each subvector serving as an element of the main vector have the same descriptor, including descriptors for its elements. By implication, then, all the subvectors must have the same number of elements of the same type.

Whether a matrix is viewed as a "column of rows" or a "row of columns" is relatively unimportant. Most common is the column-of-rows structure in which each element of the main vector is a subvector representing one row of the original matrix, as illustrated in Fig. 3-6. This representation is known as *row-major order*. In general an array of any number of dimensions is organized in row-major order when the array is first divided into a vector of subvectors for each element in the range of the first subscript, then each of these subvectors is subdivided into sub-sub-vectors for each element in the range of the second subscript, etc.

Storage Representation. A sequential storage representation is immediate from the logical organization of arrays as *vectors of vectors*. For a matrix organized in row-major order the elements of the first row are stored first, followed by the elements of the second row, etc., as in Fig. 3-7. In the storage representation the logical division into rows, of course, is not explicit; the storage representation is simply one long sequence of bit strings, each representing one element of the matrix. For arrays of higher dimension the same representation extends easily to allow a *vector of vectors of vectors . . .* to any number of levels.

A[1]	(A[1])[1]	(A[1])[2]	(A[1])[3]	(A[1])[4]

A[1,1]	A[1,2]	A[1,3]	A[1,4]
A[2,1]	A[2,2]	A[2,3]	A[2,4]
A[3,1]	A[3,2]	A[3,3]	A[3,4]

A[2]	(A[2])[1]	(A[2])[2]	(A[2])[3]	(A[2])[4]

A[3]	(A[3])[1]	(A[3])[2]	(A[3])[3]	(A[3])[4]

3 X 4 Matrix
(ordinary view)

3 X 4 Matrix as three-element
vector of four-element vectors

Fig. 3-6. Two views of the logical organization of a matrix.

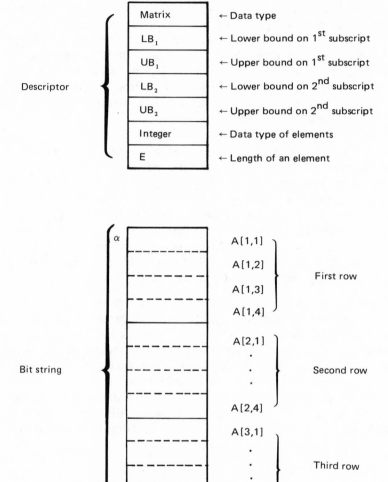

Fig. 3-7. Matrix storage structure with full descriptor.

What sort of descriptor is needed to allow the decoding of such a bit string? As with vectors we need a descriptor for the basic elementary items in the array, e.g., a type flag for **integer, real, Boolean,** etc. In addition, for each new dimension of the array there in general may be an upper and lower bound on the subscript range specified, and of course a primary type flag is necessary designating *array* and the number of dimensions (see Fig. 3-7). These basic descriptor components may be combined in various ways as required for efficient accessing, or sometimes eliminated from the run-time representation altogether where some of the descriptor checking can be completed at compile time, as we shall see below.

Accessing. Multidimensional array accessing may be done using an accessing formula that is a direct extension of that used for vectors. If A is a matrix with M rows and N columns and A is stored in row-major order, then the location of element $A[I,J]$ is given by

$$locn\ A[I,J] = \alpha + (I - LB_1) \times S + (J - LB_2) \times E \qquad (3\text{-}2)$$

where S = length of a row = $(UB_2 - LB_2 + 1) \times E$
   LB_1 = lower bound on first subscript
   $LB_2,\ UB_2$ = lower and upper bounds, respectively, on the second subscript

Collecting constant terms, this simplifies to

$$locn\ A[I,J] = \alpha - K + I \times S + J \times E$$

with $K = LB_1 \times S + LB_2 \times E$. Note that K, S, α and E are fixed when the array is created and thus need be computed only once and stored. The worst-case computation necessary on each access then becomes

$$locn\ A[I,J] = \alpha' + I \times S + J \times E$$

where $\alpha' = \alpha - K$. The generalization of these formulas to higher dimensions is straightforward (see Problem 3-2).

3-9. HETEROGENEOUS FIXED-SIZE ARRAYS, RECORDS, AND STRUCTURES

The restriction to homogeneity in an array is often too stringent to allow convenient representation of problem data. For example, in a two-dimensional array of two columns used as a table, it is often useful to have the first column composed of data of one type and the second column representing data of a second type, as, for example, in a table of integer part numbers and their unit prices or a table of state names and their populations. More generally a linear array of elements of different types may represent, for example, an employee record in a business application, with the individual elements representing employee name, age, salary, address, etc. A *two-dimensional* structure composed of a linear sequence of such employee records would represent perhaps all the employees of a single company, or a division of a company, with higher dimensions representing larger institutional groupings of employees. Heterogeneous fixed-length arrays allow more natural representation of such problem data. In contrast with homogeneous arrays, the presence or absence of declarations for heterogeneous arrays leads to different storage representations.

Heterogeneous Linear Arrays with Declarations

The *records* of COBOL and the *structures* of PL/I are the most common examples of this type of linear array. Consider the PL/I declaration

```
DECLARE 1 EMPLOYEE,
        2 NAME CHARACTER(15),
        2 AGE FIXED,
        2 SALARY FLOAT;
```

The declaration defines a heterogeneous linear array of three elements. The first is a character string, the second an integer, and the third a real number. The logical organization of such a linear array is identical with that of a vector, with the exception of the varying data types of the elements. The PL/I declaration exhibits one further characteristic of the usual heterogeneous declared array: the use of *noninteger subscripts*. Instead of the integer subscripts used in referencing in a vector, we have the symbolic subscripts NAME, AGE, and SALARY. To access the second element of the array, for example, one writes AGE OF EMPLOYEE, or EMPLOYEE.AGE. This subscripting technique is discussed further below.

Storage Structure. The storage representation for linear arrays of this type is similar to that for vectors. A sequential representation is used, with the bit strings representing individual elements stored sequentially in a single block in memory. The descriptor for such an array must necessarily be more complex than that for a vector because of the variation in data types of the elements. A full descriptor would consist of (1) the data type "heterogeneous linear array," (2) the number of elements, and (3) a descriptor for each element. However, the presence of the complete declaration during translation, together with the restrictions on accessing to be discussed below, make storage of a full descriptor unnecessary in the usual case. Figure 3-8 illustrates this storage structure.

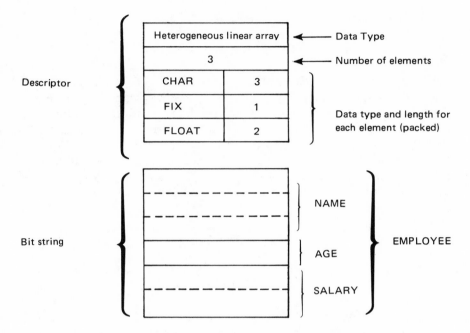

Fig. 3-8. Heterogeneous linear array with full descriptor.

Accessing. Accessing in a heterogeneous linear array is rather different from accessing in a vector. In a vector the integer subscripts serve a double purpose. They not only allow individual elements of the vector to be accessed at random but also make it convenient to process the entire vector sequentially by use of an integer variable as a pointer. The variable is initialized to designate the first vector element and is then incremented to point to each vector element in turn as processing proceeds. This sort of sequential processing is basic when working with vectors. Sequential processing is seldom appropriate when working with heterogeneous linear arrays, however, because the variations in data type of the elements do not allow uniform treatment by a single process. As a result it is only the *random accessibility* of elements that is important. Moreover, there is little reason to allow the computation of a subscript during execution, e.g., allowing a reference to EMPLOYEE.I, where the value of I is computed during execution. Such computed subscripts are of value mainly in the sort of sequential processing used with vectors. The use of integer subscripts is thus unnecessary in heterogeneous arrays; instead each element need only have a unique "subscript" distinguishing it from other elements in the same array. Because of their mnemonic value, arbitrary identifiers are ordinarily used as subscripts in such arrays, as in the PL/I example above.

The basic accessing formula in a heterogeneous linear array is

$$locn\ A[I]\ =\ \alpha\ +\ \sum_{j=1}^{I-1}\ \text{length of }A[j]$$

where the summation is necessary because of the possibly different lengths of each of the elements. The computation necessary at run time is trivial, however, because of the declaration and the fact that each reference to an element of a heterogeneous array in a program must now appear as the array name and a *constant* subscript, e.g., EMPLOYEE.AGE. Given the constant subscript and the full declaration, the summation in the accessing formula may be performed during translation, with the run-time computation resolving to the simple

$$locn\ A[I] = \alpha + K_I$$

where

$$K_I\ =\ \sum_{j=1}^{I-1}\ \text{length of }A[j]$$

At run time the precomputed sums K_I for those array elements, I, actually accessed form the only descriptor needed.

Multidimensional Heterogeneous Arrays with Declarations

The extension of heterogeneous linear arrays to multidimensional arrays is straightforward. As usual we simply allow each element of the linear array to be another heterogeneous linear array. Because each of these subarrays may have different descriptors, and thus different numbers of elements of different types, the resulting structure has the form of a tree. Consider the following PL/I structure definition:

```
1 EMPLOYEE,
    2 NAME,
        3 LAST CHARACTER(10),
        3 FIRST CHARACTER(15),
        3 MIDDLE CHARACTER(1),
    2 AGE FIXED(2),
    2 ADDRESS,
        3 STREET,
            4 NUMBER FIXED(5),
            4 ST-NAME CHARACTER(20),
        3 CITY CHARACTER(15),
        3 STATE CHARACTER(10),
        3 ZIP FIXED(5);
```

Note that the declaration syntax resembles that of an outline, with major headings, subheads, etc. The structure resulting from this declaration is composed of a single linear array named EMPLOYEE with three elements. One of these elements, AGE, is an elementary data item, a single number. The other two, NAME and ADDRESS, are each themselves heterogeneous arrays, of three and four elements, respectively. The first element of ADDRESS, STREET, is itself an array of two items.

The storage structure for the above array is given in Fig. 3-9. As with multidimensional homogeneous arrays, storage is in row-major order. Subscripts for accessing are again restricted to constants, and thus the entire accessing computation for retrieving any element in such a structure may be reduced at compile time to the simple addition of a constant to the *base address* designating the location of the structure in memory.

Heterogeneous Linear Arrays without Declarations

Different storage representations and accessing techniques are ordinarily used for heterogeneous arrays when no declarations are given. Not only may the type of each element in such an array differ, but it is assumed that each assignment of a new value to an element may change the type of element stored there. Thus the type, and in particular the length, of each array element may vary dynamically during execution. The arrays in SNOBOL4 are typical.

Logical Organization. The logical organization of such an array does not differ from that of other linear arrays: It is a simple sequence of elements of varying types.

Storage Structure. What storage representation is appropriate for a linear array whose elements may vary dynamically in length during execution? Clearly the simple sequential representation used for linear arrays heretofore is not adequate, because each new assignment may require that a longer bit string be inserted in place of a shorter one, causing other elements of the array also to be repositioned. Note that the number of elements in the array is fixed throughout execution; it is only the length of individual elements that may vary. Under these conditions the following representation is appropriate: Represent the array as *a vector of pointers to values*, and store the bit strings representing the values elsewhere in memory, in arbitrary locations. The vector of pointers may now be stored sequentially, because the size of each pointer is constant regardless of the type of value to which it points.

Descriptors for each element of the array must be stored during

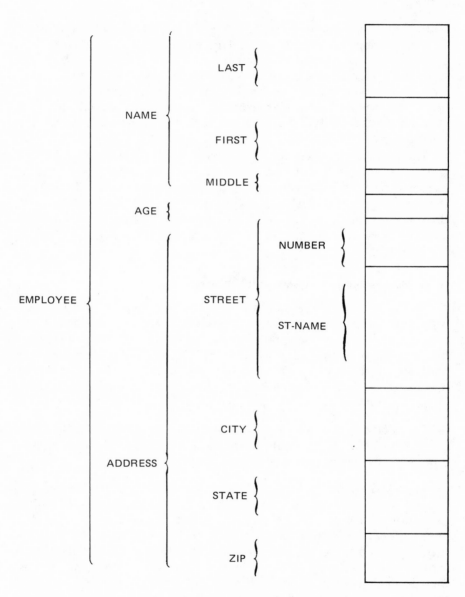

Fig. 3-9. Storage representation for a multidimensional PL/I structure (without descriptor).

execution, since no descriptors are known at compile time. These descriptors might be stored along with the bit strings for each individual element. More commonly if the descriptors are small, they may be stored along with each pointer in the vector of pointers. This representation is illustrated in Fig. 3-10. The array itself requires a

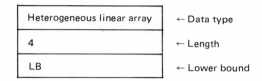

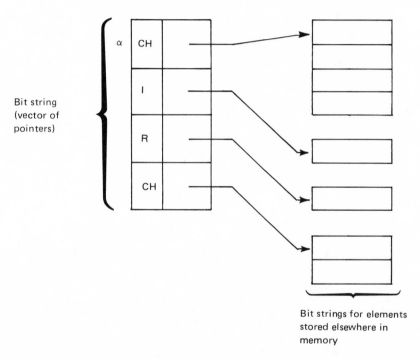

Fig. 3-10. Heterogeneous linear array with run-time descriptor.

descriptor specifying (1) the *linear array* data type, (2) the number of elements, and (3) the lower bound on the subscript range, if not assumed to be 1.

Accessing. The representation as a vector of pointers makes accessing individual elements straightforward. To access $A[I]$ the position of the Ith pointer in the vector of pointers is computed exactly as for an ordinary vector. This pointer then gives the location in memory of the bit string representing the value. Integer subscripts are ordinarily used because other forms would require explicit storage of subscripts along with the array (but see the discussion of *property lists* in Section 3-10).

**Multidimensional Heterogeneous Arrays without
Declarations**

Multidimensional heterogeneous arrays may be created readily through direct application of the homogeneous array techniques of Section 3-8 to heterogeneous arrays represented as arrays of pointers to individual elements. An alternative is to allow a pointer in a linear array of pointers to point to another linear array of pointers rather than to an elementary data item. Such a representation is widely used but appears most often in the case of variable-size arrays, which are taken up in the next section. Where the length of the array is fixed, the first mentioned representation allows efficient access to individual elements through the same accessing formula used for homogeneous arrays.

3-10. VARIABLE-SIZE ARRAYS

Often the demands of problem data representation preclude the use of fixed-size arrays. The data may be entering from an input device and their extent not be known, or they may be generated internally within a program in an unpredictable manner. To allow the natural representation and manipulation of such data, many languages allow linear arrays to grow and shrink in size dynamically during program execution. Such variable-size arrays are known by many names: *stacks*, *queues*, *sets*, *lists*, and *tables*, to name a few. The logical organization of such arrays tends not to be substantially different from their fixed-size counterparts; however, the fact of their variable size makes different storage representations and accessing techniques appropriate, in particular the technique of *linked storage representation*, which has been little used heretofore.

Storage representation for variable-size arrays is closely tied to the manner in which the array may grow and shrink. In the case of fixed-size arrays the operation of accessing was our central concern. With variable-size arrays we must also consider the basic operations of *insertion* of new elements and *deletion* of existing elements. In fixed-size arrays each element could be individually accessed by subscript. Accessing in variable-size arrays tends to be *relative*: Get the element *after* (or *before*) this one, get the *last* element, etc. Accessing by subscript is far less common and less important because each array element may change its position as the array changes in size.

Variable-size arrays must of necessity utilize run-time descriptors because of the dynamic changes in the structures during execution. Thus we can gain only minor benefits in general through the use of declarations. In addition the homogeneous-heterogeneous distinction is relatively unimportant because variations in element types cause little additional difficulty.

Stacks

A *stack* (also known as a *pushdown list* or *LIFO—*last-in/first-out—*list*) is the simplest variety of variable-size linear array. Insertion and deletion of elements is restricted to a single end of the stack, termed the *top* of the stack. Accessing is usually restricted to the top stack element. The term *stack* is descriptive of the manner in which the array grows and shrinks, for example, as a stack of plates might grow and shrink through plates being added and removed only at the top. Stacks are an extremely important data structure that we shall encounter many times in the following chapters.

Storage Structure. Two basic storage representations—one sequential and the other linked—are widely used for stacks. The sequential representation is used most often when only one or two stacks must be represented or where a reasonably small bound on the size of each stack is known in advance. The linked representation is more generally applicable to an arbitrary number of stacks. In either case we assume that the elements of the stack are either homo-geneous or have been replaced by pointers to the actual elements so that they appear homogeneous.

The sequential stack representation requires that a block of storage be reserved that is large enough for the current stack elements and contains in addition enough space so that the stack may grow to its maximum size without overflowing the block. The first element of the block is a *stack-top pointer* that always points to the current top of the stack. When this pointer points to its own position the stack is *empty.* As elements are added to the stack they (or their pointers) are placed in consecutive locations within the reserved block and the stack-top pointer is updated appropriately. When an element is deleted it must always be deleted from the top of the stack, and thus it suffices to simply decrement the stack-top pointer appropriately. Access to the top element of the stack is done indirectly through the stack-top pointer. Figure 3-11 illustrates this storage structure.

Two stacks may be represented sequentially with a single reserved block by having the stacks grow toward each other from opposite

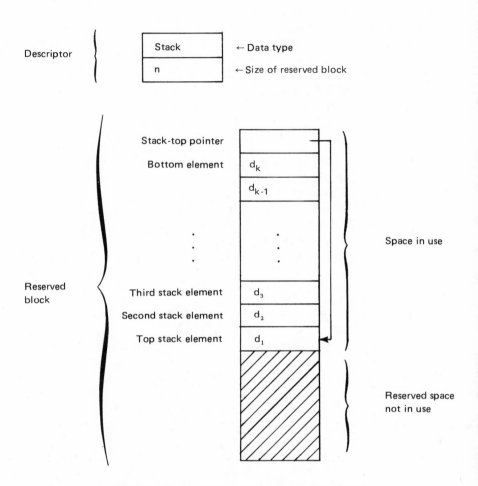

Fig. 3-11. Sequential storage representation for a stack.

ends of the block. Of course, multiple stacks may be represented in the same manner, utilizing one reserved block for each pair of stacks, but the waste in reserved storage and the difficulty in accommodating overflow of one stack usually make the second alternative—linked representation—more desirable.

The linked stack representation allows the stack elements to be scattered throughout memory. Because the sequence of elements does not then correspond to the built-in sequence of memory words, it is necessary to store with each stack element a pointer to the location of the next stack element. The stack then becomes a linked sequence of locations, as illustrated in Fig. 3-12. A pointer to the first location of the stack must be maintained in a stack-top pointer as before. Insertion and deletion of elements is simple, as illustrated

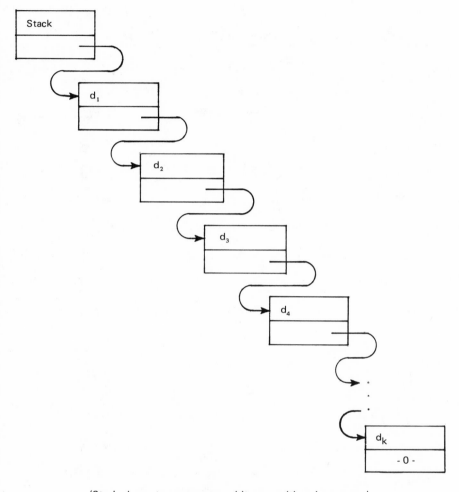

(Stack elements may occupy arbitrary positions in memory)

Fig. 3-12. Linked storage representation for a stack.

in Fig. 3-13. Although the linked representation requires extra storage for the links between elements, space for a new element may be taken from any available position in memory. No prior reservation of storage space is necessary.

Queues

A *queue* (also known as a *FIFO*—first-in/first-out—*list*) differs from a stack only in that insertion of new elements is restricted to the bottom rather than the top. Thus a queue grows at the bottom

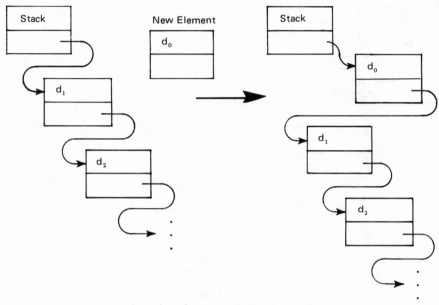

Insertion of new top element in a stack

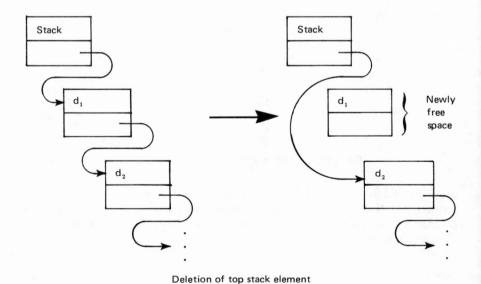

Deletion of top stack element

Fig. 3-13. Insertion and deletion in a linked stack.

and shrinks at the top. Accessing is commonly restricted to the top element.

Storage Structure. Both sequential and linked storage representations for queues are used. As with stacks the sequential representation requires a block of reserved storage within which the queue may grow and shrink. Two access pointers are maintained: a *top pointer*, which always points to the current top of the queue, and a *bottom pointer*, which always points to the current bottom plus 1 (the location for the next insertion of a new element). The queue grows circularly within the reserved block, so that when the bottom pointer reaches the end of the block it is incremented *end-around* back to the beginning of the block. When deletion of an element causes the top and bottom pointers to coincide the queue is empty. The queue overflows the reserved block when insertion of an element causes the bottom pointer to catch up with the top pointer. Figure 3-14 illustrates this representation.

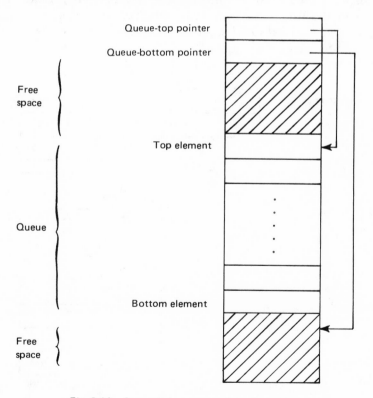

Fig. 3-14. Sequential representation of a queue.

Linked storage representation for queues is similar to that for stacks, with the addition of a bottom pointer to allow easy addition of items to the bottom of the queue (see Fig. 3-15).

Lists

A variable-size linear array in which insertions and deletions may be made at arbitrary points is usually termed a *list* (or *linked list*). Accessing of elements in a list is usually restricted to the first element and the next (or sometimes previous) element after a given one. Thus it is possible to access any list element, but only by working down the list from the first element.

Storage Structure. Linked storage representation for lists is almost a necessity because of the possibility of random insertions and deletions. The two most common linked representations are

1. *Singly linked representation.* Each list element is linked to its successor in the list, and a pointer to the first element is maintained, usually in a special *list head* location. This representation is identical to that used for stacks in Fig. 3-12.

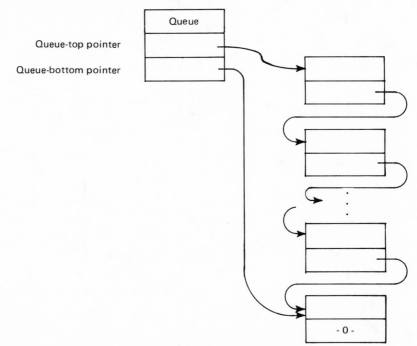

Fig. 3-15. Linked representation of a queue.

2. *Doubly linked representation.* Each list element is linked to both its successor and predecessor in the list. Pointers to both the first and last elements of the list are maintained in a list head location. See Fig. 3-16.

The singly linked representation has the defect of allowing the list to be traversed in only one direction. Thus it is simple to move down the list from its first element by following the pointers stored with each element, but it is not possible to move back up the list to an element passed by previously. The doubly linked representation is

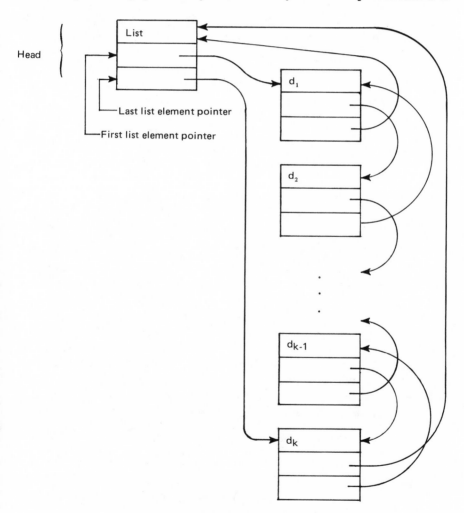

Fig. 3-16. Doubly linked list representation.

used primarily when this restriction on direction of traversal is too stringent. In other cases the extra storage for the double pointers is usually not warranted.

Property Lists

With stacks, queues, and lists, accessing using subscripts is not generally allowed. A very important class of structures is obtained by providing accessing through arbitrary identifier subscripts. Recall the use of mnemonic subscripts such as NAME, AGE, and SALARY to identify elements of the heterogeneous arrays of Section 3-9. We wish to provide similar subscripts with variable-size arrays. This requires that each insertion of an element into such an array also include a specification of the subscript by which the element is to be accessed. The resulting data structure has the form of a set of subscript-value pairs. Usually the ordering in such a structure is not significant because all accessing is done through the provided subscripts. Linear arrays of this sort are found in many languages under varying names, most commonly *property lists* (as in LISP, Chapter 14). In SNOBOL4 these structures are called *tables*, and occasionally in other languages *description lists* or *attribute-value lists*.

Applications of property lists are surprisingly widespread. In list-processing languages such as LISP, property lists often are the basic data structure used in complex applications, despite the basis of the language in ordinary linked lists.

Storage Structure. The most common storage representation for property lists is a linked list with the subscripts and values alternating in a single long sequence. Insertion or deletion of a subscript-value pair is then accomplished through the insertion or deletion of two elements into the linked list—operations that are easily performed. Accessing an element given its subscript requires a search down the list, checking only the subscript elements, until the desired subscript is found. The next list element is then the desired value. Figure 3-17 illustrates this structure. A mixed sequential and linked representation is used in SNOBOL4; see Problem 3-8.

Multidimensional Variable-Size Arrays

Extension of variable-size linear arrays to multidimensional structures follows the following simple rule: Allow an element of an array to be a pointer to another array. Most commonly this is allowed when a linked storage representation is used for linear arrays.

The three most common varieties of such structures are

1. *Trees.* At most one pointer to a given linear array (list) may be stored in another array, and no circular linkage structures are allowed. Thus each list is a sublist of only one list.

2. *List structures.* Multiple pointers to a given array are allowed, but no circular linkages may be created. Thus a given list may be a sublist of more than one list as long as circularity is avoided.

3. *Directed graphs.* Multiple pointers and arbitrary circular linkages are allowed.

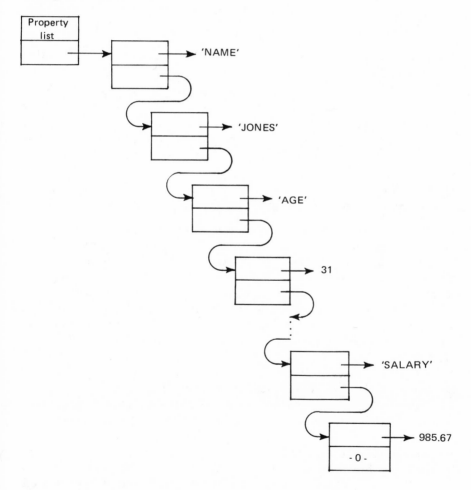

Fig. 3-17. Linked storage representation for property lists.

Storage Structure. Little new is added by these extensions, other than to make processing more complex. The pointer-based storage representation is illustrated in Fig. 3-18.

3-11. SETS

Logically a set may be viewed as in mathematics: an *unordered* collection of *distinct* elements. In contrast a linear array is an ordered collection of possibly nondistinct elements. Three operations on sets are basic:

1. *Membership test.* Is data item *x* a member of set *S*?

2. *Addition of an element.* Add data item *x* to set *S*, provided it is not already a member of *S*.

3. *Deletion of an element.* Delete data item *x* from set *S*.

Note that accessing by subscript or relative position plays no part in set processing. In programming languages the term *set* is often applied to a data structure representing an *ordered* set. Such ordered sets are actually a restricted form of list and need no special consideration. The unordered set, however, admits two specialized storage representations that merit attention.

Storage Structure. Clearly a set may be represented as a variable-size linear array, using one of the storage representations suggested for stacks, queues, or linked lists. In such a representation, however, insertion, deletion, and membership operations must each search the storage structure for the desired element before they act. It is desirable to find a storage representation that allows the basic set operations to be performed without a search. The most common such representation is based on the technique known as *scatter storage* or *hash coding*. A block of storage (sometimes termed the *hash table*) is reserved for the set, much as we reserved a block for storage of a stack or queue. Rather than storing elements of the set in sequential locations within this block, however, the elements are scattered randomly through the block. The trick is to store each new element in such a way that its presence or absence can later be immediately determined without a search of the block.

Consider how this may be done. Suppose that we wish to add a new element *x*, represented by bit string B_x, to the set *S*, represented by the block of storage M_S. First we must determine if *x* is already a member of *S*, and if not, add it to the set. We determine a position

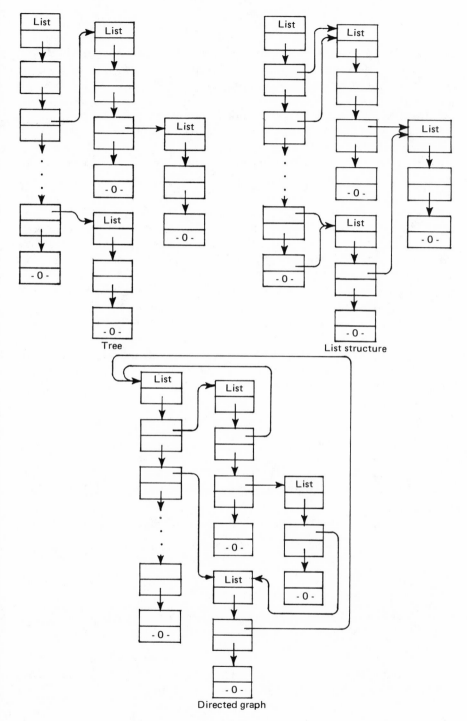

Fig. 3-18. Linked representation of trees, list structures, and graphs.

for B_x within the block M_S by the application of a *hashing function*
to the bit string B_x. The hashing function "hashes" (chops up into
little pieces and mixes together) the bit string B_x and then extracts a
hash address I_x from the result. This hash address is used as an index
pointing to a position in the block M_S. We look at that position in
the block, and if x is already in the set, then it must be stored at that
position. If not, then we store the bit string B_x at the location
designated by I_x. Any later attempt to find if x is a member of S will
be answered by hashing the new bit string B_x representing x,
obtaining I_x, accessing the block M_S at that position, and finding the
previously stored string B_x. No search of the table is ever needed.

Exactly how the hashing function works is not critical as long as
it is relatively fast and generates hash addresses that are fairly randomly distributed. An example will illustrate the idea more directly.
Suppose that we allocate a block of 1024 words (a block length
equal to a power of 2 for a binary computer is most convenient) for
the block M_S and suppose that the data items to be stored are
character strings represented by double-word bit strings. We may
represent a set of up to 512 distinct elements within this block.
Suppose that the starting address of the block in memory is α. An
appropriate hash address for such a table would be a string I_x of nine
bits, since then the formula

$$\alpha + 2 \times I_x$$

would always generate an address within the block. We might
compute I_x from a given two-word-long bit string B_x by the
following algorithm: Assume that B_x is stored in words a and b; then

1. Multiply a and b, giving c (two-word product).

2. Add together the two words of c, giving d,

3. Square d, giving e,

4. Extract the center nine bits of e, giving I_x.

Different hashing functions are appropriate depending on the
properties of the bit string representations of the data to be stored.

Even the best hashing function cannot in general guarantee that
different data items will generate different hash addresses when
hashed. While it is desirable that the hashing function spread the
generated hash addresses throughout the block as much as possible,
almost inevitably two data items may be hashed to the same hash

address, leading to a *collision*. A collision occurs when we have a data item to be added to the set, go to the block at the designated hash address, and find the block entry at that point filled with a data item *different from the one to be stored* (but which just happened to hash to the same hash address). Many techniques for handling collisions are known; for example:

1. *Rehashing*. We might modify the original bit string B_x (e.g., by multiplication by a constant), and then rehash the result, generating a new hash address. If another collision occurs, we rehash again until either B_x is found or an empty block location is encountered.

2. *Sequential scan*. From the original point of the collision in the block we might begin a sequential (end-around) search until either B_x is found or an empty block location is encountered.

3. *Bucketing*. In place of direct storage in the block we might substitute pointers to linked *bucket lists* of the elements having the same hash addresses. After hashing B_x and retrieving the pointer to the appropriate bucket list, we search the list for B_x, and if not found, add it to the end of the list.

Hashing is the basic technique for set storage where the universe of possible elements of the set is large. Where the universe is small a simpler storage representation using a single bit string is appropriate. Suppose that there are N elements in the universe. Order these elements arbitrarily as e_1, e_2, ..., e_N. A set of elements chosen from this universe may then be represented by a bit string of length N where the ith bit in the string is a 1 if e_i is in the set and 0 if not. The bit string represents the *characteristic function* of the set. With this representation, insertion of an element into a set consists only of setting the appropriate bit to a 1, deletion consists of setting the appropriate bit to 0, and membership may be determined simply by interrogating the appropriate bit. Most conventional hardware includes logical **and** and **or** operations on bit strings that may be directly and efficiently used to perform these operations. This hardware support provides the basic rationale for the bit string storage structure.

In addition to the bit strings representing sets chosen from the universe the universe itself must be represented as an ordered set in a separate vector, so that the position of any given element x in the universe, and thus the position of the bit representing x in the bit strings, may be determined. However, this vector may often be set up and used only during compilation and not stored during execution.

3-12. EXTERNAL DATA FILES

Data may be stored on external storage media either for purposes of input-output or for temporary *scratch storage* when not enough central memory is available. Such external files tend to have relatively simple organizations. Most common is the sequential file. Also seen are the indexed sequential and random access organizations. COBOL and PL/I provide the widest variety of external file organizations of the languages described in Part II.

Sequential Files

Sequential files are the common data files used for input and output in every language. In such files the basic unit of data is usually the character. Binary files are sometimes used where the data are not to be read or printed externally, but the structures are essentially identical with the character file, and so only the character file is considered here.

Logical Organization. A sequential file is organized as a linear sequence of *records*, each a character string, and ends with a special *end-of-file* record. Records are often restricted to a fixed size. In addition each file incorporates a *current record pointer* which points to the record within the file that was last read or written. The file may be accessed only through the current record pointer. For example, a READ operation reads in the record pointed to and advances the current record pointer to point to the next record, and a WRITE operation advances the pointer and then adds a new record to the file.

An important class of sequential files consists of those files in which the records have been ordered by the values of a *record key* data item stored as a part of each record. For example, a file of employee payroll records in a business application might be ordered on the basis of a special "employee number" record key (perhaps just the employee's social security number). Such ordered sequential files arise naturally in applications where the records of multiple files are to be processed simultaneously. In computing a large business payroll, for example, a *master file* of employee salary records and a *detail file* of particulars for the latest pay period (hours worked by each hourly employee, new employees, terminated employees, etc.) must both serve as input. Before the payroll computation for a particular employee can be made, the relevant record from each file must be read into memory. If both master and detail files are ordered on the same record key, then the two files can be processed sequentially in one pass, reading only one record from each into memory at a time. The records of an ordered sequential file that was not originally created as an ordered file must be sorted into the appropriate order before processing begins. Most computer installations have special file-sorting programs available for this purpose, and languages such as COBOL, which are intended for applications in which ordered files are needed, may include a special SORT primitive operation. The fact that a sequential file is ordered does not in general affect its storage representation.

Storage Representation. The storage representation for a file is closely tied to the particular storage medium used, which may be magnetic tape, drum, disk, or other mass storage device. Commonly the file appears as a bit string broken into substrings, usually confusingly called *physical records*. Each physical record on the storage device contains a number of the *logical records* of the file and corresponds to a unit of external storage that may be efficiently copied to central memory.

The representation of a file also includes a block of storage in central memory called a *buffer*, which is used as a queue (see Fig. 3-19). Typically the buffer is chosen to be large enough to hold two or more physical records. Input or output of data is a two-stage process with the buffer serving as temporary storage. During input, physical records of data are transferred from the external storage medium to the buffer as space becomes available. The current record pointer of the file is maintained as a pointer to the location in the buffer where the last used logical record ends (the top of the queue). The READ operation transfers the next logical record from the buffer to the designated programmer-defined data structures. As the buffer is emptied by READ operations, successive physical records are read from the external storage as needed and added to the bottom of the queue. The advantage of this organization is that it allows the actual transfer of physical records into the buffer to overlap the intramemory transfer of logical data records to data structures, utilizing the parallel input capabilities of most hardware computers.

During output essentially the inverse technique is used: Data are transferred into the buffer in logical record units in response to program WRITE statements. When enough data have been collected to form a physical record, the data are actually transferred to the external storage medium. In either case three pointers must be

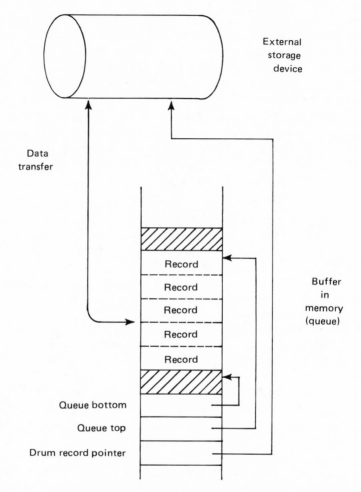

External
storage
device

Data
transfer

Record

Record

Record

Record

Record

Buffer
in
memory
(queue)

Queue bottom

Queue top

Drum record pointer

Queue top   =   logical current record pointer, points to next file record to be used
Queue bottom   =   location in buffer where next file record is to be located when read

Fig. 3-19. Storage structure for a sequential file.

maintained in central memory: a *logical* current record pointer
pointing to the position of the last read or written record in the
buffer (the queue top), a *physical* current record pointer pointing to
the location of the last physical record read or written on the
external storage medium, and a pointer to the location in the buffer
where the next physical record is to be read (the queue bottom).

The above is one common storage structure for sequential files.

The exact storage structure that is most efficient depends greatly on the properties of the hardware: the amount of central memory, hardware support of parallelism in I-O operations, physical record sizes, etc.

Random Access Files

In a sequential file the records must be accessed in sequence in the order in which they appear on the file. While limited facilities to advance or backspace the current record pointer are usually available, such operations tend to be expensive. Where random access to the records of a file is desirable, a different file organization is required.

Logical Organization. A random access file is organized as a set of unordered records. Access is through an *address* that indicates the position of the record on the external device, such as a disk track address. Thus the file appears much like a linear array of records, each accessible only through its hardware-provided address. No current record pointer is necessary because each access requires specification of the address of the desired record.

Storage Structure. A random access file must be stored on an external device such as a disk or drum that allows random access to physical records. Each file record is stored on an addressable portion of the storage device, and the hardware address is used to access the record. This simple organization often results in inefficient use of the storage device, and the indexed sequential organization is used instead.

Indexed Sequential Files

An indexed sequential file is a compromise between the pure sequential and the pure random access file organizations.

Logical Organization. An indexed sequential file is organized like an ordered sequential file. Each record contains a record key data item that is used to order the records of the file. Random accessing of records is allowed, using the record key as a subscript, and the file may also be processed sequentially from any given random access point.

Storage Structure. The file is structured as an ordinary sequential file, with the records grouped into physical records appropriate for the storage device being used. However, each file also includes a special record called an *index*. The index contains one entry for each physical record on the storage device. Each entry consists of the record key value for the last logical record within that physical record on the storage device. Index entries are ordered by increasing (or decreasing) record key values. To randomly access the record with record key value I in the file, the index is searched to find the index entry with the next largest (or equal) record key value. The associated hardware address in the index specifies the position on the storage device of the physical record containing the desired logical record. The entire physical record is then read into the buffer and a search is made for the appropriate logical record. The effect is that random access is only slightly slower than with the pure random access organization, the physical record size of the storage device may be utilized appropriately, and, moreover, once having located a desired record the following (or preceding) records may be processed sequentially with little additional cost.

3-13. INTERPRETABLE DATA STRUCTURES:
PROGRAMS, PATTERNS, AND FORMATS

Certain types of data in programming languages exist for no other purpose than to serve as inputs to *interpreters* that vary their processing of other data according to the specifications of the interpretable data structure. Programs themselves, in their run-time representation, are the key example of such structures. As noted in Chapter 2 a program serves as input data to the interpreter (software or hardware) of a virtual computer. The interpreter varies its processing of the *actual data*—numbers, arrays, lists, etc.—according to the specifications of the input program. Programs occasionally are also processible as ordinary data (e.g., in LISP), but most often their only use is as input to the interpreter of the virtual computer.

Patterns (as found in SNOBOL4) and formats are two simpler examples of data structures used for similar purposes. A *pattern*, in the SNOBOL4 sense, is a data structure set up to guide a pattern-matching operation. The pattern-matching operation accepts a pattern and a character string as input and searches the character string for a substring of the type specified by the pattern. Patterns may not be manipulated as ordinary data structures in SNOBOL4; they may only be created, incorporated as parts of larger patterns, and input to the pattern-matching operation. A *format*, as used for input-output in FORTRAN and other languages, is a pattern-like data structure that is applicable only to the conversion between external character string representations of data on input-output files and internal storage representations of data in memory. The format given to an input-output operation is "interpreted" by the operation as a guide to how to convert between external and internal representations for numbers and other data.

Storage Structure. The basic rule for storage representation of these data structures is that the representation should be efficiently interpretable. Formats are the simplest of these structures and are ordinarily represented in their original character string syntax and decoded only as necessary during input-output processing. This representation makes it relatively easy to create and read in new formats during program execution. The cost in execution speed caused by repeated decoding of the same format is high, however.

Patterns in SNOBOL4 are commonly stored in a prefix representation similar to that often used for arithmetic expressions (because they are syntactically defined as expressions in SNOBOL4). Prefix representation is discussed in more detail in Chapter 5.

Programs remain as the major interpretable data structure. Of course the most common storage representation for programs is in the form of machine code sequences. A compiler translates the original character string program representation into a sequential block of machine code. The hardware interpreter may then be used to efficiently decode and interpret this storage representation. Where the interpreter is software-simulated, other program representations in storage are possible. For example, in LISP the storage representation of a program is in the form of a list structure, as described in Section 3-10. Chapter 14 describes this program representation in somewhat greater detail. The LISP representation of programs as list structures has the advantage that programs may be operated upon by the ordinary LISP list-processing operations, in addition to serving as input to the LISP software interpreter.

Because representations of interpretable data structures are closely tied to the demands of the processes that interpret them, few general concepts in their representation are possible—each structure tends to an idiosyncratic representation tailored to its interpreting process. As a result we shall not attempt to go into these representations in depth.

3-14. REPRESENTATION OF ONE DATA
STRUCTURE TYPE USING ANOTHER:
EXTENSIBLE DATA STRUCTURES

We shall turn now to a subject that will be a recurrent theme in the remaining chapters: the extension of a language to include concepts not incorporated directly in the language initially. In this case we are concerned with data structures and the question of language facilities for definition of new data structure types. The importance of facilities for extending the language to new data structures stems from our underlying conception of the programmer's task. Given a particular problem to solve on a computer the programmer has the task of representing the problem data in the programming language he chooses to use. Most commonly the problem data does not in fact slide easily into a data representation provided directly by the language; it must be forced. The programmer must develop a representation for the problem data using the structures provided by the language as a basis. In a very real sense he is extending the language to include the data structures appropriate for his problem. The language itself may help or hinder this extension process and may make the resulting structures easy or difficult to process depending on the degree of flexibility of the base structures in the language and the ease of processing these structures in nonstandard ways. Of course almost any language allows problem data representations to be synthesized to some extent, but languages vary widely in the facilities provided and in the ease with which such extensions may be accomplished.

A simple example will help to clarify the problems involved. Suppose that one has access only to FORTRAN as a programming language. The data structures in FORTRAN are the simple homogeneous fixed-size arrays with full declarations discussed in Section 3-8, represented in storage by the usual sequential representation. Suppose that the problem to be solved requires lists of integers that dynamically vary in size through insertions and deletions. Analysis of the problem indicates that a linked list data structure is most appropriate. To represent this sort of data in FORTRAN requires an extension of FORTRAN to include a linked list data structure. The extension can be made, but the FORTRAN language provides little help.

Linked lists may be represented using the basic FORTRAN vector data structure as follows. We first set up one large vector, M, which will serve to represent a *memory*. Subscripts of vector elements serve as addresses or pointers for the *locations* (vector elements) in this memory. Since subscripts are integers, they may be stored in the same vectors as the integer data in the lists; thus the vector M should be of type **integer**. Now the linked lists may be represented in this vector M using the same storage representation suggested in Section 3-10. Each list element consists of an integer data value and an integer subscript serving as a pointer in M to the location of the next data item in the list. Each list element thus takes two consecutive locations within the vector M. This representation is illustrated in Figure 3-20. Although this representation of lists is straightforward, the lists cannot be used effectively unless the programmer also writes a set of subprograms to perform appropriate list-processing operations and, more importantly, designs a storage management system for the vector M that allows storage to be allocated, recovered, and reused as needed during list processing. Some techniques for doing this are discussed in Chapter 7. Note that the FORTRAN language provides no help outside of provision for ordinary subprogram definitions. The problem for the programmer lies in the amount of work involved in making this extension to FORTRAN—obviously only a fairly large problem to be programmed would make this extension worthwhile. An alternative would be to use a prepro-

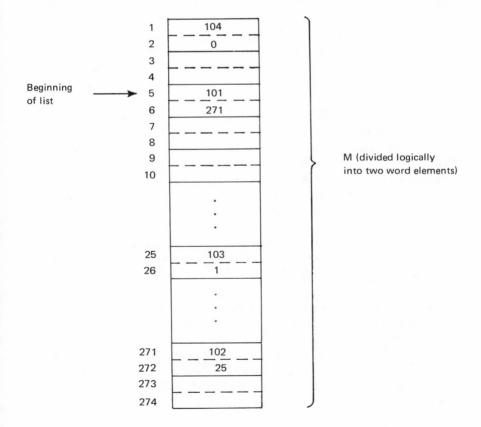

Fig. 3-20. The list (101,102,103,104) represented as a linked list in a FORTRAN vector.

grammed package of routines, such as the SLIP package (Weizenbaum [1963]), which extends FORTRAN to include a linked list
structure.

The FORTRAN example illustrates how almost any language may
be extended, through a substantial programming effort, to include a
new type of data structure. The need for such extensibility, at least
to a limited extent, exists in almost every program written, and in
most cases the "brute force" approach used above, in which the
programmer assumes the entire burden of making the extension, is
too difficult and time-consuming to be practical. Some few languages
provide built-in facilities for extensions that considerably ease the
burden on the programmer. The SNOBOL4 *programmer-defined data
types* and the PL/I *BASED variables* are two examples of such
features to be found in Part II. In neither case are the facilities
ideal—the SNOBOL4 features are entirely run-time software-
simulated and thus costly, and the PL/I features are rather error
prone—but both represent an important facet of language design.

Both the SNOBOL4 and PL/I approaches are built on the same
conceptual foundation: Complex data structures are to be constructed from *nodes* which are heterogeneous fixed-size linear arrays.
Nodes are linked together by pointers stored in one array and
pointing to others. The basic heterogeneous array nodes are as
described in Section 3-9 and are represented in a sequential block in
storage. Individual elements may be accessed by subscripts that are
arbitrary identifiers. The language provides facilities for definition of
various node types (different array structures), for creation of
individual nodes of a given type as needed, for linking nodes together
with pointers, for accessing elements of nodes and following pointers
between nodes, and for handling the necessary storage management
for the allocation, recovery, and reuse of storage. The programmer
need take responsibility only for defining the node types needed, for
creating nodes as needed, and for hooking them together as
appropriate. As a result the extension of PL/I or SNOBOL4 to
include linked lists and the appropriate operations is relatively
trivial—the sort of thing one might do in the normal course of writing
a program of average size.

Chapters 13 and 15 provide somewhat more detail on the PL/I
and SNOBOL4 features for extensible data structures. As such
features are still relatively uncommon in programming languages, we
shall not pursue the topic further. It is likely that extensibility of this
sort will play a larger role in future languages.

3-15. REFERENCES AND SUGGESTIONS
FOR FURTHER READING

The three volumes by Knuth [1968, 1969, 1973] contain a wealth of material on data structures and their manipulation: Volume 1 for various types of arrays (including variable-size arrays), Volume 2 for number representations, and Volume 3 for hash coding techniques. More elementary general treatments of data structures may be found in Harrison [1973], Berztiss [1971], Elson [1973], and Stone [1972]. Ledgard [1971] also treats data structuring issues in his survey of language design problems. D'Imperio [1969] surveys a variety of data structures based on linked representations, with particular emphasis on their storage structures. An elementary introduction to linked list processing is found in Foster [1967]. Galler and Perlis [1970] develop data structures in the course of a more general development of programming language concepts.

Two papers by Hoare [1968, 1972] are extremely important in their emphasis on the relation between language design and data structure handling. The earlier paper considers general language mechanisms for data structures composed of heterogeneous arrays linked by pointers, with particular emphasis on the use of declarations to ensure efficient and secure processing. The latter paper extends the same concerns to the development of a general-purpose, unified set of data structures and processing techniques.

The proceedings of a recent symposium on data structures in programming languages (Tou and Wegner[1971]) provides a useful entry point to research on data structures. Many research papers on various aspects of data structures may also be found in the *Communications of the ACM*.

The area of extensible data structures has received substantial attention. Ph.D. theses by Standish [1967] and Wegbreit [1970] have been particularly influential. A recent symposium proceedings (Schuman [1971]) provides a good introduction to current research.

3-16. PROBLEMS

3-1. Give an intuitive explanation of the matrix-accessing formula (3-2), using the view of a matrix as a vector of vectors. In what sense is the formula a natural extension of formula (3-1) for accessing vectors?

3-2. Extend the storage structure and accessing formula (3-2) for matrices to homogeneous fixed-size arrays of arbitrary dimension. Find the most efficient accessing formula, in the sense of the formula that requires the least amount of computation for each access. What intermediate calculations need to be made at the time the array is created?

3-3. Many computations using matrices involve sequential processing of all the elements of a single row or column. The loop in which the processing is done likely involves references to $A[I,J]$ with the subscript I or J increased by one each time through the loop. In such cases it is inefficient to compute $locn\ A[I,J]$ independently on each loop; instead (assuming subscript I is the one which is varying) $locn\ A[I,J]$ may be computed more simply from $locn\ A[I-1,J]$. Give the formula for computing $locn$ $A[I,J]$ in terms of $locn$ $A[I-1,J]$. Extend this formula to arrays of arbitrary dimension where an arbitrary subscript is the one being incremented.

3-4. Figure 3-3 illustrates two real number representations for floating-point numbers with a run-time type descriptor. One uses extra space to gain speed in arithmetic; the other sacrifices speed for a more compact storage structure. Design two similar representations for your local computer, assuming the run-time descriptor requires at most 6 bits. Write the programs necessary for addition, subtraction, multiplication, and division of numbers in these forms. Compare the relative advantages and disadvantages of the two representations.

3-5. In the language SIMSCRIPT a multidimensional homogeneous array is represented as a vector of pointers that point to other vectors of pointers, etc., to as many levels as the array has dimensions. A 3 × 4 matrix of numbers, for example, is represented by a vector of three pointers, each of which points to another vector of four numbers. Give an algorithm for accessing $A[I,J]$ when such a representation is used. Compare the relative efficiency of accessing and storage use between this representation and the usual sequential representation of Section 3-8. Consider both the case of matrices and arrays of higher dimension.

3-6. A *deque* (double-ended queue) is a queue extended to allow insertions, deletions, and accessing at both ends. Design sequential and linked storage representations for deques, and write the algorithms for insertion, deletion, and accessing. What is wrong with using the linked representation of Fig. 3-15 for deques?

3-7. Give algorithms for the three operations INSERT—BEFORE (X,E), INSERT—AFTER (X,E), and DELETE (E) on doubly linked lists, where E is a pointer to an element of a doubly linked list and X is a pointer to a new element to be inserted.

3-8. In SNOBOL4 a property list, or *table* in SNOBOL4 terminology, is created by a statement such as

$$X = \text{TABLE}(50,20)$$

Tables are stored using mixed sequential and linked representation. An initial block big enough for 50 subscript-value pairs is set up by the statement above, and a pointer to the block is assigned as the value of X. Subscript-value pairs are entered into the table by an assignment such as

$$X[AGE] = 52$$

which enters the pair $(AGE,52)$ into the table if the subscript AGE is not already present. If AGE is found, then its value is changed to 52. When 50 pairs have been entered into the initially allocated block, a new block big enough for 20 pairs (the second parameter on the call to the TABLE function) is allocated and linked to the first block. New pairs are now put in the new block until it is full, at which time another block for 20 pairs is allocated. Deletion of a pair is not allowed. Design a detailed storage structure appropriate for such tables, including run-time descriptor, and then give an algorithm for execution of the assignment given above on an arbitrary table.

3-9. When processing a tree it is common to use a stack to store temporarily pointers to subtrees which have not yet been traversed. The technique is basically as follows: Begin at the root (the head of the main list), progress down the main list until a branch point is reached, pick one of the branch paths to continue down, and store a pointer to the other in the stack. When the end of a path is reached, take the top pointer from the stack, and continue down that path. The stack initially contains only the pointer to the root of the tree. Design an algorithm for processing a tree in this manner, assuming the tree representation of Fig. 3-18 and a stack represented sequentially. How is the maximum size of the stack related to the properties of the tree; i.e., can you predict how big a block of storage should be reserved for the stack by looking at the size and shape of the tree to be processed?

3-10. A property list might be represented as a set rather than a list because elements are accessed randomly by subscript rather than sequentially. Design a storage representation for property lists using the scatter storage technique of Section 3-11.

3-11. *Concatenation* is a central operation on character strings.
  a. Assuming the representation of Fig. 3-4 for character strings of variable length with a declared bound, design a concatenation operation CAT1. CAT1 is called with three parameters A, B, and C. A and B are pointers to the two storage blocks containing the strings to be concatenated, and C is the receiving block, which initially contains some other character string. The string composed of the characters of string B concatenated to the characters of string A is to be stored in block C (with the appropriate descriptor, of course). Blocks A and B are to be unchanged by the operation.

b. Strings without a declared bound may also be stored sequentially using the same storage representation, with the maximum length deleted from the descriptor. Design an appropriate storage structure assuming that characters may be packed four per word. Then design the concatenation operation CAT2. CAT2 has two parameters, A and B, representing the strings to be concatenated, and returns a pointer to a new block of storage containing the concatenated strings. Assume that CAT2 calls a function ALLOCATE(N) that returns a pointer to a newly allocated block of N words of storage.

c. Design CAT3, a routine that concatenates strings represented as linked lists in the manner of Fig. 3-4.

3-12. In hash coding methods for set storage, both the rehashing and sequential scan techniques for handling collisions encounter difficulties if deletions from the set are allowed. Explain the difficulties encountered.

3-13. A *cross section* of a homogeneous multidimensional array is a subarray obtained by fixing one or more subscripts and letting the other subscripts vary through their ranges. For example, if A is a matrix, then any row or column of A is a cross section. In PL/I an array cross section is designated by a subscripted variable with * in one or more subscript positions. Thus $A[3,*]$ designates the third row of A, $A[*,4]$ designates the fourth column of A, and $A[*,*]$ is the entire array. Assume that arrays are stored in row-major order sequentially in the usual way. It is desirable that a descriptor for cross sections of arrays be used that allows the same accessing formula to be used for cross sections that is used for ordinary arrays.

a. Design a run-time descriptor for linear array cross sections (e.g., rows or columns of matrices) that has this property. The descriptor should contain the elements α, LB, and E needed to compute the location of the Ith element of the cross section according to the usual vector accessing formula $\alpha + (I - LB) * E$.

b. Design a run-time descriptor for two-dimensional cross sections (e.g., planes of three-dimensional arrays) that has this property.

3-14. a. Describe the elementary data types that are built into the hardware of your local computer. Determine whether any hardware data types carry descriptors.

b. Design a complete set of descriptors for the hardware data types. Each descriptor should include enough information so that it is possible to determine from the descriptor alone the location, length, and format of the data item it describes.

c. Design a *storage structure* for the descriptors whose logical organization was set up in part b. Since you do not wish to get into the problem of descriptors for descriptors, design the storage structure so that descriptors are *self-describing*; i.e., given the location of the first bit (on a binary computer) of any descriptor it should be possible to determine the length and format of the descriptor without additional information.

3-15. In PL/I and COBOL homogeneous arrays and fully declared heterogeneous arrays may be combined into mixed multidimensional arrays; i.e., elements of homogeneous arrays may be heterogeneous arrays and vice versa. For example, each element of a ten-element vector V might be a heterogeneous three-element linear array with elements NAME, AGE, and SALARY. Design a storage structure for such mixed arrays assuming only real, integer, and character string (fixed-length) as the basic data types. What sort of run-time descriptor is required?

3-16. In many SNOBOL4 implementations the set of character strings that exist at any point during program execution are kept in a *central strings table*. This table is organized as a hash table in which each entry is a pointer to a linked bucket list. A *double-hashing* scheme is used to test for membership of a given string X in the set. X is hashed twice to produce both a hash address, which is used to index the central table to obtain a pointer to the appropriate bucket, and a *bucket order number*. Each entry on a bucket list is composed of a bucket order number and a pointer to a string. Entries on a given bucket list are ordered by bucket order number. To determine if X is stored in the bucket designated by its hash address, the bucket is searched, matching X's bucket order number against those in the bucket list until either a match is found or a bucket order number greater than that of X is found. In the latter case X is immediately inserted in the list, and otherwise a character-by-character match of X with any other strings in the list with the same bucket order number is required. Program this double-hashing scheme, assuming that strings are stored in sequential blocks with a length descriptor. The function coded would accept a pointer to a string as input, look up the string in the table, enter it if it is not found, and return the address of the old entry if found and the address of the new entry if not.

3-17. Some computers have been constructed with hardware data descriptors. Survey the use of hardware data descriptors (a good starting point would be the paper by Feustal [1973]). Of the different types of data structures described in this chapter, how many have been implemented directly in hardware?

4 OPERATIONS

Operations form the complement of data in programming: Data represent the passive component, the stored information, and operations represent the active component, that which creates, destroys, and transforms the data. The control structures of the next two chapters serve as the glue by which data and operations are bound together in sequences in such a way that each operation operates on the proper data at the proper time.

4-1. GENERAL CHARACTERISTICS OF OPERATIONS

Operations may be of two sorts: *operations on programmer-defined data* and *operations on system-defined data*. The former include those usually thought of as *operations* by the programmer—addition, subtraction, square root, test for equality, etc. The latter include those usually viewed as part of the control structure of the language—goto's, subprogram calls, naming of data structures, parameter transmission, etc. In this chapter operations on programmer-defined data are the primary concern. Operations on system-defined data are discussed as appropriate during description of the simulation of various programming language structures.

Operations on programmer-defined data may be further subdivided into *primitive operations*, operations built in to the language, and programmer-defined operations or *subprograms*. This chapter considers subprograms only briefly. In Chapters 5 and 6, the control structures involved in the definition of subprograms are considered at length.

Primitive operations in programming languages exist in great profusion. Almost every programming language contains a few that are unique. Some, such as arithmetic operations, reflect hardware primitives, while others, such as pattern matching, may entail extensive software simulation. As with data structures, there is little point in attempting a comprehensive survey of primitive operations in languages. Only a few basic concepts serve to adequately categorize most operations. The discussion is based on these, and while many of the most common types of primitives are treated, there is no attempt to be comprehensive. For similar reasons no algorithms for the various operations are discussed. It is not our purpose to describe in detail how any particular operations are performed but rather to analyze the general concepts that serve as the foundation for the design of detailed algorithms.

Syntax for Operations

Primitive operations are represented in programs in a variety of ways. The standard infix notation for arithmetic operations, e.g., $X + Y$, comes immediately to mind, but many other notations are in use. Some of the basic notations for the representation of operations within expressions are taken up in the next chapter in the context of sequence control within expressions. Often special syntactic forms are provided for important operations. For example, input-output operations have special statement forms in most languages, and declarations in languages like ALGOL often serve as well to specify operations of data structure creation. Other operations are invoked implicitly; for example, conversions between different data types in mixed-mode expressions are often automatically invoked. The particular syntactic representation for the same operation tends to vary widely between languages, even for simple arithmetic operations (e.g., + in ALGOL and FORTRAN becomes PLUS in LISP and ADD in COBOL). As usual the particular syntax used for an operation is of relatively little concern; it is the underlying semantics that matters.

Operations and Functions

An operation in a programming language is logically a *mathematical function*: For a given set of input operands it has a well-defined and uniquely determined result. Each operation has a *domain*, the set of possible input operands on which it is defined, and a *range*, the set of possible results that it may produce. In mathematics it is common to define a function by specifying its domain and range and an algorithm for mapping the former into the latter. Unfortunately in programming it is far more common to have only a partial specification for an operation. The determination of the domain and range of a given operation, much less the algorithms on which it is based, may be exceedingly complex. There are four main factors that combine to obscure the definition of many programming language operations:

1. *Operations that are undefined for certain inputs.* An operation that apparently is defined over some domain may in fact contain error stops, infinite loops, or other internal structures that cause it to be undefined for certain inputs in the domain. The exact domain on which an operation is undefined may be extremely difficult to specify, as, for example, the sets of numbers that cause underflow or overflow in arithmetic operations.

2. *Implicit operands.* An operation in a program ordinarily appears with a set of explicit operands, e.g., in the form of a list of arguments. However, the operation may access other implicit operands through the use of global variables or other nonlocal identifier references, access to system-defined data, or the like. Complete determination of all the data that may affect the result of an operation is often obscured by such implicit inputs.

3. *Side effects (implicit results).* An operation may return an explicit result, as in the sum returned as the result of an addition, but may also modify the values stored in other data structures, both programmer- and system-defined. Such implicit results are termed *side effects.* The most common type of side effect is that produced by the assignment operation. The main result of this operation is the modification of a value stored in a data structure; the explicit result of the assignment operation may be taken to be the same as the value stored (as in APL) or may simply be ignored (as in FORTRAN or ALGOL). A second type of side effect occurs in a subprogram that modifies its input parameters. Side effects are a basic part of many operations, particularly those that modify data structures. Their presence makes exact specification of the range of an operation difficult.

4. *Self-modification.* One of the most problematic aspects of programming language operations is the potential for self-modification: An operation may modify its own internal structure, either its local data or its own code, so that on two successive executions with the same operands it produces different results. A common example is in the *random number generator* found as an operation in many languages. Typically this operation takes a

constant operand (unless it is being reinitialized) and yet returns a different result each time it is executed. Of course the operation not only returns a result each time it is executed but also modifies an internal *seed* number that affects its result on the next execution. Self-modification through changes in local internal data is common in operations; self-modification through actual modifications in the code of an operation is less common but possible in languages like LISP and SNOBOL4.

The complexity of programming language operation definitions is one reason that attempts to treat programming languages with the tools of ordinary mathematics have not been highly successful. The resulting formal structures have been too complex to analyze easily. As languages are understood more fully and their design made less complex, a true mathematics of programming languages will no doubt develop. However, the informal treatment of this chapter is the most satisfactory for our purposes in treating present programming language operations.

Operations and Declarations

Information declared about the properties of operations is used for much the same purposes as information declared about the properties of data structures: storage management and static type checking. Explicit declarations for operations are ordinarily necessary only for subprograms; with primitive operations the properties of each operation are part of the language definition (or of its implementation). For example, in the assignment

$$X := Y + Z \mid U$$

it helps little to know the types of X, Y, Z, and U during translation if the division operator is defined so that it may produce an integer or a real value depending on whether the quotient of Z and U is an integer. Static type checking is possible only if the result of the division is invariant or depends only on the types of its operands. In the assignment

$$X := Y + FN(Z, U)$$

a similar data type must be known for the result of the function subprogram FN. In this case an explicit declaration of result type for the subprogram FN would usually be required as part of its definition.

Operations and Storage Management

While the internal workings of particular operations are of
relatively little interest here, one aspect of their behavior is critical:
their effect on storage management. An operation may require an
allocation of storage for its results; it may free the storage used by its
operands; or both. An operation may be termed *elementary* if its
storage demands are fixed and not dependent on its operands, as, for
example, an arithmetic operation that always produces a result of
known type (and thus size) for any two operands. A *creation*
operation requires allocation of storage, a *destruction* operation frees
storage, and a *modification* operation may do both.

4-2. ELEMENTARY OPERATIONS

Every language has a built-in set of elementary primitives that
perform basic operations on simple data types, e.g., arithmetic
operations, logical operations, and data type conversions.

Arithmetic Operations

The basic arithmetic operations of addition, subtraction, multiplication, division and exponentiation are primitive in almost every
language. In languages used in scientific computing, such as PL/I,
FORTRAN, and ALGOL, extended sets of operations including
square root, the trigonometric operations, and other specialized
operations are likely to be found as well. The basic characteristics of
an arithmetic operation are

1. The operands and result are numbers, and

2. The operation is a simple function, possibly with error stops,
but with no implicit inputs, side effects, or self-modification.

A primary difference among languages is whether static type
checking of operands for arithmetic operations is possible. Where
types are declared and static type checking is possible, type-specific
operations may be used at run time and ordinarily no run-time
descriptors for numbers are needed. If dynamic type checking is
necessary, then generic operations and run-time descriptors must be
used.

The basic addition, subtraction, multiplication, and division
operations are usually represented in type-specific forms directly in

the hardware. Others, such as exponentiation, square root, and the trigonometric functions, must be software-simulated. In either case the use of type-specific rather than generic operations at run time is likely to be substantially more efficient.

Examples. Representative examples from various languages

1. *ALGOL division.* Syntax: infix / or ÷, e.g., X / Y or X ÷ Y. Properties: Types of operands are given by declaration—/ takes operands of either type **real** or **integer**; ÷ takes operands only of type **integer**. Type of result is invariant: / always produces a **real** result, and ÷ an **integer** result. May be translated into type-specific hardware (or software-simulated) division operation.

2. *LISP addition.* Syntax: prefix PLUS with an arbitrary number of arguments, e.g., (PLUS X Y Z). Properties: Operands may be type **real** or **integer**. Result is type **integer** if all operands are **integer**, and otherwise type **real**. No declarations are provided. PLUS is a generic addition operation that requires run-time checking of operand type descriptors and appropriate type conversions before actual addition.

3. *COBOL multiplication.* Syntax: statement form with many options. Basic form: MULTIPLY X BY Y GIVING Z. Properties: Types of operands are variable but specified by declarations in the program. Type of result is the declared type of the receiving operand, e.g., Z in the statement above. May be translated into a type-specific hardware multiplication, but extensive conversions of both operands and result may be required. Because of declarations, the conversions necessary may be determined during translation.

4. *FORTRAN square root.* Syntax: Prefix SQRT, e.g., SQRT(X). Properties: Type of operand must be **real**; type of result is **real**. Software-simulated where a hardware square root operation is not provided.

5. *APL addition.* Syntax: infix +, e.g. X + Y. Properties: Operands may be single numbers or arbitrary number arrays of same shape and size. Result is a single number or array of the same shape. Requires allocation of storage for result array. No declarations are provided; neither the size nor the shape of the result array may be predicted. Generic nonelementary addition operation: requires run-time type checking and storage allocation.

Relational Operations (Predicates)

The relational tests on numbers—equal, not-equal, less-than, greater-than, less-than-or-equal, greater-than-or-equal—are a second set of primitives found in most languages. As with arithmetic operations these may be translated into type-specific or generic versions, with at least partial hardware support for the type-specific operations usually provided. The relational operations take the form of simple functions, accepting two numbers as operands and producing a Boolean value (**true** or **false**) as a result.

Relational operations may be extended to character strings when much sorting of character string data is done. A collating sequence (see Section 3-7) is defined that induces an ordering on character strings (an extension of the usual alphabetic ordering). One string is then less-than another if it precedes it in this ordering.

Examples. Representative examples from various languages:

1. *ALGOL less-than.* Syntax: infix $<$, e.g., X $<$ Y. Properties: Operands may be type **integer** or **real**; result is always type **Boolean**. Declarations for operands allow translation into type-specific hardware operation.

2. *SNOBOL4 lexically-greater-than.* Syntax: prefix LGT, e.g., LGT(X,Y). Properties: Operands must both be character strings or numbers (which are converted to strings); result is an implicit Boolean value (a success-failure signal) that may be used to control branching in the same statement. Ordering of strings is controlled by a collating sequence, available through the keyword &ALPHABET, whose value is a string containing all the characters in their defined collating sequence. Generic operation: checks types of operands and makes conversions as necessary before testing.

Boolean Operations

Boolean operations are primitive in many languages. A Boolean operation accepts only Boolean values (true-false or 0-1) as operands and produces a single Boolean value as a result. The basic operations are *and, or* and *not,* but more extended sets are sometimes included (e.g., in ALGOL and APL) such as Boolean *equivalence, implication, exclusive or, nand* (not-and) and *nor* (not-or).

Boolean operations are often extended to bit strings. For example, the *and* of two bit strings of the same length is a bit string of equal length whose every bit is determined by taking the *and* of the two corresponding bits in the operand strings.

Type Conversion Operations

Type conversion operations, used to convert data items between different representations, are important in many languages. COBOL and PL/I in Part II provide extensive sets of primitive type conversions. Type conversion operations may be invoked directly, e.g., the ALGOL *entier* operation that converts a real number to an integer, but more commonly they are invoked implicitly when type conflicts arise in attempts to apply other operations. Many languages automatically provide type conversion for numbers represented as integers, reals, double-precision reals, character strings containing only digits, signs and decimal points, etc. Adjustment of the lengths of character or bit strings through truncation or addition of blanks or zeros is also a form of type conversion. COBOL and PL/I also provide a wide range of conversions for numbers in character string form by addition of explicit decimal points, dollar signs, suppression of leading zeros, etc.

4-3. ASSIGNMENT

Assignment is the basic operation of data structure modification. Assignment differs from the other operations considered to this point in that it works through side effects rather than as a simple function; i.e., it produces no function value in the usual way but instead modifies one of its operands. As operands assignment requires (1) a data value to be stored and (2) a pointer to a location in a data structure in which the data value is to be stored. Given these operands the assignment operation simply modifies the given data structure location to contain the given value. In the process the major area of difficulty is that of descriptor handling.

Suppose that we wish to assign value V to location L, and the descriptor of V differs from that of the value currently stored in L. For example, L may contain an integer while V is a real, or both may be character strings, but V is longer than that stored in L. Two distinct techniques for handling the conflict are possible:

1. Convert V to have the same descriptor as that of L's current value; i.e., keep L of *invariant data type*, and store the converted value as the new value of L, or

2. Let the data type of L's value vary by assigning V as the new value of L without conversion.

The first approach is typical of languages that provide program declarations for data structures. Because data types are fixed by declaration in the program, they cannot be allowed to vary during execution, and thus assignment must involve type conversions where there are conflicts. For example, in FORTRAN, ALGOL, and PL/I, assignment includes type conversion where necessary. The advantage, of course, is that obtained from declarations in general, as discussed in Section 3-4: better storage management (because the sizes of values do not vary dynamically), static type checking, faster access, etc. The second approach, variable data types, is typical of SNOBOL4 and APL (in part). The advantages are in flexibility and elimination of unnecessary data type conversions.

Almost every language contains an explicit *assignment statement*, but assignment occurs as an operation in many other contexts as well. Input-output operations, for example, involve assignment of new input values to data structures or assignment of new data to an output file; SNOBOL4 pattern matching or the COBOL arithmetic operations both may involve assignment.

Examples. Representative examples from various languages:

1. *ALGOL assignment.* Syntax: $V := E$, where V evaluates to a location and E to a value. Properties: The data type of V remains fixed; the value of E is converted to the data type of V. Both data types are known from declarations during translation so the conversions necessary may be determined during translation.

2. *COBOL MOVE.* Syntax: MOVE X TO Y. Properties: Simple assignment statement; both X and Y designate locations. The value of X is converted to the data type of Y. This conversion may be very complex, but declarations for X and Y allow the necessary conversion to be determined during translation.

3. *APL assignment (specification).* Syntax: $X \leftarrow E$. Properties: Generic assignment operation; no declarations for X or E are given; the operator must check types and take various actions at run time. If X is unsubscripted, then the value of E, which may be an entire array, replaces the current value of X and no conversion is done; X takes the type of E. If X is subscripted, then the value of E is assigned to the designated locations in the existing value (array) of X; type of X remains unchanged.

4. *SNOBOL4 input operation.* Syntax: any reference to the special variable INPUT. Properties: implicit assignment. Whenever an attempt to access the value of INPUT is made, program execution is interrupted and the next record on the standard input file is assigned as the new value of INPUT.

4-4. DATA STRUCTURE CREATION AND ELEMENT INSERTION

Operations that create new data structures or that enlarge existing structures through the insertion of new elements are of primary importance in every language. Such operations require allocation of new storage and because of this are central in the design of the storage management mechanisms that underlie a language implementation.

The creation of a data structure involves four basic steps: (1) creation of a descriptor for the structure, (2) allocation of storage for the structure itself (i.e., the bit string), (3) specification of the values of the elements of the structure, and (4) creation of an access path to the structure. Insertion operations usually involve storage allocation for the new elements, specification of their values, and sometimes adjustment of pointers to effect the insertion into an existing structure.

The four steps in structure creation are straightforward. We have discussed at length in Chapter 3 the descriptors and element-value bit strings necessary for various data structures. Creation of an access path to a new structure is done either through association of the structure with an identifier, its *name*, in some referencing environment (see Chapter 6) or through storing a pointer to the structure in some other existing already-accessible structure.

Examples. There is great variation in the manner in which creation and insertion operations are handled in different languages. Some examples will clarify the different approaches:

1. *FORTRAN arrays.* A DIMENSION declaration is used to create arrays, e.g., the declaration DIMENSION A(20) specifies that a vector of 20 real numbers is to be created. The vector descriptor may be created during compilation from information available in the declaration. Storage is allocated during loading at the end of translation but before execution begins. Access paths are also set up during translation. Ordinarily the vector is created *empty*, with undefined element values that are filled by assignments during execution. Alternatively, element values may be specified at compile time using a DATA statement.

2. *ALGOL arrays.* A program declaration specifies the point of array creation during execution, which must be on entry to a

subprogram or block, e.g., the declaration **real array** $A[1:20]$ at the beginning of a block specifies that a vector of 20 elements is to be created on entry to that block during execution. The declarations allow partial descriptors to be constructed during translation. The creation of the array on block entry involves creation of the remainder of the descriptor, allocation of storage, and creation of an access path to the array by naming it. The newly created array is empty, with undefined element values that must be filled in by assignment to individual array elements.

3. *APL arrays.* Arrays are created by many different APL operators, e.g., any arithmetic operator applied to two arrays of the same shape and size creates a new array as its value. Creation here involves simultaneous allocation of storage, creation of the descriptor, and specification of all element values. However, the array creation operations return only a pointer to the new array; no permanent access path is created. The new array may be immediately input to another operation, in which case it exists only temporarily and is then destroyed, or it may be *named*, by assignment of the pointer to an identifier, and thus retained for later use.

4. *PL/I BASED structures.* A program declaration specifies the structure descriptor, and its position in the program delimits the segment of program execution within which structure creation may occur. For example, the declaration

```
1 STRUCT BASED (P),
  2 X FIXED,
  2 Y FLOAT;
```

at the beginning of a block or subprogram specifies a descriptor for a *structure type*, STRUCT. Structures of this type may be created only within the block or subprogram where the declaration appears. Allocation of storage for the structure and creation of an access path is done separately during execution using a statement such as

```
ALLOCATE STRUCT SET(P);
```

ALLOCATE statements may be executed at arbitrary points during execution within the block or subprogram. Each creates a new data structure with the descriptor specified by the declaration, and each may be made accessible through a pointer stored in an already-accessible variable such as P. Each newly created structure of type STRUCT is initially empty. Values for the elements X and Y must be filled in by assignment.

5. *SNOBOL4 programmer-defined data types.* All creation steps are done during execution. A descriptor must first be created through execution of a call on the DATA built-in primitive. The DATA primitive also sets up functions for the creation of structures with the new descriptor and for accessing the elements of the structures after their creation. For example;

$$DATA('STRUCT(X,Y)')$$

creates a descriptor similar to the PL/I structure descriptor for a heterogeneous linear array of two elements. Three functions are also set up by this statement: function STRUCT for creation of structures of type STRUCT and functions X and Y for accessing the elements of structures of type STRUCT. A later statement,

$$STRUCT(2,3.102)$$

causes storage to be allocated for a structure with the descriptor specified by STRUCT and also specifies the initial values for the elements of the structure: 2 and 3.102. However, no access path is created; only a pointer to the new structure is returned as the value of the function STRUCT. An access path may be created by assignment of this pointer as the value of an existing variable or data structure element, e.g., by

$$Z = STRUCT(2,3.102)$$

6. *LISP CONS insertion.* The LISP CONS operation inserts a new element containing a descriptor and two pointers at the head of an existing linked list. For example, (CONS X L) takes as operands two pointers, X and L. X points to the value of the new list element; L points to the head of the list to which X is to be added. CONS requests storage for a new list element and fills the element with the two operand pointers X and L and a standard descriptor specifying the data type *list element.* If L is the special symbol NIL, then CONS effectively creates a new list of the single element X. No permanent access path to the new element is created; the returned pointer must be stored immediately as the value of another list element elsewhere or used as an input to another operation. CONS operations may be executed at arbitrary points during program execution.

The above examples give some idea of the variety of conceptions of how to design data structure creation and insertion operations.

Note that languages such as LISP, SNOBOL4, APL, and PL/I that allow data structure creation to occur at arbitrary points during execution essentially are forced to utilize one of the very flexible but relatively inefficient *heap* storage management techniques discussed in Chapter 7. FORTRAN and ALGOL, by restrictions on the points at which creation may take place, allow much simpler storage management schemes to be used. The problem, of course, is that of balancing the conflicting goals of flexibility and efficiency.

4-5. DATA STRUCTURE DESTRUCTION AND ELEMENT DELETION

In discussing destruction operations on data structures one must be careful to distinguish the operation of *destruction*, which makes a data structure logically inaccessible, from the operation of *recovery of storage* for the structure. In many languages the two are quite separate; for example, storage for structures that have been destroyed is often recovered only when it is actually needed for creation or modification of other structures later during execution. The LISP garbage collection mechanism is a good example of such a storage recovery technique.

An additional difficulty in the discussion of the destruction operation is that it usually is implicit. Seldom does a language provide an explicit operation which a programmer may use to destroy an existing data structure (the PL/I FREE operation is a notable exception). Instead the simpler operation of destroying an access path to a structure is available. The structure is "destroyed" when all access paths to it have been destroyed, at which time the storage locations allocated for it may be recovered and reused.

Let us look in greater detail at the operation of destroying an access path to a structure. When a data structure is created, an access path to the structure must also be created; otherwise there would be no way to get to the new structure. The usual way to do this is either to name it by associating it with an identifier or to store a pointer to it in another structure. During the lifetime of the structure the initially created access path may be augmented by other access paths, e.g., through other identifier associations (as when an array is transmitted to a subprogram and given a formal parameter name). Multiple access paths to a single structure are quite common. In general it is difficult and time-consuming to keep track of the various access paths to a structure, so often one cannot tell easily when accessing a structure through one path whether there may be other access paths to the structure. This leads to the central problem of destruction. Suppose that the programmer is allowed to explicitly indicate when a particular data structure is to be destroyed. He must specify an access path to the structure, and the destruction operation may readily destroy that access path as well as the structure itself. However, if there are any other access paths to the structure still in existence, then a serious situation arises: Destroying the structure leaves these other access paths leading into an undefined region of storage. Such access paths to nonexistent structures are commonly termed *dangling references*.

Dangling references are caused by recovering storage for a destroyed structure "too soon," before all access paths have been destroyed. The complementary problem is that of *garbage*. Dangling references may be avoided by using a destruction operation that destroys an access path without returning the allocated storage for reuse until the last access path is destroyed. However, owing to the difficulty of keeping tabs on all the access paths to a given structure, it may be that all the access paths to a structure become lost without the structure itself being returned to free storage. In this case the structure is said to have become *garbage*. A garbage structure is one which exists but to which no access paths exist and which thus cannot be used. The difficulty with garbage structures is the recovery of the storage they occupy. If during program execution many garbage structures accumulate in memory without being recovered, it is possible that the program will be unable to continue because of a lack of available storage.

Dangling references and garbage are two key problems in the design of operations that destroy data structures. Similar problems arise in the case of operations that delete elements from data structures. We shall consider in detail techniques for avoiding garbage and dangling references in Chapter 7 in the overall context of storage management mechanisms. Most languages adopt the convention that a data structure cannot be explicitly destroyed by the programmer. Instead he may destroy only access paths, and the structure is implicitly destroyed when all access paths have been lost. The language implementation assumes responsibility for the actual release of the storage for the structure when it is determined that no access paths exist.

Examples. Two examples will serve to illustrate the possible approaches:

1. *ALGOL.* In ALGOL each data structure (array or simple variable) when created is immediately associated with its *primary*

identifier, the identifier given in the declaration for the structure at the beginning of some program block. This serves as the primary access path to the structure. This access path exists throughout execution of the block and is destroyed when the block is exited. During execution of the block the structure may be transmitted to subprograms and thus become associated with other identifiers. However, owing to the nature of subprogram calls and returns, such associations must inevitably be destroyed before exit from the original block in which the array was declared. Thus on exit from the original block it is known that the association of the array with its primary identifier is the only association still in existence. When this association is destroyed, the array must become garbage, and the storage allocated for it may be recovered.

2. *LISP*. In LISP each list data structure, after creation, may be referenced through a variety of associations, through identifiers or through pointers in other lists of which it may be a sublist. There may also be access paths to subparts of the list. It is possible to create and destroy such access paths at will during execution of a program. At any time the last access path to a list may be destroyed, but in general there is no simple way to determine when this occurs. Since it is difficult to determine when a particular list has become garbage, no storage recovery is done for any list at the time of destruction of an access path. Instead garbage structures may be generated and may continue to exist in memory even though they cannot be accessed. When available storage is depleted and storage for destroyed structures must be recovered in order for program execution to continue, a complex *garbage collection* operation is performed that traces down all existing access paths to all lists and tags those lists that are still accessible. All other memory locations are then assumed to belong to garbage lists, and they are recovered for reuse. Here the creation of dangling references is carefully avoided—but at the expense of performing a complete check of all possible access paths to a structure before being able to decide that it in fact has become garbage and that its storage is recoverable.

These two examples indicate the problems of designing languages to avoid dangling references. In ALGOL the design allows a simple determination of when a structure has been destroyed—but at the cost of some fairly rigid rules regarding creation of alternative access paths to a structure. In LISP there is great flexibility in creation of alternative access paths but no simple way to determine when a structure has become garbage.

4-6. PATTERN MATCHING

Most operations on data structures either affect the whole structure, e.g., creation and destruction, or are given designated elements of the structure with which to operate, e.g., assignment. *Pattern-matching operations* differ in that they determine the part of a structure on which they are to operate dynamically in terms of relations between the various elements of the structure. Two types of pattern matching may be distinguished:

1. *Simple pattern matching.* Pattern matching may be used simply to test for certain relationships of elements within the structure.

2. *Pattern matching and replacement.* Pattern matching may be used to identify a subpart of the structure, which is then to be replaced by a designated new structure. If the new structure is the null element, the result is a deletion, and if it is the original subpart plus some new data, the result is an insertion.

Pattern matching is most often used on character string data. It is the basic operation in SNOBOL4 where character string processing is central. A simple pattern-matching operation might be

Look for the substring "THE" in the string named X

In simple pattern matching the result would be a Boolean value, true or false, depending on whether the substring were found or not. Coupled with replacement, one of the following forms might be found:

1. Look for "THE" in X and replace it by the null string (delete it),

2. Look for "THE" in X and replace it by "THE END" (insert "END" after it), or

3. Look for "THE" in X and replace it by "AN" (substitution).

Simple pattern matching is an elementary (though complex) operation in that no explicit storage management is involved. Coupled with replacement the full range of storage management problems appears. It is best for our purposes to consider the simple pattern-matching operation alone and view the pattern matching with replacement operation as a combination of simple pattern matching, where the location of the matched substructure is returned as a value, and assignment.

Pattern matching may be viewed as a generalization of ordinary data structure accessing. In ordinary accessing, a set of *subscripts* are provided that designate an element of the structure. An accessing operation takes as inputs a structure and a set of subscripts and produces a pointer to the desired element of the structure. A pattern-matching operation accepts as input a structure and a *pattern*, which designates a desired element or set of elements of the structure. The pattern-matching operation then also produces a pointer to the desired elements of the structure. Pattern matching differs mainly in that

1. The desired elements may not exist in the structure.

2. The pattern need not specify the exact position of the desired elements in the structure but may specify instead their position relative to other elements in the structure.

SNOBOL4 Pattern Matching. A look at some of the features of pattern matching in SNOBOL4 will clarify how patterns are defined. In SNOBOL4 pattern matching is always applied to a character string data structure. The pattern-matching operation attempts to locate a single substring of this string that has the properties defined by the input pattern. Patterns are actually a special type of data structure that are created by pattern-defining expressions and functions built into the language. The pattern-matching operation itself is specified in a special pattern-matching statement. If X is the name of a character string and P is a pattern, then

$$X \quad P \qquad :S(L1)F(L2)$$

is a pattern-matching statement which specifies that X is to be searched for a substring that meets the specifications of pattern P, with a branch to statement L1 if such a substring is found and to L2 if not. Coupled with replacement the statement would be

$$X \quad P = Z \qquad :S(L1)F(L2)$$

which would cause the matched substring, if any, to be replaced by the string named Z.

A wide variety of built-in operations are provided in SNOBOL4 for the creation of patterns. Some of the most important are

1. Find a substring matching a given string, e.g., find "THE".

2. Find a substring of a given length, e.g., a substring of six characters.

3. Find a substring beginning in a given character position, e.g., a substring beginning at the seventh-character position.

4. Find a substring composed only of certain given characters, e.g., a substring composed only of decimal digits.

5. Find a substring composed only of characters *not* in a given set, e.g., a substring not containing any spaces or punctuation marks.

These simple pattern construction operations may be combined using the following two operations:

1. *Concatenation.* If A is a pattern and B is a pattern, then the concatenation of A and B is a pattern that matches a substring beginning with a substring matching A followed immediately by a substring matching B. For example, the pattern "Find a substring composed of the string "THE", followed by a string composed only of spaces, followed by a string containing no spaces or punctuation marks," is composed of the concatenation of three simple patterns.

2. *Alternation.* If A is a pattern and B is a pattern, then the alternation of A and B, written A|B, is a pattern which matches any substring matching either A or B. For example, the pattern "THE"|"AN"|"A" is a pattern matching any one of the strings "THE", "AN", or "A".

Pattern Matching in Input-Output. The standard input-output technique in FORTRAN and many other languages involves the use of a type of pattern matching to convert between an external file representation of data in character string form and an internal memory representation as fixed- and floating-point numbers. The pattern is defined as a *format*. During input the format specifies the pattern of fields containing numbers to be found in the input records and the internal form to which they are to be converted. Besides the format the input operation is also given a list of locations in which the converted numbers are to be stored. The reverse is done during output. The format defines the pattern of characters to be created on an output record, including conversions of numbers from internal binary to character string form, spacing between numbers, headings and comments to be inserted, etc. The patterns definable in input-output formats are usually considerably more restricted than those provided in SNOBOL4. In SNOBOL4 the basic pattern-matching capabilities may be used to format strings for input-output so that no special input-output formatting featues are needed.

Pattern Matching in Other Data Structures. Pattern-matching concepts are applicable to any type of data structure. They have been found most useful in character string processing because many character-string-processing algorithms are naturally represented with pattern-matching operations. Pattern matching in more complex data structures such as arrays and trees is less common, in part because fewer algorithms need it and in part because general pattern matching in such structures is likely to be slow and expensive in execution time (as string pattern matching is in SNOBOL4). APL includes some basic pattern-matching operations for homogeneous arrays that have proved useful. It may be that pattern-matching concepts will find wider use in new languages.

4-7. OPERATIONS ON PROGRAMS: TRANSLATION AND EXECUTION

Programs are actually a form of data, as we noted in Chapter 3. The primitive operations on programs, however, are quite different from the ordinary operations on other types of data. The most basic primitives on programs are two: translation and execution. Ordinarily translation and execution are thought of as *meta-operations* which are activated only at the operating system level. For example, to get a FORTRAN program compiled and executed one typically instructs the operating system to compile (translate) the program into executable form. The operating system retrieves the FORTRAN compiler and gives the compiler the FORTRAN program as input. Similarly the compiled program is executed by means of another command to the operating system.

Translation and execution may also appear as primitives in a language. The usual situation is this. A program P written in some language L is being executed. P either creates or reads in some data Q. The data Q represents a program that P wishes to execute. Q might be, for example, a character string representing a legal program in language L. In this case Q requires translation into executable form before it can be executed. Alternatively Q might already be in executable form if, as in LISP, the executable form for a program coincides with the usual data structure. In this case no translation would be required. In the former case P needs access to an operation TRANSLATE and an operation EXECUTE; in the latter case only the operation EXECUTE is needed. Observe how this is done in two languages: LISP and SNOBOL4.

In LISP linked list structures are the basic form of data structure. Programs also are represented in this form as a special class of list structure. A list structure that happens to have the right form may be executed as a program by giving it as an operand to the primitive operation EVAL. A program P may thus build a list structure Q and get Q executed by calling EVAL(Q). Translation of LISP programs in external character string form into internal executable form by a primitive operation is also possible. The READ operation accomplishes this as a special case of ordinary input. The program to be translated is placed in character string form in the input file. A READ operation translates the program into an internal linked list structure, which, as we have noted, is directly executable by EVAL.

The SNOBOL4 technique is somewhat different. Character strings are the basic data structure in SNOBOL4, but programs in character string form are not directly executable. Instead character strings must first be translated into executable form using a primitive operation CODE. CODE takes as operand a character string representing a legal SNOBOL4 program (with semicolons between statements) and as result produces a data structure of data type *executable code*. Data structures composed of executable code may not be further manipulated except to be executed. Execution of a code data structure is initiated by a direct **goto**, transferring control to the name of the data structure or to a labeled statement within the structure. Return from the code execution to the original program must be explicitly set up by another direct **goto** within the code structure.

Few applications actually require the ability to generate, translate, and execute programs dynamically during execution of another program, but where appropriate the facility can be extremely valuable. The difficulty of allowing programmer-controlled TRANSLATE and EXECUTE primitives is twofold: (1) Run-time translation requires that the translator be available during execution, but the translator in most cases is a large space-consuming program which it is undesirable to have in memory during execution, and (2) run-time programmer-initiated execution of newly translated programs makes difficult much of the organization of run-time activities which it is desirable to do during translation. For these reasons translation and execution as primitive operations are usually found only in languages that perform relatively simple translations and whose execution structures are largely software-simulated.

4-8. PROGRAMMER-DEFINED OPERATIONS: SUBPROGRAMS

Suppose that a programmer is not satisfied with the primitive operations built into the language he is using. He wishes to extend the language to include new operations of his own design. A language that supports such extension might be called a language with an *extensible operation set* (paralleling the extensible data structures of Section 3-14). In fact facilities for constructing new operations, in the form of subprograms, are basic in every programming language. (Applying the term *extensible operation set* to the subprogram mechanism is not standard. Ordinarily the term is restricted to more specialized mechanisms for adding operators through syntactic changes in the language.)

Discussion of subprograms is broken into a number of parts here. Control structures involving subprogram call and return and mechanisms for transferring data to and from subprograms are treated in depth in the next two chapters. Our concern in this section is more general: the overall structure of subprograms viewed as programmer-defined operations.

Subprogram Bodies. Two basic categories of subprograms may be distinguished depending on whether the subprogram is written in the same language as the main program. Most commonly subprograms are written in the same language. The body of such a subprogram ordinarily takes the same form as the main program, with only a special initial statement to distinguish it. Any algorithm that can be programmed in the language may be set into the body. A very flexible sort of extensibility is thus provided where the desired algorithm can be expressed in terms of the language-provided primitives, data structures, and control structures. Restrictions on communication between the subprogram and calling programs are usually present. We shall discuss these below.

Where the algorithm cannot be coded in terms of language-defined primitives, the second type of subprogram is useful—the subprogram coded in another language. Supbrograms of this sort are less often seen. Their utility is restricted to rather special circumstances because of the difficulty of communication between programs written in different languages and because of differences in storage management requirements. Ordinarily only precompiled

FORTRAN or assembly language subprograms with static storage requirements may be used.

Subprogram Operands and Results. Subprograms are categorized as *function subprograms* (or *functions*) if they return an explicit result and as *subroutines* if they work entirely through side effects and return no explicit result. Function subprograms are used in expressions where the result is immediately input to another operation. Subroutines must be· called separately, usually with a special CALL statement.

Operands to subprograms are termed *actual parameters* or *arguments*. Various techniques for transmission of operands to subprograms are treated in Chapter 6. Operands for subprograms tend to be relatively unrestricted; commonly an operand may be any data item, either a number or other elementary data item, or a data structure such as an array or list. In addition names of other subprograms are often permitted as operands, and sometimes also statement labels.

Results of subprograms are likely to be more restricted. Results may appear either as explicit function values or as side effects through modification of parameters or nonlocal variables. In many languages the results of subprograms are restricted so as not to interfere with storage management. For example, a common restriction in languages like FORTRAN and ALGOL is that the storage required for the result of a subprogram must be allocatable before execution of the subprogram begins. In ALGOL a subprogram may return a single number as the result or may modify in arbitrary ways the contents of existing data structures (but not change their size) but may not itself create and return a data structure as its value. Thus an ALGOL subprogram cannot set up a table and return the table as its value; instead the table must be created before the subprogram is entered. The subprogram may then fill the table (through side effects) and return control. In addition subprograms are not usually allowed to free storage for their operands. The effect of such restrictions is to allow only subprograms that serve as elementary operations; creation, destruction, or other operations involving storage management are not programmable.

In languages such as LISP, SNOBOL4, and APL in which more general storage management methods are used, subprograms may be allowed to create and return data structure values. In these languages storage allocation goes on more or less constantly during program execution for various purposes, and the boundaries of subprogram entry and exit are not particularly crucial to the storage management schemes.

Declarations and Subprograms. As with primitive operations it is important to have declarations of the type of the result of function subprogram in languages with declared data types. Typically this type declaration is made part of the definition of the subprogram, as in the ALGOL subprogram header

integer procedure $SUB(...)$;

From this declaration it may be determined that a call of SUB in an expression such as

$$X \times SUB(...) + Y$$

will have a result of type **integer**, which then allows static type checking and translation of the expression into type-specific multiplication and addition operations.

4-9. REFERENCES AND SUGGESTIONS FOR FURTHER READING

The study of operations in programming languages is perhaps best approached through the study of particular programming languages. APL (Iverson [1962] and Chapter 16) has a particularly elegant set of operations for homogeneous array processing which illustrate well the manner in which a properly chosen set of operations interact to create a simple language of great power. SNOBOL4 (Chapter 15) provides an elegant set of pattern-matching primitives, as well as a variety of operations for data structure creation. Gimpel [1973] considers the pattern-matching operation in greater depth. The design of the SLIP list-processing extension to FORTRAN (Weizenbaum [1963]) and the IPL-V language (Newell [1964]) illustrate early designs of powerful list-processing operation sets.

An alternative to the study of operation sets in particular languages is the study of operation sets appropriate to particular data structure types. The references in Chapter 3 are relevant here, because in general each writer considers the design of the operations that process a structure at the same time as the design of the structure itself.

The complexities of formal definition of programming language operations are brought out in the various approaches to formal language definition referenced in Chapter 9. Note particularly the difficulties of definition of operations that work primarily through side effects, such as assignment, and of operations that create and destroy data structures.

4-10. PROBLEMS

4-1. For a language with which you are familiar, list the primitive operations, the operands, and the results of each, and explain in what ways the operations are difficult to define as simple mathematical functions.

4-2. In studying the preliminary design of language BL you note that BL includes a stack data structure and three operations:

1. NEW-TOP(S,E), which adds the element E to the top of stack S,

2. POP-TOP(S), which deletes the top element of stack S, and

3. GET-TOP(S), which returns a pointer to the location in stack S of the current top element.

What is wrong with the design of these three operations? How could they be redefined to correct the problem?

4-3. Two facts about SNOBOL4 operations:
   a. The SNOBOL4 assignment operation does not copy the value assigned; thus after the statement A = B both A and B have the *same value* (i.e., each contains a pointer to the same character string).
   b. In a SNOBOL4 pattern-matching and replacement statement such as

$$X \quad P = Z$$

Z is not substituted directly for the substring matched by P in X; instead a *copy* of string X is made, the appropriate substitution of Z for the matched substring is done, and the new string is assigned as the value of X.

What is the reason for the copy being made in the pattern-matching and replacement step? What other design would avoid the problem?

5 SEQUENCE CONTROL

Control structures in a programming language provide the basic framework within which operations and data are combined into programs and sets of programs. To this point we have been concerned with data and operations in isolation; now we must consider their organization into complete executable programs. This involves two aspects, the control of the order of execution of the operations, both primitive- and user-defined, which we term *sequence control* and discuss in this chapter, and the control of the transmission of data among sets of operations, which we term *data control* and discuss in the next chapter. This division is convenient, as both subjects are rather complex, but it also serves to differentiate sharply two aspects of programming languages which are often confused.

5-1. IMPLICIT AND EXPLICIT SEQUENCE CONTROL

Many different sequence control structures are in use in various programming languages. They may be conveniently categorized in three groups:

1. Structures used in *expressions* (and thus within statements, since expressions form the basic building blocks for statements), such as precedence rules and parentheses,

2. Structures used between *statements* or groups of statements, such as conditional and iteration statements, and

3. Structures used between *subprograms*, such as subprogram calls and coroutines.

This division is necessarily somewhat imprecise. For example, some languages, such as LISP and APL, have no statements, only expressions, yet versions of the usual statement sequence control mechanisms are used.

Sequence control structures may be either implicit or explicit. *Implicit* (or default) sequence control structures are those defined by the language to be in effect unless modified by the programmer through some explicit structure. For example, most languages define the physical sequence of statements in a program as controlling the sequence in which statements are executed, unless modified by an explicit sequence control statement. Within expressions there is also commonly a language-defined hierarchy of operations that controls the order of execution of the operations in the expression when parentheses are absent. *Explicit* sequence control structures are those that the programmer may optionally use to modify the implicit sequence of operations defined by the language, as, for example, by using parentheses within expressions, or **goto** statements and statement labels.

5-2. SEQUENCE CONTROL WITHIN EXPRESSIONS

Consider the formula for computing one root of the quadratic equation

$$\text{root} = \frac{-B + \sqrt{B^2 - 4AC}}{2A}$$

This apparently simple formula actually involves at least 15 separate operations (assuming a square root primitive and counting the various data references). Coded in a typical assembly or machine language it would require at least 15 instructions, and probably far more. Moreover, the programmer would have to provide storage for and keep track of each of the 5 or 10 intermediate results generated. He would also have to worry about optimization: Can the two references to the value of B (and also A) be combined, in what order should the operations be performed to minimize temporary storage and make best use of the hardware, etc.? In a high-level language such as ALGOL, however, the formula can be coded as a single expression almost directly:

$$S := (- B + SQRT (B \uparrow 2 - 4 * A * C))/(2 * A)$$

The notation is compact and natural, and the language processor rather than the programmer concerns itself with temporary storage and optimization. It seems fair to say that the availability of expressions in high-level languages is one of their major advantages over machine and assembly languages.

Expressions are a powerful and natural device for representing sequences of operations, yet they raise new problems. While it may be tedious to write out long sequences of instructions in machine language, at least the programmer has a clear understanding of exactly the order in which the instructions will be executed. But what of the expression? Take the ALGOL expression for the quadratic formula. Is the expression correct? How do we know, for example, that the expression indicates the subtraction should take place *after* the multiplication of $4 * A * C$ rather than before? The sequence control mechanisms that operate to determine the order of operations within this expression are in fact rather complex and subtle.

Tree Structure Representation of Expressions

The basic sequence control mechanism in expressions is *functional composition*: A main operation and its operands are specified; the operands may be either constants or the results of data references or other operations, whose operands in turn may be constants or the results of data references or still other operations, to any depth. Functional composition gives an expression the characteristic structure of a tree, where the root node of the tree represents the main operation, nodes between the root and the leaves represent intermediate level operations, and the leaves represent data references (or constants). For example, the expression for the quadratic formula may be represented (using M to represent the unary minus operation) by the tree of Fig. 5-1.

The tree representation clarifies the control structure of the expression. Clearly the results of data references or operations at lower levels in the tree serve as operands for operations at higher levels in the tree, and thus these data references and operations must be evaluated (executed) first. Yet the tree representation leaves part of the order of evaluation undefined. For example, in the tree in Fig. 5-1 it is not clear whether $-B$ should be evaluated before or after $B \uparrow 2$, nor is it clear whether the two data references to the identifier B may be combined into a single reference. Unfortunately, in the presence of operations with side effects it may make a difference, as we shall see below. It is common in a language definition to define

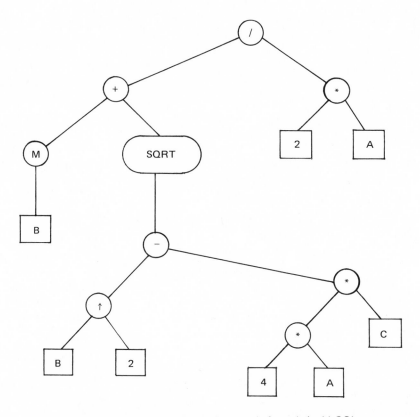

Fig. 5-1. Tree representation of quadratic formula in ALGOL.

the order of evaluation of expressions only at the level of the tree representation and to allow the language implementer to decide on the detailed order of evaluation (such as whether $-B$ or $B \uparrow 2$ comes first). Before looking at the problems that arise in determining the exact order of evaluation, however, it is appropriate to look at the various syntactic representations for expressions which are in use.

Syntax for Expressions

If we take expressions as characteristically represented by trees, then in order to use expressions within programs some linearization of trees is required; i.e., one must have a notation for writing trees as linear sequences of symbols. Let us look at the most common notations:

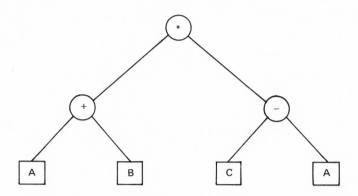

Fig. 5-2. Tree form of the simple expression $(A + B)*(C - A)$.

1. *Prefix Notation (Ordinary, Polish, and Cambridge Polish).* In *prefix* notation one writes the operation symbol first, followed by the operands in order from left to right. If an operand is itself an operation with operands, then the same rules apply. In *ordinary prefix* notation one simply encloses the sequence of operands in parentheses, separating operands by commas. The tree of Fig. 5-2 then becomes

$$* (+(A,B),-(C,A))$$

A variant of this notation is used in LISP and is sometimes termed *Cambridge Polish*. In Cambridge Polish notation the left parenthesis following an operator symbol is moved to immediately precede it and the commas separating operands are deleted. An expression then looks like a nested set of lists, where each list begins with an operator symbol followed by the lists representing the operands. In Cambridge Polish the tree of Fig. 5-2 becomes

$$(* (+ A\ B) (-\ C A))$$

A second variant, called *Polish* (or parenthesis-free) notation, allows the parentheses to be dropped altogether. If we assume that the number of operands for each operator is known and fixed, then the parentheses are unnecessary. For example, the tree of Fig. 5-2 represented in Polish notation becomes

$$* + A\ B - C\ A$$

Consider now the quadratic formula (Fig. 5-1) represented in prefix notation:

$$/(+(M(B),SQRT(-(\uparrow(B,2),*(*(4,A),C)))),*(2,A))$$ (ordinary prefix)
$$(/(+(M\ B)(SQRT(-(\uparrow B\ 2)(*(*4\ A)\ C))))(*2\ A))$$ (Cambridge Polish)
$$/+M\ B\ SQRT-\uparrow B\ 2**4\ A\ C*2\ A$$ (Polish)

The most obvious fact about these prefix expressions is that they are difficult to decipher. In fact, the Polish form of the expression cannot be deciphered at all without knowing for each symbol in the expression the number of operands it requires (treating data references as operators with no operands). The ordinary prefix and Cambridge Polish forms require large numbers of parentheses, and, of course, the notation is simply unfamiliar to those accustomed to the more common infix notation.

Prefix notation is not without value, however. In fact, ordinary prefix notation is the standard mathematical notation for most operations other than binary arithmetic and logical operations. More important, prefix notation may be used to represent operations with any number of operands, and thus it is completely general—only one syntactic rule need be learned in order to write any expression. For example, in LISP, where programs are expressions, one need master only the Cambridge Polish notation for writing expressions and one has learned most of the syntactic rules of the language. Prefix notation is also a relatively easy notation to decode mechanically, and for this reason translation of prefix expressions into simple code sequences is easily accomplished. Occasionally a prefix representation is used directly during execution as the executable form of an expression (e.g., in SNOBOL4).

2. *Postfix (Suffix or Reverse Polish) Notation.* Postfix notation is similar to prefix notation except that the operation symbol *follows* the list of operands. For example, the expression in Fig. 5-2 is represented as

$$((A,B)+,(C,A)-)*\ \text{ or }\ A\ B+C\ A-*$$

Postfix is not a common syntactic representation for expressions in programming languages, but it does have importance as the basis for a particularly valuable execution-time representation for expressions (see below).

3. *Infix Notation.* Infix notation is suitable only for binary operations, i.e., operations taking two operands. In infix notation the

operator symbol is written between the two operands. Because infix notation for the basic arithmetic, relational, and logical operations is so commonly used in ordinary mathematics, the notation for these operations has been widely adopted in programming languages and in some cases extended to other operations as well. In infix form the tree of Fig. 5-2 is represented

$$(A + B) * (C - A)$$

Although infix notation is common, its use in a programming language leads to a number of unique problems:

a. Because infix notation is suitable only for binary operators, a language cannot use only infix notation but must necessarily combine infix and prefix (or postfix) notations. The mixture makes translation correspondingly more complex.

b. When more than one infix operator appears in an expression the notation is inherently ambiguous unless parentheses are used. For example, the infix expression

$$A * B + C$$

might represent either of the trees of Fig. 5-3.

Parentheses may be used to explicitly indicate the grouping of operators and operands, as in $(A * B) + C$ or $A * (B + C)$, but in complex expressions the resulting deep nests of parentheses become confusing. For this reason languages commonly introduce implicit control rules that make most uses of parentheses unnecessary. The two common types of implicit rules are

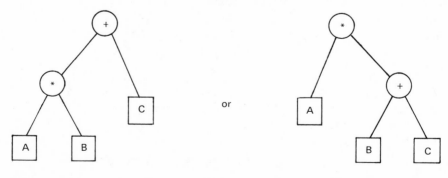

Fig. 5-3.

i. *Hierarchy of operations (precedence rules).* The operators that may occur in expressions are placed in a hierarchy or precedence order. The ALGOL hierarchy is typical (see Table 5-1).

Table 5-1   ALGOL Hierarchy of Operations

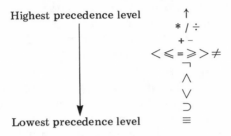

Highest precedence level

Lowest precedence level

In an expression involving operators from more than one level in the hierarchy the implicit rule is that operators with higher precedence are to be executed first. Thus in $A * B + C$, $*$ is above $+$ in the hierarchy and will be executed first.

ii. *Associativity.* In an expression involving operations at the same level in the hierarchy an additional implicit rule for associativity is needed to completely define the order of operations. For example, in $A - B - C$, is the first or second subtraction to be performed first? Left-to-right associativity is the most common implicit rule, so that $A - B - C$ is treated as $(A - B) - C$. However, in APL associativity is from right to left: $A - B - C$ is treated as $A - (B - C) = A - B + C$.

Each of the notations for expressions that we have mentioned has its own particular difficulties. Infix notation with the implicit precedence and associativity rules and explicit use of parentheses (when required) gives a rather natural representation for most arithmetic, relational, and logical expressions. However, the need for the complex implicit rules and the necessary use of prefix (or other) notation for nonbinary operations makes the translation of such expressions complex. Infix notation without the implicit rules (i.e., with full parenthesization) is cumbersome because of the large number of parentheses required. However, both Cambridge Polish and ordinary mathematical prefix notation share this problem with parentheses. The Polish notation avoids use of parentheses altogether, but one must know in advance the number of operands required for each operator, a condition that is often difficult to satisfy when programmer-defined operations are involved. In addition the lack of any structuring cues makes reading complex Polish form expressions exceedingly difficult. All the prefix notations share the advantage of applying equally to operations with differing numbers of operands.

The major and minor differences in notation among languages make the situation even more difficult. In APL, for example, infix notation is used for both primitive and programmer-defined operations, but without a hierarchy of operations, and with right-to-left rather than left-to-right associativity. LISP uses only Cambridge Polish. Many languages adopt infix notation for the basic arithmetic, logical, and relational operations; Polish prefix notation for built-in unary operators like negation and logical **not**; and ordinary mathematical prefix notation for everything else, including both programmer-defined operations and some built-in functions such as *sine* and *cosine*. SNOBOL4 represents relational operations in ordinary prefix notation but adds a considerable number of new unary and binary operators in Polish prefix and infix notation, respectively. It is apparent that no general agreement exists on the best notation for expressions in programming languages.

Translation of Expressions into Tree Representations

Translating an expression from its syntactic representation in a program text into its executable form is most easily conceptualized as a two-stage process. First the expression is translated into its tree representation, and then the tree is translated into a sequence of executable instructions. The first stage is ordinarily concerned only with establishing the basic tree control structure of the expression, utilizing the implicit rules of precedence and associativity when the expression involves infix notation. In the second stage the detailed decisions concerning order of evaluation are made, including optimization of the evaluation process. Both stages of expression translation have received extended study because both are of central importance in the construction of compilers for high-level languages. The first stage is part of the syntactic analysis phase of compilation; the second falls into the code generation phase. A detailed study of the problems involved in either stage is subject for a book on the details of compilation techniques, but a brief discussion is given in Chapter 9.

Understanding of techniques for the translation from expressions to tree representations has been greatly enlarged by the study of formal grammars and syntax-directed compilation techniques. Many of the practical techniques in use, although based indirectly on the tree representation, avoid explicit construction of the tree and instead produce directly an executable form of the expression.

Execution-Time Representations of Expressions

Various run-time representations of expressions are in use in language implementations. Because of the difficulty of decoding expressions in their original form in the program text, especially where infix notation is used, it is commonplace to translate into an executable form that may be easily decoded during execution. The most important alternatives in use are

1. *Machine code sequences.* The most common technique is to simply translate expressions into actual machine code. The ordering of the instructions reflects the sequence control structure of the original expression. On conventional computers such machine code sequences must make use of explicit temporary storage locations to hold intermediate results. Machine code representation, of course, allows use of the hardware interpreter, providing very fast execution.

2. *Tree structures.* Expressions may be executed directly in their natural tree structure representation, using a software interpreter. Execution may then be accomplished by a simple tree traversal. This is the basic technique used in (software-interpreted) LISP, where entire programs are represented as tree structures during execution.

3. *Prefix or postfix form.* Expressions in prefix or postfix form may be executed by relatively simple interpretation algorithms that scan the expression from left to right. Postfix representation is particularly useful here, as the order of symbols in the postfix expression corresponds closely to the order in which the various operations must be executed. In some actual computers based on a stack organization, such as the Burroughs B5500, the actual machine code is essentially represented in postfix form. Prefix representation is the executable form of programs in SNOBOL4 in most implementations. Execution is by a left-to-right scan, with each operation calling the interpreter recursively to evaluate its operands.

Evaluation of Tree Representations of Expressions

Although translation from expressions in programs into tree representations occasionally causes difficulty, the basic translation procedure is straightforward. The second stage, in which the tree is translated into an executable sequence of primitive operations, involves most of the subtle questions of order of evaluation. It is not our concern here to study directly algorithms for the generation of executable code from the tree representation but rather to consider the problems of order of evaluation which arise in determining exactly the code to generate.

Problem 1. Uniform Evaluation Rules. In evaluating an expression, or in generating code for its evaluation, one would expect the following uniform evaluation rule to apply regardless of the operations involved or of the complexity of the expression: For each operation node in the expression tree, first evaluate (or generate code to evaluate) each of its operands, and then apply the operation (or generate code to apply the operation) to the evaluated operands. The exact order in which these evaluations occur should not matter, so that the order of evaluation of operands or of independent operations may be chosen to optimize use of temporary storage or other machine features. Under this evaluation rule, for the expression of Fig. 5-2 either of the following orders of evaluation would be acceptable:

Order 1:

1. Fetch the value of A, obtaining a.

2. Fetch the value of B, obtaining b.

3. Add a and b, obtaining d.

4. Fetch the value of C, obtaining c.

5. Subtract a from c, obtaining e.

6. Multiply d and e, obtaining f, the value of the expression.

Order 2:

1. Fetch the value of C, obtaining c.

2. Fetch the value of B, obtaining b.

3. Fetch the value of A, obtaining a.

4. Subtract a from c, obtaining e.

5. Add a and b, obtaining d.

6. Multiply d and e, obtaining f.

This is all quite natural, and one would like to adopt the uniform

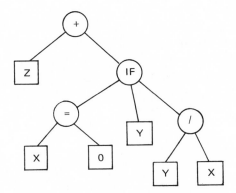

Fig. 5-4. An expression containing a conditional.

evaluation rule mentioned. Unfortunately it is not always correct to evaluate the operands before applying the operation. The best example is the case of expressions containing conditionals, for example, in ALGOL: $Z + ($ if $X = 0$ then Y else $Y / X)$. One would like to treat such a conditional simply as an operation with a "funny syntax" and three operands, as in Fig. 5-4. In fact in LISP this is exactly what is done, utilizing the Cambridge Polish notation for conditionals as well as for all other operations. But now the problem with the uniform evaluation rule appears. If we evaluate the operands of the conditional operator IF in Fig. 5-4, we produce the effect of doing exactly what the conditional is set up to avoid, namely dividing Y by X even if X is zero. Clearly, in this case we do not wish all the operands evaluated before the operation is applied. Instead we need to pass the operands (or at least the last two operands) to the operation IF *unevaluated* and let the operation determine the order of evaluation.

The problem with conditionals suggests that perhaps an alternative uniform evaluation rule would be better: *Never* evaluate operands before applying the operation; instead always pass the operands unevaluated and let the operation decide if evaluation is needed. In fact, it may be shown that this evaluation rule works in all cases and thus theoretically would serve. However, implementation turns out to be impractical in most cases, for how is one to simulate the passing of unevaluated operands to operations? While it can be done, it requires substantial software simulation to accomplish. Moreover, as the need for unevaluated operands commonly arises only in a few cases it is difficult to justify the expense of simulation.

The two uniform evaluation rules suggested above correspond to two common techniques for passing parameters to subprograms, transmission *by value* and *by name*, respectively. The details of these concepts and their simulation are discussed in greater depth in the next chapter when parameter transmission is taken up. For our purposes here it suffices to point out that no simple uniform evaluation rule for expressions (or for generating code for expressions) is satisfactory. In language implementations one commonly finds a mixture of the two techniques. For example, in LISP, functions (operations) are split into two categories (EXPR-SUBR and FEXPR-FSUBR) depending on whether the function receives evaluated or unevaluated operands. In SNOBOL4 programmer-defined operations (subprograms) always receive evaluated operands while language-defined primitive operations receive unevaluated operands. ALGOL primitive operations receive evaluated operands, with conditionals being simulated by in-line code sequences, but programmer-defined subprograms may receive both evaluated and unevaluated operands.

Problem 2. Side Effects. The use of operations with side effects (or which are self-modifying) in expressions is the basis of a long-standing controversy in programming language design. Consider the expression

$$A * FUN(X) + A$$

Before the multiplication can be performed the value of A must be fetched and $FUN(X)$ must be evaluated. The addition requires the value of A and the result of the multiplication. It is clearly desirable to fetch the value of A only once and simply use it in two places in the computation. Moreover, it should make no difference whether $FUN(X)$ is evaluated before or after the value of A is fetched. However, if FUN has the side effect of changing the value of A, then the exact order of evaluation is critical. For example, if A has the value 1 on beginning evaluation of the expression and $FUN(X)$ evaluates to 3 and, as a side effect, increases the value of A by 1, then different orders of evaluation might produce any of the results 4, 5, 7, or 8.

Two positions on the use of side effects in expressions have emerged. One position is that side effects should be outlawed in expressions, either by disallowing functions with side effects altogether or simply by making undefined the value of any expression in which side effects might affect the value (e.g., the value of the expression above). Another view is that side effects should be allowed and that the language definition should make it clear exactly what the order of evaluation of an expression is to be so that the programmer can make proper use of side effects in his code. The difficulty with this latter position is that it makes many kinds of optimization impossible. In many language definitions the question is simply ignored altogether, with the unfortunate result that different implementations provide conflicting interpretations.

Statements, of course, must be allowed to have side effects. For example, the assignment operation necessarily produces a side effect—a change in the value of a variable or data structure element. And clearly we expect the side effects produced by one statement to affect the inputs of the next statement in sequence. The problem is whether this sort of interdependence through side effects should be allowed below the statement level, in expressions. If disallowed, we need to specify the order of evaluation in expressions only to the tree representation level; expression evaluation, for the programmer, is without "tricks"; and optimization of expression evaluation sequences by the translator is possible. However, if optimization is not a prime concern, it is often valuable to allow side effects and specify the order of evaluation completely. In this case we lose much of the reason for distinguishing between statements and expressions in a language. In a number of languages, notably LISP, APL, BLISS (Wulf [1971]), and EULER (Wirth and Weber [1966]), the distinction between expressions and statements has in fact almost or entirely disappeared. For the programmer this represents a valuable simplification. Thus there is no dominant position on side effects in expressions—either approach has its adherents. In this regard it is of interest that Niklaus Wirth in the design of EULER dropped the statement-expression distinction, allowing side effects throughout, but in the later design of PASCAL (Wirth [1971b]) reintroduced the distinction, while at the same time disallowing side effects in expressions.

Problem 3. Error Conditions. A special kind of side effect is involved in the case of operations that may fail and generate an error condition. Unlike ordinary side effects, which are usually restricted to programmer-defined functions, error conditions may arise in many primitive operations (overflow or underflow on arithmetic operations, divide by zero, etc.). It is undesirable to outlaw side effects of this sort, yet the meaning, and even the occurrence of such error conditions, may be affected by differences in the order of evaluation of expression components. In such situations the programmer may need precise control of the order of evaluation, yet the demand for optimization may preclude this (see Problem 5-5). The solution to these difficulties tends to be essentially ad hoc and varies from language to language and implementation to implementation.

5-3. SEQUENCE CONTROL BETWEEN STATEMENTS

In this section we shall take up the basic mechanisms in use for controlling the sequence in which individual statements are executed within a program, leaving for the following section the larger sequence control structures concerned with programs and subprograms.

Implicit Statement Sequence Control

The most common implicit rule governing the execution order of statements is the rule that execution proceeds according to the physical order of statements within a program. Execution begins with the first statement. When execution of the first statement is complete, the second statement is executed, followed by the third, etc.

This implicit rule is typical of every language in Part II, but more complex implicit sequence control rules are fairly common in special-purpose languages. When complex control structures are typical of an application area, the programmer's burden may be considerably reduced if the implicit rules in the language reflect these natural structures.

Parallel Execution

A less common form of statement sequence control is the specification that a group of statements are to be executed in parallel. This concept is seen in the ALGOL 68 (Van Wijngaarden et al. [1969]) *collateral* execution. If the statements in an ALGOL 68 program segment are separated by commas rather than the usual semicolons, then the statements are to be executed (conceptually) in parallel. Thus, for example, the statements $S_1, S_2, S_3, \ldots, S_n$ have the flow chart of Fig. 5-5. Parallel execution would be simulated by sequential execution on a conventional computer, of course, but the order of execution may be optimized since it is irrelevant to the result.

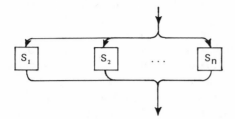

Fig. 5-5.

Labels and Goto Statements

The ability to label statements and then transfer control explicitly to a labeled statement from another point in a program is common to most programming languages. The transfer of control is most often indicated by use of a **goto** statement, although other notations are common. For convenience we shall adopt the term **goto** *statement* to refer to any notation for the explicit transfer of control to a labeled statement from elsewhere in a program. This form of explicit control mechanism is both straightforward to use and efficient to execute since, at least in its simple form, it reflects the basic underlying structure of conventional computers, in which each instruction word has an address and the hardware has a built-in *jump instruction* that transfers control to a designated address. Besides the basic **goto** statement, many languages include various augmented forms of **goto** based on the use of labels as data.

It is convenient to identify three basic approaches to the use of statement labels and **goto** statements:

1. *Labels as local syntactic tags in programs during transla-tion.* The simplest approach is to restrict the use of labels and **goto** statements to situations that may be directly translated into the hardware *instruction word address/jump instruction* construct. Such restricted use allows simple and efficient simulation of the label/**goto** structure. To set up such a simulation it must be possible for the translator to equate each label with an execution-time address so that **goto** statements may be translated into equivalent jump instructions. Typically the translator sets up a table of labels during translation. Each label in the table is paired with its equivalent (relative) run-time address while the executable program form is being generated. When translation is complete the table of labels is discarded. FORTRAN provides the best example of this approach. Within each FORTRAN subprogram, statement labels are unique. No references to statement labels within a subprogram are possible from outside it; if a referenced statement label does not exist within the same subpro-gram, it is considered an error. In FORTRAN it is always possible to

translate labels into relative machine addresses before execution begins.

2. *Labels as restricted data items at run time but without run-time computation of labels.* A more complex approach is to allow statement labels to be represented at run time as a restricted type of data. The most important restriction is to avoid constructs that allow statement labels to be read in or computed at run time, because such constructs would necessarily require that a table of statement labels and pointers to corresponding code positions be maintained during program execution. Within this restriction the language may still allow label variables and arrays, references to nonlocal labels, and label parameters to subprograms. ALGOL is typical of languages allowing use of labels at this intermediate level. Two ALGOL constructs preclude the simple translation of labels into equivalent machine addresses: (1) **goto** statements may reference nonlocal statement labels, and (2) **goto** statements may reference formal parameters of type **label**. In the presence of recursive subprograms both these constructs require that a label be represented during execution by a pair composed of the location of the corresponding machine code instruction and a pointer to an *activation record*. These complexities are taken up at length in Chapter 6. The important point to note here is that the *hardware address—jump instruction* structure cannot be used directly for all ALGOL constructs, making it necessary to move to partial software simulation of the label/**goto** structure during execution of ALGOL programs.

3. *Labels as unrestricted data items during execution.* The most general approach is to accept statement labels as simply another data type during execution by allowing labels to be read in or computed as needed, as, for example, in

.

.

.

READ X
.

.

.

GO TO X
.

.

.

To allow this generality it must be possible to determine during execution for each label the corresponding position in the executable form of the program. Thus a run-time table of labels and code positions is required. SNOBOL4 and APL are typical of languages taking this approach. In APL, programs are ordinarily executed in a form very similar to their input form, with line numbers attached to the statements. The line numbers represent a simple run-time label table, and thus it is natural to utilize this table to allow run-time computation of labels. Labels are restricted to integers, and any integer-valued expression may be used in a goto statement. A similar situation exists in SNOBOL4, but here labels are character strings. A run-time table of labels is set up during translation, and during execution any string-valued expression may be used in a goto, resulting in a table look-up to find the associated position in the executable code.

The Goto Controversy

Although every language in Part II allows the use of labels and goto statements in programs, considerable controversy surrounds their continued inclusion in new languages. In a number of new languages the use of labels and gotos has been either sharply curtailed or completely eliminated. Consideration of the problems surrounding gotos provides an insight into the criteria for and importance of the other sequence control mechanisms provided by a language.

Disadvantages of Goto *Statements.* Goto statements create difficulties both for the programmer and for the implementor. For programmers it is widely acknowledged that heavy use of gotos in a program is evidence of poor program design. A program that relies on gotos for sequence control is commonly difficult to debug and even more difficult to understand and maintain. The difficulty lies in following the structure of a program. As one traces through a program any labeled statement poses a problem, because control might transfer to that statement from any place in the program, and there is no way to determine where this might happen without scanning the entire program. Similarly when a group of goto statements is reached control may go off in many directions, and there is no simple way to tell how the various directions are related. Contrast this with the structure of a typical ALGOL conditional statement:

$$\text{if } \langle test \rangle \text{ then } \langle statements \rangle \text{ else } \langle statements \rangle;$$

In such a statement it is easy to see the overall structure of the branching by simply finding the **then**, **else**, and terminating semicolon. The two statement sequences bracketed by these delimiters specify exactly what is to be done in case the ⟨*test*⟩ is true or false. The typical test and **goto** conditional statement provides none of this logical structure:

if ⟨*test*⟩ then goto *L1* else goto *L2*

In such a statement one can determine only that control branches; there is no simple way of knowing if the two possible paths ever rejoin, much less what statements are executed in each case. It is this lack of structure associated with the use of **goto**s and labels to which many object. It is worth noting in this regard that it is not uncommon in large programming projects, where many different people will be writing programs and using and maintaining programs written by others, to set strict standards on the use of **goto** statements, so that the resulting programs will be properly structured even though **goto** statements may still be used.

For the implementor of a language the use of labels and **goto**s creates an additional set of problems, although the base cause is still the same—the difficulty of analyzing the possible paths of control in a program. In designing a compiler for a language where run-time efficiency is important, such as FORTRAN or ALGOL, one of the important design goals is the production of *optimized* executable code. Optimization depends importantly on the control structure of a program, and when **goto**s and labels are used heavily it is difficult for a compiler to analyze the control structure without extensive computation.

Advantages of **Gotos** *and Labels.* There are, of course, also advantages associated with the use of **goto**s and labels in languages. Important among these is the direct hardware support of simple forms of this sequence control mechanism on conventional computers. Second, the **goto**—label structure is completely general purpose—if you have **goto**s and labels, then you theoretically need nothing else; other sequence control mechanisms only add convenience. Without **goto**s and labels a variety of other mechanisms have to be substituted. The **goto**-label structure also serves as a useful building block for simulation of other control structures. For example, one may simulate coroutines or case statements in FORTRAN using the **goto**.

Can **Gotos** *and Labels be eliminated*? Obviously the **goto**/label control structure is basic in many languages. In fact, in some languages, e.g., APL and assembly languages, it is almost the only explicit mechanism available for controlling the sequence in which statements are executed (outside of subprogram calls). On the other hand, there are languages, most notably "pure" LISP (without the PROG feature) and the systems programming language BLISS (Wulf et al. [1971]), with no labels and gotos at all. We might answer the question on a purely theoretical level, and say "yes, it is well known that recursion is by itself a completely general control mechanism." Thus in pure LISP, with only recursive subprogram calls, nothing is lost theoretically by the lack of labels and gotos. Yet this clearly is not sufficient as an answer. In practice can one really write any program without gotos? And if so, then what is to be used for control instead? One cannot help but note that one of the first extensions to pure LISP was the addition of a label and goto control structure (the PROG feature).

The feasibility of eliminating gotos in programs depends strongly on the variety of alternative control structures available. In most languages with a fairly rich alternative control structure, e.g., ALGOL or PL/I, it is seldom that a goto—label structure is required in a program as the natural representation of an algorithm. In such languages the use of gotos is indeed usually evidence of poor program design, a point which is often stressed to students of these languages. Without a fairly rich set of alternatives such as conditional statements, iteration statements, recursive subprograms, etc., one may eliminate gotos only at the cost of gross distortion of the natural structure of many programs. Even in ALGOL the elimination of all gotos in a program may be possible only by introducing major distortions of the algorithm; in FORTRAN it is all but impossible. We may take it as a point of good program design in any language that each use of a goto and label should be scrutinized to determine whether an alternative construction may not be more appropriate. However, the complete elimination of gotos and labels requires a language with a rich set of alternative control structures and may still be of doubtful advantage.

Conditional and Case Statements

Our discussion now turns to other control structures that serve to supplement or replace the goto/label construct in programs. The basic *test and branch* or *conditional statement* is found in every language. In its simplest form the conditional statement appears as a *test and* goto, but more sophisticated forms do not rely on the goto.

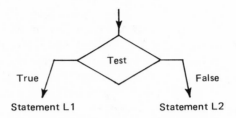

Fig. 5-6. Test and **goto** statement flow chart.

A variant of some importance is found in the *case statement* of many recent languages. Conditional and case statements are ordinarily translated directly into sequences of simpler (hardware) primitives using **goto**s and labels so that software simulation is not necessary.

Test and **Goto.** The simplest form of conditional statement is the *test and* **goto**, in which the alternatives to which control is to be transferred are specified only by statement labels. The basic structure is

if ⟨*test*⟩ **then go to** *L1* **else go to** *L2*

representing the flow chart of Fig. 5-6, although many variants are in use. FORTRAN, SNOBOL4, and APL, as well as most assembly languages, rely largely on this type of conditional branching.

The test and **goto** statement, because it relies on the **goto** and label structure, has the same disadvantage: Its use may lead to poorly structured programs.

Test, Branch, and Join. A more sophisticated form of conditional than the simple test and **goto** is the *test, branch, and join*, typified by the ALGOL

if ⟨*test*⟩ **then** ⟨*statement sequence*₁⟩ **else** ⟨*statement sequence*₂⟩;

which in flow chart form is Fig. 5-7. In this conditional, rather than designating the statements to which control is to transfer by statement labels, the entire statement sequences are embedded within the structure of the statement itself. Thus it is immediately clear from examination of the statement what is to be done in each case and where control in either case rejoins a single common stream. Such a structure is much more amenable to analysis, both by the programmer and by a compiler, than the test and **goto**. Owing to its more

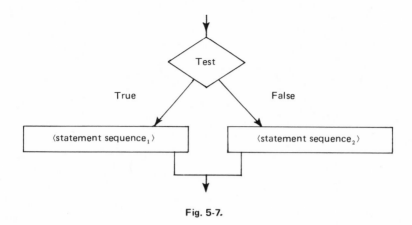

Fig. 5-7.

easily analyzed structure, the test, branch, and join statement is to be preferred to the test and **goto** in most algorithms.

Case Statements. A case statement, available in many recent languages such as ALGOL 68 and PASCAL, is an extension of both the test, branch, and join statement, the *computed* **goto** of FORTRAN (Chapter 10), and the *switch* of ALGOL (Chapter 11). Typically the **case** statement takes the form

> **case** ⟨*expression*⟩ **of**
> ⟨*statement sequence*₁⟩;
> ⟨*statement sequence*₂⟩;
> .
> .
> .
> ⟨*statement sequence*ₖ⟩;

The ⟨*expression*⟩ evaluates to an integer in the range $1, 2, \ldots, k$, and the corresponding ⟨*statement sequence*⟩ is executed. Thus we have the flow chart of Fig. 5-8. The case statement is a conditional statement with a programmer-specified n-way branch, as opposed to the two-way branching characteristic of simple conditionals. Note, however, that the case statement, unlike the FORTRAN computed **goto** or the ALGOL switch, provides this flexibility without introducing the need for statement labels. In addition, the various alternative groups of statements to be executed in each case are embedded explicitly in the statement structure, making analysis of

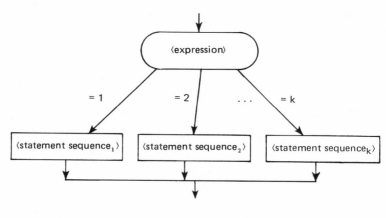

Fig. 5-8.

case statements straightforward. Availability of the case statement in a language leads again to a reduction in the need for **gotos** and labels in programs.

Iteration Statements

Iteration statements, such as the FORTRAN and PL/I DO statement, ALGOL **for** statement, and variants of the COBOL PERFORM statement, provide another major alternative control structure in many languages. Unlike conditionals, which are always required in some form, iteration statements may often be replaced by sequences of simpler statements in a program. In fact it is not uncommon to find the semantics of iteration statements defined in terms of such equivalent sequences of simpler statements, as is done in the definition of the ALGOL **for** statement in the ALGOL report (Naur [1963]).

The basic structure of an iteration statement consists of a *body* and a *head*. The body is ordinarily composed of an arbitrary sequence of statements; the head consists of an expression designating the number of times the body is to be executed. Although the bodies of iteration statements are fairly unrestricted, many variants of head structure may be seen. Let us look at some typical ones.

Simple Repetition. The simplest type of iteration statement head specifies that the body is to be executed some fixed number of times. The COBOL PERFORM statement is typical.

PERFORM *body* 12 TIMES.   or   PERFORM *body* K TIMES.

In this simple form the body is simply executed 12 times, or the current value of K times. This seems straightforward, yet already there is a subtle question that arises in the second form of the statement. The problem concerns the point of evaluation of the variable K. Is K evaluated only once before the first execution of the body, or is K evaluated before *each* execution of the body? The result will be the same unless the value of K is changed within the body. If this happens, the result can be very confusing; e.g., the iteration may never terminate if the value of K were to be increased each time through the body. For this simple iteration statement it is reasonable to assume that K is evaluated once only before execution begins. A second question of concern: What if the initial value of K is negative or zero? Should we simply skip execution of the body, execute it once, or treat it as an error condition and halt execution of the program altogether?

Although these questions may seem like hairsplitting for this simple iteration statement, the same questions arise in each form of the statement, and thus it is important to look at them in their simplest form here. In each case it is important to ask (1) when is the termination test made, and (2) when are the variables used in the statement head evaluated.

Repetition While Condition Holds. A somewhat more complex iteration may be constructed using a *repeat while* head. A typical form is

while ⟨test⟩ do ⟨body⟩

The meaning of this construct may be represented by the flow chart of Fig. 5-9. In this form of iteration statement the test expression is reevaluated each time after finishing execution of the body. Note also that here it is to be. expected that execution of the body will change some of the values of variables appearing in the test

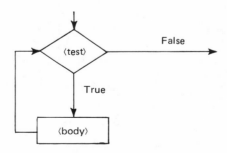

Fig. 5-9.

expression; otherwise the iteration, once begun, would never terminate.

Repetition While Incrementing a Counter. The third alternative form of iteration statement of interest, and the most important in many languages, is the statement whose head specifies a variable which serves as a counter or index during the iteration. An initial value, final value, and increment are specified in the head, and the body is executed repeatedly using first the initial value as the value of the index variable, then the initial value plus the increment, then the initial value plus twice the increment, etc., until the final value is reached. In FORTRAN this is the only form of iteration statement available. The ALGOL **for** statement illustrates the typical structure

for $I := 1$ **step** 2 **until** 30 **do** $\langle body \rangle$

The meaning of this statement is defined by the flow chart of Fig. 5-10. In its general form both the initial value, final value, and increment may be given by arbitrary expressions, as in

for $K := N\text{-}1$ **step** $2\times(W\text{-}1)$ **until** $M\times N$ **do** $\langle body \rangle$

Again the question arises as to when the termination test is made and when and how often the various expressions are evaluated. Here the question is of central importance additionally for the language implementor because such iteration statements are prime candidates for optimization, and the answers may affect greatly the sorts of

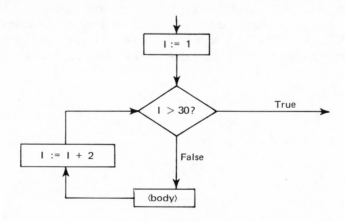

Fig. 5-10.

optimizations which can be performed. As we shall see in Section 5-5 this form of the iteration statement is basic in most languages in which arrays are important data structures because it represents the natural statement for setting up element-by-element processing of arrays.

Many other variants of the iteration statement are in use. We shall not attempt to survey them all. ALGOL, PL/I, and COBOL in Part II illustrate additional possibilities. The iteration statement forms another major alternative to the **goto**/label mechanism. As with conditionals the iteration statement requires no use of statement labels, and the overall structure of the statement is readily analyzable. For these reasons the iteration statement is the preferred sequence control mechanism for loop structures in programs.

5-4. SUBPROGRAM SEQUENCE CONTROL

In this section our concern is with mechanisms for controlling the sequence in which sets of programs and subprograms are executed. The simple subprogram CALL and RETURN statement structure is common to almost all programming languages, but more sophisticated control structures involving recursion, interrupts, coroutines, tasks, and scheduling of subprogram calls are also important.

Simple Subprogram Call-Return Structure

We are accustomed in programming to mentally structuring our sets of programs and subprograms into hierarchies. A program is composed of a single main program, which during execution may call various subprograms, which in turn may each call other sub-subprograms, and so forth to any depth. Each subprogram at some point is expected to terminate its execution and return control to the program which called it. During execution of a subprogram, execution of the calling program is temporarily halted. When execution of the subprogram is completed, execution of the calling program resumes at the point immediately following the call of the subprogram. This control structure is often explained by the *copy rule*: The effect of the subprogram CALL statement is the same as would be obtained if the CALL statement were replaced by a copy of the body of the subprogram (with suitable substitutions for parameters and conflicting identifiers) before execution. Viewed in this way subprogram calls may be considered as control structures that simply make it unnecessary to copy large numbers of identical or nearly identical statements that occur in more than one place in a program. However, if a particular subprogram turned out to be very short (e.g., only one or two statements), then we could actually apply the copy rule explicitly and replace the subprogram call by *in-line* code during translation. In fact, this sort of replacement of subprogram calls by in-line code is often done in compilers for languages like FORTRAN when simple standard function subprograms are involved (computation of the absolute value of a number is a typical example).

The copy rule view of subprograms involves many implicit assumptions that warrant detailed consideration. However, let us first look at the implementation of simple subprogram calls on conventional computers. Simulation of copy-rule-defined subprogram calls and returns is straightforward. Conventional computers ordinarily support such calls directly with a hardware *return jump* instruction that causes a jump to a designated location (the *entry point* of the subprogram) and at the same time stores the location of the next instruction of the calling program (the *return point*) into another location, usually a register or the location immediately preceding the entry point. Even without direct hardware support this mechanism is easily simulated by using instruction addresses and jump instructions. It is necessary only to associate with each subprogram a location for storing the return point of the calling subprogram. When another program calls the subprogram it must first store the appropriate return point in the called subprogram's return point location. The called subprogram returns control to the calling subprogram by simply transferring control to this return point. Figure 5-11 illustrates a typical form of this simulation.

The copy rule leads to a view of subprograms as a simple notational convenience. As a practical matter it is convenient to write the subprogram once and call it from a number of different places in a program rather than copying the statements anew each time. Moreover, there is a storage advantage during program execution because the executable form of the statements need be stored only once. Perhaps more importantly it is a major organizational tool. When designing the calling program the detailed design of the subprograms need not be done at the same time; one need only insert a subprogram call and specify arguments and results. The detailed design of the subprogram may be left until later. The program-subprogram structure is the most prominent organizational technique in programming. Clearly, even as a notational convenience subprograms are invaluable. Yet the copy rule implication that

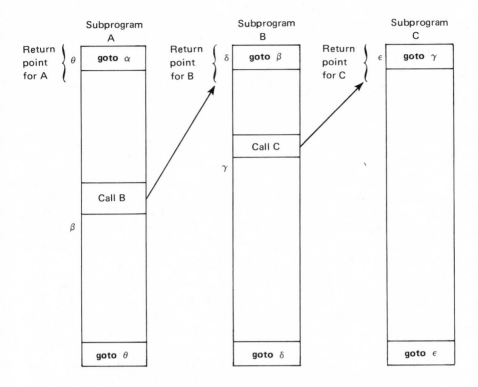

Subprogram C is in execution; A and B are in suspended execution

Fig. 5-11. Simulation of simple subprogram call-return mechanism.

replacement of subprogram calls by subprogram bodies during translation is always possible (even if often undesirable) is simplistic. Implicit in the copy rule are a number of assumptions about sequence control structures and subprograms that are too stringent and may profitably be relaxed. Let us look at some of these:

1. *Subprograms cannot be recursive.* A subprogram is *directly recursive* if it contains a call on itself (e.g., if subprogram B contains the statement CALL B); it is *indirectly recursive* if it calls another subprogram that calls the original subprogram or that initiates a further chain of subprogram calls that eventually leads back to a call of the original subprogram. In the case of simple nonrecursive subprogram calls we may apply the copy rule during translation to replace subprogram calls by copies of the subprogram body and completely eliminate the need for the separate subprogram (in

principle, not in practice). But if the subprogram is directly recursive, then this is not possible even in principle, because the substitution of subprogram call for subprogram body is obviously unending: Each substitution which deletes a CALL statement introduces a new call on the same subprogram, for which another substitution is necessary, etc. Indirect recursion may allow some subprograms to be deleted but must lead eventually to making others directly recursive.

2. *Explicit CALL statements are required.* For the copy rule to apply, each point of call of a subprogram must be explicitly indicated in the program to be translated.

3. *Subprograms must execute completely at each call.* Implicit in the copy rule is the assumption that each subprogram is executed from its beginning to its logical end each time it is called. If called a second time, the subprogram begins execution anew and again executes to its logical end before returning control.

4. *Single execution sequence.* At any point during execution of a program-subprogram hierarchy exactly one program has control. Execution proceeds in a single sequence from calling program to called subprogram and back to calling program. If we halt execution at some point, we may always identify one program that is in execution (i.e., that has control), a set of others whose execution has been temporarily suspended (the calling program, its calling program, etc.), and the remainder, which have either never been called or which have completely executed.

5. *Immediate transfer of control at point of call.* An explicit CALL statement in a program indicates that control is to transfer directly to the subprogram at that point, and thus copying the body into the calling program has the same effect.

Relaxation of any one of these assumptions leads to subprogram control structures that cannot be easily understood in terms of the copy rule and that moreover cannot be simulated during program execution with the simple *return jump* hardware structure provided in most conventional computers, a structure which is grounded in the copy rule approach. Of the major languages discussed in Part II, only FORTRAN and COBOL are based directly on the copy rule view of subprograms. Each of the others allows more flexible structures and thus requires some software simulation of the subprogram calling structure during execution. In the following we shall consider the various subprogram control structures that result from the relaxation of each of the above five assumptions in turn.

Note that the emphasis is strictly on sequence control structure here, i.e., on the mechanisms for transfer of control between programs and subprograms. Closely tied to each of these sequence control structures is the question of data control: parameter transmission, global and local variables, etc. These topics are taken up separately in the next chapter so as not to confuse our focus on the sequence control mechanisms themselves. For example, even simple subprogram calls ordinarily arise in two forms, the *function call*, for subprograms that return values directly, and the *procedure* or *subroutine call*, for subprograms that operate only through side effects on shared data. Function calls are ordinarily embedded in expressions, while procedure calls require a separate statement. These distinctions are based on methods of data control, however, and thus are taken up in the next chapter. For our purposes in this chapter the two types of subprograms are identical in the sequence control structures they require, and thus we do not distinguish the two cases.

Subprogram Definitions and Subprogram Activations

Before considering the various alternative control structures involving subprograms, the important distinction between a *definition* and an *activation* of a subprogram must be made. To this point the term *subprogram* has been used in reference both to the *subprogram definition*, the representation of a subprogram as written by the programmer and as input to the translator, and to the *subprogram activation*, the representation of the subprogram during execution. For the simple subprogram call-return control structure this confusion is permissible, for there is conceptually a single subprogram involved at both translation time and execution time.

The distinction becomes crucial when we begin to consider recursive subprograms and other more general subprogram control structures. Consider a subprogram A that calls subprogram B, and suppose that B then calls subprogram A recursively. During execution of A after the recursive call from B there exist two activations of A. Subprogram A was activated initially when first called (from elsewhere in the program). During execution of this activation of A the call to B occurred, and the execution of this activation of A was suspended. Similarly execution of the activation of B was suspended when A was called recursively. The recursive call on A creates a *new activation* of A, entirely independent of the original activation. Conceptually this second activation may be viewed as an entirely new copy of A, but a copy created dynamically at the point of call during execution, rather than during translation as with our original copy rule. When execution of the second activation of A is complete, control returns to B and then perhaps back to the first activation of A. Alternatively subprogram calls in the second activation of A may lead to further recursive activations of both A and B. Thus during execution many different activations of a subprogram may exist, each appearing as an independent copy derived from the same subprogram definition in the original program text.

The subprogram *definition* serves as a template for constructing subprogram *activations* during execution. Typically the translator translates the subprogram definition into a *fixed part* containing the executable code, constants, and other program elements that are the same in every activation, and an *activation record template* representing that part of the subprogram that varies between activations. When the subprogram is called during execution the template is used to construct an *activation record* for the new activation of the subprogram. Typically the activation record contains space for the local data of the subprogram, parameters, return point, temporary storage, and various items of system information. The activation record together with the fixed part of the subprogram constitute an *activation* of the subprogram.

In this chapter we shall consider only that part of the activation record of a subprogram that is directly involved in sequence control, most often the subprogram return point. The next chapter considers the aspects of activation records pertinent to data control, such as local data and parameters. In Chapter 7 the full structure of an activation record is considered in the context of storage management.

For simple nonrecursive subprograms, as, for example, in FORTRAN, at most one activation of each subprogram may exist at any point during execution. In this case, and ignoring all but the return point component of an activation record, it is feasible to simply allocate space during translation for a single activation record (one return point) along with the fixed program part. This organization is the basis for the simulation of the simple call-return control structure discussed above.

Recursive Subprograms

Recursion, in the form of recursive subprogram calls, is one of the most important sequence control structures in programming. Many algorithms are most naturally represented using recursion. In LISP, recursion, together with simple operation sequences and branching, is the major sequence control mechanism, rather than the iteration (looping) of most other languages. In fact, in pure LISP, iteration is not allowed; recursion is the only mechanism available for repeating a sequence of operations.

If we relax assumption 1 and allow recursive subprogram calls, the programmer notices little difference at the language level because ordinarily no distinction is made syntactically between recursive and nonrecursive subprogram calls. However, while recursive calls may not change the language syntax, the simulation necessary for implementing recursive calls is substantially different from that for nonrecursive calls. Recursive calling structures are seldom supported directly by the hardware and thus must be largely software-simulated, leading to a major difference in run-time efficiency between the nonrecursive and recursive mechanisms.

Recall that for the run-time simulation of nonrecursive calls we needed a single return point location associated with each subprogram. For recursive calls this single location does not suffice. To see the difficulty, consider a subprogram A which calls a subprogram B which in turn calls itself recursively. When A calls B it stores its return point in the return point location associated with B. But when B calls itself recursively it stores a new return point in its own return point location. This new return point specifies the return point from the recursive call of B to the original call of B. But, of course, storing the new return point destroys the return point to A originally stored in B's return point location. Thus while return from the recursive call is possible, return from the original call can no longer be effected. Indirect recursion results in similar difficulties, as illustrated in Fig. 5-12.

The difficulty is simply explained in terms of subprogram activations. For each activation of a given subprogram it is necessary to store a return point, because each activation may have been initiated from a different place (call statement or function reference). With recursion there may be arbitrarily many activations of the same subprogram. Obviously, a single return point location cannot suffice. Moreover, it also does not suffice to allocate a fixed block of storage for return points because the maximum size of this block cannot in general be predicted. Instead we need a *stack* for return point storage, a stack which can expand as needed during execution.

Associating a stack with each subprogram for return point storage allows a simple simulation for recursive calls. The stack is used as follows during execution. On the first (nonrecursive) call to a subprogram we save the return point in the first stack location. On the first recursive call, we store the return point for this call in the second stack location. On the second recursive call, we use the third

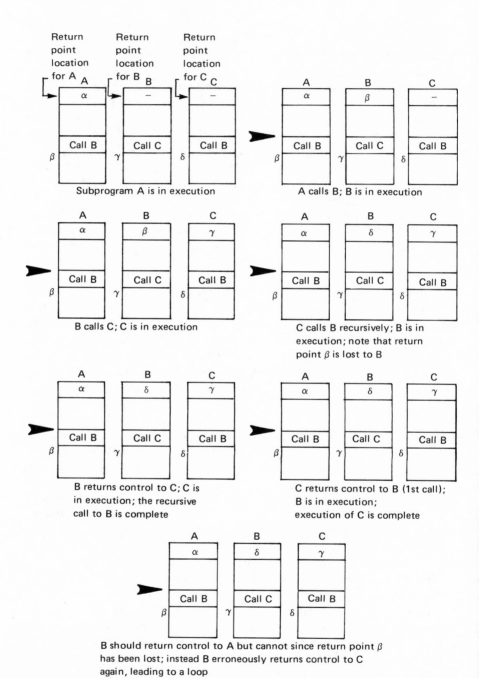

Fig. 5-12. The problem of simulation of recursive subprogram calls with simple call-return structure.

stack location, and so forth. When we complete execution of the subprogram and wish to return, we must find the last stack entry made and use that as the appropriate return location, deleting that return location from the stack to expose the one below it for use in returning from the next level of recursion. In this way the stack of return locations allows the subprogram to unwind the nest of recursive calls correctly, returning at the end to the original calling program. Each stack location serves as a simple activation record for an activation of the subprogram (since we are ignoring local variables, parameters, etc.)

The basic simulation mechanism of associating a stack of return points with *each* subprogram may be simplified by using instead a *central stack* of return points for all subprograms. Subprogram calls obey the last-in—first-out rule: At any point during execution the next subprogram to return control to its calling program must be the last one entered. This last-in—first-out structure allows a central stack to be used as follows: Whenever a subprogram *B* is called, the calling program *A* stacks the appropriate return point on top of the central stack. If *B* calls *C*, then *B* stacks the return point for *C* again on the same stack. If *C* calls *B* recursively, then *C* again stacks the return point for *B* on the central stack. Suppose now that *B* completes execution (on the recursive call). To return, *B* simply retrieves the top return point from the central stack, deletes it from the stack, and returns control to that location, which will be the appropriate point in *C*. When *C* is finished it again goes to the central stack and retrieves the current top return point, deletes it from the stack, and returns control to the designated return point, which now is the appropriate location in *B*. In this manner the calling structure is unwound correctly. Note that the central stack need contain only return points; it need not contain a designator of which subprogram is to use which return point, as this is implicit in the last-in—first-out nature of the subprogram call-return structure. Thus rather than separate stacks for each subprogram it suffices to have only a single stack of all return points. Figure 5-13 illustrates this use of a central stack.

The run-time simulation of recursive subprogram calls introduces a cost, because ordinarily the hardware provided return-jump mechanism cannot be used directly, necessitating software simulation of the stacking and unstacking of return points. Provision must also be made for management of the run-time stack, consideration of stack overflow, etc. The result is a substantial overhead. Oftentimes in compilers concerned with optimization of execution speed an attempt will be made to distinguish between recursive and nonrecursive subprograms so that the simpler hardware-supported return-jump

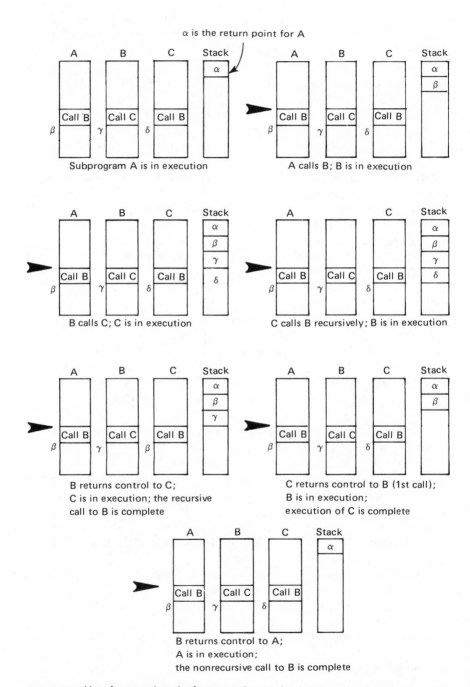

Fig. 5-13. Use of a central stack of return points to simulate recursive subprogram calls.

structure may be used for nonrecursive subprograms. Occasionally (e.g., in PL/I) the programmer is required to explicitly distinguish between recursive and nonrecursive subprograms in his coding, for example, by heading definitions of recursive subprograms with the tag *recursive*.

Interrupts (Traps)

An important alternative control structure is obtained by relaxing the rule that subprogram calls must be explicitly indicated in the calling program at the point of call. In many situations provision for explicit call statements is undesirable. Typically cases occur in which a subprogram should be called when a particular condition arises, rather than when execution of a program reaches a particular point. For example,

1. *Error conditions.* Call a subprogram to process an error such as an arithmetic operation overflow or reference to an array element with a subscript out of bounds.

2. *Conditions which arise unpredictably during normal program execution.* Call a subprogram to handle special output headings at the end of a printer page or to process an end-of-file indicator on an input file.

3. *Tracing and monitoring during program testing.* Call a subprogram to print trace output during program testing when a subprogram is entered or exited or when the value of a variable changes.

While it may often be possible to explicitly test for conditions of these types in a program and explicitly call the appropriate subprogram, the *interrupt* control structure with its implicit call is much simpler. Typically the interrupt control structure is divided into two parts:

1. *Specification of the interrupt routine* (the subprogram to be called when the condition arises) *and its association with a particular condition.* This specification often takes the form of a declaration at the beginning of a program of the form

ON *condition* CALL *subprogram*

as, for example, ON OVERFLOW CALL SUB.

2. *Enabling* (and *disabling*) *of interrupt condition checking.* It is seldom desirable to have continuous checking throughout program

execution. More commonly the programmer is provided with facilities for turning the checking on and off at different points during execution (as, for example, turning tracing on during execution of untested routines and off on return to tested portions of a program). In PL/I this is accomplished by the use of special tags on statements or groups of statements, as, for example,

$$\text{ON OVERFLOW CALL SUB;}$$

$$\cdot$$
$$\cdot$$
$$\cdot$$

$$\text{(OVERFLOW):} \quad X = Y * Z + W;$$

$$\cdot$$
$$\cdot$$
$$\cdot$$

Interrupt routine SUB will be called only if overflow occurs during execution of a statement tagged (OVERFLOW). In SNOBOL4 interrupt enabling is accomplished in part through the use of special *key-word* variables which must be set to nonzero values to enable various kinds of trace interrupts. Other interrupt conditions are logically monitored continuously, such as end-of-file conditions.

The advantage of the interrupt control structure is that concern for extraordinary conditions may be moved out of the main line of program flow so as not to obscure the basic algorithm. In addition many of the uses of interrupts (e.g., in tracing or testing for certain error conditions) are peculiar to program testing. In these cases the implicit testing and subprogram calls involved may easily be deleted when program testing is complete without modifying the main body of the program.

Implementation of the interrupt control structure on conventional computers is often partially hardware-supported, in that most computers provide built-in monitoring for certain types of error conditions (e.g., arithmetic overflow, end-of-file) with provision for control to be transferred to an interrupt routine when the condition occurs. However, more often interrupt condition checking must be software-simulated (e.g., tracing, end of page, subscripts out of bounds). This simulation takes two main forms. In languages such as PL/I in which programs are compiled into machine code the translator may explicitly insert code (when an interrupt is enabled) for checking the interrupt condition and branching to the interrupt routine whenever an operation is executed which could cause that condition. Thus, for example, at each array reference that could have a subscript out of bounds, an explicit "test for subscript out of bounds" instruction sequence is inserted in the translated program. In languages such as SNOBOL4 that are implemented by a software interpreter it is more common to have the interpreter check for the condition and for the *enabled* status continuously during program execution. The latter technique is somewhat more flexible than the former. However, it requires that execution of each program be monitored, regardless of whether interrupts are enabled or not. The former technique has the advantage that the explicit code for condition checking is inserted only into that part of a program in which an interrupt condition is explicitly enabled. If no interrupts are enabled, then there is no cost during program execution.

The topic of interrupt conditions and interrupt routines is more directly a major concern in assembly language programming and operating systems. Relatively few high-level languages have attempted to include broad interrupt facilities, although many languages provide various special features based on an interrupt control structure (e.g., the trace features in SNOBOL4). PL/I has perhaps the most extensive language features in this area. Many subtle questions arise in the design of general interrupt control structures. For example, how are interrupt conditions that arise during execution of an interrupt routine to be handled, what is the proper method for return of control to the interrupted routine when error conditions are involved, and how is the interrupt routine to gain access to the relevant data in the interrupted routine, especially when the data are in error? Some of these topics are taken up in the problems and in Chapter 6.

Coroutines

Suppose that we drop assumption 3 and admit subprograms that do not execute completely before returning control to their calling programs. Such subprograms are termed *coroutines*. When a coroutine receives control from another subprogram it ordinarily executes only partially. The execution of the coroutine is suspended when it returns control, and at a later point the calling program may "resume" execution of the coroutine from the point at which execution was suspended.

Note the symmetry which has now been introduced into the *calling program/called program* structure. If A calls subprogram B as a coroutine, then B executes for awhile and returns control to A, just as any ordinary subprogram would do. When A again passes control to B, now by a *resume* call, B again executes for awhile and returns control to A, just as an ordinary subprogram. Thus to A, B appears as an ordinary subprogram. But now the situation is very similar viewed from subprogram B. B, in the middle of execution, gives control to A. A executes for awhile and returns control to B. B continues execution for awhile and returns control to A. A executes for awhile and returns control to B. From subprogram B, A appears very much like an ordinary subprogram. The name *coroutine* derives from this symmetry. Rather than a calling program and a called program, the two programs appear more as equals—two subprograms swapping control back and forth as each executes, with no one of them clearly controlling the other. Figure 5-14 illustrates the control transfer between two coroutines.

From two coroutines it is natural to extend this sequence control structure to a set of coroutines. The coroutine A in execution may transfer control to another coroutine B with a statement of the form

resume B

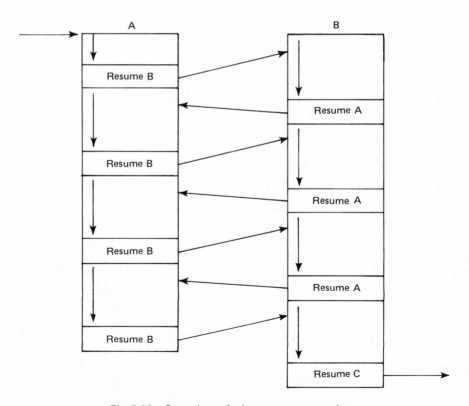

Fig. 5-14. Control transfer between two coroutines.

Let us take the simplest case in which coroutines may be activated only by **resume** statements (interpreting a **resume** call of a coroutine which has not yet been activated or which has completed its execution to indicate an ordinary subprogram call). The **resume** statement acts very much like an ordinary subprogram call except that the entry point to the subprogram is variable. However, note that there is now no analogue of the **return** statement, with its special property that the routine to which control is to be returned is not specified. Instead the **resume** statement always specifies explicitly which of the other coroutines is to receive control. Simulation of this coroutine control structure is simple under these restrictions. As with simple subprograms only a single storage location is needed for the control information in each routine. However, unlike simple subprograms, the control location associated with a coroutine is used to store the resume point *for that coroutine*. Execution of a **resume** B statement in coroutine A then involves two steps:

1. The location of the statement following the **resume** statement in A is stored in the resume point location for A.

2. The resume point location for B is accessed to obtain the location in B at which execution of B should be resumed.

Thus essentially each coroutine stores its own resume point. Control structures in which routines may be called either as coroutines or ordinary subprograms and in which coroutines may be recursive (i.e., in which more than one activation of a coroutine may exist simultaneously) require more complex simulations. Problem 5-12 explores some of these structures.

Coroutines are not currently a common control structure in programming languages outside of discrete simulation languages (see below). However, they provide a control structure in many algorithms that is more natural than the ordinary subprogram hierarchy. Moreover, the simple coroutine structure may be readily simulated in most languages using the **goto** statement and a *resume point* variable specifying the label of the statement at which execution is to resume (see Problem 5-13).

Coroutines provide two organizational structures for programs that differ from those provided by the usual subprogram hierarchy: partial execution of subprograms and division into subprograms without a hierarchical structure. Two examples serve to illustrate these concepts.

Consider first a program to play a complex four-handed card game such as bridge. The game includes a number of phases: dealing, bidding, and playing each of 13 tricks. In a program to play this game there is a natural division of the program into four *player* subprograms that involve the bidding and playing strategies of each of the four players, and a *house* program that deals, determines the order of play, the winner of each trick, the winner of each hand, and keeps track of the score. We might consider the house routine as the main program and utilize the usual subprogram hierarchy. The house routine would then have to pass control individually to each player routine in the proper sequence during bidding and playing. Each player routine would bid or play a card as appropriate and return control to the house routine, which would then call the next player, etc. However, this structure is rather unnatural because the house routine really only needs to operate at the end of each round of bidding or playing. And in addition the house routine has difficulty setting up the calling sequence for the player subprograms because the playing sequence differs from trick to trick—a different player routine is called first on different tricks. One additional facet makes the usual subprogram structure inappropriate: Each player routine obviously must only partially execute on each call because each player's strategy is in fact distributed over the entire sequence of bidding and playing. On each call a player routine must update his strategy data (based on what the other player routines have done since the last call) and proceed to choose a card or bid based on this updated information. At the next call the player routine must continue from the point at which the previous call ended.

Organizing the bridge-playing program as a set of one house and four player coroutines provides a more appropriate organization. Because each coroutine resumes execution always from the point at which it last terminated, the continuation of player strategies from phase to phase of the game is directly representable (with ordinary subprograms it requires special flags and branching). Moreover, because the coroutines are "equals" sharing control, the transfers of control during play of the game are more directly representable. Each player coroutine always passes control to the player routine on its *left* unless it is the end of a trick or round of bidding, in which case it passes control to the house coroutine. The house coroutine receives control only when it has something to do and need only pass control to the appropriate player coroutine after determining which player is to play next.

Our second example of the use of coroutines is in the organization of a compiler. In fact the coroutine concept first appeared in print in a paper by Conway [1963] describing the organization of a COBOL compiler. Typically a compiler is a large complex program logically split into a number of phases—lexical analysis, syntactic analysis, semantic analysis, optimization, and code generation (see Chapter 9). This division provides a natural basis for organization of the compiler into subprograms (actually sets of subprograms) for performing each of these phases. In compiling a program it is not desirable to completely perform any one of these processes before beginning the others. For example, one does not want to do a complete lexical analysis before beginning the syntactic analysis or a complete syntactic analysis before generating any code. Instead the natural control flow requires constant shifting of control between the different parts of the compiler—a portion of the program to be compiled is lexically, syntactically, and semantically analyzed, code is generated and optimized, and then another cycle begins. However, this cycle may be interrupted by many special situations, e.g., the semantic analyzer may detect a macro to be expanded and may request the lexical and syntactic analyzers to process the macro body, the syntactic analyzer may detect an error and request special semantic processing not leading to code generation, etc. Moreover, each of the separate parts of the compiler must only partially execute each time it receives control and must keep track of its current processing point when it transfers control to another part, so that it can later resume where it left off. This compiler structure is naturally organized as a set of coroutines.

Tasks and Parallel Execution

Dropping assumption 4, a single execution sequence, leads to the concept of subprograms executed in parallel by separate independent processors. In PL/I such parallel subprograms are termed *tasks*, a term we shall use here.

The basic idea behind tasks is quite simple. Consider a subprogram A being executed in the normal fashion. If A calls subprogram B, then ordinarily execution of A is suspended while B is executed. However, if B is called as a task, then execution of A *continues* while B is being executed. The original single execution sequence has now split into two parallel execution sequences. Continuing, either A or B or both may initiate further tasks, allowing any number of parallel execution sequences to coexist. The PL/I statement for initiation of a task B from a task A is simply

$$\text{CALL } B(\text{parameters}) \text{ TASK}$$

Task A is referred to as the *attaching task* and task B as the *attached subtask*.

Initiation of a task is straightforward, but clearly there is no need to return control to the attaching task, for of course control was never relinquished. It is natural for the attached subtask to simply terminate. However, as both tasks A and B are executed in parallel and their execution is in no way synchronized, termination of subtask B must be coupled with some signal to A, for otherwise A would have no way of knowing when B had terminated. B can signal termination to A by setting a flag in some variable to which both have access. In PL/I provision for this flag is built-in. The shared variable is termed an *event variable* and is created at the time the subtask is created. For example, the statement

CALL B(parameters)   EVENT(FLAG)

creates subtask B and a variable FLAG which is initialized to *in execution*. When execution of subtask B is completed, the value of FLAG is changed to *terminated*. FLAG may be tested by the attaching task A or A may simply wait for termination of B using the statement

WAIT(FLAG)

This provides a simple direct technique for synchronization of A and B.

Although conceptually the task control structure implies separate processors for each task operating in parallel, simulation of tasks may be accomplished on a conventional computer by interleaving execution of portions of each task. Interleaving requires a higher-level system monitor routine that is capable of first executing one task for awhile, then switching control to another for awhile, then to another, etc., recognizing the case in which one task is awaiting completion of another. The resulting partial execution of each task with control swapping back and forth is quite similar to the coroutine structure, except that the transfer of control is system-initiated rather than programmer-initiated.

The task concept has many applications in programming. As an example, consider a program A which inputs and processes some data, generating some tables of new data to be output. Once the tables are computed the actual formatting and outputting of the data may itself be a complex process that is logically independent of the actual computation of the tables. It is natural in such a situation to view the *input-and-process* routine A as a separate task from the *format-and-output* routine B. Once the tables are created and given to B, task A may continue with its operation of reading and processing the next batch of input data while B is formatting and outputting the previous tables. When A is ready to again fill the tables with the newly processed data it must check to see that task B has terminated by testing the variable serving as a termination flag.

Note the difficulty of handling this program structure with ordinary subprograms. The program is naturally split into the two phases A and B. Yet if B were an ordinary subprogram, then A would have to await completion of all the outputting before beginning to input the next batch of data. A coroutine structure would be somewhat better, but the programmer would be responsible for determining exactly how to interleave the execution phases of A and B. The virtue of the task structure here is that it frees the programmer from concern with these problems, leaving the detailed decisions of how best to interleave execution of the two tasks to the language processor and operating system. From the viewpoint of the language implementor this is also desirable, because often the hardware supports parallel execution of input-output processes directly, so that the task structure may allow the language processor to make more efficient use of the underlying hardware.

The task control structure leads during execution to a tree of subprogram activations. Initially there is a single main program in execution. During the course of its execution it may create activations of a number of subtasks, each of which in turn may create other subtasks, etc., as illustrated in Fig. 5-15. Each of the nodes on this tree represents a task, and conceptually each is executing in parallel with all the others. As various of the subtasks complete execution they terminate and that node of the tree is deleted. Although this control structure is conceptually simple, parallel execution and synchronization of subprograms in general becomes extremely complex when the various tasks are sharing data or competing for shared resources. For example, two tasks may deadlock and be unable to continue execution unless data and resource sharing is carefully coordinated. These topics, however, are more appropriately taken up in the study of operating systems. Facilities for parallel execution are as yet rather rare in high-level languages.

Scheduled Subprograms

The concept of subprogram scheduling results from relaxation of the assumption that execution of a subprogram should always be initiated immediately upon its call. One may think of an ordinary subprogram call statement as specifying that the called subprogram is to be scheduled for execution immediately, without completing execution of the calling program. Completion of execution of the calling program is rescheduled to occur immediately on termination of the subprogram. The interrupt control structure may be viewed also as a means of subprogram scheduling. The interrupt routine is scheduled to be executed when a certain condition (the interrupt condition) arises.

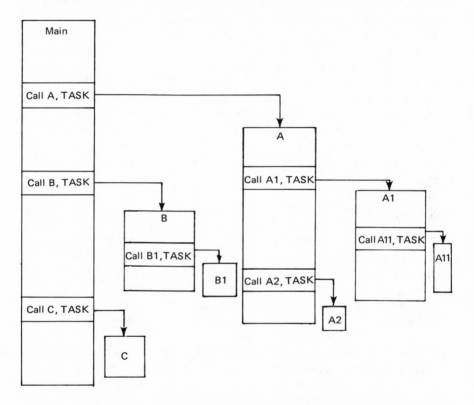

Fig. 5-15. A tree of parallel subprogram activations during execution.

Generalizing further, other subprogram scheduling techniques come immediately to mind:

1. Schedule subprograms to be executed before or after other subprograms, as, for example; CALL B AFTER A, which would schedule execution of subprogram B after execution of subprogram A is completed.

2. Schedule subprograms to be executed when an arbitrary Boolean expression becomes true, as, for example;

$$CALL\ B\ WHEN\ X = 5 \wedge Z \rangle 0$$

Such scheduling provides a sort of generalized interrupt feature—B is called whenever the values of Z and X are changed to satisfy the given conditions.

3. Schedule subprograms on the basis of a simulated *time scale*, as, for example, CALL B AT TIME = 25 or CALL B AT TIME = CURRENT-TIME + 10. Such scheduling allows a general interleaving of subprogram calls scheduled from different sources.

4. Schedule subprograms according to a priority designation, as, for example, CALL B WITH PRIORITY 7, which would activate B when no other subprogram with higher priority had been scheduled.

Generalized subprogram scheduling is a feature of programming languages designed for discrete system simulation, such as GPSS (see Maisel and Gnugnoli [1972]), SIMSCRIPT (Kiviat et al. [1969]), SIMULA (Dahl and Nygaard [1966]), and SOL (Knuth and McNeley [1964]) although the concepts have wide applicability. Each of the above scheduling techniques appears in at least one of the simulation languages mentioned. The most important technique in system simulation is that of 3, scheduling based on a simulated time scale. We shall emphasize this technique in our discussion.

When we speak of subprogram scheduling we mean scheduling of subprogram *activations*, because this scheduling is a run-time activity in which the same subprogram may be scheduled to be activated at many different points during execution. In generalized subprogram scheduling the programmer no longer writes a main program. Instead the main program is a system-defined *scheduler program* that typically maintains a list of currently scheduled subprogram activations, ordered in the sequence in which they are to be executed. Statements are provided in the language through which subprogram activations may be inserted into this list during execution. The scheduler operates by calling each subprogram on the list in the indicated sequence. When execution of one subprogram terminates, execution of the next subprogram on the list is initiated. Usually provision is also made for ordinary subprogram calls, sometimes simply by allowing a subprogram to suspend its own execution and schedule immediate execution of another subprogram.

In simulation languages the most common approach to subprogram scheduling is based on a type of generalized coroutine. Execution of a single subprogram activation proceeds in a series of *active* and *passive* phases. During an active phase the subprogram has control and is being executed; in a passive phase the subprogram has transferred control elsewhere and is awaiting a resume call. However, rather than each coroutine directly transferring control to another coroutine when it switches from active to passive, control is returned to the scheduler, which then transfers control to the next subprogram on its list of scheduled activations. This transfer of control may take the form of a resume call if the subprogram is already partially executed, or an entirely new activation of the subprogram may be initiated.

The coroutine scheduling concept is particularly direct using a simulated time scale. Assume that each active phase of execution of a subprogram may be scheduled to occur at any point on an integer time scale beginning at time $T = 0$. T is a simple integer variable which always contains the value of the current time on the simulated scale. Execution of an active phase of a subprogram always occurs instantaneously on this simulated time scale; i.e., the value of T does not change during execution of an active phase of a subprogram. When a subprogram completes an active phase and returns control to the scheduler, the scheduler updates the value of T to that at which the next subprogram on the list of scheduled subprograms is to be activated and transfers control to that subprogram. The newly activated routine partially executes and returns control to the scheduler, which again updates T and activates the next routine on the list.

In discrete system simulation one is typically concerned with simulation of a network of complex interactions, many of which are occurring in parallel, as, for example, in the simulation of a manufacturing assembly line or in the simulation of a business office. The goal in the computer simulation is to construct a model of the actual situation which may be run on the computer to gather statistics and other information about the system being simulated. For example, a simulation of an assembly line might be used to gather statistics about the result of a particular organization of work stations and allocation of men to work stations in the line (perhaps to determine where bottlenecks or idle positions occur). By simulating a variety of different configurations of the assembly line, information may be gathered about the optimal configuration.

The coroutine-based scheduling control structure is typical of GPSS, SIMULA, and SOL. The concepts appear somewhat differently in each of these languages. The control statements available to control scheduling of subprogram activations and reactivations also vary widely, although based on similar concepts. The SIMSCRIPT language provides another approach based on simple subprograms rather than coroutines. An excellent survey paper by Dahl [1968] discusses in detail these concepts and their various implementations in simulation languages.

Subprogram scheduling based on a linear time scale and a scheduler executive program requires a considerably more complicated run-time simulation than any of the other control structures mentioned in this chapter. In general no explicit hardware support is provided, so that the entire control structure must be software-simulated. The scheduler's list of scheduled subprograms may be represented most easily by a linked list of *event notices*. Use of explicit links rather than sequential storage is necessary because, in general, insertions and deletions at arbitrary points in the list are possible through execution of scheduling statements in a subprogram. Each event notice in the list must in general contain (1) the time at which the subprogram is to be activated or resumed and (2) the activation record for the subprogram, containing the resume point and the values of local variables, parameters, and other items of data peculiar to the activation. The details vary considerably depending on the language and the exact form of the scheduling operations allowed.

5-5. DATA STRUCTURES, OPERATIONS, AND SEQUENCE CONTROL

While most of the sequence control mechanisms discussed in this chapter are *general-purpose* in the sense that they occur in most programming languages regardless of the data structures or operations used in the language, it is not appropriate to leave the subject without considering the close relationship betweeen sequence control mechanisms and the data structures and operations in a language. While a variety of sequence control mechanisms may contribute to the *generality* of a language, a most important component of the *naturalness* of a programming language comes from the choice of the appropriate sequence control mechanisms for the data structures and operations available. For example, FORTRAN and ALGOL would be crippled without the iteration statement, yet APL gets along quite well without it. Similarly LISP without recursive subprogram calls is unthinkable, yet FORTRAN allows no recursion, and in ALGOL, although permitted, recursion is of fairly minor impact. Why is this so? The answer has to do with the appropriateness of iteration for element-by-element array processing and of recursion for list structure processing.

The grouping of data items together into structures has many advantages in programming, but clearly one of the major ones is the ability to process the elements of such a structure in sequence, applying the same operations to each element in turn. Array processing is a typical case. In a language like FORTRAN or ALGOL where the homogeneous array is the basic data structure, one of the most common program structures is a loop that involves a sequential scan of all or part of an array, taking each element in turn and applying the same sequence of tests and operations to it. We use a simple integer variable as a pointer into the array, an index, which takes on successively the subscripts of the appropriate array elements as values. The DO statement of FORTRAN or the **for** statement of ALGOL reflect this natural structure, allowing such loops and index variables to be set up, initialized, incremented, and tested easily. Because sequential processing of arrays, element by element, is such a common process in these languages, these iteration statements are heavily used, and their omission would greatly weaken these languages.

In APL the basic data structures are also homogeneous arrays, as in FORTRAN and ALGOL, yet APL has no iteration statement, and in fact such a statement would be relatively unimportant even were it included. The reason is that sequential element-by-element array processing in APL is uncommon. Most of the operators work directly on entire arrays as operands. While these operations may internally process the array sequentially, to the programmer this is hidden. Instead APL programs ordinarily involve relatively little statement-level control structure at all. Thus the iteration statement does not provide the natural sequence control mechanism for processing arrays in APL.

In LISP the basic data structures are dynamic trees (list structures). Again sequential processing of these structures is an important aspect of many LISP programs. But iteration using index variables with integer values is not the natural sequence control mechanism. The elements of LISP trees cannot be referenced by integer subscripts, and the structures are quite irregular in shape. These facts preclude the iteration statement as an effective mechanism for sequential processing of list structures. Instead in LISP it is recursion that provides the natural sequence control mechanism. One processes a tree recursively by first applying the tests and operations to each element of the main list, and whenever an element of this list is itself a sublist, then one simply invokes the process recursively to process this sublist. Basically one uses the recursive subprogram structure to "keep track" of a position in the list structure.

As data structures increase in complexity from the simple homogeneous arrays of FORTRAN and ALGOL or the list structures of LISP to more complex structures involving elements interconnected in irregular fashion, the "natural" sequence control mechanisms become more obscure. Consideration of mechanisms appropriate to processing such general data structures clarifies the nature of the relation between data and sequence control.

Readers. One of the simplest approaches is that of the data structure *reader*, a term introduced by Weizenbaum [1963] in his *symmetric list processing* language SLIP. A simple reader may be viewed as just a pointer to an element of a data structure. One processes a data structure using a reader by first initializing the reader to point to the desired *first* element of the structure. The reader is then "advanced" through the structure, pointing in sequence to various elements of the structure. At each point one may access (read off) the element pointed to by the reader for processing. For a simple linear array an integer variable serves as a most appropriate reader, and incrementing or decrementing the value of this variable is a perfectly adequate way of advancing the reader. An iteration statement which allows such an *array reader* to be set up together with a specification for how to initialize it and advance it through the structure then becomes a powerful and natural array-processing mechanism.

For a list structure (tree) a simple stack-structured reader is appropriate. The list structure reader either advances down the main list or "descends" into a sublist, saving its place in the main list on the reader stack. Within a sublist other descents into sublists may be necessary using further stack locations. Then as the reader "ascends" through the structure the information stored on the stack is used to unwind the processing, assuring return to the proper point on each list after sublist processing is complete. In fact, Weizenbaum's original use of readers in SLIP was in the processing of list structures using stack-structured readers. Note that sequential processing of list structures using recursion in LISP is essentially a use of the central system stack (used to store subprogram return points and local variables) to simulate a stack-structured reader for list structures. Because this may be easily done in LISP, recursion becomes the natural processing technique for list structures.

Another example occurs in SNOBOL4 pattern matching with strings. The pattern-matching algorithm in SNOBOL4 acts to set up a string reader called the *cursor* for the string being matched. Pattern matching may be viewed in part as a technique for setting up and moving this cursor through the string by means of various implicit pattern matching operations.

Generators. A second approach to the sequential processing of data structures is found in the concept of *generator*, introduced in the list-processing language IPL-V (Newell [1964]). A generator is a subprogram *A* which accepts as input (1) a data structure and (2) another subprogram *B* to be applied to the various elements of the data structure in sequence. The generator subprogram processes the data structure in some arbitrary manner, producing a sequence of elements from the structure. As each element is produced the subprogram *B* is called with the generated element as its input. When *B* returns, it signals either *continue* or *halt* to the generator subprogram. The generator then proceeds to generate the next element of the structure for processing by *B*, or it halts and returns control to the original program.

The generator concept appears in LISP in the form of *functionals*, of which *mapcar* is typical. *Mapcar*(L,F) generates each element of the input list L in sequence and applies the function F to it. LISP functionals, however, always generate the entire sequence of list elements and are unaffected by the value returned by the function F. These generator functions in LISP provide an alternative to the use of recursion to set up *readers* for list structures.

Readers and generators may be used to set up control structures for data structure processing that are not easily constructed in many languages directly. For example, in languages such as FORTRAN and ALGOL in which the iteration statement is ordinarily used to set up array readers, there is a problem with algorithms that require multiple readers on the same array which advance independently. The structure of the FORTRAN DO statement or the ALGOL for statement allows only one index to be set up in a statement. A second statement may be used to set up a second index but the second index must be completely nested within the first, i.e., the second index must cycle completely for each step of the first index, making it impossible to advance the indices independently. As a result when two independent indices into an array are required the iteration statement is used only to set up one index, and the other is simulated using an integer variable initialized and incremented separately. A similar case arises in LISP if two readers are needed to point to different elements of a list structure, and the readers can be advanced independently. Because recursion may be easily used to simulate only one of these readers, it becomes cumbersome to set up and manipulate the other.

The reader and generator concepts are complementary. Each is an approach to the solution of the same problem. Readers seem a more natural concept where the sequence of elements to be processed is found by a rather direct scan through one or a set of data structures. Generators, on the other hand, seem more natural when there is only a single sequence of elements involved but the sequence is to be derived in a rather complex manner from the data structure. Generators are also natural when the sequence to be processed is not a sequence of elements from some data structure but instead may be generated directly from some computation, e.g., a sequence of prime numbers or a sequence of permutations.

We have emphasized the concepts of readers and generators here, not only because they are useful in their own right in thinking about algorithms, but also because they lend insight into the reasons for the utility, or lack of it, in various control structures in programming languages. In analyzing a language it is often useful to consider the data structures provided by the language together with the control structures, asking whether the control structures provided allow natural construction of readers or generators for the data structures.

5-6. REFERENCES AND SUGGESTIONS FOR FURTHER READING

A great deal has been written on the subject of sequence control structures in programming languages. The general texts by Harrison [1973], Wegner [1968], and Elson [1973] provide somewhat different approaches to many of the same topics discussed in this chapter. The survey paper by Fisher [1972] provides an excellent introduction to recent research on statement and subprogram-level control structures.

Techniques for efficient translation and evaluation of expressions are a central topic in compiler design. Aho and Ullman [1972] treat the subject formally in depth. Hopgood [1969] and Gries [1971] provide more pragmatic discussions of the topic. The problem of side effects in expression evaluation stirred considerable controversy in the design of ALGOL; see Knuth [1967] and ASA [1963].

The **goto** controversy came to the surface after a famous letter by Dijkstra [1968a]. The November 1972 issue of *SIGPLAN Notices* (Leavenworth[1972]) contains a discussion and a number of papers on the subject. See also the paper by Wulf [1971] describing his experience with BLISS, a language without **goto**s. Peterson et al. [1973] and Knuth and Floyd [1971] provide more theoretical treatments of the subject.

Recursion is the subject of a monograph by Barron [1968], and, of course, it is a common programming structure in many languages, especially LISP (Chapter 14). General coroutine structures are discussed in Dahl and Hoare [1972]. Subprogram scheduling in discrete simulation languages is a central topic in the survey by Dahl [1968].

The important subject of control structures for parallel processing has been somewhat slighted in this chapter. The control of parallel processes is a central topic in operating systems design and is increasingly important in high-level programming languages. A paper by Dijkstra [1968b] is important here. Also see Wirth [1969] for a discussion of the relation between parallel processing and interrupt structures.

Two important but more specialized control structures that have not been treated here are *decision tables*, the subject of a special issue of *SIGPLAN Notices* (Silberg [1971]) and *backtracking*, including *nondeterministic algorithms* (Prenner, et al. [1972] and Floyd [1967]). A general technique for the implementation of subprogram control structures, including coroutines and backtracking, is the subject of an important paper by Bobrow and Wegbreit [1973].

5-7. PROBLEMS

5-1. *Translation of infix expressions to postfix.* One common compilation technique for expressions is to translate infix expressions first into a postfix (reverse Polish) form. The reverse Polish is then translated directly into machine code or optimized and then translated into machine code. The translation into reverse Polish is based on use of a stack and a table of precedences. Consider a simple expression composed only of identifiers and binary infix operators, such as A * B + C / D - E. Assuming the usual hierarchy of infix operations (e.g., as given in Table 5-1) the translation algorithm is based on a simple left-to-right scan of the infix expression using two processing rules:

1. Identifiers are moved directly into the output reverse Polish string as they are encountered.

2. Operators are stacked on an intermediate stack with a number indicating their precedence level in the hierarchy. Before an operator is stacked all operators on the top of the stack with higher precedence are first deleted from the stack one by one and moved into the output reverse Polish string.

For the expression above the output reverse Polish string is

A B * C D / + E -

  a. Give a flow chart for this translation algorithm in the simple case of
      expressions containing only identifiers and the binary arithmetic infix
      operators $+, -, *, /$, and $\uparrow$.
  b. Expand the algorithm of part a to include expressions with
      parentheses. Note that the parentheses do not appear in the output
      string, although, of course, they control the order in which the
      output string is generated.
  c. Expand the algorithm of part a to include the unary operator $-$
      (negation) in Polish prefix notation. What is an appropriate pre-
      cedence for unary $-$?
  d. Expand the algorithm of part a to include function calls in ordinary
      mathematical notation, e.g., SIN(X) or MAX(A,B,C). What pre-
      cedence is appropriate for such function calls?

5.2. Give the tree representation of the following expressions:
  a. $-(A - B \uparrow C) * D / E \uparrow F + G$
  b. $A * B \geqslant C - D \uparrow -E / F$
  c. $A / B / C = D \uparrow E - F \wedge G > H * J$
  d. $\neg A - B > C \wedge (D < E \vee F) \vee \neg G \wedge H = J$

      Case 1 (ALGOL). Assume the ALGOL hierarchy of operations
      from Table 5-1 and left-to-right associativity.
      Case 2 (APL). Assume that all operators have equal precedence,
      that associativity is from right to left, and that parentheses indicate
      grouping in the usual way.

5-3. Give the representation of the expressions in Problem 5-2 in Cambridge
      Polish and Polish prefix representations. Assume the ALGOL hierarchy of
      operations of Table 5-1 and left-to-right associativity. In the Polish form,
      subscript each operator symbol with an integer specifying the number of
      operands of the operator. For example, $((-A) * B) - C$ becomes
      $-_2 *_2 -_1 ABC$.

5-4. In the discussion of side effects in expression evaluation the expression
      A*FUN(X)+A was considered. Under the assumption that A has the value
      1 on beginning evaluation of the expression and FUN(X) evaluates to 3
      and increases the value of A by 1, then the expression may evaluate to
      any of the values 4, 5, 7, or 8, depending on the order of evaluation. List
      evaluation sequences which produce each of these values.

5-5. *Evaluation of expressions involving logical or.* Consider the expression

$$(A) \vee (B)$$

      where A and B are arbitrary logical or relational expressions. If
      subexpression A evaluates to *true*, then it is desirable for efficiency to
      avoid evaluation of B, as the result of the entire expression must be true
      in any case. As B may itself be a complex expression the savings may be
      substantial. A useful optimization rule is the following: Evaluate the

shorter or "simpler" of A and B; if the value is *true*, skip evaluation of the other expression. Explain the potential complications to the programmer caused by such optimization in a language like FORTRAN or ALGOL.

5-6. Give a simple algorithm for left-to-right evaluation of arithmetic expressions in postfix form when only simple variables, constants, and binary arithmetic operations are involved. The evaluation rule should use a stack for temporary storage of intermediate results.

5-7. Give an algorithm for evaluation of arithmetic expressions represented in tree form, assuming that only simple variables, constants, and binary arithmetic operations are involved. Base the algorithm on a reader which initially points to the root of the tree and which "walks" through the tree, pointing to the various nodes in sequence. The algorithm should use a stack for temporary storage of intermediate results.

5-8. *Simulation of computed statement numbers in FORTRAN.* Even though FORTRAN does not allow statement numbers to be read in or computed during execution, it is not difficult to simulate this structure in FORTRAN. Suppose that A is a FORTRAN subprogram in which it is desirable to be able to compute statement numbers and then transfer to the appropriate statement within A on the basis of the computed statement number. Design a set of statements to be added to A to provide a simulation for this feature, so that, for example, one may write

SUBROUTINE A (. . .)
.
.
.
M = L(3) + 17
.
.
.

(statements which transfer control to the
statement in A whose number corresponds to
the computed value of M, i.e., which simulate
a GO TO M statement)
.
.
.

END

5-9. Consider the following ALGOL program segment:

(initialization) $SUM := 0; J := 1; N := 20;$

(iteration head)   **for** $I := 1$ **step** J **until** N **do**

(iteration body)   **begin** $SUM := SUM+A[I]; J := J+I; N := N-J$ **end**;

Which elements of the array A will be summed under each of the following evaluation strategies for evaluation of the variables J and N in the iteration head?

a. Evaluate both J and N once on initial entry to the iteration statement.

b. Evaluate J once on initial entry; evaluate N once on entry and again after each execution of the body

c. Evaluate N once on initial entry; evaluate J once on entry and again after each execution of the body.

d. Evaluate both J and N on entry and reevaluate after each execution of the body.

5-10. In subprograms called because of interrupts, a return of control to the point of the interrupt is not always appropriate. In general, the interrupt may have occurred when some operation is only partially executed, and it may be impossible or undesirable to return control exactly to the point of interrupt and complete the execution of the partially executed operation. Discuss the alternative return points which might be appropriate in case of the following interrupt conditions:

a. Overflow on an integer multiplication.

b. Second subscript out of range in a reference to an element of a three-dimensional array.

c. End-of-page condition after output of the second line of a four-line block of printing.

d. Nonnumeric character encountered during conversion of a character string to internal binary integer representation.

e. End-of-file encountered on an input file during a READ statement.

5-11. What restrictions must be placed on the enabling of interrupt condition checking to allow use of the simple single return point location in interrupt routines? If no restrictions are placed on interrupt enabling, what run-time structures are necessary to handle return points for interrupt routines?

5-12. *Recursive coroutines.* Consider a language in which subprogram execution may be initiated with an ordinary CALL or may be resumed with a coroutine RESUME. For example, if A and B are subprograms and A calls B, then control transfers to B as in an ordinary subprogram call. B may then return control to A either through a RETURN in the usual way or through a coroutine RESUME A command. In addition, B may initiate another activation of A through a recursive call of A using the statement CALL A. If A is called recursively, then A may later call B recursively, setting up another activation of B, or A may return control to B through a RETURN or a RESUME B command. Of course, there may be many subprograms and each may contain CALLs or RESUMEs on any of the others.

a. Define precisely a reasonable interpretation for the statements RESUME and RETURN in this context of recursive coroutines, assuming that CALL always initiates a new activation of the called subprogram as with ordinary recursive subprograms. Note that each subprogram may have been activated recursively a number of times and that the subprogram being executed may have been initially called from one subprogram and then later resumed from another. Thus it is not immediately obvious where control is to be transferred when a RETURN or RESUME is encountered.

b. Design a simulation for this control structure on a conventional computer. Specify the storage requirements for return and/or resume points and the manner in which this information is used during execution of the CALL, RESUME, and RETURN statements.

5-13. One of the arguments favoring retention of statement labels and goto statements is that other control structures may often be simulated using these primitive features. Simulation of simple coroutines in FORTRAN is an example. Design a simulation for coroutines in FORTRAN using the CALL statement, the ASSIGN statement (e.g., ASSIGN 20 to L;—where 20 is a statement number), and the *assigned* goto GO TO L, (list of statement numbers). The simulation should operate so that the CALL statement actually acts like a RESUME statement for subprograms in which the coroutine simulation is being used.

5-14. An alternative view of a data structure generator is as a coroutine-generator. A coroutine-generator is a coroutine which on initial activation is given a data structure as input parameter and returns the first element of the sequence of elements. On each subsequent resume call it generates the next element of the sequence and returns it. Design such a generator for

a. Generating the main diagonal on a FORTRAN, ALGOL, or PL/I matrix.

b. Generating the integer-valued leaf nodes on a LISP tree.

c. Generating the nodes breadth-first on a LISP tree. For example, the nodes in numbered order from the following tree:

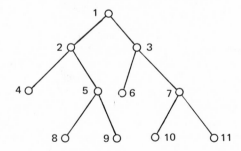

6 DATA CONTROL

When writing a program one ordinarily is well aware of the operations that the program must execute and their sequence, but seldom is the same true of the operands for those operations. For example, an ALGOL program contains

$$X := Y + Z \times 2$$

Simple inspection indicates three operations in sequence: a multiplication, an addition, and an assignment. But what of the operands for these operations? One operand of the multiplication is clearly the number 2, but the other operands are marked only by the identifiers Y, Z, and X, and these obviously are not the operands but only designate the operands in some manner. Y might designate a real number, an integer, or the name of a parameterless subprogram to be executed to compute the operand. Or perhaps the programmer has erred and Y designates a Boolean value or a string or serves as a statement label. Y may designate a value computed nearby, perhaps in the preceding statement, but equally as likely it may designate a value computed at some point much earlier in the computation, separated by many levels of subprogram call from the assignment where it is used. To make matters worse, Y may be used as a name in different ways in different sections of the program. Which use of Y is current here? In a nutshell, the central problem of data control is the problem of what Y means in each execution of such an assignment statement. Because Y may be a nonlocal variable, the problem involves scope rules for declarations; because Y may be a formal parameter, the problem involves techniques for parameter transmission; and because Y may name a parameterless subprogram, the problem involves mechanisms for returning results from subprograms. Each of these topics is taken up in turn in the following sections.

6-1. BASIC DATA CONTROL CONCEPTS

There is a striking contrast between the basic indirectness and potential ambiguity of data control and the explicitness of most sequence control. One must know the operations and their sequence or else one can hardly write a program, and so ordinarily the operations and sequence control structures are set into the program when it is written. Yet if at each step one also knew the operands for the operations, then writing the program would be pointless. One writes a program in order to apply the same basic sequences of operations to a variety of different data sets at different times. Thus references to data in a program must necessarily be indirect for the most part; when writing the program we do not know what the data will be. It is in this necessary indirectness that the potential for ambiguity in data references arises.

In conventional computer hardware the solution to the data control problem is particularly simple. The computer is designed with a fixed set of data storage locations (memory words and working registers), each of which may contain a single data item. Each location is designated by a unique name (memory address or register designator). Machine language operations must specify exactly the name of the location in which the operand is to be found or the result stored. Thus whenever a particular instruction is executed the operands for the operation are to be found in the same storage locations. This hardware organization is an example of a data control organization fixed at the time of definition of the machine language. The machine language programmer has no control over the association of names and storage locations; his programs must use the associations built into the hardware.

It is apparent that this hardware data control structure is entirely too inflexible. Some hardware features modify this structure partially, for example, by allowing the operand of an operation to be specified by a base address plus the contents of an index register. However, one must move to an assembly language to obtain a significantly more flexible data control structure. The assembly language programmer may choose his own names for data locations and need not specify which location is to be associated with which name, leaving this decision up to the assembler and loader.

Assembly language data control is still too restrictive, however. High-level languages, among other advantages, typically provide much more flexible data control structures, allowing multiple uses of the same name as well as multiple names for the same data location. The mismatch between conventional hardware and high-level programming languages is particularly apparent here. Software simulation of data control structures is the rule in implementations of high-level languages.

Names and Identifiers

The central concern in data control is the question of the meaning of names. Taken very generally the term *name* may designate any expression in a program used to specify an operand for an operation. Used in this sense data control overlaps some of the questions of previous chapters. For example, an operand for an addition operation may be designated by giving an expression to be evaluated to compute the operand, as in $(U/V-A*B)+...$ or $SQRT(2*Z)+...$. In part, the meaning of such an expression name is tied to questions of sequence control (see Section 5-2). What is yet to be discussed is the meaning of references to simple identifiers, such as U, V, Z, and $SQRT$. Another aspect of *names* which has been partially discussed previously is that of subscripted variables, names for elements of data structures, e.g., $A[2,3]$, $B[I]$, or $EMPLOYEE.SALARY$. In Chapter 3 the distinction between referencing and accessing in subscripted variables was made. *Referencing* is the operation that determines which structure is associated with a particular structure name (e.g., A, B, or $EMPLOYEE$). *Accessing* is the operation which computes the designated element location in the structure given the subscripts and the access point to the entire structure found by a referencing operation. Accessing is discussed at length in Chapter 3. Referencing is a central concern in this chapter.

Restricting our concern with names to cases that have not arisen in other contexts leaves us for the most part with questions of "simple" noncomposite names. Simple names include

1. Names for simple variables.

2. Names for data structures, including input-output files.

3. Literals, i.e., names for data constants.

4. Subprogram names.

5. Primitive operation symbols, e.g., +, *.

6. Statement labels.

7. Formal parameters.

Two of these cases are relatively trivial. The meaning of literals and primitive operation symbols is ordinarily fixed in the language definition. Thus the programmer has no control over whether 10 represents ten (decimal), eight (octal), or two (binary) or whether + represents addition. Some exceptions exist, as, for example, in SNOBOL4's OPSYN feature, which allows programmer redefinition of primitive operation symbols. However, these cases are relatively rare and add few new concepts. The remaining cases of simple variables, data structure names, subprogram names, statement labels, and formal parameters provide our central focus. Rules for the syntax of such names differ between languages and between classes within the same language. For simplicity the term *identifier* is used for a simple name of any of these types in the discussion here.

Identifier Associations and Data Control Primitives

Data control is concerned in large part with *associations* (sometimes called *bindings*) between identifiers and program or data elements. Each association may be represented as a pair consisting of the identifier and its associated element or a pointer to the element. For our purposes here this simple view is sufficient. In language implementations a variety of representations for identifier associations at run time may be used.

During execution of a program the associations for a particular identifier, say X, typically follow the pattern:

1. *Create first association.* An initial association for X is created by a declaration at the start of execution of the main program, or on entry to a subprogram.

2. *Reference association.* A reference to X in the program invokes a *referencing operation* which uses the association created for X to retrieve the associated program or data element (or a pointer to the element).

3. *Deactivate association.* Control is passed to another part of the program, causing the association for X to be deactivated. While inactive the association for X continues to exist but cannot be referenced. Deactivation is often caused by subprogram calls.

4. *Reactivate association.* The association for X is reactivated as a result of control returning to an appropriate program segment. The

association may again be referenced. Deactivation and reactivation may occur many times.

5. *Destroy association.* The association for X is destroyed and may no longer be referenced.

6. *Repeat steps 1-5.* Another association for X may be created, referenced, etc.

It is simplest to assume that a given identifier has at most one active association at any point during program execution, so that a reference to X has a unique meaning. This assumption is somewhat simplistic; various languages allow multiple identifier associations to be active simultaneously, using context to determine which association is appropriate for any given reference. For example, in SNOBOL4 the statement

$$X = X(2) \ :(X)$$

references X as a label, simple variable, and subprogram name in the same statement. Context, however, determines which association is appropriate for each reference to X. Although such situations increase the complexity of the referencing operation, no new concepts are introduced. Thus only the case in which each identifier has at most one active association at any point need be considered in detail.

To associate an identifier with a data or program element requires an operation, termed a *naming* operation. Naming necessarily precedes referencing, for the naming operation sets up an association for an identifier, while the referencing operation uses the association to retrieve the object associated with a particular identifier. The operation of destroying an association for an identifier may be termed *unnaming*. Note that naming is distinct from *creating*, an operation discussed in Chapter 4. The two often occur together and thus are sometimes confused. The ALGOL declaration **real** X, for example, specifies both that a simple variable is to be created and that it is to be named X (i.e., the identifier X is to be associated with it). Similarly the declaration **array** $A[M:N]$ creates an array and names it A. Creating may be separate from naming, however, as in the SNOBOL4 function call

ARRAY(10)

which creates an array and returns a pointer to it. The created array is not named by the creation function ARRAY. Naming without creating is exemplified in argument transmission where the formal parameter identifier is associated with the corresponding actual parameter data object.

As with creating and naming, the operations of data structure destruction and unnaming may also be separated. Recall from Chapter 4 the problems of dangling references and garbage associated with the destruction of data structures. Dangling references arise when a data structure is destroyed before all the access paths to that structure have been destroyed. A primary source of access paths to data structures is through identifier associations. If a data structure is destroyed while still named, i.e., while still associated with an identifier, then a later attempt to reference the structure through that name will leave the referencing operation "dangling"—thus the term *dangling reference*. However, dangling references may also be created when pointers to a destroyed structure exist in other structures, and thus the problem is more general than simply one of data control.

Similarly garbage is often, although not exclusively, a question of data structure unnaming. Garbage arises when all access paths to a data structure (or part of a structure) are lost without the storage for the structure being recovered. The unnaming operation destroys access paths through identifier associations and thus may lead to garbage creation. However, garbage may be created in other ways as well, for example, by destroying pointers stored in other data structures. The general problem of the prevention and recovery of garbage is taken up in the next chapter in the context of storage management.

The operations of activation and deactivation of identifier associations are often confused with the operations of naming and unnaming. For an association to be used in referencing it must both *exist* (as a result of a naming operation) and be *active*. Inactive associations are those that exist but that temporarily cannot be referenced. The ALGOL block structure provides a typical example of the distinction. On block entry in ALGOL each declaration serves as a naming operation, creating a new association between an identifier and a simple variable, array, subprogram, or switch. Simultaneously any previously existing associations for the declared identifiers are *deactivated*. Referencing within the block uses the newly created active association for each identifier. Block exit causes unnaming for the identifier associations created on entry and *reactivation* of the associations deactivated on entry.

Five major data control operations concerned with identifier associations have now been discussed:

1. *Naming.* The operation of creating an association between an identifier and a program or data object.

2. *Unnaming.* The operation of destroying an association between an identifier and its associated object.

3. *Activating.* The operation of making active an existing association between an identifier and a program or data object and thus making the association available for use in referencing.

4. *Deactivating.* The operation of making inactive an existing association between identifier and program or data object.

5. *Referencing.* The operation of retrieving the data or program object currently associated with a given identifier using the unique currently active association for the identifier.

6-2. REFERENCING ENVIRONMENTS AND SCOPE RULES

A useful concept in the study of data control is that of *referencing environment*. At any point during execution of a program a certain set of identifier associations is active. The set of active associations is termed the *referencing environment* of that program point. Whenever a reference to an identifier occurs it is the referencing environment which determines the appropriate association for that reference. The operations of naming, unnaming, activating, and deactivating modify referencing environments. Our concern is with the pattern of referencing environments that occur during execution of programs in various languages.

A *scope rule* is a rule for determining referencing environments in a program. A scope rule ordinarily specifies the pattern of activation, deactivation, and unnaming associated with a particular naming operation, thus defining the points during program execution when a particular identifier association is active (i.e., is part of the referencing environment).

Static and Dynamic Scope

Scope rules are usually classified as dynamic or static. A *dynamic scope rule* defines scope in terms of program execution. A typical dynamic scope rule specifies that the referencing environment at any point during program execution is determined by the most recent naming operation for each identifier, as, for example, in SNOBOL4.

A *static scope rule* defines scope in terms of the structure of the program when written, at translation time. For example, in ALGOL the referencing environment at any point during execution of a program is determined not by the pattern of naming during execution but by the pattern of declarations in enclosing blocks in the original program. In the following sections various static and dynamic scope rules are studied in depth. In general, dynamic scope rules are relatively easy to implement, but static scope rules, although more difficult to implement, allow production of considerably more efficient executable code. Static scope rules tend to be characteristic of languages such as FORTRAN, ALGOL, and PL/I in which execution speed is important, while dynamic scope rules are more common in software-interpreted languages such as SNOBOL4, LISP, and APL.

Global, Local, and Nonlocal References

References to identifiers are classified as *local references* if they use an association active only within the block or subprogram currently being executed. For example, in ALGOL a local reference is a reference to an identifier declared in the most recently entered block. A *global reference* is a reference to an association active throughout program execution. References to subprogram names in FORTRAN are examples of global references, as are references in ALGOL to identifiers declared in the outermost block. A *nonlocal reference*, as the name indicates, is any reference which is not local. In FORTRAN references are only local or global. In ALGOL nonlocal references may include references to identifiers declared in intermediate-level blocks between the outermost block and the innermost.

It is convenient also to use the term *local referencing environment* (or simply *local environment*) to designate those local associations introduced at the last change in referencing environment. The *nonlocal referencing environment* is the remainder of the referencing environment at any point. Typically the local environment of a subprogram contains formal parameters and local variables declared in the head of the subprogram. The nonlocal environment contains identifier associations that are shared with other subprograms.

The concepts necessary for an extended look at data control in programming languages are now at hand. Data control structures are almost always tied to subprograms. For this reason most of the discussion of various approaches to data control is organized in terms of the various subprogram control structures discussed in Chapter 5—simple nonrecursive subprograms, recursive subprograms, coroutines, interrupt routines, etc.

6-3. BLOCK STRUCTURE

The concept of block structure as found in *block-structured languages* such as ALGOL and PL/I deserves special mention. In a block-structured language each program or subprogram is organized as a set of nested blocks, usually delimited as in ALGOL by the symbols **begin** and **end**. Figure 6-1 shows schematically the structure of a typical ALGOL program. Each block begins with a set of declarations which serve two purposes:

1. *Naming.* Each declaration sets up associations for one or more identifiers. These form the local referencing environment for the block.

2. *Data structure creation.* Some of the declarations may also define data structures or simple variables to be created on block entry.

begin integer X,Y; **array** A [- - -] ;

    (statements)

    begin real U,V; **procedure** SUB ( ) . . . defn of SUB . . . ;

        (statements)

        begin Boolean U,Z;

            (statements)

        end

        (statements)

    end

    (statements)

end

Fig. 6-1. Block structure of a typical ALGOL program.

When properly handled, block structure allows use of a particularly straightforward stack-based storage management scheme (described in the next chapter), as well as providing a rather flexible data control structure. In addition block structure lends itself to use of static scope rules, thus allowing production of more efficient executable code. Because of these advantages, block structure has been adopted in a variety of languages.

Block structure may be considered as providing a special data control structure, operating within subprograms, which allows changes of referencing environment at arbitrary points during subprogram execution rather than only on entry and exit. However, a better view is to treat a block as a simple parameterless subprogram that has actually been coded in line at the point of call; i.e., the subprogram call statement has been replaced by the body of the subprogram. This view is preferable because the same problems arise in both blocks and simple parameterless subprograms and thus the cases may profitably be considered together.

6-4. SIMPLE PARAMETERLESS SUBPROGRAMS: LOCAL ENVIRONMENTS

Let us begin with simple data control structures and progress to the more complex cases. Consider first the usual subprogram hierarchy—a main program and set of subprograms which call each other in the ordinary manner. For the moment we shall ignore parameters and assume that recursive calls are not allowed. Blocks in block-structured languages as well as subprograms in FORTRAN and COBOL, ignoring parameters, fall into this category.

A subprogram has a local environment, consisting of those identifier associations that are activated on entry to the subprogram. The local environment ordinarily consists of the identifiers declared in the head of the subprogram (as well as formal parameters, but they are considered later). In addition a subprogram may have a nonlocal referencing environment, consisting of associations shared with other subprograms. Our first focus is on the local environment.

The different local environments of a set of subprograms may utilize many of the same identifiers but with different associations in each environment. As control is transferred back and forth between the subprograms the current referencing environment must be modified to reflect the appropriate local environment for referencing in each subprogram. Suppose that P, Q, and R are three subprograms such that P calls Q, which calls R, in a simple nested manner. Let us focus on the local environment for Q, and ask the following questions:

1. What is the initial local environment set up on entry to Q from P?

2. What happens to the local environment of Q when Q calls R?

3. What is the local environment of Q when control returns from R?

4. What happens to the local environment of Q when Q returns control to P?

Questions 2 and 3 are perhaps the easiest to answer. Rather clearly the local environment of Q should be *deactivated* (but not destroyed) when R is called and *reactivated* on return from R. This choice corresponds with our intuitive notion that a subprogram call is only a temporary interruption of execution of the calling program.

Questions 1 and 4 lead to greater difficulty. In fact there is no generally accepted rule, but rather two distinct answers to these questions in general use:

Approach 1. Deactivate the local environment on return to the calling program and reactivate it on reentry to the subprogram. This solution is found in FORTRAN and COBOL. The local environment may be set up (i.e., local naming done) either during translation or on the first entry to Q. When Q returns control to P after its execution, the local environment is deactivated but retained. When Q is called again, the same local environment is reactivated, and all variables have their old values, etc.

Retention of local environments between calls provides a sort of symmetry between subprograms. We may think of each subprogram as having its own attached local environment that exists throughout execution of the entire set of subprograms. For convenience think of these local environments as being set up initially by the translator. When execution begins the local environment of the main program is active, and the local environment of each subprogram is inactive. When the main program calls a subprogram such as P, then the local environment of P becomes active and that of the main program inactive. As control continues to pass between subprograms the appropriate local environments are activated and deactivated in turn, but no local environment is ever destroyed.

Approach 2. Destroy the local environment on return to the calling program and create a new one on reentry. A quite different solution is found in ALGOL (without **own**), LISP, SNOBOL4, and APL. When a subprogram is called, an entirely new local environment is created. When control is passed back to the calling program, the local environment is destroyed. Reentry to the subprogram causes creation of another local environment. If we recall the distinction between a subprogram definition and a subprogram activation (see Chapter 5), this approach amounts to setting up a new local environment for each activation of the subprogram. Approach 1 is based on a single local environment for each defined subprogram regardless of the number of activations of the subprogram during execution.

Simulation of Local Environments

It is appropriate to think of a local environment as represented during execution by a table of local associations. Each entry in the table specifies an identifier and a pointer to the program or data element with which it is currently associated. Thus if identifier A is associated with an array in the local environment of subprogram Q, then the table contains an entry for A and a pointer to the array (or the array itself). For a simple variable named X the table contains an entry for X and a pointer to the location containing the value of X (or the value directly). Identifiers which serve as subprogram names or statement labels present special difficulties; these cases are taken up in Section 6-9. Figure 6-2 shows a local environment table for a typical ALGOL block.

Retained Local Environments. Let us first consider the simulation appropriate for approach 1 to the handling of local environments. Each subprogram has a single local environment that exists

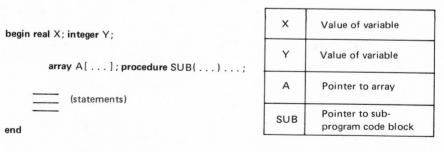

begin real X; integer Y;

    array A[. . .]; procedure SUB(. . .) . . . ;

    (statements)

end

Block declaration

X	Value of variable
Y	Value of variable
A	Pointer to array
SUB	Pointer to sub-program code block

Table

Fig. 6-2. Simple local environment table for an ALGOL block.

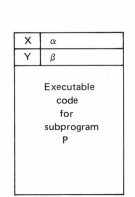

B	α'
A	β'
U	γ'
X	δ'

Z	α''
Y	β''
A	γ''
W	δ''
V	ϵ''

X	α
Y	β

Executable
code
for
subprogram
P

Executable
code
for
subprogram
Q

Executable
code
for
subprogram
R

Fig. 6-3. Simple simulation for retained local environments.

throughout execution regardless of the number of activations of the subprogram. In this case it is appropriate to store the local environment table for a subprogram with the code for the subprogram as in Fig. 6-3. If these tables are set up during translation along with the block of executable code, then the referencing operation may be made quite efficient. Suppose that the program contains a reference to X. During translation it may be determined that the association for X is the fourth entry, for example, in the local environment table. The referencing operation then, rather than searching the table for X at execution time, may be set up to directly access the association for X. The referencing computation takes the base address of the table and adds a fixed *offset* to access the fourth entry. Now the table no longer needs to contain the identifiers themselves because the identifiers are never used during execution— no search of the table is ever necessary.

The simulation outlined above is typical of FORTRAN. In FORTRAN each subprogram during execution has an associated *local data block* which contains simple variables and arrays local to that subprogram. Each reference to a local variable or array in the subprogram is replaced during compilation by a direct *base address + offset* computation. The original identifiers in the program are not present during execution. Figure 6-4 illustrates this simplified structure.

Pairing the environment table with the executable code for a subprogram allows automatic shifting of the local environment

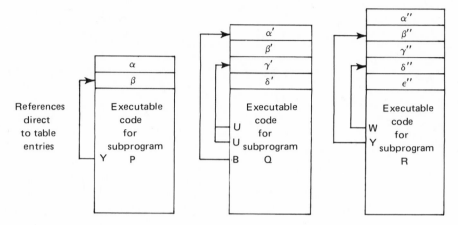

Fig. 6-4. Simplified local environment tables and referencing in FORTRAN.

during execution as control passes from subprogram to subprogram. Because each reference in a subprogram directly accesses the associated table defining the local environment, a subprogram call or return requires no explicit shifting of environment. In a sense the environment shifts have been *compiled in* to the executable code during translation and are implicit during execution.

Identifiers may not always be eliminated from the local environment table of a subprogram. Some languages, such as SNOBOL4 and LISP, allow an identifier to be read in during execution of a program and then used in a reference (e.g., using the $ operator in SNOBOL4). In such cases the identifiers must appear explicitly in the table, even though it may still be possible to compute direct accesses for most references.

Destroyed and Recreated Local Environments. Simulation of approach 2 in which the local environment is destroyed on subprogram exit and recreated on reentry may also utilize, in this simple situation, a local environment table paired with the code for the subprogram. The identifiers in the table remain the same between calls, but their associated values are destroyed on exit and new ones created on reentry. However, this solution does not generalize to recursive subprograms, and thus an alternative simulation is indicated where support of recursive calls is the ultimate goal.

The alternative simulation is based on use of a *central stack* of local environment tables. No space for an environment table is reserved with the code for a subprogram. Instead space is used in the

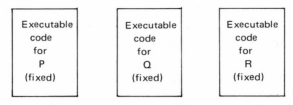

Fixed code blocks

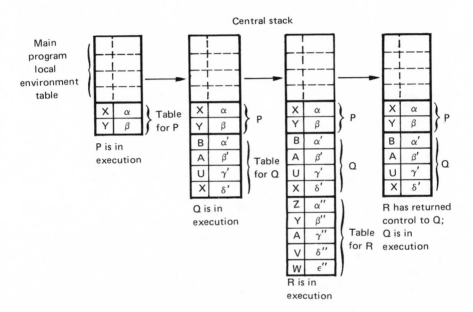

Fig. 6-5. Use of a central stack of local environment tables

central stack as needed for those subprograms which have actually been called. Initially the stack contains only the table for the main program. When the main program calls subprogram P the table for P is created and entered at the top of the stack. If P calls Q, then Q's table is stacked on top of P's. When Q terminates and returns control to P then Q's table is deleted from the stack. This stack simulation is illustrated in Fig. 6-5.

Referencing of local identifiers using the central stack is much the same as with the other technique. Although now the association table for subprogram P is not created until P is entered during execution, it is still possible to determine during translation the relative position of the association for X within the association table.

Rather than search the table for the association for X during execution the reference to X may be compiled to directly access the appropriate table entry using the computation *base address of table + offset*. The base address of the table now varies during execution because the association table of P may be at different positions in the central stack on different executions of P (if P is called from more than one routine). The offset for X remains fixed. Again, if the language design does not allow creation of new identifiers during execution, then the identifiers themselves need not appear in the table, for they are not needed in referencing.

Advantages and Disadvantages. Both of the approaches to handling of local identifiers that we have discussed here are used in a substantial number of widely used languages. PL/I and ALGOL provide for some version of both techniques. Clearly each technique has advantages not shared by the other. Consider the situation from the programmer's viewpoint. Approach 1, in which local environments are retained from call to call, allows the programmer to write subprograms which are *self-modifying* (in the sense of Chapter 4) in that their results on each call are partially determined by their inputs and partially by the local data values computed during previous executions. Approach 2, in which local environments are destroyed on exit, does not allow any local data to be carried over from one call to the next. Subprograms in this case cannot be self-modifying; their actions may only be influenced by their inputs and by shared data, not by retained local data.

There are many cases in which approach 1 is the more natural. For example, consider a subprogram which is to maintain a table. Given an input parameter, it is to look up the input in the table, return the index of the entry if the input is already in the table, and otherwise enter the input and return the index of the new entry. Using approach 1 the table may be local to the subprogram. Since the table is retained from call to call, entries may be accumulated in the table over a sequence of calls. Approach 2 forces the table to be destroyed after each return from the subprogram if it is local. Thus the tabling routine cannot build the table over a sequence of calls unless it is defined to be nonlocal to the subprogram.

While approach 1 is perhaps the better technique in this simple case, it does not generalize as well to allow shared associations and recursion, as we shall see in the following sections. Approach 1 is somewhat more efficient to use in that no explicit change of environment is necessary when transferring control between subprograms. Approach 2 requires allocation and recovery of space on the central stack on each entry and exit of a subprogram at some cost in execution speed. However, approach 2 provides a savings in storage space in that association tables exist only for those subprograms which are in execution or suspended execution. Association tables for all subprograms exist throughout execution in approach 1. Other advantages and disadvantages will become apparent as we try to generalize these approaches in the sections which follow.

6-5. SIMPLE PARAMETERLESS SUBPROGRAMS: NONLOCAL ENVIRONMENTS

Although data are ordinarily shared between subprograms through parameter transmission, there are numerous occasions in which parameters are not particularly useful. Consider a set of subprograms all making use of a common table of data. Each subprogram needs access to the table, yet transmitting the table as a parameter each time is not only inefficient but conceptually inelegant as well. Every language in Part II provides mechanisms for subprograms to share data without using parameters. Such data sharing is usually based on sharing of identifier associations. If subprograms P, Q, and R all need access to the same variable X, then it is appropriate to simply allow the identifier X to have the same association in each subprogram. The association for X is then no longer part of the local environment for any one of the subprograms but has become a common part of the nonlocal environment of each of the subprograms. Data sharing through *nonlocal environments* is an important alternative to the use of direct sharing through parameter transmission. How are nonlocal environments for subprograms to be handled? Two basic approaches exist:

1. *Explicit specification of nonlocal environments.* The most direct approach requires explicit creation of shared associations. The PL/I EXTERNAL attribute provides such a feature. If two PL/I subprograms, P and Q, tag the same identifier X as EXTERNAL, then a global association is created for X which may be referenced in both P and Q (and any other subprogram that declares X as EXTERNAL). The FORTRAN COMMON block provides a slightly different structure. A COMMON block consists of a set of variables and arrays grouped into a single named *block*. The block name is global, but the identifiers associated with the individual variables and arrays are not. Any subprogram may gain access to a particular COMMON block by an explicit declaration using the appropriate

block name. If, in addition, the identical COMMON block declaration (including identical identifiers for the individual variables and arrays) is included in each subprogram sharing the same block, as is common practice in FORTRAN, the effect is as though the individual identifier associations were shared, so that a reference to nonlocal X has the same association in each subprogram. The basic rule in explicit specification of nonlocal environments is that on subprogram entry a certain set of explicitly designated nonlocal associations is to be activated, as well as the usual local associations. On subprogram exit the same nonlocal associations are to be deactivated (but never destroyed).

2. *Implicit creation of nonlocal environments.* A more common approach provides for the implicit creation of a nonlocal environment for a subprogram when it is entered. The implicit nonlocal environment contains a set of associations shared with other subprograms. If a subprogram contains a reference to X, and no local association for X exists, then the reference is taken to be nonlocal and the association for X in the implicit nonlocal environment is retrieved. But what is the implicit nonlocal environment to be? Suppose that P calls Q which calls R and that R contains a nonlocal reference to X. Both P and Q, and any number of other subprograms, may have a local association for X. In the absence of any explicit designation of which of these associations is to be used, what would be the appropriate choice? Three possibilities are

a. *Use the most recent association in the calling chain..* If Q calls R, and Q has an association for X, then this association could be used when the nonlocal reference in R is encountered. If Q has no association for X, then we search back down the calling chain until some subprogram is found which has an association for X. This structure corresponds to the view that when a subprogram is called, an association for an identifier in the *calling program* is deactivated only if the same identifier occurs in the local environment of the *called routine.* The complete referencing environment of each subprogram then consists of its local environment plus the complete environment of the calling program with conflicting associations deactivated. Note that as a result the nonlocal environment of a subprogram is not fixed but varies depending on the point of call.

b. *Use the (global) associations in the main program.* We might consider that only associations in the main program may be shared, because they are intuitively global. Thus the nonlocal environment of a subprogram could consist only of the local environment of the main program with associations that conflict with local associations deactivated.

c. *Use a set of associations determined by the static program structure.* A third most important alternative, that of using the *static* structure of the program at compile time to determine the nonlocal environment, is taken up in Section 6-6.

Simulation of Nonlocal Environments

When nonlocal associations are explicitly specified in each subprogram the ordinary technique is to have the translator (usually the linking loader) collect these into a central table, with nonlocal references in each routine modified during loading to access this table. In cases where the data or program element which is the object of an association is also known at load time, e.g., subprogram code blocks, references may be set directly to the program or data object without the intervening association table. The translation process, particularly the loading and linking of independently translated subprograms, is made more complex by the necessity to collect and merge nonlocal associations explicitly declared in each subprogram. However, referencing during execution is straightforward, and because the nonlocal environment for all subprograms is the same, there is no need to shift nonlocal environments as control passes from subprogram to subprogram.

The use of the main program local environment as the implicit nonlocal environment for all subprograms leads to a similar simulation. The location of the execution-time association table for the main program is always fixed, being either associated directly with the code for the main program or being positioned at the bottom of the central stack, depending on the simulation of local environments used. The basic referencing rule when referencing an identifier X is as follows: First check the local subprogram environment for X; if not found, then find X in the local environment of the main program. Where both local environments are known at translation time, references may be computed directly as a base address + offset, and no search is required.

Simulation of implicit nonlocal environments based on use of the most recent association in the calling chain is more complex. Assume that local environments are to be created and destroyed on subprogram entry and exit, and that a central stack is used for the association tables during execution. A simple referencing rule may then be invoked: The appropriate association for a reference to X is

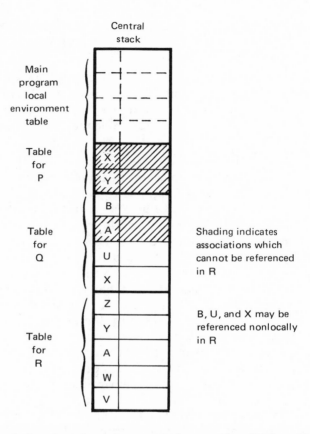

Fig. 6-6. Active referencing environment during execution of R (from Fig. 6-5).

found by searching the stack from the top down (i.e., search the local association table first). The first association found for X in the stack is that most recently created, and thus is the proper one. Implicitly this directed search ignores conflicting associations created earlier in the subprogram calling chain. This referencing technique is illustrated in Fig. 6-6 for the example of Fig. 6-5. The LISP A-list described in Chapter 14 is based on this simulation.

A search down the subprogram calling chain may also be used where association tables are attached to the subprogram code block rather than being stored in a central stack. The search must utilize the chain of subprogram return points generated during subprogram calls to guide the search to the appropriate sequence of local association tables.

Either of these techniques for simulation of the *most recent association* form of implicit nonlocal environment introduces major execution-time inefficiency. It is the requirement of the *search* for the most recent association which causes the difficulty. First, the search takes time. Local references may still be handled by the efficient base address + offset technique, but each nonlocal reference must invoke a search down a chain of local association tables. Because this chain is determined dynamically during execution and may vary between calls of the same routine, there is no way to avoid actually searching the chain. For example, suppose that subprogram R contains a nonlocal reference to X. On one call, R may be called from Q, which has a local association for X. On the next call R may be called from P, which has no association for X, and then some association for X farther back in the calling chain is needed. On yet a later call R may be called from S and the calling chain may contain no association for X at all, causing a referencing error halt. The search also reintroduces the necessity of storing the identifiers themselves in the local association tables, because the position of the association for X may differ in each local table. Thus no base address + offset computation is possible in nonlocal referencing.

How may searching for nonlocal references be avoided? Assuming we wish to retain the most recent association form of implicit nonlocal environment, a trade-off between the cost of referencing and the cost of subprogram entry and exit (plus some additional space) may be utilized. Note that both the simulations that required the search were direct extensions from the basic local environment simulations of the preceding section. Local environment tables were either stacked or stored directly with subprogram code, and the search to satisfy nonlocal references simply passed back through these local tables in the reverse order of call. As a result subprogram entry and exit were not more costly, but the nonlocal referencing was expensive because of the search. One might argue that ordinarily nonlocal referencing is likely to occur more frequently than subprogram entry and exit, i.e., the nonlocal environment is likely to be used more frequently than it is modified. In such circumstances a shift of the cost from referencing to subprogram entry and exit may be advantageous. The following simulation accomplishes this goal.

The new simulation involves augmentation of either of the local environment table simulations of the preceding section to include a central table common to all subprograms, the *central referencing environment table*. For simplicity we shall consider here the case in which local associations are not retained between calls but instead are created and destroyed on a central stack. This is the usual situation; the alternative based on retention of local environments is taken up in Problem 6-11.

The central table is set up to contain at all times during program execution *all the currently active identifier associations*, regardless of whether they are local or nonlocal. If we assume, also for simplicity, that the set of identifiers referenced in any of the subprograms may be determined during translation, then the central table is initialized to contain one entry for each identifier, regardless of the number of different subprograms in which that identifier appears. Each entry in the table also contains an *activation flag* which indicates whether or not that particular identifier has an active association, as well as space for a pointer to the object of the association.

All referencing in subprograms is direct to this central table using the base address + offset scheme described previously. Since the current association for identifier X is always located at the same place in the central table, regardless of the subprogram in which the reference occurs, and regardless of whether the reference is local or nonlocal, this simple referencing computation is adequate. Each reference requires only that the activation flag in the entry be checked to ensure that the association in the table is currently active. By use of the central table we have obtained our objective of relatively efficient nonlocal referencing without search.

Subprogram entry and exit is more costly, because each change in referencing environment requires modification of the central table. When subprogram *P* calls *Q*, the central table must be modified to reflect the new local environment for *Q*. Thus each entry corresponding to a local identifier for *Q* must be modified to incorporate the new local association for *Q*. At the same time if the old table entry for an identifier was active, the entry must be saved so that it may be reactivated when *Q* exits to *P*. Because the entries that require modification are likely to be scattered throughout the central table, this modification must be done piecemeal, entry by entry. On exit from *Q*, the associations deactivated and saved on entry to *Q* must be restored and reactivated. Again an execution-time stack is required, as in the earlier simulations, but it is used here as a *hidden stack* to store the deactivated associations. As each local identifier association is updated on entry to *Q*, the old association is stacked in a block on the hidden stack. On return from *Q* the top block of associations on the stack is restored into the appropriate positions in the central table. This central table simulation is shown in Fig. 6-7. An additional advantage accrues when using the central table if the language does not allow new references to be generated during execution. In this case, as was the case earlier in regards to local tables, the identifiers themselves may be dropped from the table, for they will never be used, having been replaced by the base address + offset computation. (In a sense the identifier is simply represented by its table offset during execution).

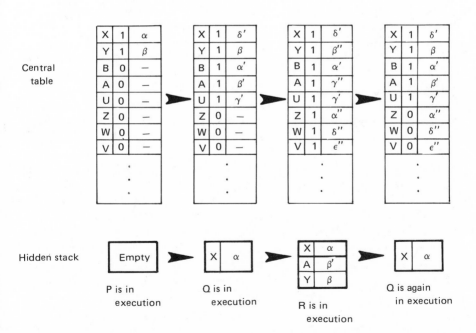

Basic referencing organization using central table

Table and stack transformation during execution (refer to Fig. 6-5)

Fig. 6-7. The central environment table simulation.

The central environment table has many variants. The SNOBOL4 implementation described in Chapter 15 is based on this simulation. Other variants are taken up in the problems at the end of this chapter.

6-6. NONLOCAL ENVIRONMENTS BASED ON STATIC PROGRAM STRUCTURE

ALGOL, PL/I, and many other languages utilize a technique for definition of nonlocal subprogram environments that differs substantially from those mentioned in the preceding section. This technique, which is based on the compile-time (static) program structure, warrants a separate discussion because of its complexity and importance.

Before discussing the technique, let us look first at some of the shortcomings of the simpler techniques of the preceding section. Two techniques, explicit specification of shared associations and implicit use of the main program's local environment, allow only a single *global* nonlocal environment common to all subprograms. Thus every reference is either local or global. This restricted case may be readily simulated but is rather inflexible. It is desirable to allow different routines to share associations without making them global to all routines. The third technique mentioned, that of using the most recent association, allows greater flexibility and in addition corresponds rather closely to our intuition about the meaning of nonlocal references in most cases. Unfortunately the most recent association technique has a major flaw in *compiled* languages such as ALGOL and PL/I where execution speed is a primary factor.

Consider the ALGOL program of Fig. 6-8. Subprogram P is called in two places, from statement $L1$ and also statement $L2$. Consider the assignment $X := X + Y$ in P. Because P contains no declaration for X or Y, the references in the assignment statement are nonlocal. Suppose that ALGOL used the most recent association rule; then on the first call of P from statement $L1$ both X and Y are **real** variables, but on the second call from statement $L2$ both are **integer** variables. Accordingly a real addition is required in the first case and an integer addition in the second. This run-time variability requires a run-time type check followed by a branch to the appropriate addition operation. Run-time type checking, however, is manifestly undesirable because of the time required to make the test and the space required to store the extra code. The result: A substantial and

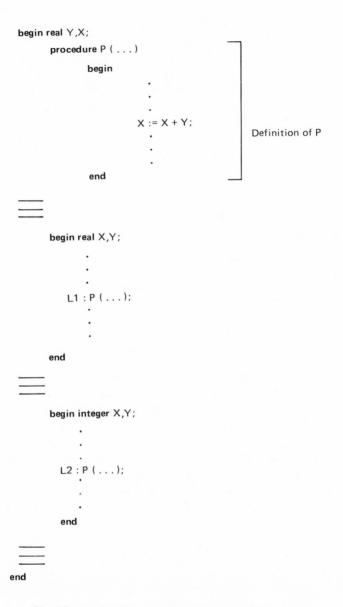

Fig. 6-8. An ALGOL procedure with nonlocal references.

unavoidable run-time cost if the most recent association rule is adopted in defining nonlocal environments. In languages such as LISP, SNOBOL4, and APL the rule is used because run-time type checking is needed anyway. However, in ALGOL and PL/I the cost at run time is too high. An alternative which allows type checking to be done during translation is desirable.

The alternative adopted in ALGOL, and subsequently incorporated into PL/I and other languages, is rather subtle. If static (compile-time) type checking is to be possible for nonlocal references, then each nonlocal reference must be paired uniquely with a declaration *during translation*. To provide this pairing we must move back to the syntactic representation of sets of subprograms (and blocks) and introduce the concept of a syntactic nesting of definitions of subprograms. To this point we have said nothing about the syntax of subprogram definition. We assumed that a set of subprograms had been defined somehow and concerned ourselves only with the problems of run-time identifier associations. Now, however, we wish to associate type descriptors (at least) with identifiers during translation. We accomplish this as follows. First we adopt a nested syntax for subprogram and block definitions, so that a program consists of an outermost block containing nested block and subprogram definitions as in ALGOL. A typical program structure in ALGOL then looks like Fig. 6-8. Now we adopt the following rule for referencing nonlocal identifiers: The variable referenced by a nonlocal identifier in a block or subprogram definition is that variable declared within the innermost *physically containing* block or subprogram in the program *as written*. Now in our old example of Fig. 6-8, Y in procedure P is a reference to the variable Y declared in the outermost block, not to either of the variables Y declared in blocks from which P is called.

Using this rule of referencing based on the compile-time nesting of subprogram and block definitions we can always associate each identifier with a declaration at compile time and thus avoid run-time type checking. The compile-time nesting of block and subprogram definitions is usually termed the *static block structure* of the program.

Simulation. The use of static block structure to determine the implicit nonlocal environment of a subprogram imposes a cost in the complexity of the run-time simulation needed. The usual simulation is based on a central stack of local environment tables, suitably modified to allow referencing based on the static block structure of the original program. We shall discuss this simulation here, leaving other simulations to be developed in the problems. This simulation is typical of many ALGOL implementations and is based on the assumption that local data are not retained between subprogram calls.

Recall from Section 6-4 the simple stack-based simulation for local environment tables. Initially the stack contains only the local environment table for the main program. As each subprogram is entered a local environment table is created on top of the stack, and on exit the top environment table on the stack is deleted. Assuming that subprogram calls are strictly nested in a last-in—first-out fashion, we may always be sure that the top local environment table on the stack at subprogram exit is the table for that subprogram. Referencing of local variables utilizes the base address + offset computation, where the base address is always that of the top local table on the stack. This part of the original simulation is still adequate.

Nonlocal referencing brings major problems, however. Consider Fig. 6-8 again. Figure 6-9 shows the contents of the stack when execution reaches the assignment $X := X + Y$ on the first call of P. Note the difficulty of referencing the appropriate association for Y because the appropriate association is not the most recently created. It no longer suffices to simply search down the stack. The problem is that the sequence of local tables in the stack represents the *dynamic nesting* of subprogram *activations*, the nesting based on the execution-time calling chain. But it is the *static nesting* of subprogram *definitions* which now determines the nonlocal environment, and the stack as currently structured contains no information about static nesting.

To complete the simulation it is necessary to represent the static

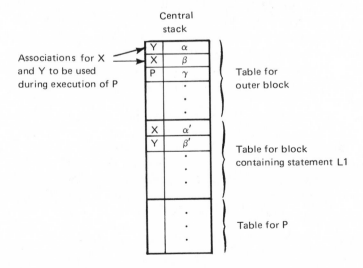

Fig. 6-9. Environment table stack during execution of P (Fig. 6-8).

block structure during execution in such a way that it may be used to control nonlocal referencing. Observe that in many respects the rule for nonlocal referencing in this case is similar to that for nonlocal referencing using the most recent association rule: To find the association to satisfy a reference to X we search a chain of local environment tables until an association for X is found. However, the chain of local environment tables to search is not that composed of *all* the local tables currently in the stack but only those currently in the stack *which represent blocks or subprograms whose definition statically encloses the current subprogram definition in the original program text*. The search then is still down the tables in the stack, but only a subset of those tables are actually part of the referencing environment.

Static Chain Simulation. These observations lead to the most direct simulation of the referencing environment: the *static chain* technique. Suppose that we modify the local environment tables in the stack slightly so that each table begins with a special entry, called the *static chain pointer*. This static chain pointer always contains the base address of another local table further down the stack. The table pointed to is the table representing the local environment of the statically enclosing block or subprogram in the original program.

The static chain pointers form the basis for a simple referencing scheme. To satisfy a reference to X we begin with the current local environment on top of the stack. If no association for X is found in the local environment, then we follow the static chain pointer in that local table down the stack to a second table. If X is not in that table, the search continues down the static chain pointers until a local table is found with an association for X. The first one found is the correct association. Figure 6-10 illustrates the static chain for the ALGOL program of Fig. 6-8.

At any point during program execution the static chain pointers in the stack actually structure the local environment tables into a tree, as illustrated in Fig. 6-11. The referencing operation always begins looking for an association at one of the leaves of the tree, progressing down the branches toward the root in the search. One leaf of the tree is always the current local environment (the table on top of the stack), and it is from this leaf that the referencing search begins.

If a nonlocal reference involves a *search* of a sequence of local environment tables, then we have returned to one of the problems which caused difficulty before. Recall that one of the reasons for introducing the additional complexity of referencing based on the

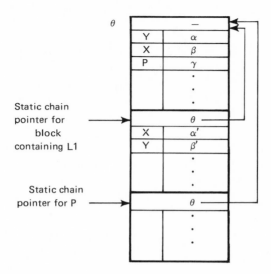

Fig. 6-10. Environment table stack of Fig. 6-9 with static chain pointers.

static block structure was execution efficiency, yet searching to satisfy references at run time is most inefficient. However, the search here may be eliminated without difficulty. To see how, we need a few preliminary observations.

First note that, for any subprogram Q, when Q is in execution (and its local environment table is therefore on top of the stack) the length of the static chain leading from Q's local table down the stack (and ultimately to the table for the main program) is *constant*. This length is constant regardless of the current size of the stack and regardless of the point of call of Q. Of course, the reason is simply that the length of the static chain is equal to the depth of static nesting of subprogram Q's definition back in the original program at compile time, and this depth of nesting is fixed throughout execution. For example, if Q is defined within a block which is directly contained within the outermost block of the program, then the static chain for Q during execution always has length 3: Q's local table, the local table for the directly containing block, and the local table for the outermost block (the main program). In Fig. 6-8 and 6-10, for example, the static chain for P always has length 2.

Second, note that in this chain of constant length a nonlocal reference will always be satisfied at exactly the same point in the chain. For example, in Fig. 6-10 the nonlocal reference to X in P will always be satisfied in the second table in the chain. Again this fact is a simple reflection of the static program structure. The number of

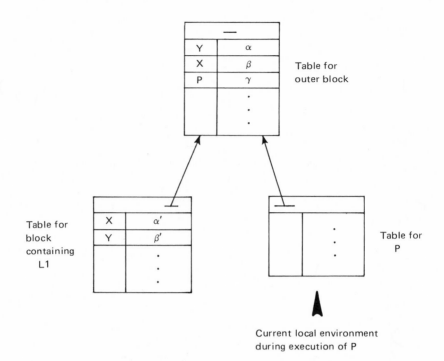

Fig. 6-11. Tree of local environment tables during execution of P.

levels of static nesting that one must go out from the definition of P to find the declaration for X is fixed at compile time.

Third, note that the position in the chain at which a nonlocal reference will be satisfied may be determined at compile time. For example, we may determine at compile time that a reference to X in P will be found in the second table down the static chain during execution. In addition, we know at compile time the relative position of X in that local table. Thus, for example, at *compile time* we can conclude that the association for X will be the second entry in the second table down the static chain during execution.

The basis for a fairly efficient referencing operation is now apparent. Instead of explicitly searching down the static chain for an identifier, we need only skip down the chain a fixed number of tables, and then use the simple base address + offset computation to pick out the appropriate entry in the table. In fact, under the usual assumption that new references cannot be generated during execution, we no longer need the identifiers represented explicitly at all, because no search is used. Instead it is natural to represent an identifier in the form of a pair, (chain position, offset), during execution. For example, if X, referenced in P, is to be found as the third entry in the second table down the chain, then in the compiled code for P, X may be represented by the pair (2,3). This representation provides a rather simple referencing algorithm.

The static chain technique allows straightforward entry and exit of subprograms. When a subprogram is called, its local environment table must be installed on top of the stack and the appropriate static chain pointer installed, pointing to a local table further down the stack. On exit it is necessary only to delete the top local table from the stack; no special action is needed. But how is the appropriate static chain pointer to install on entry to be determined? Suppose that subprogram P is called from subprogram Q and that P was defined in the original program within block B. When P is entered the appropriate static chain pointer is back to the local table for block B. At the point of call the local table for Q is on top of the stack and that for P is to be stacked on top of Q's. How is it determined that the proper pointer is the one to B? Observe that the identifier P, the subprogram name, is itself referenced nonlocally in Q. If P is represented by the pair (3,2), then the association of identifier P with a pointer to its compiled code is to be found in the table three steps down the static chain for Q, at the second table entry. But that local table in which the entry for P appears must be the table for block B. Thus when we reference P at the point of subprogram call (in Q) we can also easily retrieve the appropriate static chain pointer to insert into the local table for P when it is set up. This structure is illustrated in Fig. 6-12.

The Display Simulation. The necessity of following the static chain for each nonlocal reference is a drawback of the above technique. We may avoid this referencing cost by using an alternative simulation, but only at a cost on subprogram entry and exit. In this simulation the static chain is represented separately from the main stack. The current static chain is stored separately in a special "little stack," termed a *display*. The display contains a sequence of pointers to local tables in the main stack. At any given point during execution the display contains the same sequence of pointers that would have occurred in the static chain currently being used for nonlocal referencing in the old static chain model. Figure 6-13 illustrates the display for the example of Fig. 6-12.

Referencing using a display is particularly simple. Let us adopt a slightly modified representation for identifiers during execution. Again pairs of integers are to be used, but let the 3 in a pair like (3,2) represent the number of steps back from the *end* of the chain to the

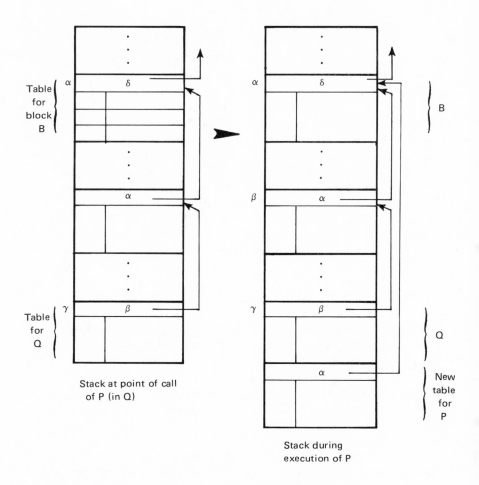

Stack at point of call
of P (in Q)

Stack during
execution of P

Fig. 6-12. Static chain creation during subprogram entry.

appropriate local table (rather than down from the start of the chain as before). The second integer in the pair still represents the offset in the table. Now given a nonlocal reference such as (3,2) the appropriate association is found in two steps:

1. Consider the first entry (3) as a subscript into the display. Thus *display* [3] contains a pointer to the appropriate local table, i.e., the base address of the local table.

2. Compute the location of the appropriate table entry as base address + offset, where the offset is the second entry in the pair.

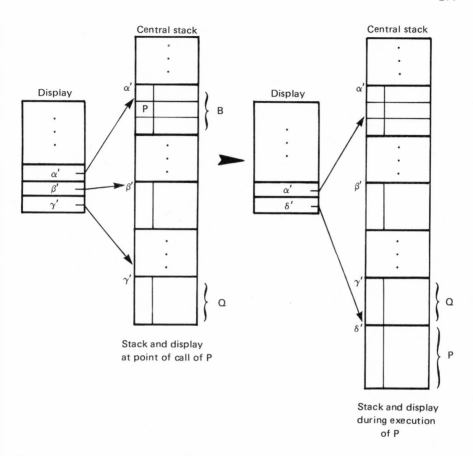

Fig. 6-13. Display modification during subprogram entry.

Ordinarily these two steps combine into one using indirect addressing through the display entry. In addition, it is often possible to place the display directly in high-speed registers during execution, thus giving only one memory access per identifier reference.

Although referencing is simplified using a display, subprogram entry and exit are more difficult. The display must be modified on each entry and exit to reflect the *currently active* static chain at all times. Consider again the subprogram P, defined in block B, which was called from subprogram Q. At the point of call the display contains the static chain for Q. This static chain contains a pointer to the local table for B (otherwise Q could not reference P). The static chain for P contains only the local table for P and the old chain from B down. Thus on entry to P the contents of the display from the entry for B to the top must be saved and later restored on exit. Ordinarily this partial static chain would be stored on the central stack with the local table for Q. The cost of saving and restoring the display is greater than with the simple static chain technique.

Advantages and Disadvantages of Nonlocal Referencing Techniques

In this and the preceding sections various approaches to the sharing of associations through explicit and implicit nonlocal environments have been surveyed. The languages in Part II utilize these techniques, and various modifications, in many different ways. There clearly is no general agreement as to the "best" way to handle nonlocal referencing. Let us consider the three main techniques: (1) explicit designation of nonlocal associations, (2) implicit nonlocal environment using the *most recent association*, and (3) implicit nonlocal environment using the *static block structure.*

Explicit designation has the advantage of simplicity of simulation (at least as ordinarily set up), as only a single global environment is defined. In addition, explicit designation is likely to provide good error protection, as references which are neither local nor explicitly designated nonlocal may be detected during translation. Explicit designation, on the other hand, is less flexible in that only a single level of nonlocal referencing is provided. Also it may require a substantial amount of extra declaration when much nonlocal referencing is done.

Implicit most recent association environments are perhaps the most elegant, as they correspond closely to our intuitive understandings of the meanings of identifiers in mathematics (for example, as modeled in the lambda calculus). They are simple to understand and to simulate, but they may force type checking during execution, causing substantial inefficiency.

Static block structure environments allow static type checking and fairly efficient simulation during execution. However, they force the sort of nested block and subprogram definition characteristic of ALGOL programs, and thus the technique cannot easily be extended to separately translated subprograms (a problem not shared with either of the other techniques).

6-7. RECURSIVE PARAMETERLESS SUBPROGRAMS

More general subprogram control structures lead to variations on the data control structures described for simple subprograms. In the preceding sections we have identified two basic approaches to local environments:

1. Retention of local environments between calls.

2. Destruction and recreation of local environments between calls.

and three basic approaches to nonlocal environments:

1. Explicit specification.

2. Implicit dynamic (most recent association) specification.

3. Implicit static (static block structure) specification.

How do recursive subprograms affect the choice of referencing environments? Recall from Section 5-4 the distinction between subprogram *definition* and *activation*, which is central in recursion. A recursive subprogram may exist in many simultaneous activations at any point during execution. The referencing environment in different activations of the same subprogram in general may be different. Thus we are confronted with the problem of defining the referencing environment for *each activation* of a subprogram.

Local Environments. Each activation of a recursive subprogram should have its own local environment. For example, if X is a local variable in P, and P calls itself recursively, then we expect a new local variable named X in each activation of P. This fact implies creation of a new local environment on each call. Similarly when control leaves P the local environment should be destroyed. Retention between calls is also a possible technique, interpreting retention to mean that a single local environment is set up which is used by all activations of a given subprogram. However, retention is not particularly useful in recursion because one ordinarily desires a new set of local associations at each level of recursion. Thus recursion usually implies destruction and recreation of local environments on subprogram entry and exit. With either technique no special simulation is required to handle local environments. When the central stack simulation is used, however, the same stack may be used to store subprogram return points (see Section 5-4).

Nonlocal Environments. Nonlocal referencing in recursive subprograms causes no particular problem in any of the three approaches to nonlocal environments. Each extends immediately to recursion. Consider a nonlocal reference to X in some activation of a recursive subprogram P. In the explicitly specified nonlocal environment, X is global and thus exists in only one activation. In the static block structure technique the reference to X will retrieve the association for X in the most recent activation of the subprogram in which X was declared. The most recent association technique, of course, retrieves the association in the most recent activation in the calling chain.

6-8. REFERENCING ENVIRONMENTS IN COROUTINES, INTERRUPT ROUTINES, TASKS, AND SCHEDULED SUBPROGRAMS

Control structures more general than simple subprograms with recursion present new referencing environment requirements. We shall discuss the problems briefly, without attempting a thorough treatment.

Coroutines

Local environments in coroutines obviously need to be retained from one RESUME call to the next; otherwise the coroutine would not be able to resume at the appropriate point in its computation. Nonlocal environments are more troublesome. Conceptually a set of coroutines operate all on the same level; there is no calling program-called program hierarchy. For this reason the most recent association implicit environment is unnatural; there is no calling chain on which to base a search for the appropriate reference. Either explicit specification or implicit static specification is appropriate. As few languages have incorporated coroutines directly, there is little experience to draw on here.

Interrupt Routines

Subprograms initiated by interrupts present a different set of referencing problems. Local environments might be handled with any of the approaches mentioned. Nonlocal referencing in interrupt routines is particularly important, however. Consider the typical case of an interrupt routine P which is to be executed when a particular type of error occurs in subprogram Q, say, for example, a subscript-out-of-range error. If P is to function adequately, it must have access to information about the array associated with the error, its bounds, the values of the subscripts in the reference, etc. In general these will be local to Q. Thus it is desirable that P have access to Q's local environment, or at least to some of the information available through that environment. As a second example, consider a trace routine that is to be activated whenever a particular sub-program is called. Again, the trace routine needs access to the local environment of the calling program if it is to output the current values of variables in that program. How is this access to be provided? One simple solution is that used in PL/I. Rather than allowing the interrupt routine direct access to the local environment of the subprogram in which the interrupt occurred, certain fixed pieces of data which are central to the processing of the particular type of interrupt are transferred to a global environment (language-defined). The interrupt routine may access this global environment but not the local environment where the interrupt occurred. This simple technique is adequate in many cases. Relatively little is known about general techniques for referencing in interrupt routines.

Tasks

Parallel execution (tasks) again creates little difficulty in local environments. Under the usual assumption that multiple activations of the same subprogram may be executing in parallel it is natural to create a new local environment when a task is initiated and destroy it when the task terminates.

Nonlocal referencing is not difficult conceptually but may cause problems in storage management. Suppose that P calls Q as a separate task to be executed in parallel. The nonlocal environment of Q, if not defined explicitly, would be either the environment of P (in the most recent association technique) or some part of the environment of P (in the static block structure technique). The problem is that as both P and Q continue to execute, each may be expected to enter new blocks or call other subprograms, thus generating separate chains of new local environments. In the stack simulation, initiation of a new task leads to a fork in the stack. Each branch of the fork continues to grow as execution of the two parallel subprograms continues. Of course, each may initiate other tasks, causing further splitting of the stack. In general, a tree structure results. When a task terminates, that branch of the tree, from the leaf down to the last branch point, must be deleted. Because this tree structure grows and shrinks unpredictably during execution, a general storage manage-ment mechanism is required to simulate it; the simple stack technique no longer suffices.

Scheduled Subprograms

General subprogram scheduling, as is found in simulation languages, causes the most difficulty in referencing. Each subprogram may exist simultaneously in many activations, each in various stages of execution. Termination of any activation of a subprogram may occur at an arbitrary point relative to other activations of the same subprogram and other subprograms. Thus there is no nicely nested pattern to subprogram calls and terminations. In addition, subprogram activations may be suspended and reactivated in a general coroutine-like manner. The result is an essentially random pattern of subprogram activation, suspension, reactivation, and termination.

Clearly deletion of lcoal environments is natural here on subprogram termination. But what is appropriate for nonlocal environments? We might use the dynamic environment at the point of call (more appropriately, point of *scheduling*), but that environment may no longer exist when the scheduled subprogram actually begins execution. An environment based on the static program structure does not answer the question of which activation is to be used. And a single global environment is somewhat inflexible, for it leaves the programmer to entirely control the sharing of data between subprograms.

No single solution is likely to be entirely adequate in this case. Different simulation languages provide different mechanisms. GPSS, for example, allows each activation of a routine (called a *transaction*) to access only local or global environments. The programmer must coordinate the sharing of data through the global environment common to all transactions.

6-9. SUBPROGRAMS WITH PARAMETERS: PARAMETER TRANSMISSION TECHNIQUES

Communication between subprograms through parameters is more common than communication through nonlocal environments. The intent—allowing data and program elements to be shared between subprograms—is the same in either case. Parameters are most useful when a subprogram is to be given different data to work on each time it is called. Use of a nonlocal environment is more appropriate when the same data are used on each call. For example, if subprogram P is used on each call to enter a new data item into a table shared with other subprograms, then typically the table would be accessed through a nonlocal reference in P, but the data item would be transmitted as an explicit parameter on each call.

In discussion of parameter transmission we must distinguish between *actual parameters* (or *arguments*) and *formal parameters*. *Formal parameters* are the identifiers used in a subprogram definition to name the data or program elements transmitted into the subprogram. Formal parameters are ordinarily specified in a *formal parameter list* at the beginning of the definition of the subprogram and are invariably restricted to be simple identifiers. *Actual parameters* are the expressions used at the point of call of a subprogram to specify the data or program items to be transmitted to the subprogram. The usual syntax is to simply write actual parameters in a list following the name of the subprogram, as in $SUB(X2*Y,17)$. As discussed in Section 5-2 this is the ordinary prefix representation for operations, in which the operands follow the operation symbol. Other notations may be used, e.g., infix notation. For simplicity we shall adopt the conventional prefix representation as basic and speak of *argument lists*, although for other syntactic representations arguments may not be represented explicitly in lists.

Parameter transmission provides a mechanism for allowing a subprogram access to nonlocal data and program elements through strictly local identifiers. Through parameters one may avoid the complexities of nonlocal environments. Formal parameters are local identifiers in a subprogram and thus form part of the local referencing environment. Parameter transmission provides a means of initializing these local identifiers to nonlocal values on subprogram entry, through a simple *positional correspondence* with the actual parameters specified at the point of call. At the point of call there is an actual parameter list; at the head of the subprogram definition there is a formal parameter list. At the time of subprogram entry the first formal parameter is associated with the data or program element designated by the first actual parameter; the second formal parameter is associated with the second actual parameter; etc. In general, it is required that there be exactly as many actual as formal parameters, although many languages relax this requirement by conventions for interpreting missing or extra actual parameters. It is through use of positional correspondence between formal and actual parameter lists that we avoid the necessity to share identifier associations through nonlocal environments.

The basic concept of parameter transmission through positional correspondence in parameter lists is straightforward. The complexity here is due largely to two aspects: the variety of types of actual parameters and the variety of parameter transmission techniques. Let us begin with a description of the basic techniques for parameter transmission and then discuss the different varieties of actual parameters and their transmission using the various techniques.

Basic Parameter Transmission Techniques

In the preceding chapter we looked briefly into the problem of evaluation rules for operands to operations: Should the operand be evaluated before transmission to the operation, or should the operand be transmitted unevaluated? We are now ready to look more deeply into this problem, because parameter transmission is simply the topic of evaluation rules expanded. An actual parameter specifies an operand for a subprogram (which is only a user-defined operation). Our concern is with what operand the subprogram actually receives and the manner of its association with the formal parameter. Three main types of parameter transmission have been used in programming languages: transmission by value, transmission by reference, and transmission by name. Each leads to a different evaluation rule for actual parameters.

Transmission by Value. In parameter transmission by value the basic rule is that the actual parameter is evaluated at the point of call. The *value* of the actual parameter is then transmitted to the subprogram and becomes the initial value associated with the corresponding formal parameter. For example, in CALL SUB(X), if X is a simple variable with the value 3 at the point of call, then the value transmitted is the constant 3. The corresponding formal parameter, say Y, is initialized to the value 3, and during execution of the subprogram SUB, Y is treated as a simple local variable. The major distinguishing characteristic of transmission by value is its restriction to transmission of data *to* a subprogram. In general, a subprogram cannot transmit results back to the calling program through a parameter transmitted by value. Thus transmission by value "protects" the calling program from side effects caused by assignments to a formal parameter within the called program. Exceptions occasionally arise, e.g., in SNOBOL4 all parameters are transmitted by value, but results may be returned through parameters by invoking indirect referencing through a variable name transmitted as a string.

Transmission by Reference (Location or Simple Name). In transmission by reference a pointer is transmitted, usually a pointer to a data location containing the value. In CALL SUB(X), for example, transmission by reference would lead to transmission of a pointer to the location of variable X in the calling program, in contrast to the value of variable X which was transmitted in the transmission by value technique. The corresponding formal parameter Y in SUB is initialized to contain the pointer to X. Each reference to Y in SUB is treated as a reference to the location of X. Any assignment to Y in SUB will change the value of X back in the calling program. Thus transmission by reference allows data to be transmitted both into and back from subprograms.

Transmission by Name. The basic concept in parameter transmission by name is that of leaving actual parameters *unevaluated until the point of use* in the called subprogram. The parameters are to be transmitted unevaluated, and the called subprogram determines when, if ever, they are actually evaluated. Recall from our earlier discussion of uniform evaluation rules that this possibility was useful in treating operations such as the *if-then-else* conditional as ordinary operations. In primitive operations the technique is occasionally useful; in programmer-defined subprograms its utility is more problematic because of the cost of simulation. Parameter transmission by name plays a major role in ALGOL and is of considerable theoretical importance. It has not been widely used outside of ALGOL, being replaced in later languages by more appropriate mechanisms based on subprograms as actual parameters.

The basic transmission by name rule may be stated in terms of substitution: The actual parameter is to be substituted everywhere for the formal parameter in the body of the called program before execution of the subprogram begins. While this seems straightforward, consider the problem of even the simple CALL SUB(X). If the formal parameter in SUB is Y, then X is to be substituted for Y throughout SUB before SUB is executed. But this is not enough, because when we come to a reference to X during execution of SUB, the association for X referenced is that *back in the calling program*, not the association in SUB (if any). When X is substituted for Y we must also indicate a different referencing environment for use in referencing X. This is precisely the problem which arises with subprogram parameters in general, a topic which we shall take up in detail below.

Not surprisingly, the basic technique for simulating transmission by name is to treat actual parameters as simple parameterless subprograms (traditionally called *thunks*, a name coined by Ingerman [1961]). This technique allows a uniform handling of the problems of referencing environments for both *by name* parameters and subprogram parameters. Whenever a formal parameter corresponding to a by name actual parameter is referenced in a subprogram, the thunk compiled for that parameter is executed, resulting in the evaluation of the actual parameter in the proper referencing environment and the return of the resulting value (or location) as the value of the thunk.

Actual Parameter Types and Parameter Transmission

Different actual parameter types usually receive different treatment depending on whether transmission is by value, reference, or name. Understanding of the differences in effect between the three transmission mechanisms is aided by considering the various actual parameter types individually.

Simple Variables. (1) *By value.* The variable is evaluated at the point of call (i.e., the location associated with the variable name in the referencing environment at the point of call is found, and the contents of that location retrieved) and the value is transmitted to the subprogram. The value becomes the initial value of the corresponding formal parameter, which then is treated as a local simple variable throughout subprogram execution. An assignment to the formal parameter does not change the value of the actual parameter variable back in the calling program. (2) *By reference.* The location associated with the variable name in the referencing environment at the point of call is found. A pointer to this location is transmitted. A reference to the formal parameter in the called subprogram is treated as an indirect reference to the actual parameter location through this pointer. Assignment to the formal parameter changes the value of the actual parameter in the calling program. (3) *By name.* This case may be treated as transmission by reference.

Constants. (1) *By value.* The constant is transmitted and set as the initial value of the formal parameter. (2) *By reference.* A storage location for the constant is allocated and initialized to the constant value. A pointer to this location is transmitted. Note: Assignments to the formal parameter may cause difficulties if each actual parameter constant is not allocated a separate storage location. For example, suppose that SUB is called by CALL SUB(1,2,1), that the constant 1 is stored only once, and that two pointers to the location are transmitted as actual parameters. If the corresponding formal parameter list in SUB is (X,Y,Z), then an assignment to X may change the value of Z inadvertently. This error is prevalent in many implementations of FORTRAN where all uses of a constant in any subprogram are translated into references to a single location containing the constant. It becomes possible to change the value of a constant 1 to 2 during a subprogram call, so that any later reference to the constant 1, e.g., in X := X+1, evaluates to 2. (3) *By name*. This case may be treated as transmission by reference or value (but assignments to the formal parameter should be prohibited).

Expressions (Other than Special Cases Listed Separately). (1) *By value*. The expression is evaluated at the point of call and the resulting value transmitted. The formal parameter is treated as a local simple variable initialized to the transmitted value. (2) *By reference*. The expression is evaluated at the point of call and the value stored in a reserved location. A pointer to this location is transmitted. (3) *By name*. The expression must be reevaluated each time the corresponding formal parameter is referenced in the subprogram. A thunk is compiled which evaluates the expression in the environment of the calling program and returns the value of the expression as its value. A pointer to the thunk is transmitted. Assignments to the formal parameter are prohibited.

Subscripted Variables with Constant Subscripts. (1) *By value*. The designated data structure element is retrieved and its value transmitted. The formal parameter acts as a simple initialized local variable in the subprogram. (2) *By reference*. The location of the designated data structure element is retrieved and a pointer to this location transmitted. The formal parameter is treated identically as for a simple variable actual parameter. (3) *By name*. This case may be treated as identical to transmission by reference.

Subscripted Variables with Nonconstant (expression) Subscripts. (1) *By value*. The subscript expressions are evaluated at the point of call, the designated data structure element is accessed, and its value is transmitted. (2) *By reference*. The subscript expressions are evaluated at the point of call and the designated data structure element is accessed. A pointer to the location of the element is transmitted. The formal parameter is treated identically as for a simple variable actual parameter. (3) *By name*. The subscript expressions must be reevaluated each time the formal parameter is referenced in the called subprogram, and a possibly different data structure element must be accessed. A thunk is compiled which evaluates the subscript expressions in the environment of the calling program and returns a pointer to the appropriate data structure location. Assignment to the formal parameter in the subprogram is allowed, but the thunk must be evaluated and assignment made to the location returned as its value.

Data Structures (Other than Simple Variables). (1) By value. When a data structure name, e.g., the name of an array, is given as an actual parameter, the interpretation is problematic. What is the "value" of an array? The interpretation adopted in ALGOL is that the array must be *copied* at the point of call, and a pointer to the copy must be transmitted to the subprogram. More commonly the treatment is identical to that of transmission by reference: A pointer to the designated data structure is transmitted. The advantage of copying the structure (the ALGOL interpretation) is that the original array is protected; assignments to the formal parameter (suitably subscripted) in the subprogram will modify the copy, not the original array. The disadvantage of copying is in the substantial extra storage required. *(2) By reference.* The data structure associated with the actual parameter identifier at the point of call is retrieved, and a pointer to the structure is transmitted. References to the associated formal parameter in the subprogram must be suitably subscripted to allow proper accessing of elements. Assignments to the subscripted formal parameter will modify the actual parameter data structure. Assignments to the formal parameter when unsubscripted are not allowed. *(3) By name.* This case may be treated as transmission by reference.

Subprograms (Including "By Name" Parameters Compiled into Thunks). When a subprogram name is used as an actual parameter a special case arises. The distinction between transmission by name, value, or reference essentially disappears: One expects a pointer to the block of executable code for the subprogram to be transmitted, perhaps also with a nonlocal referencing environment specification. The same technique applies when a by name actual parameter is compiled into a thunk. A pointer to the code for the thunk is transmitted, together with a specification of the nonlocal referencing environment in which the thunk is to be executed. In general, a thunk contains *only* nonlocal references, and thus the referencing environment specification is critical. An ordinary subprogram *may* contain nonlocal references. If not, there is no problem in its execution through a reference to the formal parameter; it suffices to simply transmit a pointer to the code. However, if it does contain nonlocal references, then the specification of nonlocal referencing environment is important.

The difficulty with nonlocal references in subprogram parameters is the following: When a reference to the formal parameter causes execution of the subprogram actual parameter, the appropriate referencing environment is not that which is "natural" at the point of call. Instead it is usually the case that a different nonlocal referencing environment must be set up especially for execution of the subprogram. Where nonlocal environment specification is explicit (as in FORTRAN) there is no difficulty because all nonlocal references are ordinarily global and thus independent of the point of call or transmission. Where the nonlocal environment is implicit, however, reinstating the proper nonlocal environment at the point of call may be complex.

Consider first the most recent association rule for nonlocal environments. Suppose that subprogram Q, which contains a nonlocal reference to X, is transmitted by subprogram P to subprogram R as a parameter. R then calls Q using the appropriate formal parameter. Suppose also that P and R each have a local association for X. When Q references X, should it get P's X or R's X? In SNOBOL4 it would get R's X; in some implementations of LISP it would get P's. Simplicity of implementation would dictate the former. Recall the simple directed search of the stack of environment tables (or the direct look-up in a central environment table) associated with the most recent association rule. Without modification we could apply this same technique during execution of Q, always retrieving R's local association if present. The difficulty with adoption of this simple interpretation is that it is rather unnatural for the programmer. Suppose that subprogram R with local variable X is a simple *generator* routine which accepts an array and a subprogram name as its two arguments. R is to apply the subprogram to each element of the array in sequence. The programmer calls R at one point in his program as CALL $R(A,Q)$, and perhaps later as CALL $R(B,Q')$. Suppose that Q and Q' contain nonlocal references to X and Z, respectively. Execution of Q' by R proceeds without difficulty: The reference to Z retrieves the association in effect at the point of call of R. But during execution of Q each reference to X inadvertently retrieves the association for local variable X in R. Since this X is supposedly unknown to the user of R, a subtle error has arisen which is difficult to detect. Clearly during execution of Q and Q' by R it is desirable to reinstate the referencing environment that existed at the point where Q or Q' were transmitted to R as parameters. This would ensure that the local environment of R would not interfere with nonlocal referencing in Q and Q'.

How is this reinstatement of the referencing environment at the point of call to be simulated? Suppose that the simple stack of local environment tables is being used. When Q is transmitted as a

parameter to R we wish to record its nonlocal referencing environment at the point of transmission and transmit that information as
part of the parameter Q itself (along with the usual pointer to the
code for Q). Then whenever Q is called by R (or other subprograms
which R may call) using the associated formal parameter, the
appropriate nonlocal environment for Q may be restored before
execution of Q is initiated. When Q is transmitted as a parameter the
environment existing at the point of transmission may be designated
by a simple pointer to the current top of the stack. The actual
parameter Q then is represented as a pair: (code pointer, environment pointer). When Q is actually called through the formal
parameter the environment pointer for Q is installed to represent the
top of the stack during execution of Q, and the code pointer is used
as the point to begin execution.

Let us consider now the static block structure specification for
nonlocal environments. Recall that the nonlocal environment in this
case depends on the point of definition of a subprogram in the
original program during translation. Assume that the static chain
mechanism is used to determine nonlocal referencing environments
during execution. When Q is transmitted to R as a parameter, its
referencing environment at the point of transmission is determined
by the static chain appropriate to its point of definition. If we
transmit with Q a pointer to the head of this static chain and
reinstate this pointer when Q is called in R, then the reinstatement of
the appropriate nonlocal environment for Q is effectively achieved.
Again Q is represented as a pair, (code pointer, environment pointer),
during argument transmission, with the environment pointer pointing
to the local environment table of the point of definition of Q. This
table is determined in exactly the same manner as if Q were being
called instead of R at the point where Q appears as a parameter.

Labels. Statement labels as actual parameters cause difficulties
somewhat similar to those caused by subprogram parameters. Again
there is no real distinction between transmission by name, value, or
reference; one expects a pointer to a code position to be transmitted.
In the called subprogram a **goto** the formal parameter leads to an
ambiguity. When control is transferred to the statement labeled by
the actual parameter, what is to be the referencing environment in
effect (i.e., which activation of the subprogram containing the label
is to receive control)? The usual interpretation is that the referencing
environment in effect after the **goto** is to be that which would have
resulted had the **goto** been executed at the point where the label was
transmitted as a parameter. Thus a label parameter must carry with it

a designation of the referencing environment in effect at the point of transmission, exactly as with a subprogram parameter. The label parameter may be represented as a pair, (code pointer, environment pointer), with the called subprogram reinstating the appropriate environment (using the environment pointer) before executing a goto.

Example 6-1. The complexities of nonlocal referencing in the presence of subprogram and label parameters may be best understood by study of an example. Consider the ALGOL program, B, of Fig. 6-14 (adapted from a program given by Johnston [1971]). The reader should stop at this point and attempt to determine the result of the program himself before proceeding. Recall that nonlocal referencing in ALGOL is controlled by the static block structure rule.

For the simulation of referencing environments during execution of B we shall adopt the static chain representation of Section 6-6. There are four separate local environments involved, for B, P, Q_{top} (declared within P), and Q_{bot} (declared below P). Each local environment may be represented by a local environment table containing one entry for each identifier declared (or used, in the case of labels) within the block or subprogram. These base table formats

```
Line
  1    B: begin integer N;
  2           procedure P(X,C); value C; procedure X; integer C; begin
  3               procedure Q(T); label T; begin
  4                   N := N + C;
  5                   X(K);
  6                   goto T
  7               end proc Q;
  8           J: if C > N then X(J) else P(Q,C+1);
  9           K: N := N + C;
 10               goto L
 11           end proc P;
 12           procedure Q(L); label L; begin
 13               N := N + 1;
 14               goto L
 15           end proc Q;
 16           N := 3;
 17           P(Q,4);
 18       L: print (N)
 19    end block B;
```

Fig. 6-14. An ALGOL program with label and procedure parameters.

Static chain pointer	
N	
P	
Q	
L	
R.P.	

Local table for B

Static chain pointer	
X	
C	
Q	
J	
K	
R.P.	

Local table for P

Static chain pointer	
T	
R.P.	

Local table for Q_{top}

Static chain pointer	
L	
R.P.	

Local table for Q_{bot}

R.P. = return point location

Fig. 6-15. Local environment table formats for program of Fig. 6-14.

are shown in Fig. 6-15. Note that each table has been extended to include, as additional entries, a static chain pointer and a return point location. In this representation, return points for the sub-programs may be represented as label parameters, consisting of a pair, (code pointer, environment pointer). Return from a subprogram is equivalent to a **goto** to this label parameter, tagged *R.P.* in the local table. For clarity, identifiers are shown as directly present in the environment tables, although as explained in Section 6-6 this is not necessary in ALGOL; identifiers would ordinarily not be present explicitly.

Execution of B proceeds through the following sequence of subprogram entries and exits:

Step
1. Enter B.
2. B calls P, setting up activation P_{init} (line 17).
3. P_{init} calls Q_{bot} through formal parameter X (line 8).
4. Q_{bot} returns control to P_{init}, statement J, through formal parameter L (line 14).
5. P_{init} calls itself recursively, setting up activation P_{rec} (line 8).
6. P_{rec} calls Q_{top} through formal parameter X (line 8).
7. Q_{top} calls Q_{bot} through formal parameter X of P_{init} (line 5).
8. Q_{bot} returns control to P_{init}, statement K, through formal parameter L, also terminating the activations of P_{rec} and Q_{top} (line 14).
9. P_{init} returns control to B, statement L (line 10).

At each of these steps the referencing environment must be modified. Figure 6-16 shows the referencing environment effective between each of the steps. Note that whenever a procedure or label is transmitted as a parameter to a new subprogram activation, a pointer to the local table in which the actual parameter reference was satisfied is also transmitted. For example, in step 2 when Q_{bot} is transmitted as an actual parameter to P, a pointer to the local table B in which the association for Q was found is also transmitted. In step 3 when Q_{bot} is called by P through the formal parameter X, the static chain pointer in the table for Q_{bot} may be set to point to table B, thus installing the appropriate nonlocal environment for execution of B. The reader is encouraged to determine himself for each step how the next environment may be set up from the previous one, given only the previous environment, the table formats of Fig. 6-15, and the program statement executed. Note that the current local environment at each step is indicated by a special static chain head (SCH) pointer stored in a fixed location. The tree structure representation rather than the explicit stack representation has been used to show more clearly the various referencing environments at each point during execution. Observe that local tables are destroyed strictly in the reverse order of their creation, and thus the tables may be created and destroyed in a single stack.

6-10. TRANSMITTING RESULTS BACK FROM SUBPROGRAMS

While our main focus in the preceding sections has been on the problems of local data in subprograms and the transmission of data to subprograms either through parameters or nonlocal environments, there remains the question of transmitting results back from subprograms. Three main methods are used:

1. Function values.
2. Modifiable parameters.
3. Changes in values of nonlocal variables (side effects).

Transmitting results through modification of nonlocal variables presents no particular difficulty. We have implicitly assumed that possibility in the preceding discussion of nonlocal environments. Function values and modifiable parameters require further discussion.

Ptr(n) represents the code pointer to the executable code for the line numbered *n* in Fig. 6-14; other pointers are indicated by arrows

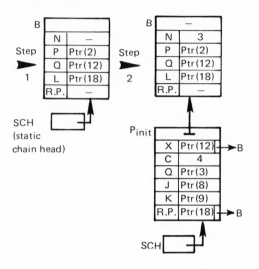

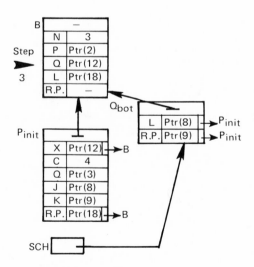

Fig. 6-16. Referencing environments during execution of program B (Fig. 6-14).

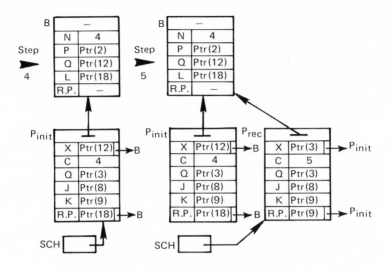

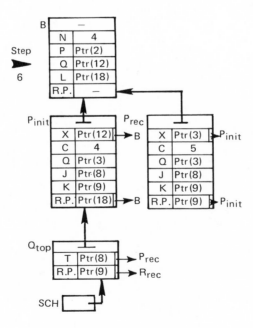

Fig. 6-16 (continued)

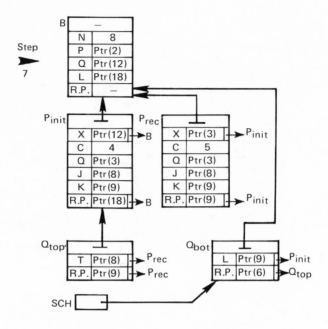

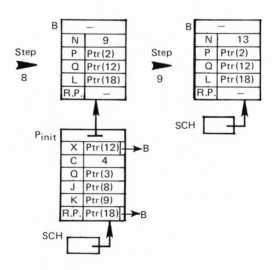

Fig. 6-16 (continued)

Modifiable Parameters

Parameters transmitted by reference may serve as a way of transmitting results back from a subprogram. This is the usual technique in FORTRAN, for example. Of course, the actual parameter must be a modifiable object, such as a simple or subscripted variable. When an assignment is made in the called subprogram to a formal parameter the result is reflected in a modified value of the corresponding actual parameter.

Parameters transmitted by name, where the actual parameter is a simple or subscripted variable, also allow results to be transmitted back from a subprogram through assignments to the corresponding formal parameter. The mechanism is more complex, however, as the actual parameters in some cases must be treated as subprograms (thunks) which return pointers to locations to which the assignment is then made.

Result Parameters. A useful alternative is provided by result parameters. A *result parameter* is a modifiable parameter in a subprogram which is used only for returning results to the calling program. The actual parameter must of course be modifiable, e.g., a simple or subscripted variable. In the called subprogram the formal parameter, tagged as a result parameter, is treated as a simple local variable throughout execution. On termination of the called subprogram, however, the final value of the formal parameter is set as the value of the corresponding actual parameter on return to the calling program.

Value-Result Parameters. It is natural to combine parameter transmission by value and result, allowing a parameter to serve both for input to and output from a subprogram. At the time of call the actual parameter is evaluated; the value transmitted becomes the initial value of the formal parameter. During execution of the called subprogram the formal parameter acts as an ordinary local variable. On exit the final value of the formal parameter is stored as the value of the corresponding actual parameter.

Value-result parameters are similar to reference parameters where the actual parameter is a simple or subscripted variable. The difference is that with reference parameters any change in the value of a formal parameter is immediately reflected as a change in the value of the corresponding actual parameter. With value-result parameters the value of the actual parameter changes only on final exit from the called subprogram.

Function Values

When a subprogram produces only a single result it is common to allow this result to be returned implicitly by treating the subprogram as a function. Often this is done by allowing the subprogram name to be treated as a variable to which assignments may be made during subprogram execution. The value of this *pseudovariable* on exit from the subprogram is returned as its *function value*. Another common technique is to explicitly designate the value to be returned by an expression at each point of exit of the subprogram, as is done in PL/I.

6-11. REFERENCES AND SUGGESTIONS FOR FURTHER READING

A central source of material on the problems of data control mechanisms and their associated implementation techniques is the volume edited by Tou and Wegner [1971]. In this volume the paper by Wegner [1971] provides a useful overview; the paper by Johnston [1971] presents the *contour model* for the representation of referencing environments, a model which is particularly useful for the clarification of environments based on static block structure; and the paper by Organick and Cleary [1971] describes a hardware implementation of a number of these concepts. Boyle and Grau [1970] treat static block structure referencing environments more theoretically.

The paper by Bobrow and Wegbreit [1973] provides an implementation structure suitable for handling referencing environments in languages using general sequence control structures such as coroutines. As a rule, in fact, most of the papers referenced in Chapter 5 that are concerned with subprogram sequence control mechanisms such as recursion, coroutines, parallel processes, and scheduled subprograms also discuss at length the related data control questions.

Parameter transmission techniques are often discussed in connection with compilation methods; see, e.g., Gries [1971]. The problems of label and procedure parameters are discussed in many of the papers in Tou and Wegner [1971] and also in papers by Reynolds [1970] and Moses [1970].

6-12. PROBLEMS

6-1. For the programs P, Q, and R, with local identifiers as given in Fig. 6-3, assume the following sequence of calls: P calls R which calls Q which calls R (recursively) which calls P (recursively).

    a. Show the contents of the central stack after this sequence of calls, as in Fig. 6-5, assuming the central stack simulation.

    b. Show the contents of the central table and the hidden stack after this sequence of calls, as in Fig. 6-7.

6-2. Explain why it is *impossible* in a language with only parameters transmitted by value or name, such as ALGOL, to write a subprogram *SWAP* of two parameters which simply swaps the values of its two parameters (which must be simple or subscripted variables). For example, *SWAP* called by *SWAP*(X,Y) should return with X having the original value of Y and Y the original value of X. Assume that *SWAP* works only for arguments of type real.

6-3. One variant of the central referencing environment table simulation of Section 6-5 is sometimes used in LISP implementations. Each identifier (atom in LISP) is paired with a separate little stack (usually part of its property list) which contains all the associations for that identifier. The current association is at the top of an identifier's stack; other associations on the stack represent inactive associations. When a subprogram is entered which has a new association for an identifier X, the new association is stacked on top of X's association stack. When execution of the subprogram is finished, the top entry on X's stack is simply deleted, restoring the old association.

    a. With this technique would a central stack still be needed? If so, what information would it need to contain?

    b. Discuss the relative advantages and disadvantages of this technique as compared to the central table technique outlined in Section 6-5.

6-4. The central referencing environment table stimulation of Section 6-5 could not be applied to a language such as ALGOL, where nonlocal referencing is based on the static block structure, as easily as it could to LISP or SNOBOL4, where nonlocal referencing uses the most recent association rule. Why?

6-5. Consider the following ALGOL-like program:

```
begin integer Y;
    procedure P(X); integer X;
        begin X := X + 1; print(X, Y)end proc P;
    Y := 1;
    P(Y);
    print(Y)
end
```

Give the three numbers printed in the case that Y is transmitted to P (a) by value, (b) by reference, and (c) by value-result.

6-6. The following ALGOL-like program appears to do very little:

```
begin integer I; integer array A[1:2];
   procedure F(X,Y); integer X,Y;
      begin    X := X + 1;
               Y := Y + 1;
               print(X,Y);
               X := X - 1;
               Y := Y - 1;
      end proc F;
      I := 1;
      A[1]  : = 5;
      A[2]  : = 10;
      F(I,A[I]);
      print(I,A[1],A[2]);
      F(A[I],I);
      print(I,A[1],A[2])
end
```

Give the ten values printed in each case when parameter transmission is as follows:

a. X and Y by reference.

b. X by reference, Y by name.

c. X by name, Y by reference.

d. X and Y by name.

6-7. What is the result of execution of B in example 6-1 if the most recent association rather than the static block structure rule is used to determine the nonlocal referencing environment?

6-8. One common restriction on actual parameter lists is that the same simple or subscripted variable cannot appear more than once in the list; e.g., CALL SUB(X,X) is not allowed. Explain the difficulties which such repeated parameters may cause for the programmer when parameter transmission is by value-result, reference, and name.

6-9. Suppose that you wished to modify ALGOL so that nonlocal referencing was based on the most recent association rule rather than the static block structure. How would the organization of the run-time central stack of environment tables have to be modified? In particular

a. What information would need to be deleted from each procedure or block local environment table in the stack?

b. What information would need to be added to each local table?

c. Describe how nonlocal referencing would work in this modified structure.

6-10. *Jensen's device.* Parameters transmitted by name allow use of a programming trick known as *Jensen's device* (discussed at length in Rutishauser [1967]). The basic idea is to transmit by name as separate parameters to a subprogram both an expression involving one or more variables and the variables themselves. By adroit changes in the values of the variables coupled with references to the formal parameter corresponding to the expression, the expression may be evaluated for many different values of the variables. A simple example of the technique is in the general-purpose summation routine SUM, defined in ALGOL as follows:

real procedure $SUM(EXPR,INDEX,LB,UB)$; value LB,UB;
    real $EXPR$; integer $INDEX,LB,UB$;
begin real $TEMP$; $TEMP := 0$;
    for $INDEX := LB$ step 1 until UB do $TEMP := TEMP + EXPR$;
    $SUM := TEMP$
end proc SUM;

In this program $EXPR$ and $INDEX$ are transmitted by name, and LB and UB by value. The call of SUM

$$SUM(A[I],I,1,25)$$

will return the sum of the first 25 elements of vector A. The call

$$SUM(A[I] \times B[I],I,1,25)$$

will return the sum of the products of the first 25 corresponding elements of vectors A and B (assuming that A and B have been appropriately declared). The call

$$SUM(C[K,2],K,-100,100)$$

will return the sum of the second column of matrix C from $C[-100,2]$ to $C[100,2]$.

  a. What call to SUM would give the sum of the elements on the main diagonal of a matrix D, declared as real array $D[1:50,1:50]$?
  b. What call to SUM would give the sum of the squares of the first 100 odd numbers?
  c. Use Jensen's device to write a general-purpose MAX routine that will return the maximum value from a set of values obtained by evaluating an arbitrary expression $EXPR$ containing an index $INDEX$ which varies over a range from LB to UB in steps of $STEP$ size (an integer).
  d. Show how the effect of Jensen's device may be obtained by using subprograms as parameters in a language without parameter transmission by name.

6-11. How must the central referencing environment table simulation of the most recent association rule for nonlocal environments be modified if local environments for subprograms are retained between calls rather than being created on each entry and destroyed on exit? Assume that no recursion is allowed.

6-12. LISP and SNOBOL4 each allow new identifiers to be added to the referencing environment of a subprogram during its execution, as global identifiers. Each language uses the most recent association rule for nonlocal referencing. Assuming that the central table simulation for referencing environments is used, explain the effect that the introduction of new identifiers has on the structure and use of the central table.

6-13. For the ALGOL program of Fig. 6-14, give the run-time representation of each identifier in each subprogram or block as an integer pair (n, k), where n represents the number of tables down the static chain and k represents the offset within that table.

6-14. Propose an appropriate method of handling local and nonlocal referencing in *recursive coroutines* (Problem 5-12). Provide arguments as to why your techniques are the appropriate ones.

6-15. In LISP it is possible for a subprogram to *construct* a new subprogram during its execution and return the new subprogram as its result. The calling program may then execute the new subprogram with appropriate parameters just as though it had always existed. Suppose that the new subprogram contains a nonlocal reference to X. The association retrieved for X during execution of the new subprogram might be

1. The association for X in effect at the point of *call* of the new subprogram, or

2. The association for X in effect at the point of *creation* of the subprogram.

Explain how each of these two choices might be simulated if the central stack method and the most recent association rule are used in LISP for the simulation of referencing.

7 STORAGE MANAGEMENT

Storage is one of the scarce resources in any computing system. Storage management is one of the central concerns of the programmer, language implementor, and language designer. In this chapter the various problems and techniques in storage management are considered in their relation to programming language design.

7-1. INTRODUCTION

Programming language design is strongly influenced by storage management considerations. Typically languages contain many features or restrictions which may be explained only by a desire on the part of the designers to allow one or another storage management technique to be used. Take, for example, the restriction in FORTRAN to nonrecursive subprogram calls. Recursive calls could be allowed in FORTRAN without change in the syntax, but their implementation would require a run-time stack of return points, a structure necessitating dynamic storage management during execution. Without recursive calls FORTRAN may be implemented with only static storage management. ALGOL is carefully designed to allow stack-based storage management, LISP to allow garbage collection, etc.

Storage management is one of the first concerns of the language implementor as well. While each language design ordinarily permits the use of certain storage management techniques, the details of the mechanisms, and their representation in hardware and software, are the task of the implementor. For example, while the LISP design may point to a free space list and garbage collection as the appropriate basis for storage management, there are a number of different garbage collection techniques known. The implementor must choose or design one appropriate to the available hardware and software.

The programmer is also deeply concerned with storage management, but his position is somewhat anomalous. While it is of major importance to the programmer to design programs that use storage efficiently, he is likely to have little direct control over storage management. His program affects storage management only indirectly through the use or lack of use of different language features. His position is made more difficult by the tendency of both language designers and language implementors to treat storage management as a *machine-dependent* topic which should not be directly discussed in language manuals. Thus it is often difficult for a programmer to discover what storage management techniques are actually used. The cost of using different language features is often proportional to the cost of the storage management involved, and where the programmer cannot discover what storage management techniques are used he has no rational way to determine the relative costs of various algorithms for the solution of a given problem.

7-2. MAJOR RUN-TIME ELEMENTS REQUIRING STORAGE

The programmer tends to view storage management largely in terms of storage of his data structures and translated programs. However, run-time storage management encompasses many other areas besides these. Some, such as return points for subprograms, have been touched on in preceding chapters; others have not yet been mentioned explicitly. Let us look at the major program and data elements requiring storage during program execution.

Translated User Programs. A major block of storage in any system must be allocated to store the translated form of user programs, regardless of whether programs are hardware- or software-interpreted. In the former case programs will be blocks of executable machine code; in the latter case programs will be in some intermediate form.

System Run-Time Programs. Another substantial block of storage during execution must be allocated to system programs that support the execution of the user programs. These may range from simple *library routines*, such as sine, cosine, or square root functions, to software interpreters or translators present during execution. Also included here are the routines that control run-time storage management. These system programs would ordinarily be blocks of hardware-executable machine code, regardless of the executable form of user programs.

User-Defined Data Structures and Constants. Space for user data must be allocated. This includes mainly data structures declared in or created by user programs, although constants used in programs must also be stored.

Subprogram Return and (Reentry) Points. Internally generated sequence control information, such as subprogram return points, coroutine resume points, or event notices for scheduled subprograms, must be allocated storage. As noted in Chapter 5 storage of these data may require only single locations, a central stack, or other run-time storage structure.

Referencing Environments. Storage of referencing environments (identifier associations) during execution may require substantial space, as, for example, the LISP A-list (Chapter 14). Some languages, such as FORTRAN, require little or no storage for this purpose.

Temporaries in Expression Evaluation. Expression evaluation requires use of system-defined temporary storage for the intermediate results of evaluation. For example, in evaluation of the expression $X \times Y + U \times V$ the result of the first multiplication must be stored in a temporary while the second multiplication is performed. When expressions may involve recursive function calls, a potentially unlimited number of temporaries may be required to store partial results at each level of recursion.

Temporaries in Parameter Transmission. When a subprogram is called, a list of actual parameters must be evaluated and the resulting values stored in temporary storage until evaluation of the entire list is complete. Where evaluation of one parameter may require evaluation of recursive function calls a potentially unlimited amount of storage may be required, as in expression evaluation.

Input-Output Buffers. Ordinarily input and output operations work through buffers which serve as temporary storage areas where data are stored between the time of the actual physical transfer of the data to or from external storage and the program-initiated input and output operations. Often hundreds (or thousands) of memory locations must be reserved for these buffers during execution.

Miscellaneous System Data. In almost every language implementation, storage is required for various system data: tables, status information for input-output, and various miscellaneous pieces of state information (e.g., reference counts or garbage collection bits).

From this list it is clear that storage management concerns storage for much more than simply user programs and data. More importantly, much of the information requiring storage is hidden from the language user.

7-3. PROGRAMMER- AND SYSTEM-CONTROLLED STORAGE MANAGEMENT

To what extent should the programmer be allowed to directly control storage management? On the one hand, PL/I allows some direct control by the programmer through statements such as ALLOCATE and FREE, which allocate and free storage for programmer-defined data structures. On the other hand, many, if not most, high-level languages allow the programmer no direct control. Storage management is affected only implicitly through the use of various language features.

The difficulty with programmer control of storage management is twofold: It may place a large and often undesirable burden on the programmer, and it may also interfere with the necessary system-controlled storage management. No high-level language can allow the programmer to shoulder the entire storage management burden. For example, the programmer can hardly be expected to concern himself with storage for temporaries, subprogram return points, or other system data. At best he might control storage management for his data (and perhaps programs). Yet even simple allocation and freeing of storage for data structures, as in PL/I, is likely to permit generation of garbage and dangling references. Thus programmer-controlled storage management is "dangerous" to the programmer because it may lead to subtle errors or loss of access to available storage. Programmer-controlled storage management also may interfere with system-controlled storage management, in that special storage areas and storage management routines may be required for programmer-controlled storage, allowing less efficient use of storage overall.

The advantage of allowing programmer control of storage management lies in the fact that it is often extremely difficult for the system to determine when storage may be most effectively allocated and freed. The programmer, on the other hand, often knows quite precisely when a particular data structure is needed or when it is no longer needed and may be freed.

7-4. STORAGE MANAGEMENT PHASES: INITIAL ALLOCATION, RECOVERY, COMPACTION, AND REUSE

It is convenient to identify three basic aspects of storage management:

1. *Initial allocation*. At the start of execution each piece of storage may be either already allocated for some use or free. If free initially, it is available to be allocated dynamically as execution proceeds. Any storage management system requires some technique for keeping track of free storage as well as mechanisms for allocation of free storage as the need arises during execution.

2. *Recovery*. Storage which has been allocated and used for awhile and which subsequently becomes available must be recovered by the storage manager for reuse. Recovery may be very simple, as in the repositioning of a stack pointer, or very complex, as in garbage collection.

3. *Compaction and reuse.* Storage recovered may be immediately ready for reuse, or compaction may be necessary to construct large blocks of free storage from small pieces. Reuse of storage ordinarily involves the same mechanisms as initial allocation.

Many different storage management techniques are known and in use in language implementations. It is impossible to survey them all, but a relative handful suffice to represent the basic approaches. Most techniques are variants of one of these basic methods.

7-5. STATIC STORAGE MANAGEMENT

The simplest form of allocation is *static allocation*, that is, allocation during translation which remains fixed throughout execution. Ordinarily storage for user and system programs is allocated statically, as is storage for I/O buffers and various miscellaneous system data. Static allocation requires no run-time storage management software, and, of course, there is no concern for recovery and reuse.

In the usual FORTRAN implementation all storage is allocated statically. Each subprogram is compiled separately, with the compiler setting up a block of storage containing the compiled program, its data areas, temporaries, return point location, and miscellaneous items of system data. The loader allocates space in memory for these compiled blocks at load time, as well as space for system run-time routines. During program execution no storage management takes place.

Static storage allocation is efficient, because no time or space is expended for storage management during execution. However, it is incompatible with recursive subprogram calls, with data structures whose size is dependent on computed or input data, and with many other desirable language features. In the remaining sections of this chapter we shall discuss various techniques for *dynamic* (run-time) *storage management*. However, the reader should not lose sight of the importance of the static allocation method—for many programs static allocation is quite satisfactory. Two of the most widely used programming languages, FORTRAN and COBOL, are designed for strictly static storage allocation.

7-6. STACK-BASED STORAGE MANAGEMENT

The simplest run-time storage management technique is the stack-based technique. Free storage at the start of execution is set up as a sequential block in memory. As storage is allocated it is taken from sequential locations in this stack beginning at one end. Storage must be freed in the reverse order of allocation, so that a block of storage being freed is always at the top of the stack. This organization makes trivial the problems of storage recovery, compaction, and reuse.

A single *stack pointer* is basically all that is needed to control storage management. The stack pointer always points to the next available word of free storage in the stack block, representing the current top of the stack. All storage in use lies in the stack below the location pointed to by the stack pointer. All free storage lies above the pointer. When a block of k locations is to be allocated the pointer is simply moved to point k locations farther up the stack area. When a block of k locations is freed, the pointer is moved back k locations. There are no problems of compaction; compaction is automatic.

It is the strictly nested last-in—first-out structure of subprogram calls and returns in most languages that makes stack storage management an appealing technique. Many of the program and data elements requiring storage are tied to subprogram activations. Stack storage is often appropriate for both subprogram return points and local environment tables for subprograms, as discussed in previous chapters. In addition, temporaries for expression evaluation and parameter transmission may ordinarily be allocated on the basis of subprogram activations. The translator usually can determine the number of temporaries needed for each activation of a subprogram. During execution temporaries may be allocated in a stack as each new subprogram activation is initiated and deleted on termination. Also important in many languages, e.g., ALGOL, is the restriction that programmer data structures may be created only on subprogram entry and must necessarily be destroyed on exit. This organization allows stack allocation for programmer data structures as well.

Grouping those elements associated with a subprogram activation which require stack allocation into a single *activation record* is a common technique. When a subprogram is called, a new activation record is created on the top of the stack. Termination causes its deletion from the stack.

Most ALGOL implementations are built around a single central stack of activation records for subprograms (and blocks), together with a statically allocated area containing user- and system-executable programs, input-output buffers, and constants. The structure of a typical activation record for an ALGOL subprogram is shown in Fig. 7-1. The activation record contains all the variable items of information associated with a given subprogram activation. Figure 7-2 shows a typical memory organization during ALGOL execution.

The use of a stack in a LISP implementation is somewhat different. Here also subprogram (function) calls are strictly nested and a stack may be used for activation records. Each activation record contains a return point and temporaries for expression evaluation and parameter transmission. Local referencing environments (A-list entries) might also be allocated in the same stack, except that the programmer is allowed to directly manipulate these associations. Therefore they are ordinarily stored in a separate stack, represented as a linked list, called the A-list. The stack containing return points and temporaries may then be hidden from the programmer and allocated sequentially. LISP implementation requires also a *heap* storage area which is managed through a free space list and garbage collection, with a special area and storage manager for *full-word* data items such as numbers. A typical LISP memory organization is illustrated in Fig. 7-3.

The use of a stack for subprogram activation records (or partial activation records as in LISP) is characteristic of implementation of

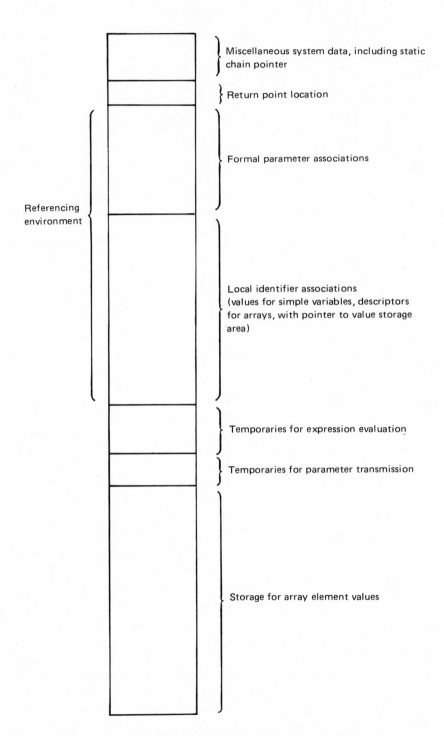

Fig. 7-1. Structure of a typical ALGOL subprogram activation record.

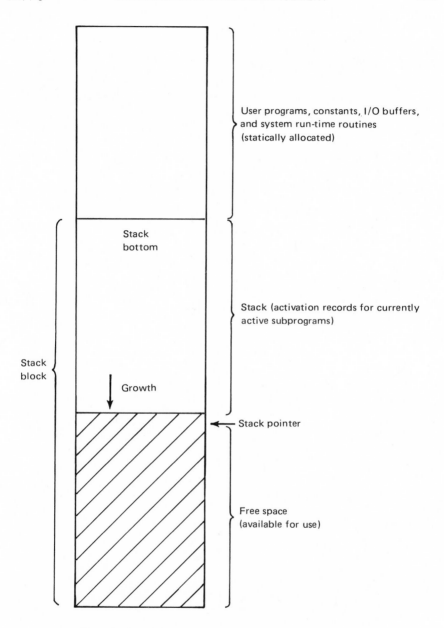

Fig. 7-2. Typical memory organization during ALGOL execution.

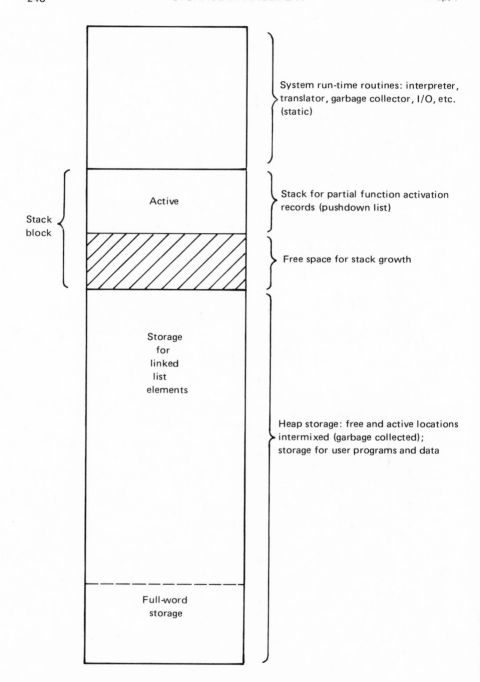

Fig. 7-3. Typical LISP memory organization during execution.

every language in Part II except FORTRAN and COBOL. Stack-based storage management is undoubtedly the most widely used technique for run-time storage management.

7-7. HEAP STORAGE MANAGEMENT: FIXED-SIZE ELEMENTS

The third basic type of storage management, besides static and stack-based management, may be termed *heap storage management*. A *heap* is a block of storage within which pieces are allocated and freed in some relatively unstructured manner. Here the problems of storage allocation, recovery, compaction, and reuse may be severe. There is no single heap storage management technique, but rather a collection of techniques for handling various aspects of heap storage management. We shall survey the basic techniques here, without attempting to be comprehensive.

The need for heap storage and storage management arises when a language requires storage to be allocated and freed at arbitrary points during program execution, as when a language allows creation, destruction, or extension of programmer data structures at arbitrary program points. For example, in SNOBOL4 two strings may be concatenated to create a new string at any arbitrary point during execution. Storage must be allocated for the new string at the time it is created. In LISP a new element may be added to an existing list structure at any point, again requiring storage to be allocated. In both SNOBOL4 and LISP, storage may also be freed at unpredictable points during execution.

It is convenient to divide heap storage management techniques into two categories depending on whether the elements allocated are always of the same fixed size or of variable size. Where fixed-size elements are used, management techniques may be considerably simplified. Compaction, in particular, is not a problem. We shall consider the fixed-size case in this section, leaving the variable-size case until the following section.

Assume that the fixed-size elements which are allocated from the heap and later recovered occupy N words of memory each. Typically N might be 1 or 2. Assuming the heap occupies a contiguous block of memory, we conceptually divide the heap block into a sequence of K elements, each N words long, where $K \times N$ = length of the heap block. This division of the heap into K fixed-size elements forms the basis for our heap storage management. Whenever an element is needed one of these is allocated from the heap. Whenever an element is freed it must be one of these original heap elements.

Initial Allocation and Reuse: Free Space Lists

Initial allocation from the heap might be accomplished with a simple *heap pointer*, similar to the stack pointer used earlier, which points to the next available free element in the heap at all times. Each time a new element is needed the heap pointer is advanced to point to the next heap element, and a pointer to the allocated element is returned. Note, however, that such a heap pointer cannot be of any help when an element is freed, because the element will in general lie at some arbitrary point back in the allocated part of the heap. Thus we are constrained to *advance* the heap pointer during allocation, using some other mechanism to keep track of storage which has been freed. Eventually the heap pointer reaches the end of the heap storage block. At that point we must begin to reuse storage back in the heap block which has been freed, moving to some new allocation technique (or compacting the free space at the end of the heap block and resetting the heap pointer, but this is seldom done with fixed-size elements).

How are we to keep track of the various elements back in the heap which have been freed? In general, these free elements will be scattered in some random pattern throughout the heap, intermixed with elements currently in use. The common technique is to maintain a linked list of these free elements, termed a *free space list*. A fixed storage location outside the heap is chosen as the head of the free space list. This location at all times contains a pointer to some free element in the heap (assuming that there is at least one). A pointer within that free element points to another free element, which links to yet another, etc.

Allocation of elements from such a free space list is simple. When an element is needed the list head location is accessed. The pointer there points to a free element which may be deleted from the list by taking the pointer it contains (which points to the second free element on the list) and storing this pointer in the list head, making this second element the new first list element. The deleted element is now available for use (Fig. 7-4).

When an element in use is freed the inverse process adds it to the head of the free space list. The pointer in the list head is stored in the newly freed element, and a pointer to this new element is stored in the list head (Fig. 7-4).

Because a free space list must be maintained anyway, it is often convenient to eliminate the heap pointer used for initial heap allocation and instead use the free space list as the source of elements

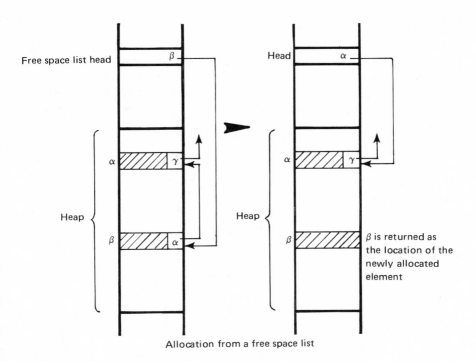

Allocation from a free space list

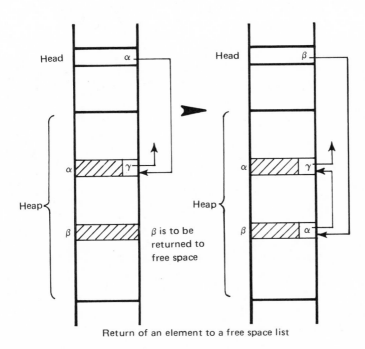

Return of an element to a free space list

Fig. 7-4. Allocation and return with a free space list.

throughout execution. To accomplish this result, all the elements in the entire heap block must be chained together into an initial free space list at the start of execution. Figure 7-5 illustrates such an initial free space list as well as the list after allocation and freeing of a number of elements.

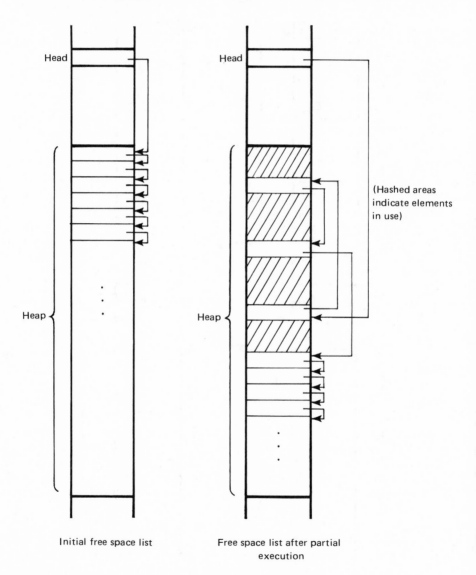

Fig. 7-5. Free space list structure .

Recovery: Explicit Return, Reference Counts, and Garbage Collection

Return of newly freed storage to the free space list is simple, provided such storage may be identified and recovered. But identification and recovery may be quite difficult. The problem lies in determining which elements in the heap are available for reuse and therefore may be returned to the free space list. Three solutions are in fairly wide use.

Explicit Return by Programmer or System. The simplest recovery technique is that of *explicit return.* When an element which has been in use becomes available for reuse it must be explicitly identified as "free" and returned to the free space list. Where the space has been used for a programmer-defined data structure the programmer is provided with a FREE or ERASE command which is used to explicitly designate data structures to be returned. Where elements are used for system purposes, such as storage of referencing environments, return points, or temporaries, or where all storage management is system-controlled, each system routine is responsible for returning space as it becomes available for reuse, through explicit call of a FREE routine with the appropriate element as a parameter.

Explicit return would seem the natural recovery technique for heap storage, but unfortunately it is not always feasible. The reasons lie with two old problems: *garbage* and *dangling references.* We first discussed these problems in Chapter 4 in connection with destruction of data structures. If a structure is destroyed (and the storage freed) before all access paths to the structure have been destroyed, the remaining access paths become dangling references. On the other hand, if the last access path to a structure is destroyed without the structure itself being destroyed and the storage recovered, then the structure becomes garbage. In the context of heap storage management a dangling reference is a pointer to an element that has been returned to the free space list (or a pointer to an element that has been returned and later reallocated for another purpose). A garbage element is one that is available for reuse but not on the free space list and which thus is inaccessible.

Both garbage and dangling references are potentially troublesome for a storage management system. If garbage accumulates, available storage is gradually reduced until the program may be unable to continue for lack of known free space. Dangling references may cause chaos. If a program attempts to modify through a dangling reference a structure that has already been destroyed, the contents of an element on the free space list may be modified inadvertently. If this modification overwrites the pointer linking the element to the next free space list element, the entire remainder of the free space list may become garbage. Even worse, a later attempt by the storage allocator to use the pointer in the overwritten element leads to completely unpredictable results; e.g., a piece of an executable program may be allocated as "free space" and later modified. Similar sorts of problems arise if the element pointed to by the dangling reference has already been reallocated to another use before a reference is made.

Recovery of heap storage by explicit return often leads to the potential to create garbage and dangling references. For example, consider the PL/I statements

| ALLOCATE ELEM SET(P) | (allocates an element from free space and sets variable P to contain a pointer to it) |
| P = Q | (destroys the only pointer to the element, leaving it as garbage) |

or

ALLOCATE ELEM SET(P)	
Q = P	(copies the pointer in P into Q)
FREE P - > ELEM	(destroys the element pointed to by P, freeing the storage for reuse; the pointer in Q is not destroyed, however, leaving a dangling reference)

It is easy in such cases for the programmer inadvertently to create garbage or dangling references, with the resulting sometimes dire consequences.

It may be equally difficult for the run-time system to avoid creating garbage or dangling references. For example, in LISP, linked lists are a basic data structure. One of the primitive LISP operations is CDR, which, given a pointer to one element on a linked list, returns a pointer to the next element in the list (see Fig. 7-6). The element originally pointed to *may* have been freed by the CDR operation, provided the original pointer given CDR was the only pointer to the

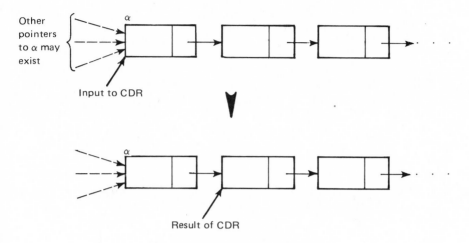

Should CDR free element α?

Fig. 7-6. The LISP CDR operation.

element. If CDR does not return the element to the free space list at this point, it becomes garbage. However, if CDR does return the element to free space and other pointers to it exist, then they become dangling references. If there is no direct way to determine whether such pointers exist, then the CDR primitive must potentially generate garbage or dangling references.

Owing to these problems with explicit return, alternative approaches are desirable. One alternative, called *garbage collection*, is to allow garbage to be created but no dangling references. Later if the free space list becomes exhausted, a *garbage collector* mechanism is invoked to identify and recover the garbage. A second alternative, that of *reference counts*, requires explicit return but provides a way of checking the number of pointers to a given element so that no dangling references are created.

Reference Counts. The use of reference counts is the simpler of the two techniques, so we shall take it up first. The basic concept is this: Within each element in the heap allow some extra space for a *reference counter*. The reference counter of an element contains at all times an integer, the *reference count*, indicating the number of pointers to that element which exist. When an element is initially allocated from the free space list its reference count is set to 1. Each time a new pointer to the element is created its reference count is increased by 1. Each time a pointer is destroyed the reference count

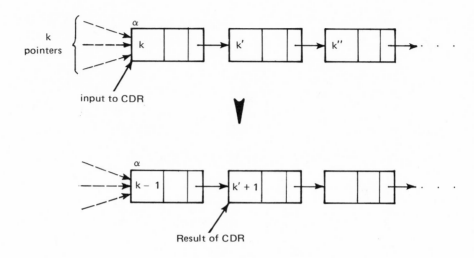

Result of CDR

If k − 1 = 0, element α may be freed safely

Fig. 7-7. The LISP CDR operation with reference counts.

is decreased by 1. When the reference count of an element reaches zero the element is free and may be returned to the free space list.

Reference counts allow both garbage and dangling references to be avoided in most situations. Consider the LISP CDR operation again (Fig. 7-6). If each list element contains a reference count, then it is simple for the CDR operation to avoid the previous difficulties. CDR must subtract 1 from the reference count of the element originally pointed to by its input. If the result leaves a reference count of zero, then the element may be returned to the free space list, and if nonzero, then the element is still pointed to by other pointers and cannot be considered free (see Fig. 7-7).

Where the programmer is allowed an explicit FREE or ERASE statement, reference counts also provide protection. The result of a FREE statement is only to decrement the reference count of the structure by 1. Only if the count then is zero is the structure actually returned to the free space list. A nonzero reference count indicates that the structure is still accessible and that the FREE command should be ignored.

The reference count technique fails in the case of circularly linked groups of elements. Consider a simple circular linked list as in Fig. 7-8, with one pointer to a list element from outside. If this pointer is destroyed, the reference count of the list element pointed to becomes 1, yet as this pointer was the only path to the structure from outside,

Pointer (stored elsewhere)

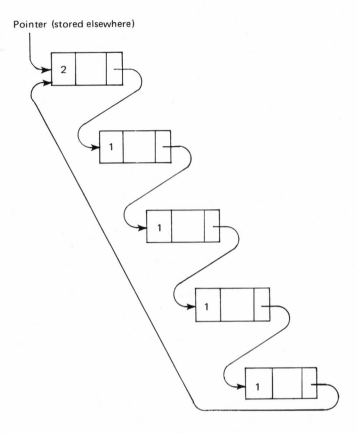

Fig. 7-8. Circular list with reference counts.

the structure as a whole has become inaccessible and thus garbage. Unfortunately, none of the list elements has a reference count of zero so no recovery is possible.

The difficulty with circular structures is not the most important difficulty associated with reference counts, however. In many cases circular structures are not allowed or occur so infrequently that the potential for garbage generation is not serious. More telling is the *cost of maintaining* the reference counts. Reference count testing, incrementing, and decrementing must go on continuously throughout execution, often causing a substantial decrease in execution efficiency. Consider, for example, the simple assignment P := Q, where P and Q are both pointer variables. Without reference counts it suffices to simply copy the pointer in Q into P. With reference counts we must do the following:

1. Access the element pointed to by P and decrement its reference count by 1. Test the resulting count, and if zero, return the element to the free space list.

2. Copy the pointer in Q into P.

3. Access the element pointed to by Q and increment its reference count by 1.

The total cost of the assignment operation has been increased substantially. Any similar operation which may create or destroy pointers must modify reference counts also. In addition, there is the cost of the extra storage for the reference counts. If extra space exists in heap elements already, this storage may be no problem. More commonly an extra location would be necessary in each element to contain the reference count. Where elements are only one or two locations in length to begin with, storage of reference counts may substantially reduce the storage available for data.

The cost of maintaining reference counts may be reduced sharply in many cases by restricting pointer use so that only certain elements may have reference counts other than 1 (or some other constant). In such a case reference counts need be maintained only for those special elements with variable reference counts. Consider, for example, a list-processing system in which each linked list is considered a separate data structure. If we provide each list with a special *header element* and allow pointers from other lists to point only to this header and never to any internal list element, then only the header element needs a reference count. The internal list elements always have a constant 1 reference count (in the case of a singly linked list, or 2 in the case of a doubly linked list). Moreover, the header reference count need only count pointers from outside the structure. This is illustrated in Fig. 7-9. Individual elements may be deleted from such a list and returned immediately to the free storage list without concern for reference counts. When the reference count of the header is reduced to zero (when a pointer stored in another list is destroyed, for example) then the entire list—header and all the elements—may be returned to the free list. Care must be taken, however, that each element of the freed list is checked for pointers to other lists. Whenever such a pointer is found the reference count of the list pointed to must be decremented and tested for zero as well.

As one restricts the use of reference counts to larger structures the cost in both storage and processing time decreases, but there is a corresponding loss in flexibility in the manner in which structures

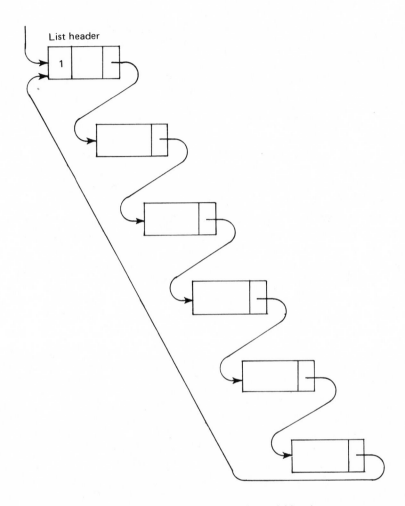

Fig. 7-9. Circular list with special header.

may be linked (because linking must be done through the header). Note also that the problem of circular linkages *within* a structure disappears; i.e., a single structure may contain circular linkages. Only circular linkages *between* structures cause difficulty.

Garbage Collection. Returning to the basic problems of garbage and dangling references, we may readily agree that dangling references are potentially far more damaging than garbage. Garbage accumulation causes a drain on the amount of usable storage, but dangling references may lead to complete chaos because of random modification of storage in use. Of course, the two problems are related: Dangling references result when storage is freed "too soon," and garbage when storage is not freed until "too late." Where it is infeasible or too costly to avoid both problems simultaneously through a mechanism such as reference counts, garbage generation is clearly to be preferred in order to avoid dangling references. It is better not to recover storage at all than to recover it too soon.

The basic philosophy behind garbage collection is simply to allow garbage to be generated in order to avoid dangling references. When the free space list is entirely exhausted and more storage is needed, the computation is suspended temporarily and an extraordinary procedure instituted, a *garbage collection*, which identifies garbage elements in the heap and returns them to the free space list. The original computation is then resumed, and garbage again accumulates until the free space list is exhausted, at which time another garbage collection is initiated, etc.

Because garbage collection is done only rarely (when the free space list is exhausted), it is allowable for the procedure to be fairly costly. Two stages are involved:

1. *Marking active elements.* In the first stage each element in the heap which is active, i.e., which is part of an accessible data structure, must be marked. Each element must contain a *garbage collection bit* set initially to "on." The marking algorithm sets the garbage collection bit of each active element "off."

2. *Collecting garbage elements.* Once the marking algorithm has marked active elements, all those remaining whose garbage collection bit is "on" are garbage and may be returned to the free space list. A simple sequential scan of the heap is sufficient. The garbage collection bit of each element is checked as it is encountered in the scan. If "off," the element is passed over; if "on," the element is linked into the free space list. All garbage collection bits are reset to "on" during the scan (to prepare for a later garbage collection).

The marking part of garbage collection is the most difficult. Since the free space list is exhausted when garbage collection is initiated, each element in the heap is either active (i.e., still in use) or garbage. Unfortunately, inspection of an element cannot indicate its status, because there is nothing intrinsic to a garbage element to indicate that it is garbage. Moreover, the presence of a pointer to an element from another heap element does not necessarily indicate that the element pointed to is active; it may be that both elements are garbage (recall the circular list of Fig. 7-8). Thus a simple scan of the heap which looks for pointers and marks the elements pointed to as active does not suffice.

When is a heap element active? Clearly, an element is active if there is a pointer to it from *outside the heap* or in another *active* heap element. If it is possible to identify all such outside pointers and mark the appropriate heap elements, then an iterative marking process may be initiated which searches these active elements for pointers to other unmarked elements. These new elements are then marked and searched for other pointers, etc. A fairly disciplined use of pointers is necessary because three critical assumptions underlie this marking process:

1. Any active element must be reachable by a chain of pointers beginning outside the heap.

2. It must be possible to identify every pointer outside the heap which points to an element inside the heap.

3. It must be possible to identify within any active heap element the fields which contain pointers to other heap elements.

If any of these assumptions are unsatisfied, then the marking process will fail to mark some active elements. The result will be recovery of active elements and thus the generation of dangling references.

The manner in which these assumptions are satisfied in a typical LISP implementation is instructive. First each heap element is formatted identically, usually with two pointer fields and a set of extra bits for system data (including a garbage collection bit). Since each heap element contains exactly two pointers, and these pointers are always in the same positions within the element, assumption 3 is satisfied. Second, there is only a small set of *system data structures* which may contain pointers into the heap (the A-list, the OB-list, the pushdown list, etc.). Marking starting from these system data structures is guaranteed to allow identification of all external pointers into the heap, as required by assumption 2. Finally it is impossible to reach a heap element other than through a chain of pointers beginning outside the heap. For example, a pointer to a heap element cannot be computed by addition of a constant to another pointer. Thus, assumption 1 is satisfied.

Satisfying the assumptions necessary for garbage collection may be difficult. Consider assumption 3. It requires that every heap element have the same format, that the position of pointers within an element be tagged, that a format designator be stored in each element, or that the marking algorithm "know" where the pointers are in any element it reaches, using some external rules about the structure of data and pointer chains. Such special requirements for garbage collection place an extra burden on the designer of a language implementation in addition to those imposed directly by the language design.

Given that the assumptions above are satisfied, how is the actual marking to be done? The basic algorithm is obvious: Begin with the pointers outside the heap and exhaustively follow chains of pointers through the heap until every active element has been marked. An algorithm with a temporary stack might be used:

1. Enter in the stack all the external pointers to heap elements. Before each pointer is stacked, test if the element to which it points is marked. If already marked, then the pointer is a duplicate and need not be stacked. If not marked, mark it.

2. Take the top stack pointer. Pop it off the stack and stack all pointers to unmarked heap elements contained in the element to which it points. As each new pointer is added to the stack, mark the element to which it points.

3. Repeat step 2 until the stack is empty.

This procedure is straightforward but immediately raises another problem: Where is space for the stack to be found? Recall that garbage collection was initiated because we were out of known free space in the heap. We might have a separate storage area for the stack, but then this space would be lost for other purposes. Moreover, this stack area would have to be rather large if we wished to ensure that garbage collection could always be completed without overflowing the stack (see Problem 7-4). As a result a stack-based marking algorithm is not entirely appropriate, although conceptually simple.

An elegant alternative is an algorithm given by Schorr and Waite [1967]. Beginning with an external pointer into the heap a pointer chain is traversed to the end. As each pointer is traversed the element reached is marked and the pointer *reversed*. When the end of a chain is reached the reversed pointers allow traversal back out of the chain. In the process, side chains are traversed in a similar manner. The algorithm requires two traversals of each pointer chain (one in each direction), but only two extra registers (rather than a stack) are needed for temporary storage. In addition, each element must have space for an extra *tag field* big enough to hold an integer equal to the length of an element.

In more detail the Schorr and Waite algorithm (slightly modified) may be described as follows. Assume for simplicity that each pointer in an active heap element is contained in a separate location within the element. (Problem 7-5 treats the case of more than one pointer per location within an element.) All heap elements have a garbage collection bit set "on" initially. The two extra registers are designated CE (for *current element*) and LE (for *last element*). Initially CE is set to contain one of the external pointers to a heap element and LE is set to NIL. Marking proceeds as follows:

1. *Mark the current element.* Test the garbage collection bit of the current element, the element pointed to by CE. If "off," then the element has already been processed; go to step 3. If "on," set it to "off" and set the tag field to zero.

2. *Follow a pointer to a new element.* Let j be the contents of the tag field of the current element. Scan the current element, beginning at the $j + 1st$ location, for pointers to other heap elements. If none are found, go to step 3. If a pointer is found in the kth location, set the tag field to k and do a circular transfer of pointers between CE, LE, and the kth location. CE gets the pointer found in the kth location, LE gets the original contents of CE, and the kth location gets the original contents of LE. Return to step 1.

3. *Retrace a chain to a preceding element.* If LE is NIL, go to step 4. Otherwise return to the element pointed to by LE. If the tag field of this element contains k, do a (reverse) circular transfer of pointers between the kth location, LE, and CE. LE gets the pointer in the kth location, CE gets the original contents of LE, and the kth location gets the pointer originally in CE. Return to step 2.

4. *Move to the next structure to be marked.* All the active elements reachable from the original external pointer have now been marked. Proceed to set CE to the next external pointer into the heap and begin again at step 1.

Figure 7-10 illustrates the marking of a list structure by this algorithm.

This algorithm is considerably less efficient than the simple stack marking algorithm since each list must be traversed twice rather than only once. Schorr and Waite suggest that a better garbage collection technique would combine the stack marking algorithm and the marking algorithm just given, using a fixed-size block as a stack until it was full and then using the latter algorithm. Many other marking algorithms are known as well; see Knuth's discussion and analysis [1968].

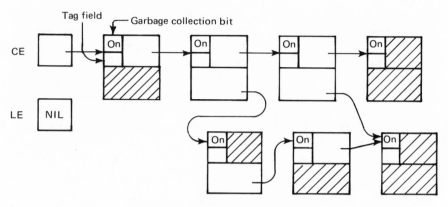

Structure at the start of marking
(fields not containing pointers are shaded)

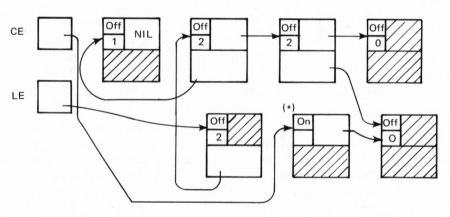

Structure during marking, immediately before marking of the element (*)

Fig. 7-10. Marking during garbage collection.

One of the striking features of garbage collection as a method of storage recovery is that its cost is *inversely* proportional to the amount of storage recovered (roughly speaking); i.e., the less storage recovered, the more it costs to garbage collect. The reason is that most of the cost of garbage collection is in the marking phase, and marking becomes more complex as the number of active elements in the heap increases. In contrast the cost of recovery using reference counts is directly proportional to the amount of storage recovered. As a result of this property of garbage collection the technique becomes very expensive when the heap is nearly full of active elements. In fact often when a program is about to use up all the heap (and thus halt for lack of storage) it will first initiate a number of expensive and relatively fruitless garbage collections, each of which produces only a few free locations which are immediately consumed when execution resumes, leading immediately to another garbage collection. The assumption is often made in designing garbage collection algorithms that any program which has almost used up the heap will almost surely soon use it up entirely, and thus a garbage collection which produces fewer than some minimum number of free locations should probably cause program termination anyway.

7-8. HEAP STORAGE MANAGEMENT: VARIABLE-SIZE ELEMENTS

Heap storage management where variable-size elements are allocated and recovered is more difficult than with fixed-size elements, although many of the same concepts apply. Variable-size elements arise in many situations. For example, if space is being used for programmer-defined data structures stored sequentially, such as arrays, then variable-size blocks of space will be required, or activation records for subprograms might be allocated in a heap (e.g., in a simulation language) in sequential blocks of varying sizes.

The major difficulties with variable-size elements concern reuse of recovered space. Even if we recover two five-word blocks of space in the heap, it may be impossible to satisfy a later request for a six-word block. This problem did not arise in the simpler case of fixed-size blocks; recovered space could always be immediately reused.

Initial Allocation and Reuse

With fixed-size elements it was appropriate to immediately split the heap into a set of elements and then base initial allocation on a free space list containing these elements. Such a technique is not acceptable with variable-size elements. Instead we wish to maintain free space in blocks of as large a size as possible. Initially then we consider the heap as simply one large block of free storage. A *heap pointer* is appropriate for initial allocation. When a block of N words is requested the heap pointer is advanced by N and the original heap pointer value returned as a pointer to the newly allocated element. As storage is freed behind the advancing heap pointer it may be collected into a free space list.

Eventually the heap pointer reaches the end of the heap block. Some of the free space back in the heap must now be reused. Two possibilities for reuse present themselves, because of the variable size of the elements:

1. Use the free space list directly for allocation, searching the list for an appropriate size block and returning any leftover space to the free list after the allocation.

2. Compact the free space by moving all the active elements to one end of the heap, leaving the free space as a single block at the end and resetting the heap pointer to the beginning of this block.

Let us look at these two possibilities in turn.

Reuse Directly from a Free Space List. The simplest approach, when a request for an N-word element is received, is to scan the free space list for a block of N or more words. A block of N words can be allocated directly. A block of more than N words must be split into two blocks, an N-word block, which is immediately allocated, and the remainder block, which is returned to the free space list. The basic idea is straightforward. A number of particular techniques for managing allocation directly from such a free space list are known:

1. *First-fit method.* When an N-word block is needed the free space list is scanned for the *first* block of N or more words, which is then split into an N-word block, and the remainder, which is returned to the free space list.

2. *Best-fit method.* When an N-word block is needed the free space list is scanned for the block with the *minimum* number of words greater than or equal to N. This block is allocated as a unit, if it has exactly N words, or is split and the remainder returned to the free space list.

The first-fit and best-fit methods may be combined if the free space list is maintained with blocks in order of *increasing size*. However, ordering by *memory location* may be more desirable for purposes of compaction (see below). Knuth [1968] analyzes both the first-fit and best-fit techniques and concludes that the first-fit method is generally to be preferred for a variety of reasons.

Recovery with Variable-Size Blocks

Before considering the memory compaction problem, let us look at techniques for recovery where variable-size blocks are involved. Relatively little is different here from the case of fixed-size blocks. Explicit return of freed space to a free space list is the simplest technique, but the problems of garbage and dangling references are again present. Reference counts may be used in the ordinary manner.

Garbage collection is also a feasible technique. Some additional problems arise with variable-size blocks, however. Garbage collection proceeds as before with a marking phase followed by a collecting phase. Marking must be based on the same pointer chain following techniques. The difficulty now is in collecting. Before, we collected by a simple sequential scan of memory, testing each element's garbage collection bit. If the bit was "on," the element was returned to the free space list; if "off," it was still active and was passed over. We should like to use the same scheme with variable-size elements, but now there is a problem in determining the boundaries between elements. Where does one element end and the next begin? Without this information the garbage cannot be collected.

The simplest solution is to maintain along with the garbage collection bit in the first word of each block, active or not, an integer *length indicator* specifying the length of the block. With the explicit length indicators present, a sequential scan of memory is again possible, looking only at the first word of each block. During this scan, adjacent free blocks may also be compacted into single blocks before being returned to the free space list, thus eliminating the partial compaction problem discussed below (see Problem 7-7).

Garbage collection may also be effectively combined with full compaction to eliminate the need for a free space list altogether. Only a simple heap pointer is needed in this case (see below).

Compaction and the Memory Fragmentation Problem

The problem that any heap storage management system using variable-size elements faces is that of memory *fragmentation*. One begins with a single large block of free space. As computation proceeds this block is progressively fragmented into smaller pieces through allocation, recovery, and reuse. If only the simple first-fit or best-fit allocation technique is used, it is apparent that free space blocks continue to split into ever smaller pieces. Ultimately one reaches a point where the storage allocator cannot honor a request for a block of N words because no sufficiently large block exists, even though the free space list contains in total far more than N words. Without some compaction of free blocks into larger blocks execution will be halted by a lack of free storage faster than necessary.

Depending on whether active blocks within the heap may be shifted in position, one of two approaches to compaction is possible:

1. *Partial compaction.* If active blocks *cannot* be shifted (or if it is too expensive to do so), then only adjacent free blocks on the free space list may be compacted.

2. *Full compaction.* If active blocks *can* be shifted, then all active blocks may be shifted to one end of the heap, leaving all free space at the other.

Partial Compaction. Partial compaction is the simplest technique. By partial compaction we mean the combining of two or more adjacent free blocks into a single larger free block. Where storage is recovered by garbage collection, partial compaction is automatic (see Problem 7-7). Where storage is freed piecemeal (through explicit return, with or without reference counts), concern with compaction is necessary. Observe that because blocks are returned to the free space list in essentially random order it is quite likely that two blocks which are adjacent in memory will become free. Because they are freed at different times, it is not apparent that they are adjacent in memory. It is desirable to compact such adjacent free blocks into single blocks as they occur. The simplest way to do this is to maintain the free space list in *order of memory location*, as in Fig. 7-11. When a block is returned to the free space list its position is found in the ordering and the preceding list entry checked to determine adjacency. If the two blocks are adjacent, they are combined into one larger block which is entered into the free space list at the same place (but only after checking that the following list entry may not also be combined into the new block).

A much faster algorithm using an unordered free space list and requiring no search of the free space list when a block is returned is possible. Knuth [1968] gives the details of the technique. The requirements are

1. A doubly linked free space list (each block containing pointers to its successor and predecessor in the list),

2. A reserved bit in the first and last word of each active heap block set to "active," and

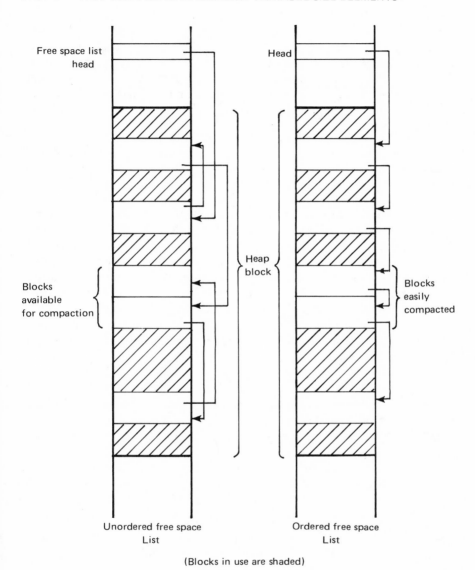

(Blocks in use are shaded)

Fig. 7-11. Ordered and unordered free space lists.

3. A similar pair of reserved bits in each free block set to "free."

The reader may easily work out the details himself (see Problem 7-8).

Full Compaction. Full compaction of the heap through shifting of all active blocks to one end is more difficult. Partial compaction may be accomplished without concern for the structure of active blocks or pointers external to the heap. The difficulty in full compaction lies in readjusting pointers to the active heap elements that are shifted to new locations. Clearly, if a block B is moved to a new location, then any pointer to B must be modified to point to B's new location. Full compaction requires

1. Identification of all external pointers to heap elements, and

2. Identification of all pointers to another heap element from an active heap element.

Unlike partial compaction, full compaction must be treated as an extraordinary procedure, as with garbage collection. The computation in progress must be suspended while compaction takes place. Full compaction has some of the other characteristics of garbage collection as well because of the need to mark active heap blocks. It is perhaps simplest to combine the two techniques, utilizing a single marking procedure followed by a compaction and a readjustment of pointers. Garbage is identified and compacted simultaneously. Such a technique is used in many SNOBOL4 implementations and is worth considering in greater detail.

The SNOBOL4 technique requires reservation within each block, whether active or free, of (1) a garbage collection bit, (2) a block-length designator, and (3) a *compaction pointer* field. Each block's compaction pointer initially points to the first location of that block. Full compaction proceeds in four steps:

1. *Marking.* Marking of active blocks proceeds exactly as in garbage collection, setting the garbage collection bit of each active block "off."

2. *Compaction pointer setting.* A sequential scan of the heap block is made, moving two pointers. One pointer, P, is advanced through the heap, pointing to the first location of each block in turn. The second, Q, initially points to the beginning of the first block. As each block is encountered by pointer P its garbage collection bit is checked. If "on," the block is garbage and P is advanced to the next block. If "off," then the block is active. Its compaction pointer is set to the current value of the pointer Q, and then both P and Q are advanced by the length of the block just checked. After being set, the compaction pointer of a block indicates the position the block *will have* after compaction.

3. *Pointer resetting.* The pointer chains followed in marking are followed again, replacing each pointer by the compaction pointer of the block pointed to, before following the original pointer.

4. *Block shifting.* A second sequential scan of memory is performed, shifting the contents of each block up to begin at the location specified by its compaction pointer (and resetting garbage collection bits). After completion of the scan all active blocks will be at one end of the heap and all free space at the other. The heap pointer may now be reset to the beginning of the free space and the suspended computation resumed. Figure 7-12 illustrates the technique.

This section has only touched on some basic heap storage management problems and techniques. Many alternative techniques are known. Knuth [1968] describes and analyzes a number of these.

7-9. REFERENCES AND SUGGESTIONS FOR FURTHER READING

Storage management considerations are a part of many of the papers concerned with control structures which are referenced in Chapters 5 and 6. The texts by Harrison [1973] and Donovan [1972] are useful general references. Gries [1971] treats stack-based storage management in some detail. Bobrow and Wegbreit [1973] consider a stack management technique for a variety of control structures.

Ross [1967] describes a general-purpose run-time storage management system used in a number of language implementations. Techniques for heap storage management have been widely studied. Knuth [1968] analyzes a number of techniques, including the important *Buddy system.* Harrison [1973] describes a number of garbage collection methods. Particular techniques are taken up in Schorr and Waite [1967], Hansen [1969], and Griswold [1972].

Storage management using both external storage and central memory is an important topic in operating systems design and is becoming increasingly important in programming language implementation. The use of *overlays* constructed by the programmer is a simple and widely used technique. However, many recent hardware designs include *virtual memory* structures based on *paging* or *segmentation* which insulate the programmer from concern with

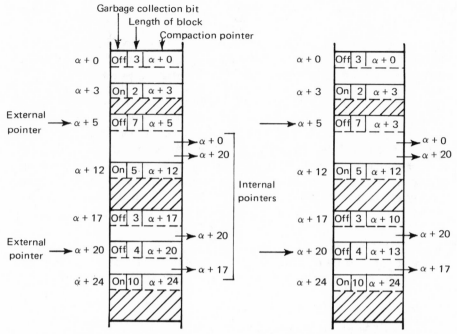

(a) Heap after marking (shading indicates garbage)

(b) Heap after compaction pointer setting

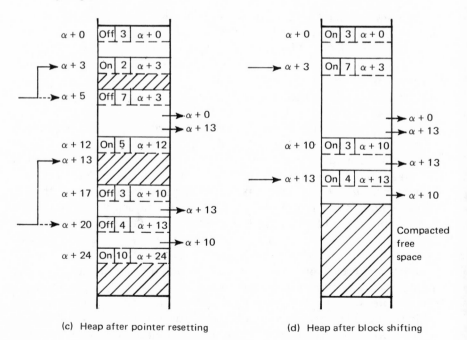

(c) Heap after pointer resetting

(d) Heap after block shifting

Fig. 7-12. Garbage collection with full compaction.

storage management. Two survey papers by Denning [1970, 1971] and a paper by Sayre [1969] serve as useful introductions to these topics. The problem of heap storage management in virtual memory systems is considered by Bobrow and Murphy [1967] and Baecker [1972], among others.

7-10. PROBLEMS

7-1. Analyze the storage management techniques used in a language implementation available to you. Consider the various elements requiring storage mentioned in Section 7-2. Are there other major run-time structures requiring storage besides those mentioned in Section 7-2?

7-2. Fill in the details of the steps in the marking of the list structure of Fig. 7-10 using the Schorr and Waite marking algorithm.

7-3. In the SLIP list-processing extension to FORTRAN each list has a special header (containing a reference count). When a list is freed, instead of returning all the list elements to the head of the free space list, only the list header is returned, and it is placed at the *end* of the free space list (using a special pointer to the end of the free space list). Thus the cost of returning a list to free space is minimal. The list elements are returned to the free space list only when the header of the list reaches the top of the free space list. What is the advantage of this technique for shifting the cost of freeing the list elements from the time of *recovery* of the list to the time of *reuse* of the storage?

7-4. Perform a worst-case analysis to determine the maximum size of the stack necessary for marking during garbage collection using the simple stack-based marking algorithm of Section 7-7. Assume that a heap element may contain at most two pointers to other heap elements, that there are at most J external pointers into the heap, and that the heap contains space for N elements altogether. How much space would have to be reserved for the garbage collection stack to ensure that garbage collection could be completed without stack overflow?

7-5. Modify the Schorr and Waite marking algorithm to allow each location within an element to contain possibly two pointers rather than only a single pointer.

7-6. *Full-word* data items such as numbers present special problems in garbage collection. Ordinarily the data themselves take up the entire heap element, with no extra bit available for garbage collection marking. It is usual in such cases to separate all such full-word elements into a special section of the heap and store all the garbage collection bits for these full-word elements in a special packed array (a *bit vector*) outside the heap. Assuming that the full-word data items are numbers (and thus contain no pointers to other heap elements), design a garbage collection algorithm which allows the possibility of pointers to full-word items in the heap. The algorithm should include marking and collecting. Maintain a separate free space list for the full-word portion of the heap.

7-7. Give an algorithm for the *collection* of marked blocks during garbage collection in a heap with variable-size elements. Assume that the first word of each block contains a garbage collection bit and a length indicator. Compact all adjacent blocks during the collection.

7-8. Without consulting Knuth's volume, design an algorithm for return of a block to free space and partial compaction using an unordered doubly linked free space list, variable-size blocks, and a reserved active-free bit in the first and last words of each block.

7-9. *APL array storage.* Design a storage management system for a heap B of variable-size blocks under the following assumptions:

1. B is used only for value storage blocks for arrays of real numbers (one word per number). Arrays always have at least two elements.

2. Each array block is accessible only through a single external pointer stored in the array descriptor. All array descriptors are stored in a block A separate from the heap B.

3. Requests for blocks to be allocated from the heap occur at random (and frequently) during execution.

4. Blocks are explicitly returned to "free" status when arrays are destroyed. This also occurs randomly and frequently during execution.

5. Permanent loss of storage through memory fragmentation cannot be tolerated. (Note that a one-word free block can never be reused.)

Your design should specify

a. The *initial organization* of the heap block B, together with any special external structures needed for storage management (e.g., free space list heads).
b. The *storage allocation* mechanism, given a request for a block of N words from B.
c. The *storage recovery* mechanism, given a call on the storage manager with the address of a block of M words to be freed.
d. The *compaction* mechanism, if any, including a specification of how it works and when it is invoked.

8 OPERATING ENVIRONMENT

In the preceding five chapters we have taken up the basic components of programming languages and their associated virtual computers. Data, operations, control structures, and storage management combine to define the internal structure of programs during execution. One important aspect has escaped other than brief mention, however: the aspect of what we shall term *operating environment*.

The operating environment of a program consists of those elements external to the program which may be used to communicate with the program, i.e., which serve as the interface between the program and the "outside world." For a typical set of programs this operating environment may consist only of a set of input devices from which data may be obtained for processing and a set of output devices on which results may be written. We might be even more restrictive and consider only the operating environment of a single subprogram. Such an environment would include not only I/O devices but also the nonlocal referencing environment of the program. However, we have considered the problems of these *internal operating environments* associated with particular subprograms at length in Chapter 6; our concern in this chapter is with the larger operating environments associated with the complete set of main program and subprograms which combined form a "program" in the usual sense.

8-1. DATA FILES

The most basic interactions of a program with its operating environment take place through data files, files used during execution for the input of new data and for the output of processed data. The structure of data files was treated in Chapter 3, and little more need be added here. Data files ordinarily appear as a special type of data structure with restricted accessing operations. Thus from the language viewpoint few new concepts are added.

Every language provides operations for transferring data to and from data files. Again input-output operations differ only in detail from other classes of operations, so that their properties raise no special difficulties.

8-2. PROGRAM FILES

Data files are part of the execution environment of a program. In contrast, program files are more often part of the operating environment of a programming language translator—which might be termed the *translation environment* of a program. A program file is usually termed *library*. The most common use of a library is to store *utility programs* which are needed by more than one programmer.

Programs in a library may exist already translated into executable form. Commonly such a library is used during the loading phase of translation. The programmer designates a library to be used. Each translated program to be loaded contains a special *loader table* designating subprograms called from this subprogram. The loader keeps track of the set of subprograms required by other subprograms and, when all programmer defined subprograms have been loaded, goes to the library to find any other subprograms needed. In this use of a library the programmer makes no explicit access to the library. Such a technique is common in implementations of FORTRAN and PL/I where separately compiled subprograms are used.

In COBOL a different technique is used. The library contains *untranslated* program segments, e.g., descriptions of data structures and common subprograms. A COPY command may be used in a program to specify a library program segment to be inserted at the point of the COPY *before* translation begins. After insertion of the library program segment the program is translated exactly as usual.

Run-time access to a program library is also available in some languages. SNOBOL4, for example, provides a LOAD statement which causes a library subprogram to be loaded and added to the list of callable subprograms during execution. The overlay features of many languages in a sense represent access to run-time program files as well.

8-3. BATCH-PROCESSING ENVIRONMENTS

Operating environments are generally characterized as *batch-processing* or *interactive* depending on whether the programmer is assumed part of the translation and execution environment of the program. Most common is the batch-processing environment. Program translation and execution are assumed to take place in an environment controlled by the computer operating system. In this environment the only accessible components are data files and occasionally program files. Some forms of access to operating system features may also be provided, e.g., to request more memory space during execution. There is assumed to be no programmer present (accessible) during program processing.

In a batch-processing environment the basic unit of program processing is a *run*, which usually consists of translation followed by execution, with perhaps parts of the program pretranslated. A run is set up through a *job control program*, a series of operating system commands that detail the various phases of translation, loading, and execution that are to take place. Files of input data must also be set up through such commands and access to program libraries obtained.

During a run, the job control program is usually interpreted statement by statement by the operating system. Each statement in the job control program specifies one step required for processing of the program: translation of the program, loading, gaining access to or creating files, program execution, etc. When the job control program has been completely executed by the operating system, the program has been completely processed and output files recovered and sent to the printer or to permanent storage within the computer system.

The details of job control languages vary widely between different operating systems. Viewed as languages, job control languages in general have a relatively simple structure and create no new problems.

The batch-processing environment assumption has an effect on the design of both a programming language and its processor. All the languages in Part II except APL assume a batch-processing environment. In the next section we shall consider the APL design in some depth. Let us look first at some of the effects of the batch-processing assumption on ordinary language design.

Effects on Language Design

The major effects are seen in the areas of error handling and input-output. In a batch-processing environment the cost of an error that halts program processing is likely to be high. Because of the absence of direct access to the programmer, the entire run must be halted, and the programmer loses a substantial amount of time correcting the error and submitting a new job to be run. It becomes desirable to build into the language fairly extensive automatic error-checking and correction features which allow errors to be handled without halting the run. As a result many languages provide extensive features for error monitoring, execution interrupts, and special error-correcting routines. In addition special debugging features such as trace and dump facilities are often provided to allow the programmer to collect detailed information about execution to aid his later debugging. In language implementation, it becomes important to design processors that can continue in reasonable ways after errors are detected. For example, compilers for such languages are usually constructed so that errors in one program segment do not halt compilation; instead the compiler attempts to either correct the error or skip over the erroneous program segment to a later segment and continue processing.

Besides the effect on language and processor features, the batch-processing environment also affects programming techniques. The programmer, to make optimal use of each run, must carefully plan how to extract as much information as possible from each run during the debugging stage. This requires careful planning and appropriate use of the special debugging features provided by the language.

In the area of input-output the batch-processing environment also affects the design of languages and processors. Most obviously, because program input-output is entirely to and from external data files, there are relatively few time constraints on this processing. Using the input-output buffering technique described in Section 3-12 the actual transfer of data from an input device to a central memory buffer may occur well before the execution of a READ statement which transfers the data to particular data structure locations. Similarly, output generated by WRITE statements may be collected in buffers and not actually transferred to the output device until enough has accumulated to make the transfer most economical. This organization allows input-output processing to be matched to the speed of the external storage device without slowing execution of the program itself. With an interactive environment input-output tends to be less flexible, because each piece of input must be generated by the programmer at his terminal device while program execution is suspended, and no buffering is possible.

There is one other critical effect of the batch-processing assumption on language design: a relative lack of concern with the overall management of the programming process. Each run of a program is viewed as a single independent task to be carried out. No concern is evidenced in the language design for the overall structure of the programmer's task of program design, coding, testing, editing, storage, and ultimately production use. These are usually considered problems for the operating system or other specialized language-independent subsystems such as editors and file managers. Although these aspects may be viewed as supporting structures and not directly a part of language design, the programmer often finds them as important in allowing rapid and correct programming as the design of the language itself. Their direct inclusion in APL has been one of the key strengths of that language.

8-4. INTERACTIVE ENVIRONMENTS

The programmer is part of an interactive operating environment. During program translation and execution he is immediately accessible through a special input-output terminal. Overall control of program processing is handled directly by the programmer from the terminal, rather than through the job control program of the batch-processing environment. For the programmer the basic unit of computer interaction is now the *terminal session* rather than the run. During a session at his terminal the programmer enters commands for program creation, editing, translation, execution, and storage as needed. During translation or execution, programs may access the usual program and data files, but more importantly they may directly interact with the programmer.

The effect of an interactive environment on the design of a language may be striking. Of course a language designed for a batch-processing environment may be adapted to an interactive environment simply by directing certain input-output to a terminal. However, where the interactive environment is assumed initially in language design, differences in input-output and error-handling features are likely to be apparent. Error handling, given the presence of the programmer, needs to be far less sophisticated, because program translation or execution may simply be interrupted, the error condition message output to the programmer's terminal, and the programmer given an opportunity to make appropriate modifications before signaling resumption (or termination) of processing. The cost of interruption of processing resulting from an error is not great in an interactive environment, and thus many more such interruptions may be tolerated. Moreover, language features such as special error-handling routines are less important.

Input-output in an interactive environment is constrained by the characteristics of interaction with the programmer at this terminal. In general most input is not set up in an input file prior to execution but rather is generated by the programmer at his terminal as needed. This fact precludes buffering data into memory in advance of the point of its actual use. Interaction presents far more serious constraints on the operating system, because the computer system cannot stop processing while waiting for the programmer to input his next command from his terminal, and neither can it delay too long executing his command once given. These constraints require a time-sharing operating system which can allocate system resources and processing time among a set of interactive users so that the computer is used to its full capacity and yet each user gets good service at his terminal. These problems, however, are beyond our concern here.

The most important characteristic of languages designed for an interactive environment is the greater concern for the overall structure of the programmer's task—the coding, testing, editing, and storage of programs, which is largely ignored in batch-processing languages. The APL design illustrates this difference sharply.

Example 8-1. The APL Operating Environment. During an APL terminal session the programmer essentially enters his "main program" line by line at the terminal. As each line is entered it is immediately executed by the APL system. The commands entered consist of a mixture of system commands, APL expressions to be evaluated immediately, definitions of subprograms and data structures to be saved for later use, and calls on subprograms defined previously. Thus the "main program" entered by the programmer contains elements both of the usual main program and of the job control program present in a batch-processing environment. The APL expressions and subprogram calls correspond to the elements of the usual main program, while the entry of subprogram definitions, data structure definitions, and system commands corresponds to the elements of the usual job control program.

Program and Data Storage

Basic to the APL operating environment is a set of permanent and temporary storage facilities for programs and data. The basic unit of storage is termed a *workspace*. A workspace consists of a set of subprogram definitions, data structures (arrays), and various pieces of system-defined status information. During a terminal session one workspace, termed the *active workspace*, is stored in central memory. As the programmer enters subprogram and array definitions through his terminal these are stored in the active workspace, which serves as temporary storage. At any point during a session a permanent copy of the active workspace may be added to the programmer's *workspace library*, which serves as the primary unit of permanent storage.

The operating environment for the APL programmer includes a set of libraries. Each programmer has his own private library of workspaces that he has created and saved. In addition there are various *public libraries*, which contain workspaces of subprograms and data accessible to every APL programmer in the system. Each programmer has full access to his own private library and to the public libraries and may also access other programmer's private libraries on a read-only basis if the proper access key is known.

Subprogram definitions are entered into the active workspace by first giving a system command specifying entry into *subprogram definition mode*, followed by specification of subprogram name and the statements forming the body of the subprogram. A second system command causes a return to normal *direct command execution mode*, and simultaneous storage of the subprogram definition in the active workspace under the given name. Data structures may be defined and saved by simply writing an expression creating the desired array (or single number or character) and assigning it to an identifier. The created array is stored in the active workspace and is accessible through the identifier.

Program Execution

Any defined subprogram may be executed during a terminal session by entering its name and a list of arguments. Such a subprogram call is executed immediately. The called subprogram may call other defined subprograms in the usual manner without restriction. During execution of a subprogram, direct interaction with the programmer at his terminal may occur in a number of ways:

1. *Direct input-output.* A subprogram may access the data structures defined in the active workspace through their identifiers in the usual way. However, a direct request for new input data may be directed to the programmer through an analogue of the usual READ command (the □ operation). When such a command is executed, subprogram execution is halted temporarily and a signal sent to the programmer's terminal requesting new input. The programmer may

then enter a data item (a number, character, or array of numbers or characters). These input data are transmitted back to the subprogram and execution is resumed. Output may also be directed to the programmer's terminal during execution, but in this case suspension of execution is not necessary. Because input direct from the programmer terminal is in small segments, no elaborate input formatting conventions are needed, and the READ operation becomes a simple request for input. The language is thus simplified by having direct and immediate access to the programmer. More formatting abilities are needed for output, but here the ability to handle character data together with the collection of APL general-purpose operators provide an adequate formatting capability without special facilities.

2. *Errors during execution.* Subprograms are not checked for errors when defined but only when executed. Thus an error detected during subprogram execution may be an ordinary syntax error or may be an execution error, e.g., a type error in operands for an operator. Any error detected immediately halts subprogram execution, and a message displaying the erroneous program statement and the error condition indicator is printed on the programmer's terminal. The programmer may now take immediate corrective action by changing stored data values, changing the definition of the subprogram, or simply terminating subprogram execution altogether. After the error is corrected, execution of the subprogram may be resumed. Because of the presence of the programmer in the operating environment during subprogram execution, this simple and direct error-handling mechanism is highly effective. The language contains no features for error handling in subprograms at all; the programmer deals with each error as it occurs.

3. *Programmed suspension of execution.* The programmer may specify before execution of a subprogram that he wishes execution to be interrupted when certain statements are reached. When such a tagged statement is reached during execution, execution is halted and control returned to the programmer. As with an error halt, the programmer may then check and modify data values or modify the subprogram definition before resuming execution. In particular this mechanism allows execution of a subprogram which is not yet completely coded. By tagging statements which are incomplete, coded parts of a subprogram may be tested before the remainder is coded.

Program Editing

Editing commands are provided so that the programmer may modify subprogram definitions as needed. These commands allow insertion, deletion, or replacement of all or part of any line in a subprogram definition, either during or after subprogram definition. In particular, editing may be performed on partially executed subprograms before execution is resumed.

The key effects of the interactive environment on the design of APL are seen in the features of the language supporting the entire range of programmer activities, including program and data definition, definition editing, and temporary and permanent storage facilities, and also in the direct use of the programmer in error handling and input-output to simplify these aspects of the language structure. More detail may be found in Chapter 16.

8-5. REFERENCES AND SUGGESTIONS FOR FURTHER READING

Many of the topics included in this chapter are also central in the design of operating systems, because in most computers the operating system is directly responsible for providing most of the operating environment for programs. The text by Watson [1970] provides many useful insights from this viewpoint. Papers by Bobrow [1972] and Teitelman [1969] provide suggestions for operating environments appropriate to support advanced work in artificial intelligence.

9 SYNTAX AND TRANSLATION

Syntax has played a relatively minor role in the preceding chapters. Instead the discussion has concentrated largely on semantic structures, with only an occasional comment on the syntactic elements used to represent the semantics. In this chapter we shall take up syntactic structure directly. There are three main aspects of this discussion: the syntactic elements themselves, the structure of the translators which process the syntax, and the formal specification of syntax.

One of the chief reasons syntax has not been more central in the discussion to this point is that many of the most important semantic elements of programs are not represented in the syntax of the program directly but appear only implicitly. For example, we have noted the use of implicit declarations, implicit data structures, implicit operations, implicit sequence control, and implicit referencing environments. If we look only at the syntax of a program, we miss much that is of central importance.

A second reason for slighting the study of program syntax is that so much here is arbitrary. Variations among languages in syntactic structures are far greater than variations in underlying semantic structures; even a brief look at the example programs for the languages in Part II shows this clearly. These variations in syntax are largely a matter of the personal taste of the language designers and deserve no extended consideration. In fact there are few generally agreed upon rules for syntactic structure in programming languages—each language designer tends to choose structures that seem natural and appropriate to him. This lack of uniformity may be seen even in the simplest case of a syntax for referencing elements of linear arrays: The first element of linear array A may be designated A(1), A[1], A<1>, (CAR A), FIRST OF A, or A.FIRST depending on the language and whether the array is homogeneous, heterogeneous, or variable-length, considering only the languages of Part II. In the larger syntactic structures—expressions, statements, declarations, and subprograms—there is even less uniformity (if that is possible).

When you undertake to master a new programming language you are likely to be confronted with an entirely new syntax masking an underlying semantics not greatly different from that of other languages with which you are familiar. This choice of a new syntax may not be entirely perverse—often the new syntactic structures are more elegant, more readable, or less error-prone or have other advantages over the familiar ones. The important thing is to move as quickly as possible to the underlying semantics of a new language. The semantic structures are likely both to be more familiar and to explain some of the reasons for syntactic peculiarities as well.

9-1. GENERAL SYNTACTIC CRITERIA

The primary purpose of syntax is to provide a notation for communication of information between the programmer and the programming language processor. It is in this context that syntax has entered the discussions of the preceding chapters—we were concerned with the information communicated by the syntax rather than the details of syntactic structure. The choice of particular syntactic structures, however, is constrained only slightly by the necessity to communicate particular items of information. For example, the fact that a particular variable has a value of type *real number* may be represented in any of a dozen different ways in a program—through an explicit declaration as in ALGOL, through an implicit *naming convention* as in FORTRAN, etc. The details of syntax are largely chosen on the basis of secondary criteria, such as readability, which are unrelated to the primary goal of communicating information to the language processor. There are a large number of such secondary criteria, but they may be roughly categorized under the general goals of making programs easy to read, easy to write, easy to translate, and unambiguous. We shall consider some of the ways that language syntactic structures may be designed to satisfy these often conflicting goals.

Readability. A program is readable if the underlying structure of the algorithm and data represented by the program is apparent from an inspection of the program text. A readable program is often said to be *self-documenting*—it is understandable without any separate documentation (although this goal is seldom achievable in practice). Readability is enhanced by such language features as natural statement formats, structured statements, liberal use of keywords and noise words, provision for embedded comments, unrestricted length identifiers, mnemonic operator symbols, free field formats, and complete data declarations. Readability, of course, cannot be guaranteed by the design of a language, because even the best design may be circumvented by poor programming. On the other hand, syntactic design can force even the best-intentioned programmer to write unreadable programs (as is often the case in APL). Of the languages in Part II the COBOL design emphasizes readability most heavily, often at the expense of ease of writing and ease of translation.

Readability is enhanced by a program syntax in which syntactic differences reflect underlying semantic differences so that program constructs which do similar things look similar, and program constructs which do radically different things look different. For example, the difference between a conditional branch, an iteration, and a **goto** control structure is made clear in most languages by the use of different statement types with different syntactic structures. In general the greater the variety of syntactic constructs used, the more easily the program structure may be made to reflect different underlying semantic structures. Languages which provide only a few different syntactic constructs in general lead to less readable programs. In APL, for example, only one statement format is provided. The differences among an assignment statement, a subprogram call, a simple **goto**, a subprogram return, a multiway conditional branch, and various other common program structures are reflected syntactically only by differences in one or a few operator symbols within a complex expression. It often requires a detailed analysis of a program to determine even its gross control structure. Moreover, a simple syntax error, such as a single incorrect character in a statement, may radically alter the meaning of a statement without rendering it syntactically incorrect. A similar problem arises in SNOBOL4, which also provides only one basic statement syntax. The presence of a single extra blank character within a SNOBOL4 statement may change the statement from a simple subprogram call to a pattern-matching statement, leading to a cascade of run-time errors in other parts of the program which can be traced back to the offending syntax error only with great difficulty. In LISP, errors in matching parentheses cause similar problems. During the program testing stage, we may well ask that a readable program not look correct when it is grossly incorrect.

Writeability. The syntactic features which make a program easy to write are often in conflict with those features which make it easy to read. Writeability is enhanced by use of concise and regular syntactic structures, while for readability a variety of more "verbose" constructs are helpful. Implicit syntactic conventions that allow declarations and operations to be left unspecified make programs shorter and easier to write but harder to read. Other features advance both goals; for example, the use of structured statements, simple natural statement formats, mnemonic operation symbols, and unrestricted identifiers usually make program writing easier by allowing the natural structure of the problem algorithms and data to be directly represented in the program.

Ease of Translation. Yet a third conflicting goal is that of making programs easy to translate into executable form. Readability and writeability are criteria directed to the needs of the human programmer. Ease of translation relates to the needs of the translator that processes the written program. The key to easy translation is regularity of structure. The LISP syntax provides an example of a program structure which is neither particularly readable nor particularly writeable but which is extremely simple to translate. The entire syntactic structure of any LISP program may be described in a few simple rules, because of the regularity of the syntax. Programs become harder to translate as the number of special syntactic constructs increases. For example, COBOL translation is made extremely difficult by the large number of statement and declaration forms allowed, even though the semantics of the language is not particularly complicated.

Lack of Ambiguity. Ambiguity is a central problem in every language design. A language definition ideally provides a unique meaning for every syntactic construct that a programmer may write. An ambiguous construction allows two or more different interpretations. The problems of ambiguity usually arise not in the structure of individual program elements but in the interplay between different structures. For example, ALGOL allows two different forms of conditional statement:

if ⟨*Boolean expression*⟩ **then** ⟨*statement*₁⟩ **else** ⟨*statement*₂⟩

and

if ⟨*Boolean expression*⟩ **then** ⟨*statement*₁⟩

The interpretation to be given to each statement form is clearly defined. However, when the two forms are combined by allowing

$\langle statement_1 \rangle$ to be another conditional statement, then the structure

if $\langle Boolean\ expression_1 \rangle$ **then if** $\langle Boolean\ expression_2 \rangle$ **then**
$\langle statement_1 \rangle$ **else** $\langle statement_2 \rangle$

is found. This statement form is ambiguous because it is not clear which of the two flowcharts of Fig. 9-1 is intended. FORTRAN syntax provides another example. A reference to $A(I,J)$ might be either a reference to an element of the two-dimensional array A or a call of the function subprogram A, because the syntax in FORTRAN for function calls and array references is the same. Similar ambiguities arise in almost every programming language.

The ambiguities in FORTRAN and ALGOL mentioned above have in fact been resolved in both languages, so that the constructions are no longer ambiguous. The manner in which this has been done is instructive. In the ALGOL conditional statement the ambiguity has been resolved by changing the syntax of the language to introduce a required **begin** . . . **end** delimiter pair around the embedded conditional statement. Thus the natural but ambiguous combination of two conditional statements has been replaced by the two less natural but unambiguous constructions

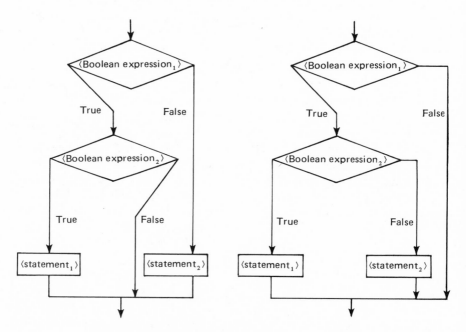

Fig. 9-1. Two interpretations of the ALGOL conditional.

if ⟨*Boolean expression*₁⟩ then begin if ⟨*Boolean expression*₂⟩ then ⟨*statement*₁⟩ end else ⟨*statement*₂⟩

and

if ⟨*Boolean expression*₁⟩ then begin if ⟨*Boolean expression*₂⟩ then ⟨*statement*₁⟩ else ⟨*statement*₂⟩ end

The same problem with combinations of conditional statements arises in PL/I, but here a second technique is used to resolve the ambiguity: An arbitrary interpretation is chosen for the ambiguous construction, in this case the final else is paired with the nearest then so that the combined statement has the same meaning as the second of the above ALGOL constructions. The ambiguity of FORTRAN function and array references is resolved by a similar rule: The construct $A(I,J)$ is assumed to be a function call if no declaration for an array A is given. Since each array must be declared prior to its use in a program, the translator may readily check whether there is in fact an array A to which the reference applies. If none is found, then the translator assumes that the construct is a call on an external function A. This assumption cannot be checked until load time when all the external functions (including library functions) are linked into the final executable program. If the loader finds no function A, then a loader error message is produced. In ALGOL a different technique is used to distinguish function calls from array references: A syntactic distinction is made—square brackets are used to enclose subscript lists in array references (e.g., $A[I,J]$) and parentheses are used to enclose parameter lists of function calls (e.g., $A(I,J)$).

Ambiguities are usually resolved by one of the two techniques: either some syntactic modification is made to distinguish ambiguous constructions (such as the begin ... end delimiters and square brackets of ALGOL) or some fixed interpretation is chosen, which may be dependent on the context, and the ambiguous syntactic construction is left intact (as in the PL/I conditionals and the FORTRAN parentheses). Either technique raises difficulties. Modifying the syntax is often only possible by introducing unnatural syntactic constructs. For example, to many beginning ALGOL programmers the need for the begin ... end delimiters in a nested ALGOL conditional is not natural, and the construct leads to many errors. Yet the alternative of providing an implicit interpretation for the ambiguous construct may lead to even more subtle errors. A beginning FORTRAN programmer, for example, is likely to be mystified at a loader error message SUBPROGRAM A NOT FOUND when all he had done was to omit inadvertently a declaration for array A.

Most languages resolve ambiguities by a combination of methods in an attempt to satisfy the other syntactic goals without ambiguity. However, many of the peculiarities of syntax of languages arise from attempts to avoid ambiguity.

9-2. SYNTACTIC ELEMENTS OF A LANGUAGE

The general syntactic style of a language is set by the choice of the various basic syntactic elements. We shall consider briefly the most prominent of these.

Character Set

The choice of character set is one of the first to be made in designing a language syntax. There are several widely used character sets, each containing a different set of special characters in addition to the basic letters and digits. Usually one of these standard sets is chosen, although occasionally a special nonstandard character set may be used, as, for example, in APL (see Chapter 16). The choice of character set is important in determining the type of input and output equipment which can be used in implementing the language. For example, the basic FORTRAN character set is available on most input and output equipment. The APL character set, on the other hand, cannot be used directly on most I/O devices.

The choice of character set is also important in determining the number of available special characters which may be used in programs and data as delimiters, operator symbols, and the like. This choice can be an important factor in making the language syntax natural and unambiguous. For example, the use of the semicolon to separate statements and declarations in ALGOL provides a natural punctuation similar to that of English and also provides a unique statement terminator. Using the FORTRAN character set without the semicolon, no suitable terminator is available. In particular neither commas nor periods may be used because of the ambiguities which arise because of other uses of these characters.

Identifiers

The basic syntax for identifiers—a string of letters and digits beginning with a letter—is widely accepted. Variations among languages are mainly in the optional inclusion of special characters such as . or - to improve readability and in length restrictions. Length restrictions, such as the FORTRAN restriction to six characters, force the use of identifiers with little mnemonic value in many cases and thus restrict program readability significantly.

Operator Symbols

Most languages use the special characters + and – to represent the two basic arithmetic operations, but beyond that there is almost no uniformity. Primitive operations may be represented entirely by special characters, as is done in APL. Alternatively identifiers may be used for all primitives, as in the LISP PLUS, TIMES, etc. Most languages adopt some combination, utilizing special characters for some operators, identifiers for others, and often also some character strings which fit in neither of these categories (for example, the FORTRAN .EQ. and **).

Key Words and Reserved Words

A *key word* is an identifier used as a fixed part of the syntax of a statement, for example, IF, THEN, and ELSE in PL/I conditional statements or DO beginning a FORTRAN iteration statement. A key word is a *reserved word* if it may not also be used as a programmer-chosen identifier. Key words serve a variety of purposes in programming languages. Commonly statements begin with a key word designating the statement type: READ, IF, GOTO, etc. Others may be used within statements as delimiters, for example, the THEN and ELSE of the PL/I conditional.

Whether key words should be reserved is largely a matter of taste. Syntactic analysis during translation is made easier by using reserved words. FORTRAN syntactic analysis, for example, is made difficult by the fact that a statement beginning with DO or IF may not actually be an iteration or conditional statement—because DO and IF are not reserved words a programmer may legitimately choose these as variable names. COBOL uses reserved words heavily, but there are so many identifiers reserved that it is difficult to remember them all, and as a result one often inadvertently chooses a reserved identifer as a variable name.

Comments and Noise Words

Most languages make provision for comments to be embedded in programs as a separate statement type which is treated as a null statement (no-op). In some cases a special bracket is provided which allows comments to be inserted anywhere. The brackets and the enclosed comment are edited out of the program before translation begins.

Noise words are optional words which may be inserted in statements to improve readability. COBOL provides many such options. For example, in the COBOL **goto** statement, written GO TO ⟨label⟩, the keyword GO is required, but TO is an optional noise word which carries no information and is used only to improve readability.

Blanks (Spaces)

Rules on the use of blanks vary widely between languages. In FORTRAN, for example, blanks are not significant anywhere except in literal character string data. Other languages use blanks as separators, so that they play an important syntactic role. In SNOBOL4 one of the primitive operations (concatenation) is represented by a blank, and the blank is also used as a separator between elements of a statement (leading to much confusion).

Delimiters and Brackets

A delimiter is a syntactic element used simply to mark the beginning or end of some syntactic unit such as a statement or expression. Brackets are paired delimiters, e.g., parentheses or **begin** . . . **end** pairs. Delimiters may be used merely to enhance readability or to simplify syntactic analysis, but more often they serve the important purpose of removing ambiguities by explicitly defining the boundaries of a particular syntactic construct.

Free and Fixed Field Formats

A syntax is free field if program statements may be written anywhere on an input line without regard for positioning on the line or for breaks between lines. A fixed field syntax utilizes the positioning on an input line to convey information. Strict fixed field syntax, where each element of a statement must appear within a given part of an input line, is most often seen in assembly languages. More commonly a partial fixed field format is used; for example, in FORTRAN the first five characters of each line are reserved for a statement label. The first character of an input line is sometimes given special significance; for example, SNOBOL4 statement labels, comments, and continuation lines are distinguished by a character in the first position of a line.

Expressions

Expressions are the basic syntactic building block from which statements (and sometimes programs) are built. The various syntactic forms for expressions have been discussed in Section 5-2 at length. We noted particularly the infix, prefix, and postfix forms and variants. Some languages, such as LISP and APL, adopt a single syntax for constructing expressions which is used uniformly. More commonly a mixture of forms is allowed, e.g., infix for arithmetic primitives, prefix for certain function calls, etc. Translation of these mixed forms is more difficult, but the expressions are usually correspondingly more readable.

Besides the obvious syntactic differences in expression forms, there is a difference among languages in the importance given to expressions. In LISP and APL, for example, the expression is the central syntactic structure—statements, if they are used at all, take the form of single expressions. Thus in APL a program is simply a sequence of expressions. In languages such as FORTRAN and COBOL, on the other hand, expressions are much less important; instead statements are the primary syntactic form, and expressions are used within statements only occasionally when a value must be computed. Most statements in these languages utilize restricted expression forms, with full expressions allowed only in assignments and for branching in conditional statements.

Statements

Statements are the most prominent syntactic component in most languages, and their syntax has a critical effect on the overall regularity, readability, and writeability of the language. Some languages adopt a single basic statement format, while others use a different syntax for each different statement type. The former approach emphasizes regularity, while the latter emphasizes readability. SNOBOL4 has only one basic statement syntax, the pattern-matching-replacement statement, from which other statement types may be derived by omitting elements of the basic statement. Similarly, each statement in APL has the form of a single expression, regardless of whether the statement is used for conditional branching, assignment, input, output, etc. Most languages lean toward the other extreme of providing different syntactic structures for each statement type. COBOL is most notable in this regard—each COBOL statement has a unique structure involving special key words, noise words, alternative constructions, optional elements, etc. The advantage of using a variety of syntactic structures, of course, is that each may be made to express in a natural way the operations involved.

A more important difference in statement structures is that between *structured* or *nested* statements and *simple* statements. A simple statement is one which contains no other embedded statements. FORTRAN, APL, and SNOBOL4 allow only simple statements. A structured statement is one which may contain embedded statements. For example, the ALGOL conditional statement

if ⟨*Boolean expression*⟩ then ⟨*unconditional statement*⟩
else ⟨*statement*⟩

is a structured statement because each of the alternatives is itself another statement. In ALGOL and PL/I structured statements are of central importance. An ALGOL program, for example, consists only of a single statement, a block. A block, however, is composed of a set of declarations and statements. The statements within a block may be simple statements—assignments, **gotos**, or subprogram calls—or they may be structured statements—conditionals, iteration statements, blocks, or just *compound statements* composed of a sequence of statements enclosed in **begin** . . . **end** delimiters. Thus an ALGOL program takes the form of a hierarchy of statements embedded within other statements at different levels. Structured statements are important in making programs more readable, because they allow the natural hierarchical organization of most algorithms to be reflected directly in the program syntax. In languages without structured statements this can be done only through subprogram hierarchies. The importance of structured statements has been pointed out also in Section 5-3 in connection with discussion of the **goto** controversy.

Overall Program-Subprogram Structure

The overall syntactic organization of main program and subprogram definitions is as varied as the other aspects of language syntax. The languages of Part II illustrate a number of the most common structures.

Separate Subprogram Definitions. FORTRAN and APL illustrate an overall organization in which each subprogram definition is treated as a separate syntactic unit. In FORTRAN each subprogram is compiled separately and the compiled programs linked at load time. In APL, programs are separately translated and are linked only when one calls another during execution. The effect of this organization is particularly apparent in FORTRAN where each subprogram is required to contain full declarations for all data elements, even for those which are in COMMON blocks and shared with other subprograms. These declarations are required because of the assumption of separate compilation.

Nested Subprogram Definitions. ALGOL (and PL/I in part) illustrates a nested program structure in which subprogram definitions appear as declarations within the main program and may themselves contain other subprogram definitions nested within their definitions to any depth. This overall program organization is related to the ALGOL emphasis on structured statements but in fact serves a different purpose. Structured statements are introduced primarily to provide a natural notation for the common hierarchical divisions in algorithm structure, but nested subprogram definitions serve instead to provide a nonlocal referencing environment for subprograms which is defined at compile time and which thus allows static type checking and compilation of efficient executable code for subprograms containing nonlocal references. Without the nesting of subprogram definitions it is either necessary to provide declarations for nonlocal variables within each subprogram definition (as is done in FORTRAN) or to defer all type checking for nonlocal references until run time. The nesting also serves the less important function of allowing subprogram names to have less than global scope.

Data Descriptions Separated from Executable Statements. An altogether different organization is found in COBOL. In most languages each subprogram definition consists of declarations for local (and sometimes nonlocal) data and a set of executable statements. In a COBOL program the data declarations and the executable statements for all subprograms are divided into two separate program *divisions*, the *data division* and the *procedure division*. A third, the *environment division*, consists of declarations concerning the external operating environment. The procedure division of a program is organized into subunits corresponding to subprogram bodies, but all data are global to all subprograms, and there is nothing corresponding to the usual local data of a subprogram. The advantage of the centralized data division containing all data declarations is that it enforces the logical independence of the data formats and the algorithms in the procedure division— minor changes in data structure can be made by modification of the data division without modifying the procedure division. It is also convenient to have the data descriptions collected in one place rather than scattered throughout the subprograms.

Unseparated Subprogram Definitions. A fourth overall program organization (or lack of organization) is illustrated by the SNOBOL4 language. No syntactic distinction is made in SNOBOL4 between main program statements and subprogram statements. A program, regardless of the number of subprograms it contains, is syntactically just a list of statements. The points where subprograms begin and end are not differentiated. In fact any statement may be part of the main program and also part of any number of subprograms at the same time, in the sense that it may be executed at one point during execution of the main program and later executed again as part of execution of a subprogram. This rather chaotic program organization is valuable only in allowing run-time translation and execution of new statements and subprograms with relatively simple mechanisms. Most SNOBOL4 programmers introduce an artificial distinction between subprogram bodies by insertion of comments or other syntactic delimiters.

9-3. STAGES IN TRANSLATION

The process of translation of a program from its original syntax into executable form is central in every programming language implementation. The translation may be quite simple, as in the case of APL or LISP programs, but more often the process is complex and requires the major share of effort in a language implementation. Most languages could be implemented with only trivial translation if one were willing to write a software interpreter (software-simulated virtual computer) and if one were willing to accept slow execution speeds. In most cases, however, efficient execution is such a desirable goal that major efforts are made to translate programs into efficiently executable structures, especially hardware-interpretable machine code. The translation process becomes progressively more complex as the executable program form becomes further removed in structure from the original program. At the extreme an optimizing compiler for a complex language like PL/I may radically alter program structures to obtain more efficient execution. Such compilers are among the most complex programs in existence.

Translator structures vary widely and are ordinarily rather ad hoc, although the syntax-directed compiler structure described below is somewhat more standardized. For the most part, however, translators are just programs, and their structures depend on the goals of the designers. It is possible, however, to identify the general stages in translation which occur in most translators.

Logically we may divide translation into two major parts: the *analysis* of the input *source program* and the *synthesis* of the executable *object program*. Within each of these parts there are further divisions, as we shall see below. In most translators these logical stages are not clearly separate but instead are mixed so that analysis and synthesis alternate, often on a statement-by-statement basis.

Analysis of the Source Program

To a translator, the source program appears initially as one long undifferentiated character string composed of thousands or tens of thousands of characters. Of course a programmer seeing such a program almost instinctively structures it into subprograms, statements, declarations, and so forth. To the translator none of this is apparent. An analysis of the structure of the program must be laboriously built up character by character during translation.

Lexical Analysis. The most basic phase of any translation is that in which the input program is subdivided into its elementary constituents: identifiers, delimiters, operator symbols, numbers, key words, noise words, blanks, comments, etc. This phase is termed *lexical analysis*, and the basic program units which result from lexical analysis are termed *lexical items*. Typically the lexical analyzer is the *input routine* for the translator, reading successive lines of input program, breaking them down into individual lexical items, and feeding these lexical items to the later stages of the translator to be used in the higher levels of analysis. The lexical analyzer must identify the type of each lexical item (number, identifier, delimiter, operator, etc.) and attach a type tag. In addition conversion to an internal representation is often made for items such as numbers (converted to internal binary fixed- or floating-point form) and identifiers (stored in a symbol table and the address of the symbol table entry used in place of the character string).

While lexical analysis is simple in concept, this phase of translation often requires a larger share of translation time than any other. This fact is in part due simply to the necessity to scan and analyze the source program character by character, but it is also true that in practice it often is difficult to determine where the boundaries between lexical items lie without rather complex context-dependent algorithms. For example, the two FORTRAN statements

$$DO\ 10\ I\ =\ 1,5$$

and

$$DO\ 10\ I\ =\ 1.5$$

have entirely different lexical structures—the first is a DO statement and the second is an assignment—but this fact cannot be discovered without fairly extensive analysis.

Syntactic Analysis (Parsing).　　The second stage in translation is *syntactic analysis* or *parsing*. Here the larger program structures are identified—statements, declarations, expressions, etc.—using the lexical items produced by the lexical analyzer. Syntactic analysis usually alternates with semantic analysis. First the syntactic analyzer identifies a sequence of lexical items forming a syntactic unit such as an expression, statement, subprogram call, or declaration. A semantic analyzer is then called to process this unit. Commonly the syntactic and semantic analyzers communicate using a stack. The syntactic analyzer enters in the stack the various elements of the syntactic unit found, and these are retrieved and processed by the semantic analyzer. A great deal of research has centered on discovery of efficient syntactic analysis techniques, particularly techniques based on the use of formal grammars (see the next section).

Semantic Analysis.　　Semantic analysis is perhaps the central phase of translation. Here the syntactic structures recognized by the syntactic analyzer are processed and the structure of the executable object code begins to take shape. Semantic analysis is thus the bridge between the analysis and synthesis parts of translation. A number of other important subsidiary functions also occur in this stage, including symbol table maintenance, most error detection, the expansion of macros, and the execution of *compile-time statements*. The semantic analyzer may actually produce the executable object code in simple translations, but more commonly the output from this stage is some internal form of the final executable program, which is then manipulated by the optimization stage of the translator before executable code is actually generated.

The semantic analyzer is ordinarily split into a set of smaller semantic analyzers, each of which handles one particular type of program construct. For example, array declarations might be handled by one analyzer, arithmetic expressions by another, and **goto** statements by another. The appropriate semantic analyzer is called by the syntactic analyzer whenever it has recognized a syntactic unit to be processed.

The semantic analyzers interact among themselves through information stored in various data structures, particularly in the central *symbol table*. For example, a semantic analyzer which processes type declarations for simple variables may often do little more than enter the declared types into the symbol table. A later semantic analyzer which processes artihmetic expressions may then use the declared types to generate the appropriate type-specific arithmetic operations for the object code. The exact functions of the semantic analyzers vary greatly depending on the language and the logical organization of the translator. Some of the most common functions may be described, however.

1. *Symbol table maintenance.* A *symbol table* is one of the central data structures in every translator. The symbol table typically contains an entry for each different identifier encountered in the source program. The lexical analyzer makes the initial entries as it scans the input program, but the semantic analyzers have primary responsibility after that. In general the symbol table entry contains more than just the identifier itself; it contains additional data concerning the attributes of that identifier: its type (simple variable, array name, subprogram name, formal parameter, etc.), type of values (integer, real, etc.), referencing environment, and whatever other information is available from the input program through declarations and usage. The semantic analyzers enter this information into the symbol table as they process declarations, subprogram headers, and program statements. Other semantic analyzers and perhaps the optimizer in the synthesis part of the translator use this information to construct efficient executable code.

The symbol table in translators for compiled languages is usually discarded at the end of translation. However, it may be retained during execution, e.g., in languages that allow new identifiers to be created at run time. APL, SNOBOL4, and LISP implementations all utilize symbol tables initially created during translation as a central run-time system-defined data structure.

2. *Insertion of implicit information.* Often in the source program, information is implicit which must be made explicit in the lower-level object program. Most of this implicit information goes under the general heading of *default conventions*—interpretations to be provided when the programmer gives no explicit specification. For example, a PL/I variable that is used but not declared is automatically provided a lengthy list of properties by default—it is of type FIXED BINARY if its name begins with I-N, it is AUTOMATIC, has scope equal to the block within which it is declared, etc. All these default specifications can be overridden by explicit programmer declarations. The task of the semantic analyzers includes the insertion (into the symbol table or the object code) of these default specifications.

3. *Error detection.* The syntactic and semantic analyzers must be prepared to handle incorrect as well as correct programs. At any point the lexical analyzer may send to the syntactic analyzer a lexical item which does not fit in the surrounding context—a statement delimiter in the middle of an expression, a declaration in the middle

of a sequence of statements, or perhaps an operator symbol where an identifier is expected. The error may be more subtle—a real variable where an integer variable is required, a subscripted variable reference with three subscripts when the array was declared to have only two dimensions, or a statement label in a **goto** statement naming a statement within an iteration statement where such jumps are disallowed. At each step in translation a multitude of such errors might occur. The semantic analyzer must not only recognize such errors when they occur and produce an appropriate error message but must also, in all but the most drastic cases, determine the appropriate way to continue with syntactic analysis of the remainder of the program. Provisions for error detection and handling in the syntactic and semantic analysis phases may require greater effort than the basic analysis itself.

4. *Macro processing and compile-time operations.* Not all languages include macro features or provision for compile-time operations. Where these are present, however, processing is usually handled during semantic analysis.

A *macro*, in its simplest form, is a piece of program text which has been separately defined and which is to be inserted into the program during translation whenever an appropriate *macro call* is encountered in the source program. Thus a macro is much like a subprogram, except that rather than being separately translated and called at run time its body is simply substituted for each call during program translation. Macros may be just simple strings to be substituted, e.g., substitution of 3.1416 for PI whenever the latter is referenced. More commonly they look much like subprograms, with parameters which must be processed before the substitution for the macro call is made.

Where macros are allowed the semantic analyzers must identify the macro calls within the source program and set up the appropriate substitution of the macro body for the call. Often this task involves interrupting the lexical and syntactic analyzers and setting them to work analyzing the string representing the macro body before proceeding with the remainder of the source string. Alternatively the macro body may have already been partially translated so that the semantic analyzer can process it directly, inserting the appropriate object code and making the appropriate table entries before continuing with analysis of the source program. The details of these processes are too complex to be taken up here. Wegner [1968] contains a more detailed discussion.

A *compile-time operation* is an operation to be performed during translation to control the translation of the source program. PL/I provides a number of such operations. The PL/I compile-time assignment provides a simple macro capability by allowing an arbitrary string to be substituted for each occurrence of an identifier. More complex compile-time operations allow parts of a program to be translated only when certain conditions are satisfied or allow groups of statements to be repeatedly translated, as though a loop were executed by the translator, reprocessing the group of statements with each iteration. Again it is the semantic analyzers which must identify and execute these compile-time operations before translation proceeds.

Synthesis of the Object Program

The final stages of translation are concerned with the construction of the executable program from the outputs produced by the semantic analyzer. This phase involves code generation necessarily and may also include optimization of the generated program. If subprograms are translated separately, or if library subprograms are used, a final linking and loading stage is needed to produce the complete program ready for execution.

Optimization. The semantic analyzer ordinarily produces as output the executable translated program represented in some internal representation such as a *Polish string* of operators and operands or a table of operator-operand sequences. From this internal representation the code generators may generate the properly formatted output object code. Before code generation, however, there is usually some optimization of the program in the internal representation. Typically the semantic analyzers generate the internal program form piecemeal as each segment of input program is analyzed. This task is done most easily if the semantic analyzers do not have to worry too much about the surrounding code which has been generated immediately before. In doing this piecemeal output, however, extremely poor code may be produced; e.g., a register may be stored at the end of one generated segment and immediately reloaded from the same location at the beginning of the next segment. Often it is desirable to allow the generation of poor code sequences by the semantic analyzers and then during optimization replace these sequences by better ones which avoid obvious inefficiencies.

Many compilers go far beyond this sort of simple optimization and analyze the program for other improvements which can be made, e.g., computing common subexpressions only once, removing constant operations from loops, optimizing the use of registers, and optimizing the calculation of array accessing formulas. Much research has been done on program optimization and many sophisticated techniques are known (see the references at the end of this chapter).

Code Generation. The code generation stage is relatively simple. The translated program in the internal representation has been optimized and must be formed into the assembly language statements, machine code, or other object program form which is to be the output of the translation. This process involves formatting the output properly from the information contained in the internal program representation. The output code may be directly executable, or there may be other translation steps to follow, e.g., assembly or linking and loading.

Linking and Loading. In this optional final stage of translation the pieces of code resulting from separate translations of subprograms are coalesced into the final executable program. The output of the preceding translation phases typically consists of executable programs in almost final form, except where the programs reference external data or other subprograms. These incomplete places in the code are specified in attached *loader tables* produced by the translator. The linking loader loads the various segments of translated code into memory and then uses the attached loader tables to link them together properly by filling in data and subprogram addresses in the code as needed. The result is the final executable program ready to be run.

We have only been able to touch on the subject of translator structure in this brief section. This aspect of programming language implementation is probably the most thoroughly understood. Extended treatments may be found in Aho and Ullman [1972], Gries [1971], Hopgood [1969], and numerous other texts.

9-4. FORMAL DEFINITION OF SYNTAX

In the formal study of programming languages the topic of syntax and syntactic analysis has received the most attention. Initially the goal of this work was that of providing precise definitions of programming language syntax for the users and implementors of the language. It quickly became apparent, however, that these syntactic definitions could also be used directly as a basis for syntactic analysis in translators. Later work has developed and analyzed a variety of techniques for syntactic analysis based on formal syntactic definitions.

A formal definition of the syntax of a programming language is usually called a *grammar*, in analogy with the common terminology for natural languages. A grammar consists of a set of definitions (termed *rules*) which specify the sequences of characters (or lexical items) that form allowable programs in the language being defined. A *formal grammar* is just a grammar specified using a strictly defined notation. The best-known type of formal grammar is the *BNF grammar* (or *context-free grammar*), which has found widespread application both in programming language definition and in natural language research. A variant of the BNF form of some importance is that used in the definition of COBOL, which for lack of a better name we shall term a *CBL* (COBOL-like) *grammar*.

BNF Grammars

The BNF (Backus-Naur form) grammer was developed for the syntactic definition of ALGOL (Naur [1963]) by John Backus [1960]. At about the same time a similar grammar form, the *context-free grammer*, was developed by linguist Noam Chomsky [1959] for the definition of natural language syntax. The BNF and context-free grammar forms are equivalent in power; the differences are essentially only notational. For this reason the terms *BNF grammar* and *context-free grammar* are usually interchangeable in discussion of syntax.

A BNF grammar is composed of a finite set of BNF grammar rules, which together define a *language*, in our case a programming language. Before looking at the form of these grammar rules, the term *language* here deserves some further explanation. Because syntax is concerned only with form rather than meaning, a (programming) *language*, considered syntactically, consists of a set of *syntactically correct programs*, each of which is simply a character string. A syntactically correct program need not make any sense semantically; that is, if it were executed, it would not need to compute anything useful, or anything at all for that matter—it may just loop immediately. In general a formal grammar for a programming language allows many such syntactically correct but semantically meaningless programs. Remember that the grammar defines only a set of *character strings* but assigns no meaning to those strings. We carry this lack of concern with meaning one step further and admit the definition: *A language is any set of* (finite-length) *character strings* (with characters chosen from some fixed finite alphabet of symbols). Under this definition ALGOL is a language (composed of all the character strings representing syntactically valid ALGOL programs), but the set of all FORTRAN assignment statements is also a language, or the set of all LISP atoms, or even the set composed of sequences of *a*s and *b*s where all the *a*s precede all the *b*s (i.e., [*ab*, *aab*, *abb*, ...]). A language may consist of only a finite set of strings, for example, the language composed of all ALGOL delimiters: **begin, end, if, then,** etc. The only restriction on a language is that each string in the language must be of finite length and must contain characters chosen from some fixed finite alphabet of symbols. The language itself may contain an infinite number of strings, of course.

A BNF grammar defines a language in a straightforward manner. In the simplest case a grammar rule may simply list the elements of a finite language. For example,

⟨*digit*⟩ ::= 0 | 1 | 2 | 3 | 4 | 5 | 6 | 7 | 8 | 9

This BNF grammar rule defines a language composed of the ten single-character strings [0, 1, 2, 3, 4, 5, 6, 7, 8, 9] by listing a set of alternatives. The above grammar rule is read "A *digit* is either a '0' or a '1' or a '2' or a . . . ." The term *digit* is called a *syntactic category*; it basically serves as a name for the language defined by the grammar rule. The symbol ::= means "is defined as" or just "is" and the vertical bar | is read "or" and separates alternatives in the definition.

Once we have defined a basic set of syntactic categories (really sublanguages), we may use these in constructing more complex languages. For example, the rule

⟨*conditional statement*⟩ :: =
       if ⟨*Boolean expression*⟩ **then** ⟨*statement*⟩ **else** ⟨*statement*⟩ |
       if ⟨*Boolean expression*⟩ **then** ⟨*statement*⟩

defines the language composed of ⟨*conditional statement*⟩s, using the syntactic categories ⟨*Boolean expression*⟩ and ⟨*statement*⟩, which must be defined in turn using other grammar rules. Note that the above rule shows two alternative forms of conditional statement (separated by the | symbol). Each alternative is constructed from the concatenation of several elements, which may be literal strings (e.g., **if** or **else**) or syntactic categories. When a syntactic category is designated it means that any string in the sublanguage defined by that category may be used at that point. For example, assuming that the syntactic category ⟨*Boolean expression*⟩ consists of a set of strings representing valid Boolean expressions, the above rule allows any one of these strings to be inserted between the **if** and **then** of a conditional statement.

Another useful form of grammar rule uses the syntactic category being defined recursively in the definition. This is the technique used in BNF rules to specify repetition. For example, the rule

⟨unsigned integer⟩ ::= ⟨digit⟩ | ⟨unsigned integer⟩⟨digit⟩

defines an unsigned integer as a sequence of ⟨digit⟩s by using the syntactic category ⟨unsigned integer⟩ recursively. The first alternative in the rule allows a single ⟨digit⟩ to appear as an ⟨unsigned integer⟩. The second alternative allows a ⟨digit⟩ to be added to the end of any string which has already been classified as an ⟨unsigned integer⟩, with the result still being classified as an ⟨unsigned integer⟩. Thus two ⟨digit⟩s in a sequence still form an ⟨unsigned integer⟩, and since this is true for two ⟨digit⟩s, it is also true for three ⟨digit⟩s in sequence, etc.

A complete BNF grammar is just a set of such grammar rules, which together define a hierarchy of sublanguages leading to the top-level syntactic category, which for a programming language is usually the category ⟨program⟩. Figure 9-2 illustrates a more complex grammar defining the syntax of a class of simple ALGOL assignment statements using the basic syntactic categories ⟨identifier⟩ and ⟨number⟩.

Functions of a BNF Grammar

The use of a formal grammar to define the syntax of a programming language is important to both the language user and the language implementor. The user may consult it to answer subtle questions about program form, punctuation, and structure. The implementor may use it to determine all the possible cases of input program structures which are allowed and thus with which his translator may have to deal. And both programmer and implementor have a common agreed upon definition which may be used to resolve disputes about allowed syntactic constructs. A formal syntactic

⟨assignment statement⟩ ::= ⟨variable⟩ := ⟨arithmetic expression⟩
⟨arithmetic expression⟩ ::= ⟨term⟩ | ⟨arithmetic expression⟩ + ⟨term⟩
                |⟨arithmetic expression⟩ − ⟨term⟩
⟨term⟩ ::= ⟨factor⟩ | ⟨term⟩ X ⟨factor⟩ | ⟨term⟩ / ⟨factor⟩
⟨factor⟩ ::= ⟨primary⟩ | ⟨factor⟩ ↑ ⟨primary⟩
⟨primary⟩ ::= ⟨variable⟩ | ⟨number⟩ |(⟨arithmetic expression⟩)
⟨variable⟩ ::= ⟨identifier⟩ | ⟨identifier⟩ [⟨subscript list⟩]
⟨subscript list⟩ ::= ⟨arithmetic expression⟩
        | ⟨subscript list⟩ , ⟨arithmetic expression⟩

Fig. 9-2. BNF grammar for simple ALGOL assignment statements.

definition also helps to eliminate minor syntactic differences between implementations of a language.

The basic function of any grammar is that of distinguishing between syntactically correct and syntactically incorrect strings. The BNF grammar form does this through the set of BNF rules, which define the set of all syntactically correct strings. To determine if a given string in fact represents a syntactically valid program in the language defined by a BNF grammar, we must use the grammar rules to construct a syntactic analysis or *parse* of the string. If the string can be successfully parsed, then it is in the language. If no way can be found of parsing the string with the given grammar rules, then the string is not in the language. Figure 9-3 illustrates the *parse tree* which results from a syntactic analysis of an ALGOL assignment statement using the BNF grammar of Fig. 9-2.

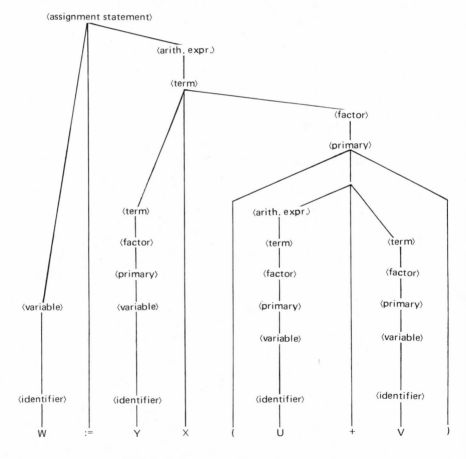

Fig. 9-3. Parse tree for an assignment statement.

While the basic function of a grammar is that of distinguishing correct and incorrect strings, BNF grammars serve a secondary function which is almost of equal practical importance. A BNF grammar assigns a structure to each string in the language defined by the grammar, as seen in Fig. 9-3. Note that the structure assigned is necessarily a tree because of the restrictions on BNF grammar rules. Each leaf of this parse tree is a single character or lexical item in the input string. Each intermediate branch point in the tree is tagged with a syntactic category which designates the class to which the subtree below it belongs. The root node of the tree is tagged with the syntactic category designating the whole language, in this case the category ⟨assignment statement⟩.

The parse tree assigned to each syntactically correct string in a language is important because it can be used to provide a sort of intuitive semantic structure for much of a program. Thus, for example, the BNF grammar for ALGOL specifies a structure for an ALGOL program as a sequence of declarations and statements, with nested blocks. The statements, in turn, are structured using expressions of various kinds, and the expressions are composed from simple and subscripted variables, primitive operators, functions calls, etc. At the lowest level even identifiers and numbers are broken down into their constituent parts. By studying the grammar for ALGOL a programmer may gain a direct insight into the various structures which combine to form correct programs. It is important to note that no grammar must *necessarily* assign the structure one would expect to a given program element. The same language may be defined by many different grammars, as may be easily seen by playing with the grammar of Fig. 9-2 a bit. Figure 9-4, for example, gives a grammar defining the same language as the grammar of Fig. 9-2, but note that the structures assigned by this new grammar are quite at odds with the structures one would intuitively assign.

The BNF grammar, in spite of its exceedingly simple structure,

```
⟨assignment statement⟩ ::= ⟨variable⟩ := ⟨arithmetic expression⟩
⟨arithmetic expression⟩ ::= ⟨term⟩ | ⟨arithmetic expression⟩ ↑ ⟨term⟩
                          | ⟨arithmetic expression⟩ X ⟨term⟩
                          | ⟨arithmetic expression⟩ + ⟨term⟩
⟨term⟩ ::= ⟨primary⟩ | ⟨term⟩ − ⟨primary⟩ | ⟨term⟩ / ⟨primary⟩
⟨primary⟩ ::= ⟨variable⟩ | ⟨number⟩ | (⟨arithmetic expression⟩)
⟨variable⟩ ::= ⟨identifier⟩ | ⟨identifier⟩ [ ⟨subscript list⟩
⟨subscript list⟩ ::= ⟨arithmetic expression⟩ ]
                   | ⟨arithmetic expression⟩ , ⟨subscript list⟩
```

Fig. 9-4. BNF grammar defining the same language as the grammar of Fig. 9-2.

can be used to do a surprisingly good job of defining the syntax of most programming languages. For example, the ALGOL BNF grammar (Naur [1963]), supplemented by only a few additional syntactic restrictions stated in English, describes the set of valid ALGOL programs very closely. The areas of syntax which cannot be defined by a BNF grammar are those which involve contextual dependence. For example, the ALGOL restrictions "the same identifier may not be declared twice in the same block," "every identifier must be declared in some block enclosing the point of its use," and "an array declared to have two dimensions cannot be referenced with three subscripts" are each unspecifiable using only a BNF grammar. It is restrictions of this sort that must be defined by an addendum to the formal BNF grammar.

The study of BNF grammars and variants has led to a powerful and elegant theory of syntax for programming languages. A wide variety of different grammar forms related to the BNF grammar has been defined and investigated. In addition the problem of parsing with BNF grammars has received wide attention, and a variety of parsing techniques has been defined and studied. From this work we have derived a deep understanding of both the strengths and weaknesses of BNF grammars and syntactic analysis using BNF grammars. The interested reader should consult Aho and Ullman [1972].

CBL (COBOL-like) Grammars: A Useful Notational Variant of BNF

Despite the power, elegance, and simplicity of BNF grammars, they are not an ideal notation for communicating the rules of programming language syntax to the practicing programmer. The primary reason is the simplicity of the BNF rule, which forces a rather unnatural representation for the common syntactic constructs of optional elements, alternative elements, and repeated elements within a grammar rule. For example, to express the simple syntactic idea "a *signed integer* is a sequence of digits preceded by an optional plus or minus" we must write in BNF a fairly complex set of recursive rules such as

$$\langle signed\ integer \rangle ::= +\ \langle integer \rangle \ | \ -\ \langle integer \rangle \ | \ \langle integer \rangle$$
$$\langle integer \rangle ::= \langle digit \rangle \ | \ \langle integer \rangle \ \langle digit \rangle$$

These notational shortcomings of BNF are largely unimportant to the theoretical development of the properties of the grammar, but many who have used BNF for syntactic description of actual languages have been moved to extend the notation in various ways to provide a more natural way of writing rules like that noted above. The most widely used of these alternative notations is that used in the definition of COBOL, which seems to have been developed independently and at about the same time as BNF. This notation has been used somewhat informally and has received little of the intensive analysis applied to BNF grammars.

As used in the COBOL definition the formal CBL grammar rules are mixed with informal English throughout, with no attempt to present an entire formal grammar for the language. It is convenient to consider the CBL rules as simply an extension of BNF which adds the following new notation:

1. Within a grammar rule, an optional element may be indicated by enclosing the element in square brackets, [....].

2. Alternative elements may be indicated by listing the alternatives vertically enclosed in braces, { ... } (replacing the vertical bar of BNF).

3. Optional alternatives may be indicated by listing the alternatives vertically enclosed in square brackets, $\left[\ldots \right]$.

4. Repeated elements may be indicated by listing one element (enclosed in brackets or braces if necessary) followed by the usual ellipsis symbol, ...

5. Required key words are underlined, and optional noise words are not.

Examples

1. $\langle signed\ integer \rangle ::= \begin{bmatrix} + \\ - \end{bmatrix} \langle digit \rangle \ldots$

2. $\langle identifier \rangle ::= \langle letter \rangle \begin{bmatrix} \langle letter \rangle \\ \langle digit \rangle \end{bmatrix} \ldots$

3. $\langle$ALGOL *conditional statement*$\rangle$ ::= **if** $\langle Boolean\ expression \rangle$ **then** $\langle unconditional\ statement \rangle$ $\left[\textbf{else}\ \langle statement \rangle\right]$

4. $\langle$COBOL ADD *statement*$\rangle$ ::= $\underline{ADD}$ $\begin{Bmatrix} \langle identifier \rangle \\ \langle number \rangle \end{Bmatrix}$

$\begin{bmatrix} , \langle identifier \rangle \\ , \langle number \rangle \end{bmatrix} \ldots \underline{TO} \langle identifier \rangle \left[\underline{ROUNDED}\right]$

$\left[, \langle identifier \rangle \left[\underline{ROUNDED}\right]\right] \ldots$

$\left[; \text{ON } \underline{SIZE}\ \underline{ERROR} \quad \langle statement \rangle\right]$

The naturalness and conciseness of this CBL grammar form compared to BNF is easily seen by viewing the difference in the definition of ⟨signed integer⟩ in the two forms or by writing a full BNF definition of the ⟨COBOL ADD statement⟩ (see Problem 9-6). Note, however, that the BNF and CBL grammar forms are equivalent in power—any language that can be defined by a grammar in one form can also be defined by a grammar in the other.

Syntax-Directed Compilers

A syntax-directed compiler is a compiler whose syntactic analysis stage is based fairly directly on a formal grammar. The syntactic analyzer of such a compiler parses the source program into units corresponding to the syntactic categories assigned by the associated formal grammar. Semantic analysis is also organized into units corresponding to syntactic categories. For example, typically the syntactic analyzer might recognize an assignment statement by building up a parse tree for the expression defining the value to be assigned and the variable to which the assignment is made. At each level in this construction, as the various pieces of the expressions are recognized, an appropriate *semantic routine* (coded as an ordinary subprogram) is called. The semantic routine performs the appropriate semantic analysis for the newly parsed construct before returning control to the syntactic analyzer to continue the parse. This structure is not far different from that described earlier—the difference is only in the use of a formal grammar to determine the organization of the syntactic and semantic analysis.

Many techniques are known for syntactic analysis based on formal grammars, especially BNF grammars which have been restricted in various ways. These techniques are described in a number of texts, e.g., Aho and Ullman [1972] and Gries [1971]. The search for efficient and general parsing methods for languages defined by different types of formal grammars has led to the development of a number of sophisticated, powerful techniques which are superior to the ad hoc methods used in early programming language translators. The interplay between theoretical research and practice in this area has been particularly successful: Most translator designs now utilize the syntax-directed compiler concepts to some degree.

In the interplay between theory and practice in syntactic analysis we see a prototype of the sort of research that we hope will ultimately underlie the entire subject of programming language design—semantics as well as syntax. The informal discussion of semantics found in Part I will likely then be replaced by more precise formal analyses which will give a depth to the subject that now is lacking. However, much research remains before this possibility becomes a reality.

9-5. REFERENCES AND SUGGESTIONS FOR FURTHER READING

The literature on the syntax and translation of programming languages is extensive. The two-volume text by Aho and Ullman [1972] surveys much of the formal mathematical theory of syntax, parsing techniques, and code optimization in the overall context of compiler construction. Gries [1971], Hopgood [1969], and McKeeman et al. [1970] provide more practical discussions of compilation methods. The brief survey paper by McClure [1972] provides a useful overview of current practice. Feldman and Gries [1968] survey a wide range of research related to syntax-directed compilation techniques.

Optimization of code produced by compilers has been the subject of numerous papers in the literature. Besides the Aho and Ullman volumes mentioned above, the book by Schaefer [1973] is useful. See also papers in the volume edited by Rustin [1972a].

The use and translation of macros in programming is an important topic not covered here. The survey by Brown [1969] and sections of Wegner [1968] and Harrison [1973] provide introductions to these concepts.

Practical considerations in the design of programming language syntax have received less attention. Sammet [1969] surveys much of the relevant material.

Formal definitions of programming languages that include semantics as well as syntax have increasingly been an important topic for research. The survey by de Bakker [1969] includes most of the early work on this topic. Three recent symposia, ACM [1972], Engeler [1971], and Rustin [1972b], provide an excellent overview of the more recent work. The *Vienna Definition Language* developed at the IBM Vienna Laboratory for the formal definition of PL/I has been the most successful definitional technique. An elementary description of this technique may be found in Wegner [1972]. Lucas and Walk [1969] and Bandat [1968] describe its application to PL/I. Lee [1972] extends the technique and describes a number of applications.

9-6. PROBLEMS

9-1. Consider the following BNF grammar rules:

$$\langle pop \rangle \quad ::= \quad [\ \langle bop \rangle \ , \ \langle \ pop \rangle] \ | \ \langle bop \rangle$$

$$\langle bop \rangle \quad ::= \quad \langle boop \rangle \ | \ (\langle pop \rangle)$$

$$\langle boop \rangle \quad ::= \quad a \ | \ b \ | c$$

For each of the strings listed below, indicate all the syntactic categories of which it is a member, if any:
a. c
b. (a)
c. $[b]$
d. $([a,b])$
e. $[(a),b]$
f. $[(a),[b,a]]$

9-2. Write a BNF grammar for the language composed of all binary numbers which contain at least three consecutive 1s (the language including the strings 000011111110100 or 1111110 but not 0011000101011).

9-3. The syntax of the *monkey* language is quite simple yet only monkeys can speak it without making mistakes. The alphabet of the language is $\{ \ a,b,d, \ \wedge \ \}$, where $\wedge$ stands for a space. The grammar is

$$\langle stop \rangle \quad ::= \quad b \ | \ d$$

$$\langle plosive \rangle \quad ::= \quad \langle stop \rangle \ a$$

$$\langle syllable \rangle \quad ::= \quad \langle plosive \rangle \ | \ \langle plosive \rangle \ \langle stop \rangle \ | \ a \ \langle plosive \rangle \ | \ a \ \langle stop \rangle$$

$$\langle word \rangle \quad ::= \quad \langle syllable \rangle \ | \ \langle syllable \rangle \ \langle word \rangle \ \langle syllable \rangle$$

$$\langle sentence \rangle \quad ::= \quad \langle word \rangle \ | \ \langle sentence \rangle \qquad \langle word \rangle$$

Which of the following speakers is the secret agent in monkey disguise?

$$\text{Ape:} \qquad ba \ \wedge \ ababadada \ \wedge \ bad \ \wedge \ dabbada$$

$$\text{Chimp:} \qquad abdabaadab \ \wedge \ ada$$

$$\text{Baboon:} \qquad dad \ \wedge \ ad \ \wedge \ abaadad \ \wedge \ badadbaad$$

9-4. Write a CBL grammar for the language defined by the BNF grammar of Fig. 9-2.

9-5. Rewrite the grammar of Fig. 9-2 to show the proper structure for expressions assuming the APL rules for operator precedence and associa-

tivity: All operators including assignment are of equal precedence and
associativity is from right to left. For example, the assignment statement
$W := Y \times W + U \times V$ should be assigned the structure

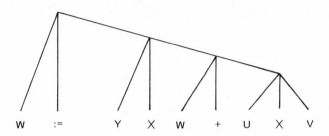

9-6. Write a BNF grammar for the COBOL ADD statement, defined using the
CBL grammar in Section 9-4.

9-7. Construct parse trees for the following assignment statements using the
BNF grammar of Fig. 9-2:
  a. $A[2] := B + 1$
  b. $A[I,J] := A[J,I]$
  c. $X := U - V \uparrow W + X / Y$
  d. $P := U / (V / (W / X))$

PART **II**   LANGUAGES

10 FORTRAN

10-1. INTRODUCTION

FORTRAN is a widely used language for scientific and numeric computing. The design of the language centers around a single primary goal: *execution efficiency*. The language structures are simple, and much of the design is rather inelegant, but the goal of execution efficiency is achieved—FORTRAN can be implemented on most computers so that execution is extremely efficient, using hardware structures almost directly for everything except input-output. Compared to ALGOL (described in the next chapter) FORTRAN has roughly the same types of data and primitive operations but is weak in control structures. The language also incorporates many minor restrictions, intended to allow more efficient execution, which add to programming difficulty and error potential. The simple structures and execution efficiency, however, have made the language a standard for much scientific computing for many years, in spite of the admitted weaknesses of the design.

The simplicity of FORTRAN in part stems from its origins. FORTRAN was the first widely used high-level programming language. The earliest versions were designed and implemented in the mid-1950s. At that point in time the utility of any high-level language was open to question by assembly language programmers. Their most serious complaint concerned the problem of execution efficiency of code compiled from a high-level language. As a result, the earliest versions of FORTRAN were oriented heavily toward execution efficiency, a feature which has never left the design. The

314

language has developed through a number of different versions, the most important of which were designated FORTRAN II and FORTRAN IV. A standard definition of each of these versions, termed *Basic FORTRAN* and *FORTRAN*, respectively, was produced about 1964, but almost every implementation of the language differs from and extends these standard definitions in some ways. The language described in this chapter is the standard FORTRAN as defined in ANSI [1966], ACM [1964], and ANSI [1971]. However, the reader should look closely at current manuals before using his local implementation of the language. Our description is also not meant to be a *complete* description of even the standard FORTRAN; in many situations some of the detailed restrictions and special cases have been omitted for clarity. A detailed history of the FORTRAN language development may be found in Sammet [1969].

10-2. BRIEF OVERVIEW OF THE LANGUAGE

A FORTRAN program consists of a main program and a set of subprograms, each of which is compiled separately from all the others, with the translated programs linked during loading. Each subprogram is compiled into a strictly statically allocated area containing the compiled executable machine code and programmer- and system-defined data areas. Shared data areas, called COMMON blocks, may also be defined. No run-time storage management is provided. Subprograms communicate only by accessing COMMON blocks, passing parameters, and passing control through nonrecursive subprogram calls. Thus almost the entire run-time structure of a FORTRAN program is fixed during translation, and only the values of simple variables and array elements vary during execution.

Data in FORTRAN encompass four number data types and Boolean values. Only simple variables and homogeneous arrays of at most three dimensions are allowed. A rather complete set of arithmetic operations and type conversions are provided, together with a basic set of relational and logical primitives. Input-output facilities are complex but restricted to sequential files.

FORTRAN statement sequence control relies heavily on statement labels and **goto** structures. Expressions and subprogram sequence control are simple. Data control is based on a strict two-level, local or global, referencing environment. Subprogram facilities are straightforward, with parameter tranmission entirely by reference.

10-3. AN ANNOTATED EXAMPLE: SUMMATION OF A VECTOR

A simple FORTRAN program for summation of a vector of real numbers is given in Fig. 10-1. The program consists of a main program and a subprogram. The subprogram, SUM, accepts a vector V and its length N as input and produces as its result the sum of the elements of the vector. The main program is a simple test program for the subprogram. The main program reads in an integer K, followed by K real numbers that are stored in a vector A. The subprogram SUM is then called to sum the vector, and the main program prints the result and returns to read in a new set of numbers until a zero is read for K. The annotations that follow refer to the line numbers on the left of the program, which are not a part of the program itself.

```
Line
 1              DIMENSION A(99)
 2       10     READ (1,5) K
 3        5     FORMAT (I2)
 4              IF(K.EQ.0) GO TO 30
 5              READ (1,15)(A(I),I=1,K)
 6       15     FORMAT (6F10.5)
 7              RES = SUM(A,K)
 8              WRITE (2,25) RES
 9       25     FORMAT (5HSUM = ,3X,F10.5)
10              GO TO 10
11       30     CONTINUE
12              END

13              FUNCTION SUM(V,N)
14              DIMENSION V(N)
15              SUM = 0
16              DO 10 I = 1,N
17       10     SUM = SUM + V(I)
18              RETURN
19              END
```

Fig. 10-1. Example FORTRAN program.

Lines 1—12. Main program definition.

Line 1. Declaration of the test vector A of 99 real number elements. The type is determined by a *naming convention* (see Section 10-4). Note that the size of the vector must be fixed to the maximum size necessary for testing (compare with the ALGOL example in Chapter 11). The vector will be created by the translator and will exist throughout program execution.

Line 2. The integer variable K is declared implicitly *by use*. It is also created by the translator and exists throughout program execution. The READ command reads a single integer from input unit 1 according to the FORMAT number 5. The integer is read in character string form and converted to the hardware integer representation before being stored as the value of K.

Line 3. The format specification for the preceding READ, specifying that the integer appears as two digits in the first two characters of the next input record.

Line 4. Control branches to statement 30 if the new value of K is zero (signaling the end of the test data).

Line 5. K real numbers are read into the first K elements of vector A. The numbers appear in character string form on external file 1 and are formatted according to the FORMAT numbered 15.

Line 6. The format for the preceding READ. The numbers appear six numbers per line, with each number in a field ten characters wide, having five digits to the right of the decimal.

Line 7. The function subprogram SUM is called and the result assigned to the new variable RES. RES is created during translation and exists throughout execution.

Lines 8—9. The value computed is printed with the heading SUM = .

Line 10. Control returns to line 2 to begin another round of input.

Line 11. This statement does nothing but merely serves as a control transfer point for the GOTO in line 4. Such statements are often necessary in FORTRAN.

Line 12. Physical and logical end of the main program.

Lines 13—19. Definition of the function subprogram SUM. This group of statements is logically entirely separate from the preceding statements and will be treated entirely independently by the FORTRAN compiler.

Line 13. The subprogram name, type, and formal parameter identifiers are declared.

Line 14. The formal parameter V is declared to be a vector with a length equal to the value of the formal parameter N on entry to SUM. This declaration allows the compiler to set up the appropriate accessing calculation for references to vector V. At run time (in most FORTRAN implementations) no checking of actual parameters for appropriate type and length is done. Thus the main program may transmit the 99-element vector A to SUM, which will treat it as a shorter vector of N elements.

Line 15. The value of the function is initialized to zero. The identifier SUM serves as a simple variable throughout execution of the function, with its final value on exit returned as the value of the function.

Line 16. An iteration loop is begun whose body extends to line 17 (in this case just the single statement). The new variable I is initialized to 1 and increased by 1 each time through the loop until it reaches the value of N.

Line 17. The sum of the elements of the vector is collected as the value of SUM.

Line 18. Logical end of the subprogram. Control returns to the calling program.

Line 19. Physical end of the subprogram.

10-4. DATA

FORTRAN provides five basic elementary data types: integer, real, double-precision, and complex numbers and Boolean (called *logical*) values. In addition, character strings may be used in certain restricted contexts, including formats (patterns) for input-output. The only data structures provided are simple variables and homogeneous arrays of up to three dimensions.

Elementary Data Items

Elementary data items may be written directly as literals in programs or may be read in from data files during program execution. Each data type is distinguished syntactically:

1. Logical (Boolean) values are written .TRUE. and .FALSE.

2. Integers are written in decimal, e.g., 210.

3. Real numbers are written in decimal with an optional

exponent, and must contain either a decimal point or an exponent, e.g., 2.102, 15.2E12, or 15E12.

4. Double-precision numbers are written as reals, except that the exponent is required and is denoted by D instead of E, e.g., 15D12.

5. Complex numbers are written as pairs of reals enclosed in parentheses, e.g., (2.102, 15E12).

Character string literals, called *Hollerith constants*, are written as a string of characters preceded by nH, where n is the decimal integer representing the number of characters, e.g., 7HTHE END.

It is presumed that the hardware representations for numbers and character strings are used at run time, except for complex numbers which are represented as pairs of reals in the obvious way.

Simple Variables and Arrays

Full descriptors for all simple variables and arrays must be declared in the program, including the type of simple variables and the shape, size, and type of elements for arrays. All data structures are created and allocated storage statically during translation, and only the values of simple variables and array elements may be changed during execution.

Simple variables are declared in one of two ways. Declaration may be *implicit*: If a variable is used without an explicit declaration, it is created automatically by the translator. Implicitly declared variables may only be of type real or integer, and this type is determined by the first letter of the variable name used: if I, J, K, L, M, or N, the type is integer; otherwise it is real. An *explicit* declaration may also be used, e.g.,

> REAL M
> DOUBLE PRECISION Q,R
> LOGICAL A,B,C

Explicit declarations for variables of types other than real and integer are required.

Arrays must be explicitly declared in a DIMENSION declaration or type declaration. The declaration specifies the number of dimensions (one, two, or three) and the upper bound on each subscript. Lower bounds are always one.

Example. DIMENSION A(10,20), K(25). This declaration defines a 10 × 20 matrix A of real numbers (the same implicit typing convention used for simple variables applies) and an integer vector K of 25 elements. Equivalently we could write

REAL A(10,20)
INTEGER K(25)

Arrays and simple variables to be shared between subprograms may also be declared in COMMON declarations (see Section 10-7).

Unlike most language definitions, the definition of FORTRAN defines the major features of the *storage representation* for arrays. Each array element occupies one storage *unit* (whose size is implementation-dependent) if the array is type real, integer, or logical, and two storage units if the array is type double-precision or complex. Vectors are stored sequentially, matrices are stored sequentially by *columns*, and three-dimensional arrays are stored as planes of columns, exactly the *reverse* of the row-major order described in Section 3-8. Storage is only for the values of array elements; no run-time descriptor is necessary.

The sequential storage representation is critical in the definition of the COMMON and EQUIVALENCE declarations. COMMON is discussed in Section 10-7 because its primary purpose is that of setting up shared data between subprograms. The EQUIVALENCE declaration allows more than one simple or subscripted variable to refer to the same storage location.

Example. EQUIVALENCE (X,Y). This declaration specifies that the simple variable names X and Y are to be associated with the same storage location. The value stored at that location may later be retrieved or modified through either of the identifiers X or Y.

Example. EQUIVALENCE (A(1,1),K(1)). This also assumes the declaration

DIMENSION A(10,20),K(21)

The EQUIVALENCE declaration defines the first element of matrix A and the first element of vector K to share the same storage unit. Because of the sequential storage representation assumed for both arrays, however, much more is actually declared implicitly: The entire 21 elements of vector K share storage with the first 21 elements of the sequential representation of matrix A, as shown in Fig. 10-2.

The intent of the EQUIVALENCE statement is to allow the *reuse* of storage reserved for variables and arrays. Because all storage is

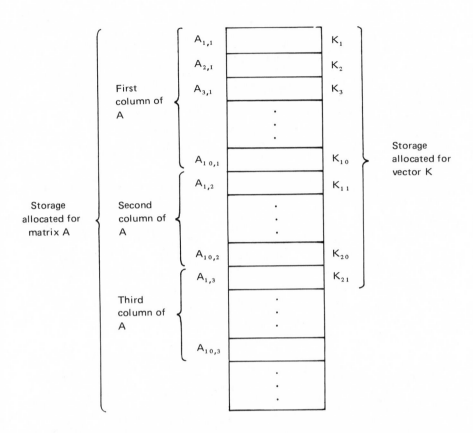

Fig. 10-2. Effect of an EQUIVALENCE statement.

allocated statically during translation in FORTRAN, an array which is used only in part of the program cannot be destroyed and the storage recovered and used to create another array. The EQUIVALENCE declaration allows the programmer to shoulder the burden of reuse of storage if he wishes. The EQUIVALENCE declaration above, for example, might be used if the programmer were planning to use matrix A only during the first part of his program and vector K only during the last part. He could then set up the storage allocated for A to be used also for K.

The EQUIVALENCE declaration, although useful in a language with only static storage management, is a poor substitute for true dynamic storage management. Essentially the burden of storage allocation and reuse is placed on the programmer, and no safeguards are provided. Note, for example, that arrays A and K are of types real and integer, respectively, in the above. It is possible to store a real number in A(1,1) and later retrieve it through K(1), thinking it an integer. No run-time descriptors are present so this error cannot be detected in most FORTRAN implementations—the programmer is left to track down a most subtle error.

External Data Files

FORTRAN provides input-output facilities only for sequential external files. These features are taken up in the next section.

10-5. OPERATIONS

FORTRAN provides an extensive set of primitives for arithmetic and for conversion between the four number data types. The basic relational and Boolean primitives are also provided. Accessing and assignment are the only operations allowed for variables and arrays (besides the compile-time creation discussed in the preceding section). Input-output operations are provided for reading and writing sequential data files. The operation set may also be extended through subprograms.

Arithmetic Operations

The basic FORTRAN arithmetic primitives (from highest precedence to lowest) are

> ** (exponentiation)
> * (multiplication), / (division)
> + (addition), - (subtraction, negation)

written in infix notation (Polish prefix for negation). These operator symbols each represent a generic arithmetic operation. The full data declarations required, however, allow static type checking and compilation into type-specific primitives in the executable program. No type conversions are performed automatically in arithmetic expressions—each operator must be provided operands of the correct type, or a syntax error is signaled.

A second set of primitives are termed the *intrinsic functions*. Included in this set are explicit type conversions between number data types (real-to-integer, real-to-double-precision, etc.), and type-specific functions for MAX, MIN, absolute value, etc., on the different number data types. Intrinsic functions are ordinarily compiled into in-line-executable code.

A third set of primitives, termed the *basic external functions*, is defined as the required routines in a library of FORTRAN-callable library functions. Included are functions for square root, trigonometric operations, logarithms, etc., each in various type-specific versions. External and intrinsic functions are called using the usual mathematical function syntax, e.g., SQRT(X) or MAX0(I,J).

Relational and Logical Operations

Relational primitives are provided for comparisons between numeric values of type integer, real, or double-precision. The operations are written in infix, using the symbols

.EQ.	(equal)
.NE.	(not-equal)
.LT.	(less-than)
.GT.	(greater-than)
.LE.	(less-than-or-equal)
.GE.	(greater-than-or-equal)

Integer values may be compared only with each other; real and double-precision values may be mixed.

The infix operations .OR. and .AND. and the prefix operation .NOT. are defined on logical values.

Accessing and Assignment

Accessing of an array element is specified using ordinary functional notation: The array name is followed by a list of one to three subscripts enclosed in parentheses, e.g., A(I,2) or B(I,J,K). Subscripts are restricted to integers, simple integer variables, or expressions of the form $c*I \pm k$, where I is a simple integer variable and c and k are integers (either c or k may be omitted). These restricted subscript expressions allow efficient run-time formulas for array accessing to be utilized (see Problem 10-2) but at some considerable loss in flexibility.

Assignment (syntax: =) is the basic operation for modifying elements of arrays and values of simple variables. Static type checking is performed, with type conversion between certain numeric data types set up implicitly when the type of the value to be assigned differs from the type declared for the variable or array element which is to be modified. For example, the assignment

$$A(3) = I - 2$$

where A is declared REAL and I INTEGER, is translated into an integer-to-real conversion followed by the assignment. Assignment cannot change any of the declared properties of an array or variable, including the length of any data element.

A number of forms of assignment statement are provided. An *arithmetic assignment statement* is used to assign a numeric value to a simple variable or array element. The value to be assigned is defined by an arbitrary arithmetic expression. For example,

$$X = Y + Z \text{ or } A(I,2) = U - V * W$$

A *logical assignment statement* is used to assign a logical (Boolean) value to a logical variable or array element, using a logical expression to define the value. For example,

$$L = X \text{ .LT. } Y \text{ .AND. } Z \text{ .GT. } 0$$

A *statement number assignment statement* is described in Section 10-6.

The language contains rather elaborate facilities for assignment of initial values to variables and arrays. Since storage for these data structures is allocated during translation, the initial value assignments are also done during translation, and no run-time cost is incurred. A *data initialization statement* is used for this purpose. The data initialization statement is composed of a list of simple and subscripted variables together with a corresponding list of initial values to be assigned. For example,

$$DATA \ X/1.0/Y/3.1416/K/20$$

defines the initial values of the variables X, Y, and K to be 1.0, 3.1416, and 20, respectively. X, Y, and K must be local variables. Initial values may be assigned to global variables and arrays (defined in COMMON blocks; see Section 10-7), but such assignments must be made using the data initialization statement within a special *block data subprogram* which consists only of the special header BLOCK DATA, followed by COMMON declarations and data initialization statements for the COMMON variables and arrays. The result of translation of such a block data subprogram is a set of loader tables which are used by the loader at the end of translation to initialize the appropriate storage locations before execution begins.

Input-Output

All external files are simple sequential files. Standard FORTRAN provides facilities to read and write such files and to reposition the current record pointer. Many FORTRAN implementations extend this basic set of operations considerably.

An external file is composed of a sequence of records together with the usual current record pointer which always points to the next record to be read (for an input file) or the next position to be written (for an output file). The current record pointer may be directly repositioned by execution of one of the statements

REWIND n

BACKSPACE n

where n is an integer identifying the file. REWIND sets the current record pointer of file n back to the beginning; BACKSPACE moves it back one record (if it is not already at the beginning). Records on a file are termed *formatted* if they consist of character strings to be read and decoded using a special *formatted READ* operation. This form is the usual one for data prepared externally. An alternative is the *unformatted* record, which may be viewed as data written out on a *scratch file* temporarily during program execution to be read in later by the same (or another) program for further processing.

READ Operations. Two READ operations are provided—one for formatted and one for unformatted records. The unformatted READ has the simple form

READ (*unit-num*) *list*

The formatted READ differs only in specifying a FORMAT statement used to control the input conversion:

READ (*unit-num*, *format-num*) *list*

The *list* is a list of simple variables, arrays elements, or array names into which values are to be read. Some examples are given in Section 10-3.

WRITE Operations. The output operations utilize the same statement format as the READ operations, with the word WRITE replacing the word READ.

The FORMAT declarations used to guide the formatted input and output operations allow a great deal of flexibility in specification of the pattern to be used. Basically the programmer may specify spacing between lines and between items in a line, number representations and number of digits to appear, and character strings to be used as headings and other explanatory data for output. On input the layout, spacing, position of decimal point in numbers, and type of conversion for numbers may be specified. The structure of such FORMAT declarations is rather complex, and the details are not of concern here. Some examples are given in Section 10-3. Formats are usually stored as character strings, without translation. During execution of a READ or WRITE statement they are interpreted by the I/O system run-time routines and used to control the I/O operation.

Subprograms

Three types of subprograms may be defined to extend the set of built-in primitives.

External Functions. Subprograms that are defined and compiled as a separate unit are termed *external functions* if they return a value. External functions are written as FORTRAN programs with a special header card which defines the function name, formal parameter list, and type of the value returned by the function. A function may only return a single number or a single Boolean value as its explicit result, although other values may be returned through side effects (changes in parameters or in COMMON variables).

External functions are called during the evaluation of arithmetic or logical expressions. The syntax is the ordinary mathematical function syntax, e.g., FN(X,Y).

External Subroutines. Subprograms that are defined and compiled as separate units are termed *external subroutines* if they return no explicit value. These are also FORTRAN programs with a special header card which specifies the subroutine name and formal parameter list, e.g.,

SUBROUTINE SUB(A,B,C)

Subroutines must return results through side effects and must be called using a special CALL statement, such as

CALL SUB(X,Y,Z)

External functions and subroutines may also be coded in other languages, e.g., assembly language.

Statement Functions. A function whose value may be computed in a single arithmetic or logical expression may be defined as a *statement function*, local to a particular subprogram. A statement function definition appears as a single declaration at the beginning of a main program or subprogram definition, following all the other declarations but before executable statements begin. The definition consists only of the function name, a formal parameter list, and the expression by which the value may be computed, e.g.,

$$FN(X,Y) = SIN(X)**2 - COS(Y)**2$$

The implicit typing rules for variable names apply to determine the type of both the formal parameters and the type of the result returned by the function (or types may be declared explicitly in the declarations of the program). The rules for type conversion of the result are exactly the same as for an assignment of the value of the expression to the function name as a variable.

Statement functions may be called as ordinary functions within expressions in the body of the program in which they are defined. They serve mainly as a shorthand in writing expressions that occur repeatedly in assignments. Because the statement function definition is local to the subprogram in which it is used, each function call is ordinarily replaced by the body of the function during translation, and no execution call and return overhead is necessary—the code is in-line within the executable program.

10-6. SEQUENCE CONTROL

The sequence control facilities of FORTRAN are straightforward.

Expressions

An expression may be used only to compute a single number or logical value. The primitives have the precedence order given below, associativity is from left to right, and parentheses may be used in the usual manner to control the order of evaluation.

$$**$$
$$*,/$$
$$+,-$$
.EQ.,.NE.,.LT.,.GT.,.LE.,.GE.
.NOT.
.AND.
.OR.

Functions may have side effects that affect the result of expression evaluation. The FORTRAN definition explicitly states that such side effects are not allowed and that any FORTRAN implementation may rearrange the order of evaluation of an expression for optimization in any manner, provided, of course, that the tree structure of the expression defined by the precedence rules and parentheses is not violated. Unfortunately, there is no way that the prohibition on side effects which affect evaluation can be enforced, because of the separate compilation of external functions. Thus it is essentially a case of "let the programmer beware"—errors caused by side effects must be detected by the programmer.

Statement Sequence Control

The order of declarations in a program is immaterial. The executable statements are always executed in their physical program sequence unless the sequence is modified by an explicit control statement.

Statement Labels. All explicit sequence control is based on statement labels and GOTOs. Statement labels are restricted to positive integers and thus have little mnemonic value. Each statement begins with a fixed length *statement number field* of five characters, which is either left blank or contains the integer statement number.

GOTO Statements. Three types of explicit GOTO statements are provided. To effect a direct transfer of control to another statement, the *unconditional* GOTO is used, e.g., GOTO 21. The *assigned* GOTO allows transfer to different statements depending on the value of a *label variable*. The statement has the form GOTO K, $(n_1, n_2, \ldots, n_p)$, where K is a simple integer variable and the n_is are statement numbers. The value of K cannot be computed but instead must be specified by a special *statement number assignment statement* of the form

$$\text{ASSIGN 21 TO K}$$

where 21 is one of the numbers in the set $n_1, n_2, \ldots, n_p$. The statement number must be given explicitly in the ASSIGN statement and cannot be computed, and in addition, the ASSIGN must appear in the same subprogram in which the assigned GOTO appears. These restrictions allow the assigned GOTO to be compiled into a simple run-time unconditional jump, with the ASSIGN statement simply filling in the address of the code for the designated statement.

A third form of GOTO allows multiway branching based on the value of an integer variable. This statement is termed a *computed* GOTO and has the form

$$\text{GOTO } (n_1, n_2, n_3, \ldots, n_p), \text{I}$$

The sequence of statement numbers $n_1, n_2, \ldots, n_p$ essentially serves as a vector of statement numbers and I as a subscript. The value of I must be in the range $1 \cdots p$, and control is transferred to the statement numbered n_I. Again this structure allows efficient execution because no run-time computation of statement numbers is involved.

Conditional Statements. Two conditional branching statements are provided in addition to the computed and assigned GOTOs described above. An *arithmetic* IF statement provides a three-way branch depending on whether the value of an arithmetic expression is negative, zero, or positive:

$$IF(expr)n_{neg}, n_{zero}, n_{pos}$$

where the *n*s are statement numbers to which control is to be transferred.

A *logical* IF statement allows only execution of a single statement if the value of a logical expression is true, using the syntax

$$IF(expr) \quad statement$$

The *statement* may not be a DO statement or another logical IF, thus disallowing any sort of nested statement structure.

Iteration Statements. The FORTRAN iteration statement is very simple in form. The header has the structure

$$DO \; stmt\text{-}num \; int\text{-}var \; = \; init\text{-}val, term\text{-}val$$

or

$$DO \; stmt\text{-}num \; int\text{-}var \; = \; init\text{-}val, term\text{-}val, increment\text{-}val$$

where *int-var* is a simple integer variable to be used as a counter during repeated executions of the body of the loop. *Init-val* is either an integer or a variable specifying the initial value of the counter, *term-val* likewise specifies the final value for the counter which terminates the loop, and *increment-val* specifies the amount to be added to the value of *int-var* each time through the loop. If omitted, the increment is 1.

The body of the loop extends from the DO statement itself to the statement which is labeled with the *stmt-num* specified in the DO statement. Execution of the loop is according to the

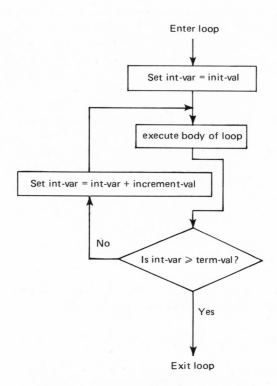

Fig. 10-3. Flow chart of DO loop execution.

flowchart of Fig. 10-3. Most of the complexities of iteration statements are avoided by the restriction that neither the value of *int-var* nor the values of variables used to specify *init-val*, *term-val*, or *increment-val* may be modified during execution of the loop. This restriction allows all the loop parameters to be calculated once on first entry to the loop and never recomputed. Usually the parameters are put in high-speed registers during loop execution for efficiency.

Subprogram Sequence Control

Only the basic call and return structure, without recursion, is provided. Function subprograms are called using the ordinary functional notation within expressions, e.g., X + FN(X,Y); subroutines are called using a separate CALL statement, e.g., CALL SUB(X,Y).

A RETURN statement in a subprogram causes a return from the subprogram when executed. The entire chain of main program and subprogram calls may be terminated by execution of a STOP statement.

This subprogram control structure may be simulated using only a single return point location for each subprogram, as explained in Section 5-4, and thus execution is very efficient, in keeping with the general FORTRAN design philosophy.

Execution may be interrupted and control passed to an unspecified external operating environment using the statement

PAUSE n

where n is an integer or omitted. A programmer is expected to inspect the number n from a console and then signal resumption of execution, but no language features support this.

10-7. DATA CONTROL

Referencing in FORTRAN is either local or global; no provision for intermediate levels of nonlocal referencing is made. All identifiers must be declared (explicitly or implicitly) in the program. These structures allow determination of each subprogram's referencing environment during translation and efficient handling of environments during execution with essentially no overhead.

Subprogram Referencing Environments

Ordinarily simple variables and arrays are local to the subprogram in which they are declared and used. The local referencing environment for each subprogram is set up during translation. During execution the associations are activated on each entry and deactivated on each exit from the subprogram; thus whenever a subprogram is reentered all local variables and arrays have the values they had on the last exit. This structure reflects the underlying run-time structure used: Storage for variables and arrays is allocated statically during translation, and references are translated into direct memory addresses (usually an offset from a base address) for the locations where the data are stored. Thus no explicit referencing environment tables need be present during execution—the environment has been "compiled into" the executable code. Because of this structure no explicit modification of referencing environment is required on subprogram entry or exit; instead the transfer of control to the subprogram implicitly changes the local referencing environment appropriately. This direct local referencing applies to simple variables, arrays, statement numbers, and I/O format statements.

If simple variables or arrays are to be shared between subprograms, they must be explicitly declared part of the global referencing environment. This global environment is not set up in terms of single variables and arrays but rather in terms of *sets of variables and arrays*, which are termed *COMMON blocks*. A COMMON block is a named block of storage and may contain the values of any number of simple variables and arrays. For example,

$$COMMON/BLK/X,Y,K(25)$$

appearing in a subprogram declares a COMMON block named BLK which contains the variables X and Y and the vector K. Assuming that X and Y have type real and K has type integer, the block BLK occupies 27 storage units in sequence in memory. Suppose that two subprograms SUB1 and SUB2 both contain the above COMMON declaration. Then the block BLK is accessible to both of them, and the identifiers X, Y, and K have the same associations (and values) in each. Any other subprogram may gain access to this same COMMON block by inclusion of the same COMMON declaration in the subprogram definition.

The effect of the COMMON declaration is effectively to allow the global referencing environment to be partitioned into *blocks*, so that every subprogram need not have access to all the global environment. The COMMON declaration allows efficient run-time processing, because any reference to a global variable in a subprogram may be immediately compiled into a base address + offset computation at run time, where the base address is the address of the beginning of the COMMON block.

The COMMON statement is most often used in an identical form in each subprogram accessing a given COMMON block. However, the structure allows other possibilities as well. Observe that is is only the *name* of a COMMON block that is actually a global identifier; the variable and array names in the COMMON statement list are *local* to the subprogram in which the statement appears; i.e., it is only the block of storage containing the values of the identifiers which is actually being shared, not the identifiers themselves. It is thus possible to have different identifiers and to organize the COMMON block differently in each subprogram which uses it. For example, if subprogram SUB1 contained the COMMON statement given above, SUB2 might contain

$$COMMON/BLK/U,V,I(5),M(4,5)$$

This COMMON block also occupies 27 storage units, and the type assigned to each element of the block is the same in each case. The second COMMON statement assigns a completely different set of identifiers and array structures to the 27 storage units, but such an assignment is valid as long as the overall length and type structure of the block is preserved.

Subprogram Parameters and Results

Parameter transmission is uniformly by reference. Actual parameters may be simple variables, literals, subscripted variables, array names, subprogram names, or arithmetic or logical expressions. The details of transmission by reference for these types of parameters are given in Section 6-9.

Results of function subprograms are transmitted by assignment within the subprogram to the name of the subprogram. The name of the subprogram acts as a local variable within the subprogram, and the last assignment made before return to the calling program is the value returned. Subprograms may return only single numbers or logical values as results.

10-8. OPERATING ENVIRONMENT

FORTRAN is designed for a batch-processing environment. Relatively little is assumed about the operating environment outside of the structure of input-output data files detailed in Section 10-5 and the assumed presence of a compile-time library of subprograms including at least the set of basic external functions noted in Section 10-5.

10-9. SYNTAX AND TRANSLATION

FORTRAN subprograms are designed to be separately compiled, with the compiled programs linked together by the loader before execution. As a result each subprogram definition contains full declarations for all global as well as local identifiers—variables and arrays in COMMON blocks, parameters, called subprograms and functions, etc. This structure allows translation of each subprogram into efficient executable code, with most error checking performed during translation.

Syntax

Program syntax is semifixed field and oriented toward punched card input. A program is a sequence of *lines*, each of 72 characters.

The first five characters of a line are reserved for the statement number, if any. Character positions 7—72 contain the statement itself, written in free format with spaces inserted as desired. If a statement is continued to a second line, character position 6 is used to designate a *continuation line*. Each program has a fairly fixed structural format consisting of an initial header card (except for the main program), followed by declarations, statement function definitions (if any), executable program statements, and a terminating END statement, in that order. Each statement and declaration begins with a key word identifying its type—DO, IF, etc.—except assignment statements and statement function definitions. FORTRAN uses only a standard basic character set, with no unusual special characters.

Individual lines of a FORTRAN program are usually easily understandable. The overall structure of programs, however, tends to be rather opaque because of the heavy use of statement labels and GOTOs in the sequence control mechanisms. Thus it is often difficult to see the overall flow of control in a FORTRAN program. Also the use of mnemonic identifiers is hampered by a restriction to six character identifiers.

Translation

Translation of most FORTRAN statements is straightforward and may proceed on a simple line-by-line basis. The only structure of any complexity in a program is the DO loop. The translator must match each DO statement with the numbered statement designated as terminating the body of the loop, and check that numerous restrictions on the structure and nesting of DO loops are satisfied.

Each FORTRAN subprogram is translated separately. The language structures are designed so that the entire storage requirements of a subprogram may be determined by the translator. The translator is thus able to set up the entire run-time structure for a subprogram as a contiguous block of memory, divided into areas of compiled code, system data, and programmer-defined data structures. Only the linkages to COMMON blocks, system run-time routines, and called subprograms cannot be filled in during initial compilation. However, these linkages may be filled in by the loader when the various separately compiled programs are assembled in memory prior to execution. The compiler, therefore, constructs the memory "image" of the block of memory for each compiled subprogram and in addition outputs a set of loader tables which define for the loader the remaining linkages between subprograms which must be filled in before execution. The necessary linkages, in general, are simple and easily made by the loader.

Error detection during translation is an important part of most FORTRAN compilers. Because extensive declarations for data are provided, and because of the relatively simple program structures involved, most errors are relatively easily detected during translation. Run-time error detection, however, is usually poor, except in *diagnostic* implementations designed for program testing. The reason is the conflict between run-time error checking and efficient execution—in general, the information necessary for run-time error checking, e.g., data types and array bounds, need not be present during execution for other purposes, and thus there is some (often substantial) extra overhead required for run-time error checking.

Optimization is a key feature of most implementations. In fact, much of the work on program optimization has grown out of attempts to optimize FORTRAN-executable machine code.

Formal Syntax

Although formal definitions of FORTRAN syntax exist (see, e.g., Burkhardt [1965]), they have been of relatively little importance in the FORTRAN development. In fact, the formal definition of standard FORTRAN does not utilize a formal grammar for syntax specification. Complete syntactic definition of FORTRAN is made complex by the semifixed field format and by the numerous minor restrictions on various constructs.

10-10. STRUCTURE OF A FORTRAN VIRTUAL COMPUTER

Simulation of a FORTRAN virtual computer on a conventional computer poses few problems. Because storage allocations are entirely static, the entire run-time memory organization may be set before execution begins. Figure 10-4 illustrates a typical run-time memory layout. The memory area is divided into blocks of varying size. Each block contains one subprogram (including compiled code and local data structures), one COMMON block, or a run-time system routine. The special *blank COMMON* block is used for the COMMON block with a null name. In the usual implementation the loader initially is stored in this block at the beginning of loading. The loader brings in each of the separately compiled subprogram and COMMON blocks, stores them in memory starting at the other end of the available area, and links them together appropriately as required by the compiler-produced loader tables. The space occupied by the loader is allocated for blank COMMON. Although this organization is hidden from the programmer, it gives the special blank COMMON

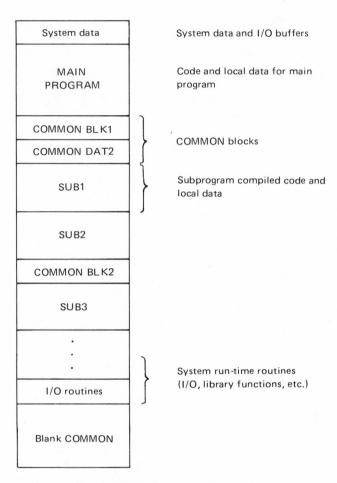

Fig. 10-4. FORTRAN run-time memory layout.

block the property that it cannot be initialized using the DATA statement (because such initialization would entail the loader loading initial values on top of itself).

Little software simulation is required for primitives except for the input-output operations. The I/O package in most implementations is a sizable set of routines which must be present in memory throughout execution. Other FORTRAN structures are compiled directly into machine code on most computers, with no need for software simulation. The run-time representations for almost all these structures have been described in the previous chapters.

10-11. REFERENCES AND SUGGESTIONS FOR FURTHER READING

Numerous texts describe the essentials of FORTRAN programming. The standard definition of the language is found in ANSI [1966]. For most purposes the more accessible preliminary definition in ACM [1964] is sufficient. Further clarification of the standard definition is provided in ANSI [1971].

Sammet [1969] provides an extensive collection of references on various aspects of the language, as well as an excellent history of its development. A paper by Backus et al. [1957] is the first published description of the language. This paper, as well as further historical commentary, is found in Rosen [1967]. Numerous papers on applications of FORTRAN have appeared in the *Communications of the ACM* and other technical journals. A *FORTRAN Bulletin* describing new developments in the evolution of the language appears periodically as part of *SIGPLAN Notices*.

10-12. PROBLEMS

10-1. State an algorithm for distinguishing FORTRAN assignment statements from other types of statements. Assignment statements begin with no key word; an identifier always begins the statement (either a simple variable or an array name). However, since the key words which begin other statements are not reserved, an identifier may be identical with a key word. Thus, for example,

$$DO\ 21\ I = 2.5$$
$$IF(J) = K - L$$

are valid assignments (recall that spaces are not significant). How may a FORTRAN translator distinguish assignments from other statement types most easily?

10-2. FORTRAN subscript expressions are restricted to the general form $C * I \pm K$ (see Section 10-5). One of the reasons is that such subscripts allow most or all of the accessing formula for an array reference to be computed in high-speed registers, with a minimum number of accesses to main memory.

    a. Determine the accessing formula which must be used for references $A(cI+k)$, $B(cI+k,dJ+\ell)$, and $C(cI+k,dJ+\ell,eK+m)$. Recall that FORTRAN arrays are stored by columns rather than rows (Section 10-4).

b. For your local computer, design a machine code sequene which performs as much of the accessing calculation as possible in high-speed registers. Try to minimize accesses to main memory. Note that only the values of I, J, and K vary during execution; the other elements in the formulas are fixed.

10-3. In an attempt to allow more efficient program execution, the definition of standard FORTRAN introduces the concept of *second-level definition* for certain variables at certain points in a program. Write a short paper explaining the concept of second-level definition and its effect on the run-time structures which may be used in a FORTRAN implementation.

10-4. A subprogram may be transmitted as a parameter from one subprogram to another in FORTRAN, e.g., by

CALL SUB1(A,B,SUB2)

in which SUB2 is a subprogram name. However, the identifier SUB2 in such a call may be ambiguous. To resolve the ambiguity an

EXTERNAL SUB2

declaration is required in the program containing the above CALL statement. Explain the cause of the ambiguity and the manner in which the EXTERNAL declaration resolves it.

10-5. Recursive subprogram calls are not permitted in FORTRAN, but most implementations do not check for such errors. Instead a recursive call will be executed properly but the program will later get into a loop when it attempts to return from the subprogram called recursively.

a. Explain the cause of the loop.

b. Design a subprogram call and return mechanism that will detect a recursive call at the time of call and generate an error message.

11 ALGOL 60

11-1. INTRODUCTION

The definition of ALGOL 60 was a key event in the history of programming languages. No other single language has had such far-reaching influence on the design and definition of languages. ALGOL has also been the central language on which much research in programming languages has been based. Oddly this importance has come about in spite of the fact that the language has never seen widespread use in the United States for practical work (although it has been widely used in Europe and at U. S. universities).

ALGOL was designed by an international committee during the late 1950s and early 1960s, culminating in the 1963 "Revised Report on the Algorithmic Language ALGOL 60" (Naur [1963]), one of the classic documents in the literature of computer science. The book by Sammet [1969] contains a thorough history of the ALGOL development.

ALGOL is usually classified as a language for scientific computations because of its emphasis on numeric data and homogeneous array data structures. Of course it is applicable to other areas as well, but the relative inflexibility of its data structures usually makes other languages more suitable.

Two outstanding characteristics make ALGOL important: the general clarity and elegance of its structure, and the manner of its definition. Of particular note are its control structures; both PL/I and later versions of FORTRAN (including the FORTRAN of Chapter 10) have benefited from the ALGOL control structure design, as have many other languages, e.g., BLISS (Wulf et al.

[1971]) and PASCAL (Wirth [1971b]). A successor to ALGOL, the language ALGOL 68, was designed by another committee under the auspices of IFIP during the late 1960s and is described in Van Wijngaarden et al. [1969].

The definition of ALGOL was the first use of a formal grammar for the definition of the syntax of a programming language. The BNF grammar form was developed specifically for the definition of ALGOL and first described in a paper by Backus [1960]. There was a careful attempt to provide a complete semantic definition of the language as well, although this part of the definition utilized no formalism (and was not without errors and ambiguities; see Knuth [1967]). The concise, elegant, and relatively complete definition of the language made it ideally suited to formal analysis and study. As a result much research in the area of programming languages has utilized ALGOL as a focus.

One further use of the language has increased its importance: It has served for many years as the primary publication language for algorithms in the *Communications of the ACM* and other journals. It is fair to state that a knowledge of ALGOL is a necessary prerequisite to much advanced work in programming languages and related areas.

11-2. BRIEF OVERVIEW OF THE LANGUAGE

ALGOL is a language designed for compilation. In the usual implementation, programs and subprograms are compiled into machine code, with only a minimum of software simulation required for some of the primitive operations. Except in a few instances the language structures are designed so that the compiler can do most of the data descriptor creation and processing and so that relatively efficient executable code can be produced, utilizing hardware structures directly wherever possible. The major exceptions are in provision for dynamic creation and destruction of data structures during execution and for dynamic changes in referencing environments based on the concept of *static block structure* as described in Section 6-6. These dynamically varying run-time structures are restricted in use, however, so that a simple stack storage allocation mechanism based on *activation records* created on entry to subprograms may be used, as described in Section 7-6. Owing to the dynamic storage allocation and referencing environment updating necessary during execution, ALGOL programs in general cannot be executed as efficiently as equivalent FORTRAN programs on conventional hardware. This is one major reason ALGOL has never supplanted FORTRAN in much scientific programming.

An ALGOL program is composed of a main program and a set of subprograms, constructed of blocks. A *block* is composed of a set of declarations followed by a sequence of statements, with the whole enclosed by the delimiters **begin** . . . **end**. The main program is simply a single block. Each subprogram definition is composed of a *header*, which declares the subprogram name, the names of the formal parameters, and types for each name, and a *body*, which in general is a block. Block boundaries determine points of data structure creation and destruction as well as the scope of all identifier associations (with minor exceptions).

The declarations beginning a block serve two main purposes:

1. Subprogram definitions must appear as *declarations* in the block before they may be called. The subprogram body is compiled into a separate segment of executable code during translation, but the association of the subprogram name with the code is set up only on entry to the block containing the definition during execution.

2. Data structures—arrays and simple variables—must be declared in the block in which they are to be used. Each declaration specifies an identifier to be associated with a data structure on entry to the block during execution. The programmer may choose whether the structure named is to be created anew on each entry and destroyed on each exit or whether it is to be retained between entries with only the identifier association deactivated on block exit and reactivated on entry.

The statements within a block center around the usual assignment statement, which may be used to assign new values to simple variables or elements of arrays. The other statement types are used for sequence control: a test-branch-join conditional statement, an iteration statement, a subprogram call statement (with recursion), and statement labels and a **goto** statement. In addition one block may appear as a *statement* within another block, allowing the definition of new identifier associations and new data structures at any point. Such associations are local to the block and may not be referenced outside the block in which they occur.

Data in ALGOL are restricted to simple homogeneous arrays of integer, real, or Boolean elements. A fairly extensive set of arithmetic, relational, and logical operations are provided.

ALGOL is the original *block-structured* language, using the static block structure to determine referencing environments throughout. The language also provides two options for transmission of actual parameters to subprograms: transmission by value or transmission by name.

11-3. AN ANNOTATED EXAMPLE: SUMMATION
OF A VECTOR

The ALGOL program of Fig. 11-1 represents a main program and a function subprogram. The subprogram sums the elements of an argument vector of real numbers. The main program serves as a driver for the subprogram, creating a vector, reading numbers into the vector, calling the subprogram to compute the sum, printing the result, and returning to create a new vector and a new set of numbers. The program is the ALGOL equivalent of the FORTRAN program of Section 10-3. The following explanation of the details of the program structure is keyed to the line numbers on the left in Fig. 11-1, which are not a part of the ALGOL program.

Line 1. The main program has the form of a block enclosed by **begin** . . . **end.** Lines 2—9 are main program declarations. Lines 10—16 are statements forming the executable part of the main program.

Line 2. The first line of the subprogram definition extending through line 8. Every subprogram must be defined as a declaration either in the main program or in another subprogram definition. Line 2 names the subprogram *SUM,* names the formal parameters *V* and

```
Line
 1              begin
 2                  procedure SUM(V,N); value N;
 3                      real array V; integer N;
 4                      begin integer I; real TEMP;
 5                          TEMP:=0;
 6                          for I:=1 step 1 until N do TEMP:=TEMP+V[I];
 7                          SUM:=TEMP
 8                      end;
 9                  integer K;
10              START: inreal(1,K);
11                      If K > 0 then
12                          begin real array A [1:K];
13                              inarray(1,A);
14                              outreal(2, SUM(A,K));
15                              goto START
16                          end
17              end
```

Fig. 11-1. Example ALGOL program.

N, and specifies that the parameter corresponding to *N* is to be transmitted by value. Transmission by name is assumed unless transmission by value is specified explicitly. The identifier *SUM* is a local identifier in the *main program* referencing environment; *V* and *N* are local to the definition of *SUM*.

Line 3. Declaration of data type for the actual parameters corresponding to the formal parameters *V* and *N*. Note the *V* is declared to correspond to an array, but no declaration of number of dimensions or subscript range is given. This information is transmitted in a run-time array descriptor with the actual parameter.

Line 4. The first line of the body of the subprogram. A subprogram body is defined to be a single statement, which may be a block delimited by **begin** . . . **end** and containing a set of statements. Since a set of statements are required for this subprogram, a new block is begun with **begin**. Declarations for two local variables *I* and *TEMP* follow. These variables will be created on entry to this block during execution and destroyed on exit; thus their lifetime is essentially that of one execution of the subprogram *SUM*.

Line 5. The := is the assignment operator. The local variable *TEMP* is initialized to zero. The newly created local variable *TEMP* has an undefined initial value; thus this initialization statement is required.

Line 6. An iteration statement which adds the array elements to the value of the local variable *TEMP* in sequence. The iteration statement header **for** *I* := 1 **step** 1 **until** *N* **do** initializes the local variable *I* to the value 1 and then executes the body *TEMP* := *TEMP* + *V* [*I*] repeatedly, incrementing the value of *I* by 1 after each execution until the value *N* is reached.

Line 7. Subprogram *SUM* is to be a function, returning a value. The value to be returned is designated within the subprogram definition by an assignment to the name of the subprogram. In this case the value returned is the value of the local variable *TEMP*, containing the sum of the elements of the operand vector *V*.

Line 8. End of definition of subprogram *SUM*. The **end** closes the block which began on line 4, completing the statement forming the body of *SUM*.

Line 9. Main program declaration of simple variable *K*. The declaration of subprogram *SUM* was the first declaration in the main program; this one completes the main program declarations.

Line 10. Beginning of the body of the main program. The statement is labeled *START* for the later **goto** at line 15. A value is read from input file 1 for variable *K*. The format of the value read is system- rather than programmer-defined. An automatic conversion of the input value to integer form is made.

Line 11. A test-branch-join conditional statement begins here with a test for a positive value of *K*. If the test is satisfied, the block following the **then** and extending to line 16 is executed. If the test is not satisfied, control passes to the statement following line 16, which happens to be the end of the program.

Line 12. Beginning of the block to be executed if the value of *K* is positive. The declaration **real array** $A[1:K]$ specifies that a vector of *K* elements is to be created on entry to this block, with subscripts running from 1 to the value of *K*. Each time execution reaches this block a new array is created.

Line 13. *K* real numbers are read in and stored in the vector *A*. Note that no length need be given for *A* because this information is carried in a run-time descriptor for *A*.

Line 14. The function subprogram *SUM* is called with vector *A* and its length *K* as parameters. The value returned is immediately an input to the subprogram *outreal*, which outputs the value to file 2.

Line 15. Control is transferred back to line 10 to begin reading a new set of test values. Since this transfer leads out of the block begun on line 12, the vector A created on entry to the block is destroyed by this transfer.

Line 16. End of the block begun on line 12, terminating the "true" branch of the conditional statement begun on line 11 as well.

Line 17. End of the main program (outermost) block.

11-4. DATA

ALGOL is quite restricted in the types of data allowed. The three elementary data types are **real, integer,** and **Boolean.** Homogeneous multidimensional arrays and simple variables form the basic data structure types available.

Real and integer numbers are represented in decimal notation in programs; at run time the appropriate hardware representation is assumed. Boolean values are represented by the special symbols **true** and **false** in programs; at run time, of course, a single-bit representation suffices.

Character strings, statement labels, and subprogram names are also treated as data types to a limited extent. Character strings (delimited by quotes) may be transmitted to subprograms as parameters but may not be otherwise utilized. Their use is primarily for such things as passing a page heading to an output routine. Labels and subprogram names may also be transmitted to subprograms as parameters and used within subprograms in the usual way.

The types of simple variables and arrays are declared at the beginning of a block. The size of arrays may be made dependent on run-time data, so that storage for arrays cannot be allocated until run time. Arrays may have an arbitrary number of dimensions, with the upper and lower bounds of each subscript range individually specified by the programmer. For example, the declaration

$$\text{integer array } A \ [-10:20,3:N+2]$$

defines a two-dimensional array of integers named A. A has 31 rows, referenced by the integers $-10, -9, -8, \ldots, -1, 0, 1, 2, \ldots, 20$, and a number of columns equal to the value of variable N at the time during execution when the block containing this declaration is entered. The columns are referenced by the integers $3, 4, \ldots, N - 1, N, N + 1, N + 2$. Arrays are represented at run time by the usual sequential representation. Once created their size is fixed until they are destroyed.

Ordinarily arrays and simple variables are created on entry to the block in which they are declared and destroyed on exit from the block, using the central stack for the required storage. The optional **own** declaration, however, allows retention of an array or variable between block executions. For example, the declaration

$$\text{own Boolean array } B \ [1:20]$$

defines a vector B of Boolean values which is to be created on first entry to the block in which the declaration appears during execution, and thereafter retained between entries to the block, so that on each subsequent block entry B will contain the same values it contained on the last previous exit. The **own** specification allows the odd situation of an **own** array which *varies* in size on each entry to a block. This variability conflicts with the stack-based storage management mechanism on which most ALGOL implementations are based and often is not implemented. Where the **own** array has fixed size it may be allocated storage in the static area along with the compiled code for the block. Then on block entry only the association of the array name with the storage area is entered into the activation record in the stack.

11-5. OPERATIONS

ALGOL contains a fairly extensive set of primitives for arithmetic, as well as the basic relational and Boolean operations. These are compiled into the equivalent hardware primitives in general.

Arithmetic Operations

The basic arithmetic primitives (from highest to lowest precedence) are

> ↑   (exponentiation)
> ×   (multiplication), / (real division), ÷ (integer division)
> +   (addition), − (subtraction, negation)

written in the usual infix notation (prefix for negation). The required declarations allow static type checking for these operations and compilation into type-specific run-time operations. Conversion between integer and real number representations is performed implicitly whenever necessary.

A set of *standard functions* is also provided which must include at least sine, cosine, square root, and a few other common functions. These are called with the usual mathematical function syntax, e.g., *sqrt*(X).

Relational and Boolean Operations

The relational primitives are

$$=, \; \neq, \; <, \; >, \; \leqslant, \; \geqslant$$

defined on real and integer values.

The Boolean primitives are

> ¬ (not)
> ∧ (and)

$\lor$ (or)
$\supset$ (implication)
$\equiv$ (equivalence)

All are written using the ordinary infix notation (prefix for not).

Accessing and Assignment

Subscripts designating array element accessing are written using square brackets, e.g., $A[2,3]$. Subscripts may be specified by an arbitrary arithmetic expression, so that multiple levels of subscripting are possible, e.g., $A[B[I], C[J+K]]$.

Assignment of new values to simple variables and single array elements is basic. The assignment operation is represented by $:=$. Automatic conversion is made between real and integer data types before assignment as required. A real or integer value to be assigned may be specified by an arbitrary arithmetic expression, which may include conditional expressions (see below). Similar expressions utilizing relational and Boolean operations may be used to compute Boolean values.

Creation and Destruction

Arrays and variables may be created on block entry and destroyed on exit, by means of a declaration at the beginning of the block (destruction is not explicitly specified), provided that the declaration does not include the **own** specification. Each time an array is created its size may change, although not its type or number of dimensions. The size is recomputed each time the array is created if the subscript ranges in the declaration contain variables. For example, the declaration

$$\text{array } A[J+K:M]$$

causes creation of a new vector A each time the block containing the declaration is entered during execution. Before storage for the vector is allocated, the values of the expressions $J+K$ and M are found to determine the subscript range for the new vector and the amount of storage needed.

One anomaly in the ALGOL design is an implicit *array copy* operation which is invoked whenever an array is transmitted *by value* to a subprogram. This idea is discussed in greater detail in Section 6-9.

Input-Output

The original ALGOL definition provided no facilities for input-output, on the basis that such facilities are necessarily too implementation-dependent to be part of the basic definition. This omission was remedied in two later proposals, IFIP [1964] and Knuth et al. [1964], both of which included basic features for sequential file processing. The former includes only a simple set of seven basic I/O primitives for input and output of numbers, arrays, and strings; the latter is more reminiscent of the complex FORTRAN formatted I/O operations. However, ALGOL implementations still tend to vary in this area, and we shall not describe any particular operation set as a result.

Subprograms

The set of built-in primitives may be extended through subprogram definition in the usual way. Subprograms may be functions, returning a single numeric or Boolean value, or they may work entirely through side effects. A wide variety of parameter types is allowed (see Section 11-7).

11-6. SEQUENCE CONTROL

ALGOL contains a rich and elegant set of sequence control structures at the expression and statement levels. Subprogram control is restricted to simple subprogram calls with recursion.

Expressions

Three types of expressions are recognized. *Arithmetic expressions* are composed of simple and subscripted variables, integer and real constants, function calls, and the primitive arithmetic operations. The usual hierarchy of operations is assumed, with left-to-right associativity, and parentheses are used for explicit control when necessary. A novel feature is the inclusion of conditionals within expressions. For example,

$$X := Y + (\text{if } A = B \text{ then } A + 1 \text{ else } A) * B$$

is a valid assignment which computes either the value $Y+(A+1)*B$ or $Y+A*B$ depending on whether $A=B$. *Boolean expressions* are similar to arithmetic expressions except that they may involve Boolean constants and variables and the relational and Boolean primitives.

Boolean expressions may also contain conditionals; e.g., a valid assignment is

$$B := (\text{if } X > 0 \text{ then } C \text{ else } D) \wedge E$$

where all the variables other than X have type Boolean. *Designational expressions* are discussed below.

ALGOL functions may have side effects that affect the value of an expression. Unfortunately the order of evaluation of variable and function references in expressions is not defined, so that the result of evaluation in such cases is implementation dependent.

ALGOL expressions may in general be translated into equivalent sequences of machine code instructions, although evaluation may require a number of conversions between integer and real number representations. Complexity arises from two situations: (1) ALGOL function calls may be recursive, and thus temporary storage required during expression evaluation must be allocated dynamically in cases where the expression includes a function call, and (2) in some cases the type of the result of an expression evaluation may not be predictable during translation, requiring run-time type checking. The latter situation arises in both conditional expressions and in cases where the types of formal parameters are not specified in a subprogram.

Statement Sequence Control

ALGOL statements are executed in sequence (within a given subprogram) until the end of the subprogram is reached or an explicit sequence control statement is executed. Conditional statements, iteration statements, and **goto**s are the explicit control mechanisms provided.

Conditional statements. Conditional statements have the form

if ⟨*Boolean expression*⟩ **then** ⟨*unconditional statement*⟩
else ⟨*statement*⟩

representing the following control structure:

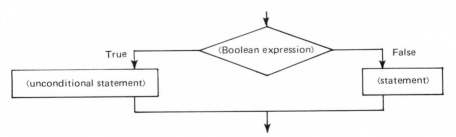

This is the classic test-branch-join structure discussed in Section 5-3. Note that the conditional uses no **gotos**; instead the boundaries of alternative sequences are explicitly delimited by the **then** ... **else** ... ; structure. The **else** ⟨*statement*⟩ portion may be omitted. When the two alternatives are combined the resulting structure is ambiguous, as discussed in Section 9-1. The solution adopted in ALGOL is to force the first ⟨*unconditional statement*⟩ to be a *compound statement*, a statement sequence enclosed in **begin** ... **end** delimiters, if it does not consist of a single unconditional statement.

Iteration Statements. ALGOL provides one of the most general iteration statements of any language described here. The **for** *statement*, as it is called, takes one of the following forms:

> **for** ⟨*variable*⟩ := ⟨*list of values*⟩ **do** ⟨*body*⟩
> **for** ⟨*variable*⟩ := ⟨*expr*⟩ **while** ⟨*Boolean expr*⟩ **do** ⟨*body*⟩
> **for** ⟨*variable*⟩ := ⟨*init-val*⟩ **step** ⟨*incr-val*⟩ **until** ⟨*final-val*⟩**do** ⟨*body*⟩

Examples

1. **for** *I* := 2,3,5,7,11,13 **do** ⟨*body*⟩. The body is executed six times, with the variable *I* assigned the values 2, 3, 5, 7, 11, and 13 on successive executions.

2. **for** *K* := *K*+1 **while** *K* ⩽ *N* ∧ *X* > 0 **do** ⟨*body*⟩. Execution of this statement follows the flow chart:

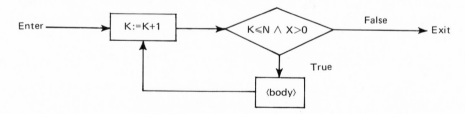

3. **for** *Q* := 1 **step** 1 **until** *N* **do** ⟨*body*⟩. The body is executed once for each integer in the range 1-*N*, with each integer assigned in turn to *Q*.

The three basic forms of **for** statement head element may be combined, as in

> **for** *I* := 2,3,7,11,15 **step** 1 **until** 20, *I*+2 **while**
> *I* ⩽ *N* ∧ *X* < 0 **do** ⟨*body*⟩

The problems of order of evaluation of variables in the **for** statement head which are discussed in Section 5-3 have never been entirely resolved in ALGOL. Knuth [1967] discusses the problem at some length. Different ALGOL implementations may use different evaluation rules, which occasionally may cause subtle differences in result if the body of a **for** statement changes the values of any of the variables referenced in the head of the statement.

Note that the **for** statement syntax requires no use of statement labels or **gotos**; as with conditional statements the various elements of the statement are delimited entirely by special key words.

Labels and **goto** *Statements.* ALGOL statements may be labeled by preceding the statement by a label and a colon. The usual **goto** statement is provided, e.g., **goto** *L2*. A number of subtleties arise in the use of **gotos** because of the block structure of programs. Statement labels need not be declared other than by use, but otherwise they are identifiers and follow the same scope rules for referencing as other identifiers. This structure means that a **goto** within a subprogram or block may cause a transfer of control to a statement outside that block or subprogram, into some enclosing block, because all the statement labels in the enclosing block are accessible from enclosed blocks or subprogram definitions. A similar situation arises when a statement label is passed as a parameter to a subprogram and used as the object of a **goto** within the subprogram. The interpretation given to such jumps to nonlocal labels is that the subprogram or block is exited normally before the control transfer is made. Thus the destruction of arrays and variables and the destruction of the referencing environment which occurs on normal exit from a block or subprogram also must occur when these nonlocal **gotos** are performed. A detailed example of these concepts and their run-time simulation is found in Section 6-9.

Switches and Designational Expressions. The basic **goto** control transfer is augmented by two additional features. A *switch*, in its simplest form, is simply a vector of statement labels. A switch declaration at the beginning of a block specifies the sequence of labels the switch contains. For example, the declaration

$$\text{switch } S \; := \; L1, L2, SY, NEXT$$

at the beginning of a block sets up a vector S containing the four statement labels $L1$, $L2$, SY, and $NEXT$. Within the block a **goto** of the form **goto** $S[2]$ may be used to transfer control to statement $L2$. The contents of a switch may not be modified during program execution, and there is no way to compute a statement label during execution. Thus the switch serves simply as a technique for programming a multiway branch, where the possible branch points may be determined at compile time. Under this restriction the compiler may compile an efficient control transfer for a switch reference.

A *designational expression* is an expression whose value is a statement label. Designational expressions may be constructed only from statement labels, switch references, and if ... then ...else conditional branching structures. The object of a **goto** is actually allowed to be any designational expression; the simple **goto** ⟨*label*⟩ is a special case. This generalization provides a more convenient syntax for branching using **goto**s. For example,

goto if $X=Y$ then $L1$ else if $X > Y$ then $L2$ else $L3$

provides a three-way branching structure. The switch structure is also extended to allow each switch element to be a designational expression rather than just a single label. For example,

switch S := $L1$, if $X=Y$ then $L2$ else $L3$, SY, $NEXT$

is a valid switch declaration. A subsequent **goto** $S[2]$ causes a transfer to statement $L2$ or $L3$ depending on whether $X=Y$.

The ALGOL features for **goto**s, switches, and designational expressions are designed so that compilation into fairly efficient executable code is possible. In particular, statement labels may not be computed during execution and thus no run-time table of statement labels is needed.

Although ALGOL provides these fairly complex features for **goto**s, it is a long-standing rule of good ALGOL programming that **goto**s should be used as seldom as possible. The other control structures, particularly the general conditionals and iteration statements, make most **goto**s avoidable. In fact the general clarity of ALGOL programs without the **goto** is probably the underlying source of the **goto** controversy discussed in Section 5-3.

Subprogram Sequence Control

ALGOL allows only simple subprogram calls with recursion. As noted above, return from a subprogram may occur either through reaching the end of the subprogram body during execution or through an explicit **goto** which transfers control to a labeled statement outside of the subprogram. No explicit *return* statement is provided. A subprogram may be called as a function within an expression or as a subroutine simply by writing the subprogram name and actual parameter list, e.g., $SUB(X, Y, Z)$, as a separate statement.

11-7. DATA CONTROL

Facilities for data control in ALGOL are much more elaborate and complex than in other early programming languages. Each block or subprogram introduces a new set of identifiers and defines their associations, which remain in effect throughout execution of the block or subprogram and are destroyed on exit. The dynamic sequence of block and procedure entries and exits during execution controls which identifier associations are in effect, but the static (compile-time) block structure controls the associations to be used in resolving references to nonlocal identifiers. This use of static block structure is described in detail in Section 6-6 and was first introduced in ALGOL.

ALGOL is rather unique in providing two argument transmission techniques: transmission by value or by name. The concepts are explained in Section 6-9. The choice of argument transmission technique is specified by listing the formal parameters to be transmitted by value in the heading of the procedure definition immediately after the list of formal parameters of the procedure, as seen in the example of Fig. 11-1.

Actual parameters may be single numbers or Boolean values, entire arrays or simple variables, subprogram names, statement labels, character strings, or arithmetic, Boolean, or designational expressions. When an expression is an actual parameter it will be transmitted unevaluated if transmission is by name, and otherwise it will be evaluated to obtain a number, Boolean value, or statement label. The complexities involved in transmission of these various types of parameters are detailed in Section 6-9.

It is in the area of data control that the largest amount of run-time simulation is needed in ALGOL. Parameter transmission by name is particularly costly since in many cases the actual parameter must be treated as a separate subprogram to be executed each time the corresponding formal parameter is referenced (see Section 6-9 for a more detailed discussion). However, the entire referencing environment based on the static program structure must also be software-simulated on conventional computers. Although techniques such as the *display* allow this to be done fairly efficiently, there is still a substantial run-time cost involved compared to the direct referencing structure used in, e.g., FORTRAN.

11-8. OPERATING ENVIRONMENT

The basic ALGOL definition specifies little about operating environment beyond the explicit mention that the body of a procedure may be defined in *code*, presumably another language. The ALGOL report specifies no input-output structures and thus even an assumption of an environment of external data files is lacking, although of course each implementation adds input-output facilities. There is no provision for calling external subprograms, nor is there provision for separate compilation of ALGOL procedures. The omission of provision for an operating environment has been one of the major weaknesses of the language. Because each implementation must necessarily supply such a specification, one of the major parts of the language becomes implementation-dependent. This dependence hinders the interchange of programs, which was one of the important goals of the original ALGOL design.

11-9. SYNTAX AND TRANSLATION

The ALGOL syntax is organized around the basic block-structured program organization, an organization first introduced in this language. A program is composed of nested blocks. Subprogram definitions appear as declarations within blocks and are themselves structured as nests of blocks. The important use of this organization to control the referencing environment has already been discussed at length. Syntactically this block structuring has the effect of clarifying the structure of a program. In contrast to FORTRAN, where no substructure within a single program other than a division into statements may be shown, the ALGOL structure allows multiple levels of organization within a given program.

This hierarchical organization principle shows up again in the extensive use of structured statements. The key control statements, conditional (**if**) and iteration (**for**) statements, contain other statements or groups of statements. In addition any sequence of statements may be grouped into a single compound statement by simply enclosing the sequence in **begin . . . end** delimiters. This organization allows the program structure to reflect directly the natural structure of many algorithms—a key feature in making programs readable.

Other facets of the ALGOL syntax are quite ordinary. Programs are written *free field*, without regard for card or other boundaries. The statement and expression forms are quite natural, utilizing simple key words and operator symbols to improve readability. In its general simplicity and clarity the ALGOL syntactic structure is rather elegant.

Formal Syntax

The two key innovations in ALGOL syntax were the block structure and the use of a formal grammar to define the syntax precisely. The BNF grammar form (Section 9-4), which has been the standard for syntactic definition of programming languages for many years, was developed for the definition of ALGOL. The formal grammar for ALGOL is quite concise, fitting on a single page, and yet it describes the language syntax remarkably well. It is this elegant and concise grammar which made ALGOL the basis for much work in parsing techniques and formal program analysis during the years following its definition.

Translation

ALGOL is designed to be compiled into efficient machine code, and to this end the language incorporates a variety of declarations for types, array shapes, function values, and the like. The structured statements and block structure make compilation more complex than, e.g., with FORTRAN. Translation is not a simple line-by-line process, because any individual conditional or iteration statement may contain any number of other statements. Thus the compiler must be prepared to interrupt processing of one if or for statement and process any number of other statements nested within, any one of which may be another if or for statement with other nested statements within it. The compiler must be considerably more complex in its ability to keep track of the progress of compilation on many different levels of nesting simultaneously.

Coupled with the problem of nested statement structure is the problem of the nested static referencing environment which results from the gross organization of a program into a hierarchy of block and subprogram definitions. The compiler must keep track of the static referencing environment (e.g., in a stack-structured symbol table) to be able to determine the type of identifiers in statements to be compiled. Optimization is also an important part of many ALGOL compilers, although the more complex program structure makes optimization somewhat more difficult than with FORTRAN.

Understanding of ALGOL compilation techniques, particularly

the problems of parsing the nested program structures, has been greatly enhanced by studies of formal grammars and their associated parsers. Many parsing techniques for languages described by the BNF grammar form are widely known.

11-10. STRUCTURE OF AN ALGOL VIRTUAL COMPUTER

Execution-time storage management in a typical ALGOL implementation is based on a static storage area and a central dynamically allocated stack. Programs are translated into blocks of executable machine code and allocated storage statically before execution begins. Figure 7-2 outlines the gross storage layout during execution in a typical ALGOL implementation. One area of storage is allocated for storage of the translated program to be executed. The program is represented in the form of actual machine code and is subdivided into segments corresponding to the various blocks and procedures of the original program. The exact form and organization of this program storage is of relatively little importance to the programmer. Part of this static storage area also contains the code for the various run-time support routines needed during execution, including code for software simulation of input-output operations and for standard functions such as sine and square root.

The other major storage area is that reserved for the execution-time stack, which is used for allocation of storage for the activation records associated with the various active or suspended blocks and subprograms during execution. As each subprogram or block is entered an activation record is created and allocated storage on the top of the stack. As each subprogram or block is exited the space allocated for the corresonding activation record is recovered. The careful design of the language permits immediate recovery of storage upon exit of the associated block or subprogram without the possibility of creating dangling references.

The activation record associated with a particular block or subprogram activation contains all the variable information associated with execution of that block or subprogram (see Fig. 7-1). In particular the activation record contains the current local identifier associations, storage for temporaries generated during evaluation of expressions, storage for descriptors and values of arrays and variables, and storage for parameter lists during transmission. The language is designed so that the size of each of these storage areas in an activation record may be determined at compile time with the single exception of the value storage for arrays. Section 7-6 contains more detail on the ALGOL stack storage management technique.

Run-time simulation of most ALGOL structures is relatively straightforward and allows direct use of hardware features in many cases. Arrays are stored sequentially with a partial descriptor, which is necessary because of the possibility of run-time computed subscript ranges. Declaration of type and number of dimensions, however, allows the accessing calculation to be compiled into the executable code. Declarations also allow type-specific operations to be utilized, usually directly available in the hardware, except in the few cases mentioned in the preceding section. The major areas requiring run-time software simulation are referencing environments, by name parameters, and input-output.

11-11.   REFERENCES AND SUGGESTIONS FOR FURTHER READING

ALGOL is undoubtedly the most widely written about programming language in existence. The definition of the language (Naur [1963], reprinted in Rosen [1967]) was preceded and followed by numerous books and articles describing the language and various aspects of its structure. The description by Rutishauser [1967] is perhaps the most thorough. Two proposals for input-output structures in ALGOL are found in Knuth et al. [1964] and IFIP [1964]. Knuth [1967] provides an enlightening description of some of the subtleties and fine points that led to difficulty in implementations of the language. Wegner [1968] and Galler and Perlis [1970] view various of the ALGOL concepts in the framework of more general programming language design questions. The history of the ALGOL development has also been rather thoroughly documented; see Sammet [1969] and Bemer [1969].

Techniques for ALGOL implementation have been widely discussed in the literature, in distinct contrast to implementations for most other languages. Randell and Russell [1964] and Grau et al. [1967] provide the most complete expositions of ALGOL implementation methods.

Numerous extensions and generalizations of the language have also been proposed. One important sequence of languages based on ALGOL has been the work of Niklaus Wirth (with various collaborators); see Wirth and Hoare [1966], Wirth and Weber [1966], and Wirth [1971b]. Included here are the important languages EULER and PASCAL. The most important ALGOL-based design, however, is found in the language ALGOL 68. This powerful and complex language was designed under the auspices of IFIP (International Federation for Information Processing) by a group headed by A. Van Wijngaarden. The formal definition of ALGOL 68 is found in Van Wijngaarden et al. [1969], but a more accessible description is provided by Lindsey and Van der Meulen [1971] and more briefly by Branquart et al. [1971]. ALGOL 68 is intended to be a successor to ALGOL 60 (hence the name) but as yet has not met with the wide acceptance accorded the original ALGOL.

11-12. PROBLEMS

11-1. Write an ALGOL arithmetic expression whose result may be either type real or type integer depending on data input during execution (i.e., an expression whose result type cannot be determined during compilation).

11-2. The original ALGOL definition allows a statement label to be a positive integer (rather than an identifier), but integer labels are seldom implemented because in combination with parameters of type label they lead to ambiguities that can be resolved only at run time at a considerable cost in execution speed. Explain the difficulties engendered by integer labels.

11-3. The key words in ALGOL statements (e.g., if, then, begin, real, procedure) are not reserved words. In fact in the ALGOL report (Naur [1963]) they are not words at all but simply single symbols in an extended alphabet. Such an extended alphabet is not directly implementable, and thus each ALGOL implementation must choose a way of writing these special symbols in terms of a smaller alphabet provided by the hardware. Suggest at least two different ways this might be done without introducing ambiguities into the language.

11-4. Explain the difficulties encountered in run-time storage management if *dynamic* own *arrays* are allowed, i.e., own arrays that vary in size on each entry to the block in which they are declared. For example, suppose that in block B the declaration

$$\text{own array } V[M{:}N]$$

appears. On each entry to block B only the elements of V with subscripts in the range m to n (where m and n are the current values of M and N, respectively) may be accessed, and any of these accessible elements that have been assigned a value during some previous activation of block B must still have the last assigned value. How does this concept conflict with the stack storage management scheme used in most ALGOL implementations?

12 COBOL

12-1. INTRODUCTION

COBOL (COmmon Business Oriented Language) is a language which has been widely used since the early 1960s for business applications of computers. As is the case with most other widely used languages, COBOL has evolved through a sequence of design revisions, beginning with the first version in 1960 and leading to the latest revision in 1972. Sammet [1969] gives an excellent history of the development of COBOL through 1968.

COBOL is perhaps the most widely implemented of the languages described in this book, but few of its design concepts have had a significant influence on later languages, with the exception of PL/I. Both of these facts may be partially attributed to its orientation toward business data processing, a major area of computer application, but one in which the problems are of a somewhat unique character: relatively simple algorithms coupled with high-volume input-output (e.g., computing the payroll for a large organization). Most of the other languages described in this book emphasize features supporting complex computations with relatively small amounts of input-output and thus do not benefit greatly from the COBOL design.

Because input-output is a prime concern in business applications programs, the COBOL design emphasizes features for specification of the properties and structure of input-output files. Another important and obvious language characteristic is the English-like syntax of the language statements (aimed at making programs readable enough to be largely self-documenting).

The widespread implementation and use of COBOL has led to efforts to standardize the language definition. The first COBOL standard definition was published in 1968; a revised and updated standard appeared in preliminary form in 1972. This chapter is based largely on the revised 1972 standard definition. The standard is organized in a modular fashion which allows the language to be implemented on a wide range of hardware. The definition consists of a *nucleus* and a set of ten *modules*, each of which has one to three *levels*. A minimal COBOL implementation consists of implementation of the features making up the lowest level of the nucleus and of each of the modules (table handling and sequential input-output are the only modules with a nonnull lowest level). Increasingly more powerful and complex COBOL implementations which include more powerful data and control structures and more complex interactions with external files may be constructed by adding higher levels of the nucleus or of some of the modules. On a small computer with limited I/O equipment the minimal COBOL may be reasonable, but for larger computers larger COBOL subsets are appropriate. In this manner the standard COBOL definition attempts to maintain flexibility in implementation without loss of standardization. COBOL programs which run on one COBOL implementation should run with only minor modification on any other COBOL implementation which includes the subset of the original implementation.

12-2. BRIEF OVERVIEW OF THE LANGUAGE

Perhaps the most striking aspect of a COBOL program is its organization into four *divisions*. This organization is largely a result of two design goals: that of separating *machine-dependent* from *machine-independent* program elements and that of separating data descriptions from algorithm descriptions, so that each might be modifiable without affecting the other. The result is a tripartite program organization: The PROCEDURE division contains the algorithms, the DATA division contains data descriptions, and the ENVIRONMENT division contains machine-dependent program specifications such as the connections between the program and external data files. A fourth IDENTIFICATION division begins each program and serves to name the program and its author and to provide other commentary as program documentation.

The COBOL design is based on an essentially static run-time structure. No run-time storage management is required, and many aspects of the language are designed to allow relatively efficient run-time structures to be used (although this goal is less important than that of hardware independence and program transportability).

Data representations in COBOL have a definite business-applications flavor but are rather flexible. The basic data structure is the multidimensional heterogeneous array, called a *record*. Records are also the basis for external data file structures, which play an extremely important role in COBOL. Records may be mixed with ordinary homogeneous arrays, so that homogeneous arrays may be components of records and vice versa. Such structures must be fully declared in a program and no run-time variability of structure size is allowed. Individual record elements, array elements, or simple variables must be declared as to type, but an almost unbounded set of possible type declarations may be constructed through PICTURE specifications. Numbers and character strings are the basic elementary data types. The language also provides rather extensive facilities for specifying the properties of external data files.

Built-in primitive operations include simple arithmetic, logical and relational primitives, and some simple character string scanning and substitution operations. Assignment, which includes automatic type conversion of the assigned value to the type of the receiving variable, is particularly important because of the large variety of possible type specifications allowed. As might be expected, a powerful set of input-output primitives are provided for accessing and manipulating various kinds of external files. These include input-output for sequential, indexed-sequential, and random access files; a SORT primitive; and a *report generator* for automatic generation of complex output formats.

Sequence control in COBOL includes a statement label—goto structure, a rather restricted **if . . . then . . . else** construct, and a PERFORM statement which serves both as a simple subprogram call statement and as an iteration statement. An interrupt facility is provided for use on various types of input-output errors. Expressions play a minor role in the language, and no programmer-defined functions are allowed. True subprograms (with parameters and local variables) are infrequently seen; they need not even be implemented in less than full COBOL. The PERFORM statement provides a call-return structure without change in referencing environment. Many (perhaps most) COBOL programs are written as a single routine using a common global referencing environment defined by the DATA DIVISION of the program.

The language is notable for its English-like syntax, which makes most programs relatively easy to read. The language provides numerous optional *noise words* which may be used to improve readability. The syntax makes COBOL programs easy but relatively tedious to write because even the simplest program becomes fairly lengthy (as is seen in the next section). Translation of COBOL into efficient executable code is a complex compilation problem, because of the number of different data representations which may be defined and the large number of options in the way in which many statements may be written. Most of the early COBOL compilers were extremely slow, but more recently improvements in compilation techniques have led to relatively fast COBOL compilers, producing fairly efficient executable code.

12-3. AN ANNOTATED EXAMPLE: SUMMING A LIST OF PRICES

The simple COBOL program illustrated in Fig. 12-1 processes an input file composed of a sequence of *item-name—price* pairs. Each input pair is listed in the output and a final count of the number of input pairs and the total of the item prices is output at the end. The following annotations refer to the line numbers to the left of the listing, which are not a part of the listing.

Lines 1—3. These lines form the IDENTIFICATION DIVISION of the program. They serve only as commentary. The PROGRAM-ID is required; the AUTHOR line is not. Line 1 is the required initial statement.

Lines 4—11. These lines form the ENVIRONMENT DIVISION of the program. Line 4 is the required initial statement.

Lines 5—7. The CONFIGURATION SECTION of the ENVIRON-MENT DIVISION. The SOURCE-COMPUTER paragraph identifies the computer on which the program is to be compiled. The OBJECT-COMPUTER paragraph specifies the computer on which the compiled program is to be executed. These designations may serve only as comments, but alternatively the compiler or run-time system may check them and abort compilation or execution if the actual configuration is not the same as that specified.

Lines 8—11. These lines form the INPUT-OUTPUT SECTION, consisting of a single FILE-CONTROL "paragraph," whose purpose is to relate the file names used within the program to actual external files. In this case the file called INP-DATA within the program will actually be the standard system input file INPUT. Similarly, the file called RESULT-FILE within the program will actually be the

Line

```
1          IDENTIFICATION DIVISION.
2          PROGRAM-ID. SUM-OF-PRICES.
3          AUTHOR. T-PRATT.
4          ENVIRONMENT DIVISION.
5          CONFIGURATION SECTION.
6          SOURCE-COMPUTER. CDC6400.
7          OBJECT-COMPUTER. CDC6400.
8          INPUT-OUTPUT SECTION.
9          FILE-CONTROL.
10              SELECT INP-DATA ASSIGN TO INPUT.
11              SELECT RESULT-FILE ASSIGN TO OUTPUT.
12         DATA DIVISION.
13         FILE SECTION.
14         FD INP-DATA LABEL RECORD IS OMITTED.
15         01  ITEM-PRICE.
16              02  ITEM PICTURE X(30).
17              02  PRICE PICTURE 9999V99.
18              02  FILLER PICTURE X(44).
19         FD RESULT-FILE LABEL RECORD IS OMITTED.
20         01  RESULT-LINE PICTURE X(132).
21         WORKING-STORAGE SECTION.
22         77 TOT PICTURE 9999999V99, VALUE 0, USAGE IS COMPUTATIONAL.
23         77 COUNT PICTURE 9999, VALUE 0, USAGE IS COMPUTATIONAL.
24         01  SUM-LINE.
25              02  FILLER VALUE  '  SUM = ' PICTURE X(12).
26              02  SUM-OUT   PICTURE   $$,$$$,$$9.99.
27              02  FILLER VALUE  '  NO. OF ITEMS ='  PICTURE X (21).
28              02  COUNT-OUT  PICTURE  ZZZ9.
29         01  ITEM-LINE.
30              02  ITEM-OUT  PICTURE  X(30).
31              02  PRICE-OUT  PICTURE  ZZZ9.99.
32         PROCEDURE DIVISION.
33         START.
34              OPEN INPUT INP-DATA AND OUTPUT RESULT-FILE.
35         READ-DATA.
36              READ INP-DATA AT END GO TO PRINT-LINE.
37              ADD PRICE TO TOT.
38              ADD 1 TO COUNT.
39              MOVE PRICE TO PRICE-OUT.
40              MOVE ITEM TO ITEM-OUT.
41              WRITE RESULT-LINE FROM ITEM-LINE.
42              GO TO READ-DATA.
43         PRINT-LINE.
44              MOVE TOT TO SUM-OUT.
45              MOVE COUNT TO COUNT-OUT.
46              WRITE RESULT-LINE FROM SUM-LINE.
47              CLOSE INP-DATA AND RESULT-FILE.
48              STOP RUN.
```

Fig. 12-1. Example COBOL program.

standard system output file OUTPUT. The names INPUT and OUTPUT are peculiar to the particular COBOL implementation being used.

Lines 12—31. These lines form the DATA DIVISION. Line 12 is the required header. The remaining lines define all the variables and data structures used in the program.

Lines 13—20. These lines form the FILE SECTION of the DATA DIVISION. Each external file used for input or output by the program must be defined, its characteristics specified, and the format (or formats) of a typical data record specified. For this program standard files are used and thus relatively little need be specified. Line 13 is the required header.

Line 14. This line begins the file description (FD) for the file named INP-DATA. Since the file is a standard input file, only the required LABEL RECORD IS clause is given, specifying that the file has no label at its beginning. The information provided here, together with that obtained from the FILE-CONTROL paragraph (line 10) enables the compiler to set up code for the proper accessing of the file at run time.

Lines 15—18. Description of a typical record in the external file INP-DATA. This declaration sets up a record data structure (heterogeneous vector) in central memory having the specified form. Each time a new logical record is read from the external file (as a character string) the input characters are stored in this data structure and then accessed through the identifiers specified in this declaration.

Line 15. The record data structure is named ITEM-PRICE. The 01 preceding the name is a *level number* used to define the hierarchical grouping of elements within the record. The level 01 indicates that a new structure definition is being initiated.

Lines 16—18. The record ITEM-PRICE contains three elements. In the usual manner of heterogeneous array declarations (see Section 3-9) each of the elements is named by a separate identifier. However, because only the first two elements, ITEM and PRICE, contain significant data here, the third element, which appears only to fill out the record definition to 80 characters (the length of a record derived from punched card input data), is named with the null name FILLER. This record data structure must be large enough to accommodate the entire record input from the external file at each READ statement, so the FILLER element is required here.

Line 16. The type of the element named ITEM is declared using a PICTURE clause. The PICTURE specification X(30) designates a simple character string data type of 30 character positions.

Line 17. The element PRICE is declared, using the PICTURE specification 9999V99, to be a number in character string form consisting of six digits (the six 9s) with the decimal point assumed between the fourth and fifth digits. Because the ITEM element is declared to occupy the first 30 characters of an input record, the PRICE element occupies the thirty-first through thirty-sixth positions. The thirty-seventh through eightieth positions (44 characters) are declared as a *filler* in the next line.

Lines 19—20. The declaration for the output file named RESULT-FILE. Because output lines of varying formats are to be output, it is convenient to define the record structure in central memory for this file to consist of a single long character string of 132 character positions, representing the length of a print line on an external printer. The actual output lines will be built up in other data structures and moved into the RESULT-LINE structure only immediately before output.

Lines 21—31. These lines make up the WORKING-STORAGE SECTION of the DATA DIVISION. Simple variables and records used only as local data structures in the program and not associated with an external file for input and output are declared here.

Line 22. A simple variable (indicated by level number 77) named TOT is declared. The value of TOT will be a positive real number less than 10 million with at most two digits to the right of the decimal. Initially TOT has the value zero. The USAGE IS COMPUTATIONAL clause specifies that TOT is primarily used in arithmetic calculations and should be stored in binary floating-point form (or other form appropriate for direct use in hardware arithmetic operations). Without the USAGE clause TOT would be stored in character string form as a string of nine digits, and it would then have to be converted to an appropriate hardware representation before each arithmetic operation, at a substantial cost in execution speed.

Line 23. Simple variable COUNT is declared as an integer less than 10,000.

Lines 24—28. These lines define a record data structure of four elements which is used to build up the character string representing the final output line printed by the program. Line 24 declares the structure name as SUM-LINE.

Line 25. The first element of the record is a character string with a fixed value consisting of six blanks followed by SUM = . Because there will never be any need to access this element individually, it is given the null name FILLER.

Line 26. The element SUM-OUT will contain the number representing the total of the individual item prices input. Because this number is to be part of the output line, the PICTURE clause specifies an appropriate output format for the number. The specification $$,$$$,$$9.99 declares that the value of SUM-OUT will be a number less than 10 million with two digits to the right of the decimal point (all but the leftmost $ counts as a 9). The decimal point will be explicitly inserted between the seventh and eighth digits, any leading zeros beyond the units position will be suppressed and replaced by blanks, commas will be inserted in the usual positions as needed, and a single $ will be printed immediately to the left of the leading digit of the number.

Lines 27—28. The remaining two elements of SUM-LINE are declared: the constant string NO. OF ITEMS, and the four-digit integer COUNT-OUT, whose value will have leading zeros replaced by blanks.

Lines 29—31. The declaration for the record ITEM-LINE, which serves as the record in which another format of output line is constructed. This line is simply the *echo print* of the input line, formatted slightly differently.

Lines 32—48. These lines form the PROCEDURE DIVISION of the program—the executable program statements. Line 32 is the required header. The division is broken into "paragraphs" by statement labels such as START and READ-DATA, which may be used as objects of GOTO control transfers.

Line 34. The external files names INP-DATA and RESULT-FILE are set up for processing. INP-DATA is to be used for input, and RESULT-FILE for output.

Line 36. The next record of file INP-DATA is read in (as a character string) and stored in the internal record data structure ITEM-PRICE associated with the file. If an end-of-file indicator is read, showing that the file has been completely processed, then control is transferred to the statement labeled PRINT-LINE.

Lines 37—38. The value of variable TOT is incremented by the newly input value of PRICE (an element of ITEM-PRICE). The value of COUNT is incremented by 1. Both TOT and COUNT are stored in the hardware number representation, but PRICE is in character string form and must be converted to hardware form before the addition.

Line 39. The newly input value of PRICE is assigned as the value of PRICE-OUT. Because the PICTURE declarations for the two elements differ, the assigned value is converted to the appropriate format for a value of PRICE-OUT.

Line 40. The character string value of ITEM is assigned to ITEM-OUT. Because the PICTUREs of the two elements are the same, no conversion is needed.

Line 41. The entire contents of record ITEM-LINE (a string of 37 characters) is copied into the record RESULT-LINE and filled out with blanks to make 132 characters. The resulting character string is output to file RESULT-FILE as the next record.

Line 42. Control is transferred back to the statement labeled READ-DATA to read the next input record (line 35).

Lines 44–45. Control is transferred here when the input file has been completely processed. The final output line is now formatted and output. Line 44 assigns the total of the item prices which has been collected in simple variable TOT to the element SUM-OUT of record SUM-LINE. Because the PICTURE declarations differ, the number is converted from internal binary format (or other hardware representation) to character string form. Line 45 specifies a similar assignment of the value of COUNT.

Line 46. The contents of record SUM-LINE are copied to record RESULT-LINE, filled out to 132 characters with blanks, and output to file RESULT-FILE.

Line 47. The two external files are "closed" to further processing.

Line 48. End of program.

12-4. DATA

All data declarations in a COBOL program are collected into the separate DATA DIVISION. This division is split into a number of *sections*, the most important of which are the WORKING-STORAGE SECTION and the FILE SECTION. The former includes declarations for each simple variable and local data structure used by the program. The latter contains similar declarations for data records transmitted between central memory and external files. In both these sections the same basic data declaration formats are used. Less commonly used sections contain formats for the optional report generator and declarations for formal parameters (in programs to be called as subprograms).

The central principle of data representation in COBOL is that all data are stored in character string form at run time, with the exception of those numeric data items explicitly declared with a USAGE IS COMPUTATIONAL clause. This character string data representation serves two important purposes. First, because COBOL is oriented toward applications with high-volume input-output, it allows data to be stored in central memory in a form which may be directly transmitted to an external file without conversion. Numbers, in particular, are not automatically converted to a hardware binary representation on input but instead are converted only when needed as operands in an arithmetic operation. Second, the character string representation allows data descriptions to be almost entirely independent of particular hardware characteristics such as word length or number representation. As a result COBOL programs are relatively easy to transport.

The character string machine-independent data declarations exact a price in execution speed because data items may be split across word boundaries and thus be difficult to access and also because numbers must be converted to the hardware representation before arithmetic operations and then the result converted back to character string form before being stored. As a compromise the language provides the optional SYNCHRONIZED declaration which forces a data item to begin or end at a word boundary (or other natural memory division) and the USAGE IS COMPUTATIONAL declaration which allows a hardware number representation to be used for a particular data item. Use of these optional declarations makes the length of data structures or individual items implementation-dependent but may have a dramatic effect on execution speed.

Elementary Data Items and Simple Variables

Every variable used in a COBOL program must be explicitly declared in the DATA DIVISION. Unlike the small fixed set of possible variable types found in most languages, COBOL allows individual type declarations to be built up in a large variety of ways. A simple variable occupies a fixed number of character positions at run time, and the declaration of the variable defines the number of character positions as well as the format of the data item.

The PICTURE Clause. The primary type declaration for a simple variable (or an element of a larger structure) is specified through a *PICTURE clause* attached to the declaration of the variable in the DATA DIVISION. The simplest form of PICTURE clause specifies only the number of character positions occupied by the data value, as in

77 VAR PICTURE XXXXXXXX.

or equivalently

77 VAR PICTURE X(8).

In these declarations, VAR is the variable name, 77 indicates a simple variable, and XXXXXXXX or X(8) specifies that the value of VAR is a string of eight characters.

A number being input as a simple sequence of digits but which represents an amount in dollars and cents might be described by the PICTURE

AMT PICTURE 9999V99

indicating a data value composed of six digits, with the decimal point positioned between the fourth and fifth digits.

For output a much more elaborate format might be desirable, e.g., if the amount is to appear on a bill or check to be mailed. An appropriate PICTURE might then be

AMT-OUT PICTURE $$$$9.99

The value of AMT-OUT is an *edited number*, a character string of seven characters composed of zero to three blanks, followed by a $, followed by one to four decimal digits, followed by a . , followed by two decimal digits. The number of blanks before the $ is determined by the number of leading zeros in the actual value. Leading zeros are suppressed and the $ "floats" to the right.

These examples illustrate only a few of the possibilities for PICTURE construction. In general, a data item may occupy any fixed number of character positions; each of these character positions may be tagged as containing a digit, a letter, or an arbitrary character; *editing* characters may be added to specify insertion of blanks, zeros, DB, CR, or one of the characters ". , $ / + -"; leading zeros may be suppressed or replaced by * ; etc.

Other Clauses for Elementary Data Items. The declaration of a variable or element of a data structure may contain other clauses in addition to the PICTURE declaration. The VALUE clause may be used to define an initial value for the variable; the JUSTIFIED clause determines left or right justification of a character string value when the value is shorter than the receiving variable. The SYNCHRONIZED and USAGE IS COMPUTATIONAL clauses have already been mentioned.

Heterogeneous Arrays (Records)

The basic data structure in COBOL is the multidimensional heterogeneous array, termed a *record*. The records used by a program must be completely declared in the DATA DIVISION of the program. Because full declarations are provided, static type checking and relatively efficient run-time storage and accessing of elements of records are possible. Records are declared using an outline format of nested levels, each with a *level number*, as described in Section 3-9. Because the arrays are heterogeneous, each element and group of elements requires a separate declaration. Elementary items are declared using the same PICTURE and other clauses described for simple variables. Each elementary item or group of items in the record receives an identifier as a name, which may be used as a subscript in accessing.

At run time a record is represented as a contiguous block of storage. If the record does not involve items declared as COMPUTATIONAL, then this storage area may be considered simply as a long character string, with the elementary item and group names serving as names for various substrings within the area. Section 3-9 describes the concepts involved at length.

Homogeneous and Mixed Arrays

Records may contain homogeneous arrays (called *tables*) of one to three dimensions as components. For example, to set up a vector of ten elements each of which is a five-digit integer the declaration might be

```
01  ARR.
    02  A OCCURS 10 TIMES PICTURE 99999.
```

ARR is the name of the entire vector; the individual elements may be referenced as A(1), A(2), . . . , A(10).

The OCCURS clause is used to declare a vector, each element of which may be an elementary data item or another record or array. If an element contains an OCCURS clause as well, then the result is a two-dimensional array. Up to three levels of such nesting are allowed. For example,

```
01  THREE-DIM-ARRAY.
    02  PLANE OCCURS 20 TIMES.
        03  ROW OCCURS 30 TIMES.
            04  ELEM OCCURS 10 TIMES PICTURE 9999.
```

defines THREE-DIM-ARRAY as a three-dimensional $20 \times 30 \times 10$ homogeneous array of four-digit integers. Individual elements are accessed by subscripting in the usual way, e.g., ELEM(7,21,3) designates the element in the seventh plane, twenty-first row, and third column. In addition, individual rows and planes may be accessed as units, e.g., PLANE(12) or ROW(4,5).

More interesting than simple homogeneous arrays are mixed records containing both homogeneous and heterogeneous components. For example, the record declared as

```
01  POPULATION-DATA.
    02  TOTAL-US-POP PICTURE 9(10).
    02  STATE OCCURS 50 TIMES.
        03  STATE-NAME PICTURE X(30).
        03  STATE-POP  PICTURE 9(9).
        03  CAPITAL-NAME PICTURE X(30).
        03  CAPITAL-POP PICTURE 9(8).
```

contains an elementary item, TOTAL-US-POP, and a vector, STATE, of 50 items, each of which is a heterogeneous array of four elements.

Most of the complexity of referencing and accessing in such mixed arrays may be dealt with at compile time because of the presence of full declarations with fixed bounds for all arrays. At run time a simple sequential representation suffices.

The REDEFINES Clause. The concept of *redefinition* of a storage area is important in COBOL. A record declaration serves both to reserve a block of storage in central memory for the record structure and to assign names and types to various subparts of the storage area. The REDEFINES clause allows more than one structure to be described for the same record storage area or part of a storage area. For example, the declaration

```
01  ARR.
    02  A OCCURS 10 TIMES PICTURE 99999.
```

reserves a block of 50 character positions, structured into a vector of 10 five-digit integers. If this declaration were immediately followed by the declaration

```
01  NEW-ARR  REDEFINES  ARR.
    02  B  PICTURE  99999.
    02  C  OCCURS  5  TIMES.
        03  D  PICTURE  XXXX.
        03  E  PICTURE  99999.
```

then the same 50-character block would also be used for the record NEW-ARR, as shown in Fig. 12-2. The REDEFINES clause allows an arbitrary number of different structures to be imposed on a single

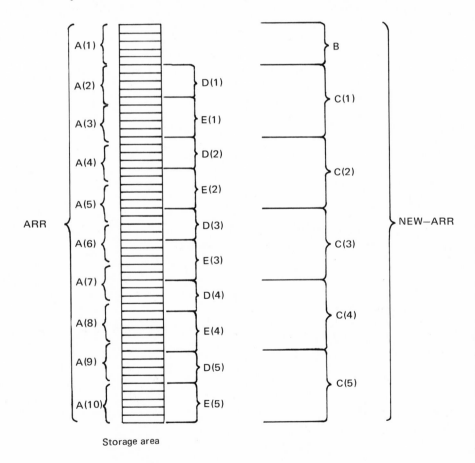

Storage area

Fig. 12-2 A storage area with multiple definitions showing the names by which various substrings may be referenced.

storage area, thus allowing a single character string to be taken apart or built up in a variety of ways.

External Files and File Declarations

The FILE SECTION of the DATA DIVISION contains a declaration for each external file accessed by the program. The declaration specifies various gross characteristics of the file and defines each format that a record on the file might assume. Additional declarations in the ENVIRONMENT DIVISION specify the particular external files to be used and certain implementation-dependent properties of the files.

Files may be sequential, indexed, or random. These different types of organization are discussed in Section 3-12. The programmer specifies the organization of the file and whether records are to be accessed sequentially or at random. In addition, declarations may specify the presence or absence of labels on the files, the contents of labels if present, the indexing key if the file is indexed, the number of buffer areas to be used during input-output (which affects the speed of input-output operations), and a variable to be used as a *status indicator* during input-output operations, so that the programmer may monitor the result of each operation.

Besides these declarations of the gross external characteristics of the file and related data areas to be used in file processing, the program specifies the internal structure of the file. In general, the file is composed of a sequence of physical records or *blocks*, each containing in turn a sequence of logical records, each of which is a simple character string. As part of the file declaration the programmer specifies the number of logical records that comprise a block and the length of a logical record. The BLOCK CONTAINS is used for the former purpose. The length of a record is defined by the record declarations which comprise the major part of the file description.

After the initial line describing the gross characteristics of the file a sequence of record declarations follow, each in exactly the same form as the record declarations found in the WORKING-STORAGE SECTION for local record data structures. The sequence of record declarations here, however, has a different significance: Each declaration describes a different format for a record which might appear on the external file. A single central storage area, called the *record area*, is allocated for the file. Its length is equal to the length of the longest record defined by any of the record declarations. Each of the record declarations essentially redefines the structure of this single record area, but no explicit REDEFINES clause is necessary.

Input is straightforward. A READ operation reads the next (or other specified) record from the external file (using an internal buffer for temporary storage). This record is a character string which is stored in the record area for the file without modification. If only a single record declaration for the file was given, as in the example of Section 12-3, then the record just input has a known format specified by the record declaration, and the programmer can proceed to access the various substrings of the record using the identifiers and type declarations defined by the record declaration. However, more generally, the file declaration may contain more than one record declaration, indicating that the external file may contain records in various formats. In this case after the record is input to the record area, the programmer must first determine its format before he can select the proper set of identifiers (specified by some one record declaration) to use in accessing the substrings of the record. This format identification is commonly done by using a *format tag* field which each format has in common, with a unique tag number designating the format of the individual record (see Problem 12-3).

The output operation is equally straightforward: A character string is copied from the record area of the file to the buffer area and ultimately to the external file. Output lines, however, are usually formatted in a record in WORKING-STORAGE and moved to the file record area only immediately before output, because this allows fixed headings and other constant data to be entered into the WORKING-STORAGE records at compile time and never modified, as illustrated in the example program of Section 12-3.

12-5. OPERATIONS

The sequence of operations which a COBOL program executes is defined in the PROCEDURE DIVISION. COBOL contains a fairly rich set of built-in primitives but only minimal facilities for programmer-defined operations (subprograms). Subprogram facilities are taken up in Sections 12-6 and 12-7.

Arithmetic, Relational, and Boolean Operations

Addition, subtraction, multiplication and division operations may be written as separate statements, e.g.,

ADD X, Y GIVING Z
DIVIDE P BY Q GIVING R REMAINDER S

or alternatively (in most cases) in more conventional form using a COMPUTE statement:

$$\text{COMPUTE } Z = X + Y$$

COMPUTE assignment statements may also include exponentiation (**). The programmer may specify whether the result assigned is to be truncated or rounded and also may specify an action to be taken in case the result is too large to fit in the receiving location, e.g.,

MULTIPLY K BY L GIVING M ROUNDED;
ON SIZE ERROR GO TO MULT-ERR

Relational and Boolean operations may be used in Boolean expressions in IF, PERFORM, and SEARCH statements. The usual arithmetic relations are provided, and these may be applied to nonnumeric data using the collating sequence defined by the implementation to determine the ordering. The Boolean operators AND, OR, and NOT are primitive. In addition, primitives are provided for testing if the value of a particular data item is strictly numeric or alphabetic.

Accessing, Assignment, and Type Conversion

Implicit type conversions caused by an attempt to store a data value in a variable with a different type declaration are an important part of COBOL. Much formatting of data for output is done through such implicit type conversions. The primitive used in making such data transfers (with their associated implicit conversions) is the simple assignment operator MOVE. The statement

MOVE A TO B

assigns a copy of the current value of A as the new value of B. The example of Section 12-3 contains numerous examples of the use of MOVE. Other COBOL statements involve assignments as well, e.g., the arithmetic statements ADD, SUBTRACT, MULTIPLY, DIVIDE, and COMPUTE.

Accessing of elements of data structures is controlled by subscripting. In heterogeneous records each element or group of elements is provided with an identifier as subscript. Elements of homogeneous arrays within records (defined using the OCCURS clause) are accessed through integer subscripts. The same identifiers may be used to designate elements within different structures. For example, there may be an element named CITY in three different records named EMPLOYEE-RECORD, NEW-EMPLOYEE, and EMPLOYER. Because such an element name by itself is ambiguous, each use of the name must be *qualified* by adding the name of some higher-level grouping (such as a record name) which will uniquely identify the desired elements, as in CITY OF NEW-EMPLOYEE or CITY OF EMPLOYER. In general, any reference is acceptable as long as it is unambiguous.

The use of the same identifer to name elements in more than one structure is made particularly useful by the *CORRESPONDING option*—the ability in COBOL to access in one step all the elements with identical names in two different structures. For example, the statement`

MOVE CORRESPONDING A TO B

will cause the value of each element of A which has a like named element in B to be assigned as the new value of that corresponding element (with the necessary implicit type conversions). The corresponding elements need not occupy identical positions within the records A and B. This accessing of corresponding elements is also possible in the ADD and SUBTRACT statements.

Input-Output and Sorting

The largest group of COBOL primitives are concerned with input-output operations. The basic operations on external files— OPEN files, CLOSE files, READ, and WRITE—are illustrated in Section 12-3. The operations ACCEPT and DISPLAY are used for input and output, respectively, to low-speed devices such as computer consoles or small terminals. On random access files REWRITE allows substitution for an existing record and DELETE allows deletion of a record.

Most data files processed by COBOL programs must be sorted before they can be processed. For example, a file of weekly payroll inputs must be sorted (perhaps by social security number) before it can be processed if the weekly inputs are to be matched to entries in a (presorted) master payroll file. Because the sorting operation is so common, most COBOL implementations include a SORT primitive which allows a file to be sorted using a given *key* element as the basis for the ordering.

Other Operations in COBOL

A variety of other primitives is provided. A SEARCH statement allows an efficient search of a homogeneous array data structure. Some simple character-string-processing primitives are provided which allow a string to be scanned for specified characters and replacements made. The optional report writer module, when available, provides a set of primitives for formatting and outputting printed matter by setting up page formats directly rather than working with single output lines as is the case with the WRITE primitive.

12-6. SEQUENCE CONTROL

COBOL sequence control structures are heavily oriented toward statement sequence control. Expressions play only a minor role in the language, and subprograms are restricted to simple calls and returns without recursion. In addition, interrupts are provided in certain special cases.

Expressions

The minimal COBOL language uses no expressions at all. In full COBOL they occur in only three places. In the COMPUTE assignment statement an arithmetic expression using the basic arithmetic operations and parentheses may be used to specify the value to be assigned. In an IF conditional statement and the SEARCH statement the condition may be specified by an expression involving arithmetic, relational, and Boolean operators in the usual manner. No provision is made for function calls within expressions, and thus expression evaluation is straightforward.

Statement Sequence Control

The executable portion of a COBOL program, the PROCEDURE DIVISION, begins with an optional set of interrupt routine definitions together with the associated interrupt conditions. Following these *declaratives* the program statements are grouped into *sentences*, the sentences into *paragraphs*, and the paragraphs (optionally) into *sections*. Each paragraph and section begins with a label which may be used as the object of a GOTO or PERFORM control transfer. Execution follows the physical statement sequence without regard to sentence, paragraph, or section boundaries unless a GOTO, PERFORM, or IF statement is used to explicitly transfer control. Particularly notable is the fact that there are no explicit subprogram boundaries within the PROCEDURE DIVISION. Paragraphs or sections may be used as simple subprograms, but control is also allowed to flow directly into the same paragraphs or sections in the normal sequence of execution.

Labels and GOTOs. A simple GOTO may transfer control to any paragraph or section label. A multiway branch using a vector of labels and a computed subscript (similar to the FORTRAN *computed GOTO*) is also provided using the syntax

GO TO L1,L2, . . . ,Ln DEPENDING ON ⟨ *identifier* ⟩

A third option allows a simple GOTO to be written as the only statement in a separate paragraph. The label specified may then be modified at run time by execution of an ALTER statement, e.g.,

ALTER L1 to PROCEED TO L25

where L1 is the label of the paragraph containing the GOTO to be modified. These facilities are essentially the same as those provided by FORTRAN.

Conditional (IF) Statements. An *if-then-else* statement similar to that found in ALGOL is provided, using the syntax

IF ⟨*condition*⟩; ⟨*statement sequence*⟩ ELSE ⟨*statement sequence*⟩.

The ⟨*condition*⟩ specified may be a relational or Boolean expression.

PERFORM Statements. The COBOL PERFORM statement serves both as an iteration statement and as a simple parameterless subprogram call. In its simplest form,

PERFORM L1. or PERFORM L1 THRU Ln.

it causes execution of a designated paragraph (or section) or sequence of paragraphs (or sections) as a simple parameterless subprogram. Control is transferred to the paragraph labeled L1; the statements in that paragraph, or in following paragraphs through paragraph Ln, are executed; and control returns to the point of call (the PERFORM statement). No parameters or local variables are involved; only control transfers occur. The other forms of PER-FORM are straightforward extensions of this basic concept. The statement

PERFORM L1 THRU Ln *k* TIMES.

serves to call the *subprogram* repeatedly *k* times. The statement

PERFORM L1 THRU Ln UNTIL ⟨condition⟩

iterates execution of the subprogram until the condition evaluates to true. The fourth version of the statement,

PERFORM L1 THRU Ln VARYING I1 FROM J1 BY K1 UNTIL ⟨condition₁⟩
                        AFTER I2 FROM J2 BY K2 UNTIL ⟨condition₂⟩
                        AFTER I3 FROM J3 BY K3 UNTIL ⟨condition₃⟩

allows iterative execution of the subprogram with from one to three loop indices moving through integer ranges. In the above statement, index I3 cycles completely for each step in the value of I2, etc.

Special Condition Checking. In addition to the basic statement sequence control structures mentioned above many COBOL statements provide for execution of one or more statements when a special condition arises during execution of the base statement. For example, each arithmetic statement may contain a suffix designating actions to be taken in case of a *size error*, an error caused by the result of the arithmetic operation being too large to fit in the designated result variable location. Thus the statement

ADD A TO B, ON SIZE ERROR PERFORM ERROR1.

would cause execution of subprogram ERROR1 should the sum of the values of A and B exceed the space allocated for B. Other special condition checks include end-of-file checking on READ statements and end-of-page checking on WRITE statements.

Subprogram Sequence Control

True subprograms play a minor role in COBOL programming. In fact, early versions of COBOL (1960–1965) included no subprogram facilities beyond the primitive structure associated with the PERFORM statement, described above. True subprograms with parameters and local referencing environments first appeared as an optional language feature in the 1968 version of the language. They are not required in any COBOL implementation. When implemented, subprograms are restricted to simple nonrecursive calls and returns.

The only other sequence control structure of interest provides a limited interrupt capability for monitoring input-output errors or end-of-file conditions (e.g., parity errors). The programmer may specify at the beginning of the PROCEDURE DIVISION a *routine* (set of paragraphs or sections) to be executed should such an I/O error occur on a given file.

12-7. DATA CONTROL

The data control mechanisms in COBOL are the most primitive of any language described in this book. This fact is basically a reflection of the lack of emphasis on subprograms in the language. The DATA DIVISION of a program sets up a single global referencing environment which is used throughout the PROCEDURE DIVISION for referencing. Although paragraphs or sections in the PRO-CEDURE DIVISION may be called like subprograms using PER-FORM, these "subprograms" must use only the common global referencing environment and may have no parameters or local identifiers. The only identifiers not appearing in the DATA DIVI-SION are the labels for paragraphs and sections in the PROCEDURE DIVISION and again these cannot be made local but are implicitly global (e.g., GO TO L1 appearing anywhere in the PROCEDURE DIVISION transfers control to the same label L1).

In versions of COBOL since 1968 the optional true subprogram facility allows subprograms (written as complete COBOL programs) to be separately compiled and to have parameters and their own local referencing environments (defined by the DATA DIVISION of each subprogram). These local environments are retained between calls, as in FORTRAN. Parameters to such subprograms are transmitted by reference, and actual parameters are restricted to single identifiers naming simple variables or records. Full declarations for the corresponding formal parameters must be provided in a special LINKAGE SECTION of the DATA DIVISION of the subprogram. No subprogram, label, expression, or constant actual parameters are allowed. The only nonlocal identifiers in COBOL are the names of separately compiled subprograms, the external file names mentioned in the ENVIRONMENT DIVISION, and a few other minor implementation-dependent identifiers. The simple data control structures used in COBOL allow all referencing to be set up at compile time. Direct access to the appropriate data locations is then possible at run time without any referencing overhead.

12-8. OPERATING ENVIRONMENT

The COBOL design is unique in attempting to separate aspects of a program which deal with the operating environment into a separate ENVIRONMENT DIVISION. The goal is to make programs transportable from one COBOL implementation to another by changing only the ENVIRONMENT DIVISION to reflect the changed operating environment in the new implementation. COBOL is designed for a batch-processing environment, and thus most of the specifications in the ENVIRONMENT DIVISION are concerned with external data files and have been discussed in the preceding sections.

12-9. SYNTAX AND TRANSLATION

The major features of the COBOL syntax have been mentioned in the preceding sections. Programs are broken into four divisions, each composed of sections, which in turn are broken into paragraphs (in the ENVIRONMENT and PROCEDURE divisions). The statement formats are English-like and many optional noise words are allowed to improve readability. The goal of this syntactic organization is a language in which programs are readable without extra documentation. However, the language design only partially accomplishes this goal. The natural English-like syntax makes individual statements or groups of statements quite readable, but the weakness of the COBOL subprogram capabilities and limited use of expressions and structured statements tend to obscure the overall organization of a program. The control structures natural to an algorithm often cannot be directly reflected in the program (FORTRAN also suffers from this defect).

Because of the relatively simple and natural syntax, COBOL programs are not particularly difficult to write, but programming in COBOL is tedious because of the large amount of code which must be produced (even for simple programs) in the form of division, section, and paragraph headers, and because of the full declarations required for each data item used. Also, every key word or noise word used in a COBOL statement is a reserved identifier which cannot be used by the programmer. The list of reserved words fills an entire printed page (about 300 words). Conflicts between programmer-chosen identifiers and reserved words are common COBOL programming errors.

Translation

The COBOL syntax is not designed for simplicity of translation. The language syntax itself, with the numerous statement types, optional elements within statement types, and variety of syntactic constructs, is difficult to parse efficiently. In addition, run-time efficiency is highly desirable in compiled COBOL programs because such programs are often compiled into executable form and then used repeatedly from their compiled form (e.g., a payroll computation program may be run every pay period for years). The language is designed to allow reasonably efficient executable code to be produced: Full declarations for all data elements are required, storage is allocated statically at the beginning of execution, and run-time variability is almost entirely restricted to modifications in the values of data elements. Thus COBOL provides the information necessary for a compiler to compile reasonably efficient code, but the task of actually producing the optimized code is made difficult by the sheer bulk of a large COBOL program. Usually a *multipass* compiler is used, which consists of a number of processing stages brought into memory one at a time in sequence to compile the input program. The initial stages perform syntactic analysis and construct tables for later stages which generate and optimize the resulting code.

Areas of particular difficulty in translation, besides the basic syntactic analysis itself, lie in the production of efficient code for input-output, data accessing, and type conversions. Because of the variety of file structures which may be used and the variety of input-output operations which may access these files, the production of efficient code for these operations is difficult. Similar problems arise with the implicit type conversions that occur so frequently in COBOL programs. The large variety of possible type specifications leads to an extremely complex set of possible conversions which might be performed and for which efficient code must be generated. Data accessing within records and arrays is made difficult by the machine independence of the data declarations in a program, which often leads to individual data elements that do not fit exactly within the natural word boundaries of the computer memory. A single data item may fall partially in one word and partially in another, for example. Generation of code for efficient accessing of such data items is often difficult but extremely important for run-time efficiency. Most COBOL programmers try to aid the compiler as much as possible by tailoring data structure definitions so that frequently accessed items fall within word boundaries in such a way that efficient hardware accessing operations may be used (the SYNCHRONIZED clause also provides aid here, although usually at some cost in space).

The COBOL Formal Grammar

The CBL grammar form discussed in Section 9-3 has been used successfully since the initial COBOL design to describe the syntax of the language. This grammar form allows a succinct and readable representation of the rather complex syntactic options of the many COBOL statement and declaration types.

12-10. STRUCTURE OF A COBOL VIRTUAL COMPUTER

The overall memory organization imposed by a COBOL program during execution is static (although overlays are often used). Thus there is no run-time storage management. Programs are compiled into machine code and executed by the hardware interpreter. Input-output operations require fairly extensive run-time software support on most computers. The most obvious area of incompatability between the COBOL virtual computer and conventional hardware, however, is in data representations. For the most part COBOL data are stored in the form of character strings, and each substring representing a data element has a complex type declaration. As mentioned in the previous section difficult problems arise in accessing data elements and converting among the different data types. Ideally, since program declarations provide the necessary descriptors, most of the checking, accessing, and type conversion setup can be handled at compile time, with only relatively simple accessing and type conversion calculations compiled into the run-time code. However, in a COBOL implementation with less optimization of compiled code, much of this processing may be done by software routines at run time, using data descriptors produced by the compiler. Some of the more specialized COBOL primitives are also software-simulated, in particular the SORT operation and the SEARCH command for searching arrays.

12-11. REFERENCES AND SUGGESTIONS FOR FURTHER READING

Many texts are available that provide an introduction to COBOL and its applications. The complete standard definition of the language is found in ANSI [1968] and the revised standard definition in ANSI [1972]. Sammet [1969] gives an excellent history of the development of the language through 1968. The more recent history is summarized in the appendix to ANSI [1972]. The automatic conversion of *decision tables* into COBOL programs is the subject of a number of recent papers; see Silberg [1971].

12-12. PROBLEMS

12-1. Explain why use of the SYNCHRONIZED clause in a data structure declaration can make the size of the structure implementation-dependent.

12-2. For the storage area of Fig. 12-2, write a record declaration that REDEFINES record ARR to allow each individual character in the storage area to be accessed by an integer subscript.

12-3. Suppose that a COBOL program for processing public school student records contains the following input file declaration:

```
FD INP-FILE LABEL RECORD IS OMITTED . . .
01  ELEM-STUDENT.
    02  GRADE PICTURE 99.
    02  NAME . . .
          .
          .
          .
01  JR-HIGH-STUDENT.
    02  GRADE PICTURE 99.
    02  SCHOOL . . .
          .
          .
          .
01  SR-HIGH-STUDENT.
    02  GRADE PICTURE 99.
    02  NAME . . .
          .
          .
          .
```

The statement READ INP-FILE causes the next record to be read from the file and stored in the record area for the file. The record may have any one of the three formats designated in the file description. Write a COBOL conditional statement that will transfer control to paragraph PARA1 if the record read is that of an ELEM-STUDENT (GRADE = 1—6), to PARA2 if the record is that of a JR-HIGH-STUDENT (GRADE = 7—9), and to PARA3 if the record is that of a SR-HIGH-STUDENT (GRADE = 10—12).

13 PL/I

13-1. INTRODUCTION

PL/I is a large, multipurpose language designed during the mid-1960s by a committee organized by the IBM Corporation. The initial goal of the committee was to design a successor to FORTRAN which would include more extensive data-structuring facilities and a more sophisticated operating environment and which would thus be applicable to a broader range of problem areas. The committee decided that FORTRAN compatibility could not be maintained if these goals were to be met and proceeded with the design of the new language that became PL/I. PL/I is applicable to a rather wide range of problem areas: scientific applications, business applications, and to some extent systems programming, as well as applications which overlap these areas.

The design of PL/I draws heavily on the earlier languages FORTRAN, ALGOL, and COBOL. PL/I contains fairly direct analogues of the FORTRAN parameter transmission mechanisms, separately compiled subprograms, formatted input-output, and COMMON blocks; of the ALGOL block structure and structured statements; and of the COBOL record-oriented input-output, heterogeneous arrays, and PICTURE type declarations. However, in each case the design of PL/I extends these earlier constructs and, in addition, supplies many new concepts, particularly in the areas of control structures and storage management.

The most significant aspects of the PL/I design stem from the attempt of the designers to balance two sets of conflicting goals: generality and flexibility without loss of execution efficiency, and ease of use for unsophisticated programmers without loss of detailed control for experienced programmers. In both cases the solution involves placing a considerable extra burden on the PL/I compiler. Generality and flexibility are obtained through the inclusion in the language of a large variety of different data structures, primitives, and control structures. To allow the compiler to produce relatively efficient executable code, however, extensive declaration of the properties of the structures used by a program is required. The variety of structures and the detailed declarations required also advanced the goal of programmer control—an experienced programmer may control the run-time structures and execution costs by careful choice of program structures and declarations. In addition, the language provides explicit storage management primitives and storage classes that allow the experienced programmer to provide detailed control of storage. The resulting language is large and complex. To make it also usable by the less experienced programmer the design adopts the philosophy of extensive *default declarations*—declarations provided by the compiler whenever the programmer fails to specify all the attributes of a data or program element. The inexperienced programmer may thus write straightforward programs without concern for many language details, and the compiler is expected to provide the necessary additional information. (Unfortunately, the default declaration concept, in practice, is sometimes more confusing than helpful to the programmer, because the default declaration provided may not be that which is expected.)

A PL/I implementation requires a fairly large amount of run-time software support, but the major emphasis is on the compiler. The language design ensures that in most cases a program contains enough declared information (explicitly or by default) that the compiler may produce relatively efficient executable code, but the large variety of program structures and options together with the complexity of the default rules make the task of actually producing efficient code from the available information extremely difficult. Most language designs either emphasize flexibility at the expense of run-time efficiency (e.g., LISP and SNOBOL4) or run-time efficiency at the expense of flexibility (e.g., FORTRAN and COBOL); PL/I attempts to gain both, but the cost is paid in language and compilation complexity.

The design of PL/I represents one extreme in design philosophy. Basically, the design attempts to meet the needs of a broad range of applications by including a wide variety of often overlapping features within a fixed framework. Relatively few features are provided for language extension; instead most of the features needed by a programmer are included directly in the language. The merits of this approach versus the smaller but more easily extensible base language have been widely debated but with no definite resolution.

13-2. BRIEF OVERVIEW OF THE LANGUAGE

A PL/I program consists of a set of separately compiled routines, each of which has a nested block structure similar to that of an ALGOL program (and each may include nested subprogram definitions). Each block or subprogram definition contains a set of declarations and a set of executable statements. Generally, each statement or declaration type has a basic form and a large number of options which the programmer may either use or omit and accept the compiler-provided default option. The resulting syntax is rather complex, and programs are not particularly easy to read or write.

PL/I contains a wide variety of elementary data types, including an extensive set of possible type specifications for numeric data. Character and bit strings, pointers, and labels may also be used. Homogeneous and heterogeneous arrays are the basic data structure types, and full declarations (with the exception of array subscript ranges) must be provided. The same structures provide the basis for a *programmer-defined data type* facility with provision for creation and destruction of new structures at arbitrary points during program execution. The language also includes extensive provision for use of external files for input-output, again with declarations of the properties of the files.

A large range of primitive operations are built into the language. The major emphasis falls on arithmetic and other numeric operations and on input-output. Extensive automatic type conversions are provided, including conversions between different hardware number representations and COBOL-like conversions between formatted character string data. Many operations may be applied to entire arrays as operands, although the facilities for array operations are not as powerful as those of APL. In addition, array *cross sections* may be treated as subarrays. Some basic string-processing operations are provided, but the programmer must control most of the associated storage management.

PL/I expressions and statement sequence control features are powerful but standard in form. Subprogram sequence control, however, includes both parallel processing (tasks) and a powerful interrupt structure, as well as ordinary subprogram calls with recursion.

Subprogram facilities are emphasized in PL/I. Subprograms may be either separately compiled, in which case a FORTRAN-like explicitly declared global referencing environment may be used, or definitions may be nested within other subprogram definitions, in which case the static block structure determines the nonlocal referencing environment. Parameters are transmitted by reference (or by value-result in some implementations). Declarations for formal parameters are required in subprograms, but extensive facilities are provided so that the programmer may either specify automatic conversions of actual parameters to match the corresponding formal parameter types or, alternatively, specify different entry points for a subprogram depending on the types of the actual parameters transmitted.

Compilation of PL/I programs is difficult because of the complexity of the language and the need to compile efficiently executable code. At run time programs are represented in machine code and hardware-interpreted, but substantial run-time software support is necessary for storage management and simulation of the large number of primitives used. Run-time storage management requires, in general, a static area, a stack, and a heap (which may be split into many small heaps by the programmer). Only the simple explicit allocation and freeing method of heap management is used, however; and the programmer is responsible for avoiding the generation of garbage or dangling references. Thus heap management is not particularly expensive in execution time.

13-3. AN ANNOTATED EXAMPLE: SUMMATION
OF A VECTOR

Figure 13-1 shows a PL/I program which is analogous to the FORTRAN and ALGOL example programs of Chapters 10 and 11, respectively. The program consists of a main program and a subprogram. The subprogram SUM is a function which sums the elements of an argument vector V of real numbers. The main program tests SUM by creating a sequence of vectors, reading in values for the vector elements, calling SUM, and then printing the value computed by SUM for each test vector. The annotations below refer to the line numbers to the left of the listing, which are not a part of the program.

Line 1. Beginning of the main program. The main program takes the form of a *procedure* (subprogram) declaration. The main program is named TEST. The OPTIONS (MAIN) attribute specifies that this procedure is the main program.

Line

```
 1        TEST: PROCEDURE OPTIONS (MAIN);
 2            START: GET LIST (K);
 3                IF K > 0 THEN BEGIN;
 4                    DECLARE  A(K) DECIMAL FLOAT;
 5                    GET LIST (A);
 6                    PUT LIST ('INPUT IS',A,'SUM IS',SUM(A));
 7                    GO TO START;
 8                END;
 9            SUM: PROCEDURE (V);
10                DECLARE V(*) DECIMAL FLOAT,
11                    TEMP DECIMAL FLOAT INITIAL (0);
12                DO I = 1 TO DIM(V,1);
13                    TEMP = TEMP + V(I); END;
14                RETURN(TEMP);
15                END SUM;
16        END TEST;
```

Fig. 13-1. Example PL/I program.

Line 2. First executable statement in the main program. The statement is labeled START. Integer variable K is declared implicitly by use. A value for the variable K is to be read in from the standard input file. The GET indicates input; the LIST indicates that the input value will appear on the external file as an ordinary decimal number separated from other data items by blanks or commas. LIST-directed input is the simplest of four basic input format options.

Line 3. A one-branch conditional statement begins here and extends to line 8. If the test K > 0 is not satisfied, then control transfers to the first executable statement following line 8, which in this case is the terminating END for the main program in line 16.

Line 4. Lines 4—8 form a BEGIN-block which is executed if the test on line 3 is satisfied. The block begins with a declaration of a vector A of K elements, where the value of K is the value just read in. The DECIMAL FLOAT specification gives the type of each element of A: real numbers represented in an appropriate hardware floating-point format internally but in decimal for input-output. A new vector A is created each time control enters this block during program execution, and the vector is destroyed on block exit.

Line 5. K values for the newly created vector A are read in from the standard input file. Again LIST-directed input is used so that the values may be entered on the file separated by blanks or commas without any special formatting.

Line 6. The input values stored in A are printed, together with the sum of the values returned by function subprogram SUM, with appropriate headings. PUT indicates output to the standard output file. LIST-directed output is used, which requires no programmer-supplied format specification. Output values are printed in a simple sequence separated by blanks.

Line 7. Control is transferred back to line 2 to begin another test loop.

Line 8. End of the BEGIN-block begun on line 3 as well as the conditional statement begun on the same line.

Lines 9—15. Definition of the function subprogram SUM. This declaration could have been placed anywhere within the body of the main program. The PL/I compiler is expected to process all declarations appearing anywhere within a program as though they had occurred at the beginning of the program.

Line 9. Beginning of the procedure named SUM, which has one formal parameter, V.

Line 10. PL/I requires declarations for all formal parameters. V is declared to be a vector of decimal floating point numbers (represented in the appropriate hardware representation). The * in the subscript list for V designates that the subscript range is to be that of the actual parameter vector transmitted to SUM.

Line 11. A local variable TEMP is declared. TEMP has type decimal floating-point, and its initial value is to be zero. A new variable TEMP, initialized to zero, is created on each entry to SUM and destroyed on exit.

Line 12. A DO iteration statement begins here and ends with the END on the next line. The function call DIM(V,1) calls a built-in primitive function which returns the size (subscript range) of the first dimension of vector V; thus it is possible to find out the dimension of a vector or array dynamically during execution. The controlled variable I is initialized to 1 and incremented by 1 each time through the loop until the size of V is reached. Note that variable I need not be explicitly declared; its use without a declaration causes the compiler to assume that it is a global fixed-point variable.

Line 13. Body of the iteration statement begun on line 12. The successive elements of V are summed using the temporary variable TEMP.

Line 14. Control is transferred back to the calling program. Since SUM is a function subprogram, an expression designating the function value to be returned is given, which in this case consists of the value of variable TEMP.

Line 15. End of the body of subprogram SUM.

Line 16. End of the main program.

13-4. DATA

PL/I contains an extensive selection of data types and primitives for accessing and modifying data elements. In general, full declarations of data types (with the exception of array subscript ranges and string lengths) are provided at compile time for each identifier, either explicitly or by default. The declarations are structured in terms of *attributes*—each declaration specifies a set of values for the various attributes which a variable or data structure may have. The compiler uses these attribute declarations to determine an appropriate run-time representation for each data item and the manner in which it is accessed and modified.

Numbers

Numbers in PL/I are classified on the basis of four attributes: (1) *mode*, which may be real or complex; (2) *scale*, which may be fixed-point or floating-point; (3) *base*, which may be decimal or binary; and (4) *precision*, which is specified in terms of the number of digits in the number. For example, the declaration

DECLARE X DECIMAL FLOAT (10)

declares identifier X to represent a simple variable whose value will be a decimal floating-point (real) number with at most ten digits. Complex numbers are represented as pairs of real numbers. Although there are four basic types of real numbers (decimal and binary fixed-point and decimal and binary floating-point) and a large number of possible specifications of precision, in fact, each number type is represented by the closest hardware number representation at run time—no run-time software simulation of real number representations and arithmetic operations is ordinarily used. Thus, for example, in the IBM 360 PL/I implementation a maximum precision for floating-point reals is specified, precision declarations beyond the maximum are not allowed, and all decimal or binary floating-point numbers with less than the maximum precision are represented using the appropriate hardware single- or double-precision floating-point representation. The variety of numeric data attributes provides, however, a hardware-independent but still rather closely controllable declaration, and the same declaration may be treated differently by different PL/I compilers.

Numeric data may also be stored in character string form. Again the programmer controls the choice of representation by the form of his declaration—to specify character representation of numbers a PICTURE declaration similar to that in COBOL is used.

Character and Bit Strings

Character strings and bit strings may be used as data values. Variables and data structure elements may be of type *character string* or *bit string*, but the declaration must specify either a fixed string length or a maximum string length. The hardware bit or character representation is utilized, and because of the required declared bounds, a fixed-size block of storage may be allocated for each string variable at run time. Character string variables may alternatively be declared using a COBOL-like PICTURE declaration. PL/I contains no explicit Boolean data type. Instead bit strings of length 1 are used.

Arrays and Structures

Homogeneous and heterogeneous multidimensional arrays are the basic data structure types of PL/I. Full compile-time declarations of dimensions and element types are required, except that the subscript ranges in homogeneous arrays may be provided at run time. The techniques for declaration, run-time storage, and accessing of such arrays are standard and are discussed in Sections 3-8 and 3-9. Heterogeneous arrays are called *structures*. They may include homogeneous arrays (*arrays*) as elements, and arrays may include structures as elements, leading to mixed arrays similar to those in COBOL.

The elements of structures are given identifiers as names; elements in arrays are accessed by integer subscript in the usual way. In addition, an array *cross section* may be accessed as a unit by using a subscripted variable with an asterisk in one or more of the subscript positions. For example, a 10 × 20 array A of five-digit integers might be declared:

DECLARE A (10,20) FIXED (5)

The third row of A is accessed by A(3,*), the fifth column by A(*,5), and the entire array by A or A(*,*). A cross section is also an array and may be treated as such in general, even though its elements may not be stored in a contiguous block of storage. Many of the PL/I primitives will accept arrays (including cross sections) as well as single data items as operands.

Two or more arrays or structures may be declared to utilize the same storage area by specifying the second to be DEFINED in terms of the first. For arrays the technique is similar to the FORTRAN EQUIVALENCE construct; for structures the technique resembles the COBOL REDEFINES construct. However, for arrays the technique is extended to allow the second array to consist of a noncontiguous set of elements of the first array. For example, if A is declared to be a 20 × 20 matrix,

DECLARE A(20,20) FLOAT;

then B may be declared to consist of the main diagonal of A by the declaration

DECLARE B (10) DEFINED A(1SUB,1SUB);

which declares B to be a vector of ten elements of A, with the element B(I) accessed using the same accessing formula as would be used for a reference to A(I,I). Thus B(1) and A(1,1) share the same storage location, as do B(2) and A(2,2), etc.

Storage Classes and Programmer-Defined Data Types

One of the attributes included in the declaration of a simple variable, array, or structure is its *storage class*: STATIC, AUTO-MATIC, CONTROLLED, or BASED. The STATIC and AUTO-MATIC classes are those ordinarily used. In these two cases the storage class attribute simply defines the lifetime of the declared structure: STATIC structures exist throughout program execution (as in FORTRAN), and AUTOMATIC structures are created on entry to the block or procedure in which the declaration occurs and are destroyed on exit (as in ALGOL).

When the CONTROLLED or BASED storage class attribute is specified, however, the significance of the declaration for the associated structure is radically modified. The declaration now becomes a *template* defining a *typical structure* in a class of structures which may be considered as a new *programmer-defined data type*. A new structure of the defined type may be created by use of an ALLOCATE statement and subsequently destroyed by a FREE statement.

The difference between the CONTROLLED and BASED attributes lies in the accessing arrangements. When ALLOCATE is used to create a new structure of a type declared as BASED, a pointer to the new structure is stored at the time of creation in a pointer variable (designated either in the ALLOCATE statement or in the original declaration). Subsequent attempts to access the structure must use this pointer as an access path. Many ALLOCATE statements may be executed in sequence, and the pointers returned may be used to link together the created structures to form arbitrary graph structures. Subsequent FREE statements must specify a pointer to the particular structure which is to be destroyed.

When a structure type is declared as CONTROLLED, on the other hand, only a single structure of the declared type may be accessed at any time during program execution. The CONTROLLED declaration basically serves to set up a stack (initially empty) of structures of the declared type. Each ALLOCATE statement creates a new structure of the specified type and pushes it down on the top of the associated stack; a FREE statement pops the top element off of the stack and destroys it. Between an ALLOCATE and FREE statement only the top structure on the stack is accessible.

There is no restriction on the complexity of the data structure declared as BASED or CONTROLLED. Thus it is possible to declare a complex multidimensional heterogeneous array data structure type and then create and manipulate a stack of such structures (by a CONTROLLED attribute) or a set of such structures accessed through pointers (by a BASED attribute). Run-time accessing is fairly efficient because the compiler has a template for a typical structure and may compile a base address + offset type of accessing formula into the executable code for each reference to an element of such a structure, leaving the base address to be determined at run time.

The storage class attributes are obviously closely related to the underlying storage management structures used: The STATIC attribute implies static storage for the associated data structure, AUTOMATIC implies a stack storage mechanism based on activation records for the associated block or procedure, and BASED and CONTROLLED imply a heap structure because the use of ALLOCATE and FREE require storage allocation and recovery at arbitrary points during execution.

Pointers

The data type POINTER is one of the elementary data types in PL/I. A simple variable or element of an array or structure may be declared to be of type POINTER and at run time may then contain a pointer to a data structure of a type declared as BASED (pointer data may also be generated for non-BASED data structures, but this is less common). The pointers to BASED structures generated by the ALLOCATE statement must be stored in POINTER variables. Each reference to a BASED variable must specify a pointer variable which contains the pointer which is to serve as the *base address* for the accessing calculation.

PL/I pointers, in general, are handled without any run-time descriptors or data type checking. This structure provides efficient execution but places the burden of ensuring correct pointer use on the programmer. In particular, dangling references and garbage may easily be generated through incorrect pointer use, and no system protection is provided.

Areas and Offsets

BASED and CONTROLLED data are allocated storage in a central heap. Because both types of data utilize pointers for access, it is not, in general, possible to output such data to an external file for later input, because the data would be returned to a new memory location, thus invalidating all the pointers involved. PL/I provides an interesting technique which allows output and subsequent input of blocks of pointer-based data without the associated pointers becoming invalidated. The PL/I programmer is allowed to set up a *mini-heap* called an *area*. An area is simply a contiguous block of storage used as a heap. Whenever a pointer to an element within an area is generated, the pointer may be set up not as an absolute memory address but rather as an "offset" from the beginning of the area; thus such pointers are called *offsets*. In general, any BASED or CONTROLLED data may be created using ALLOCATE in any desired area. The offsets produced may be treated as pointer data. However, when it is desirable to output the data stored in an area, the entire area as a simple sequential block of memory may be output. Subsequently, the stored area may be read back into new memory locations, and the offset pointers retain their original relationships.

Statement Labels

A variable or data structure element may be declared to be type LABEL. However, labels cannot be computed and as a result the compiler may convert labels to an appropriate internal run-time representation and no run-time labels table need be maintained. This topic is discussed further in Section 13-6.

Input-Output Files

PL/I provides facilities for fairly extensive declaration of the properties of external files and of the accessing methods to be used. In basic organization, an external file is treated either as a *stream*—a single sequence of bits or characters—or as a sequence of *records*, each of which is individually accessible. Input and output operations on a STREAM file always involve conversions of the data from the external form into appropriate internal memory representations, as in the FORTRAN formatted input-output operations. A RECORD file allows direct input and output of records without conversion, as in the COBOL input-output operations. RECORD files may be structured as sequential, random access, or indexed sequential; STREAM files are necessarily sequential.

13-5. OPERATIONS

The basic primitive arithmetic, relational, and Boolean operators, as well as string concatenation, are represented by infix or Polish prefix operator symbols in PL/I. However, a large additional set of primitives is also included in the form of *built-in* functions, using the ordinary mathematical prefix notation which is also used for programmer-defined functions. Certain primitives, most notably those for storage allocation and input-output, may be invoked only through use of special statement types.

Arithmetic Operations

The basic arithmetic operations are represented by the infix operators +, -, *, /, and ** (exponentiation) and prefix - (negation). In addition, a full set of built-in functions for square root, absolute value, max, min, trigonometric operations, etc., are provided. In general, each arithmetic primitive may be used with operands of any type or mixture of types which can be converted to a form appropriate for the operation. Great emphasis is placed on providing fully automatic conversion between data types. Owing to the large number of different arithmetic type specifications, the details of these automatic conversions are extremely complex. In general, static type checking is possible, numbers are represented in the appropriate hardware representation at run time, and hardware arithmetic operations are used directly. The full type declarations which are required allow the necessary type conversions to be determined at compile time, but the run-time software necessary to actually perform the conversions may be substantial.

Relational Operations

Eight primitive relational operations are provided in infix form: $=, >, <, >=, <=, \neg=, \neg<,$ and $\neg>$. Each may be applied to numbers, bit strings, or character strings (using the implementation-defined collating sequence for character ordering). Again, automatic conversion between data types is provided whenever possible.

Boolean and String Operations

There is no Boolean data type as such in PL/I; a bit string of length 1 is used instead. The basic Boolean operators, **and** (&), **or** (|), and **not** ($\neg$) are provided as operators on bit strings. In addition, a concatenation operation (||) on both character and bit strings is provided. However, concatenation is restricted by the requirement that the generated string be used immediately or else stored in a data structure or variable whose size has been fixed at the time of structure creation. Other basic string manipulation primitives are provided as built-in functions, e.g., LENGTH, which returns the length of an argument string; INDEX, which searches a string for a given substring and returns its position; and SUBSTR, which retrieves a specified substring of a given string.

Accessing and Assignment

Array elements are accessed by subscript in the ordinary manner. In structures (heterogeneous arrays) the syntax used is to write the name of the structure followed by the subscripts separated by periods. For example, if A is declared,

```
DECLARE 1  A
          2  B
              3  C  FIXED
              3  D  FLOAT
          2  E  FIXED
```

then A.B.C. refers to the element C of A. As usual, however, if the subscript identifiers alone are unambiguous, then only part of the full element designation need be given. Thus C is sufficient as a reference provided no other currently declared structure contains an element named C. Whole arrays may be accessed by name, and cross sections of homogeneous arrays may also be accessed as units and treated as arrays, as discussed in the preceding section.

The assignment operation (syntax =) provides automatic type conversion of the assigned value to the type of the receiving element. In addition, assignments may list multiple receiving locations on the left-hand side, each with a different required type conversion. For example,

$$K(2),X,Z = 2*Q$$

assigns the value of 2*Q to each of K(2), X, and Z, converting the assigned value as needed.

Certain built-in functions, termed *pseudovariables*, may also be used on the left of an assignment. For example, the SUBSTR built-in function is ordinarily used to retrieve a substring of designated length from a designated position within another string. However, SUBSTR may be used on the left of an assignment as a pseudovariable, in which case the value of the right-hand expression (which must be a string) is stored in the designated position within the receiving string. For example, the assignment

$$SUBSTR(STR1,2,5) = SUBSTR(STR2,17,5)$$

stores a copy of the five-character string beginning at the seventeenth character position in STR2 in the five character positions beginning at position 2 in STR1.

Array and Structure Operations

The primitive infix and prefix operators may be applied to array operands to produce array results, under the restriction that the arrays be identical in number of dimensions and subscript ranges. The types of array elements may differ provided that appropriate conversions can be made. For example, if A and B are two arrays of identical dimension and subscript range, then A+B results in an array of the same size, each of whose elements is the sum of the corresponding elements of A and B.

Infix and prefix operators may also be applied to structures (heterogeneous arrays) provided that both structures have the same organization (but not necessarily the same element names) and that appropriate conversion of data types of corresponding elements is possible.

The result of an array or structure expression must ordinarily be immediately assigned to another array or structure of identical shape. Assignments are made between values in the generated structure and corresponding elements in the receiving structure according to the usual rules for assignment. The array or structure assignment basically serves as a shorthand for a sequence of element-by-element assignments.

Where an expression involves structures the entire assignment may alternatively be suffixed with the phrase BY NAME. The effect is similar to the COBOL CORRESPONDING option: The operations are performed on elements which have identical names, regardless of their positions within the structures. For example, if A, B, and C are declared by

```
        DECLARE 1  A,                  DECLARE 1  B,
                   2 X FLOAT,                     2 Y FLOAT,
                   2 Y FIXED,                     2 X FIXED;
                   2 Z FLOAT;


        DECLARE 1  C,
                   2 U FIXED,
                   2 X FLOAT,
                   2 Y FLOAT;
```

then the result of the assignment

$$A = B * C, \text{ BY NAME}$$

would be the same as

```
        A.X = B.X * C.X
        A.Y = B.Y * C.Y
```

with the appropriate data type conversions performed automatically.

Creation and Destruction Operations

The rules for data structure creation and destruction are tied to the declared storage class for each structure. STATIC structures are created during compilation before execution begins and exist throughout execution. AUTOMATIC structures are created on block entry and destroyed on exit. CONTROLLED and BASED structures are created by explicit use of ALLOCATE statements during execution and are destroyed by FREE statements. Garbage and dangling references may easily be generated by misuse of ALLO-CATE and FREE. For example, if A is declared

$$\text{DECLARE A (10) FLOAT BASED (P)}$$

then the statement

ALLOCATE A

creates a vector of ten elements and stores a pointer to it in P. A subsequent ALLOCATE A creates another vector of ten elements and assigns the pointer to P, destroying the pointer to the original vector. The original vector has become garbage unless the programmer has explicitly copied the original pointer in P to some other POINTER variable. If the original ALLOCATE A statement were followed instead by

Q = P
FREE A

then the pointer to the vector stored in P would be destroyed along with the vector itself, but pointer variable Q would be left with a dangling reference, a pointer to the destroyed structure.

Input-Output Operations

For RECORD files the input-output primitives are similar to those found in COBOL. A READ statement reads the next record from the external file to an internal storage area without conversion of individual data items. A WRITE statement transmits a copy of a storage area to the external file without conversion. REWRITE and DELETE statements allow replacement or deletion of individual records in an external file. RECORD files are generally used when a large volume of input and output is required, especially when the output files produced are to be used only as input for some later processing, e.g., in updating a master file in a business application.

STREAM files are commonly used when the input-output volume is smaller and when the output is to be printed. Data received from a STREAM file are immediately converted to the appropriate type for the receiving variable or data structure; on output the inverse conversion is made. The basic STREAM input operation is the GET statement; the basic output operation is the PUT statement. However, three different *modes* of STREAM input-output are provided, which give different levels of convenience and programmer control of the conversions provided. The *EDIT-directed* mode utilizes a programmer-supplied format which specifies the exact conversions desired for each input or output data item. EDIT-directed input-output is essentially the same as the FORTRAN input-output structure discussed in Chapter 10.

The other two modes of STREAM file input-output provide greater convenience for the programmer by utilizing simple *free field* formats. The programmer need only specify the variables for which values are to be input or output. In *DATA-directed* transmission each data item on the external file consists of an identifier and a value. On input, the identifier specifies the variable to which the value is to be assigned. On output the name of the variable whose value is being output is output along with the value. DATA-directed output is useful in generating debugging printouts; both input and output are useful in programs which require only a small amount of input-output. A more generally useful alternative is *LIST-directed* input-output in which the programmer specifies a list of variable names whose values are to be transmitted. The input or output file contains only values in this case. For input the values must be on the external file in sequence separated by blanks or commas with no special formatting. Execution of a GET FILE (INPUT) LIST (X,Y,Z) statement would cause the next three values from file INPUT to be read in, converted to the appropriate types, and assigned as the values of X, Y, and Z. The output statement

PUT FILE (OUTPUT) LIST (X,Y,Z)

would cause the current values of X, Y, and Z to be output to file OUTPUT after conversion to some suitable (system-defined) output format.

Subprograms

PL/I provides extensive facilities for the definition and use of programmer-defined subprograms—both functions and subroutines. These topics are taken up in the next two sections.

13-6. SEQUENCE CONTROL

The PL/I sequence control structures within expressions and between statements are relatively straightforward. The most novel features of the language are found in the facilities for parallel processing and interrupt handling.

Expressions

Only the basic arithmetic, relational, and Boolean operations, plus concatenation of strings, are represented by infix or Polish prefix operators. Other primitives are invoked using the syntax for a programmer-defined function call. The prefix and infix operators have the hierarchy (from highest precedence to lowest)

> ** (exponentiation), prefix + and - , ¬ (Boolean *not*)
> * (multiplication), / (division)
> + (addition), - (subtraction)
> || (concatenation)
> =, >=, < =, >, <, ¬ =, ¬<, ¬>
> & (Boolean *and*)
> | (Boolean *or*)

Parentheses may be used for explicit control within expressions in the usual way. Because optimization of the order of expression evaluation is desirable during PL/I program compilation, the language definition explicitly states that the order of evaluation of sub-components of an expression is not defined (beyond the basic rule that all operands of an operator must be evaluated before the operator is applied). Calls to programmer-defined functions may produce side effects which affect the value of the expression; the results of expression evaluation in such cases are implementation-dependent.

Statement Sequence Control

Within a single subprogram, execution follows the physical executable statement sequence except where explicit control transfers are specified by the programmer. Executable statements and declarations may be interspersed, but the declarations are collected by the compiler and treated as though they all appeared at the beginning of the associated block or procedure.

Conditional Statements. An ALGOL-like IF ... THEN ... ELSE ... ; conditional statement is used, with the ELSE ... part optional. Conditional statements may be nested by using another IF as the statement following THEN or ELSE; the ambiguity introduced by nesting conditionals with optional ELSE clauses (see Section 9-1) is resolved by always matching an ELSE with the closest preceding unmatched THEN.

Iteration Statements. The iteration statement has the form

DO ⟨*test*⟩; ⟨*statement sequence*⟩ END;

where the ⟨test⟩ may take one of the two forms:

WHILE ⟨Boolean expression⟩

or

⟨variable⟩ = ⟨initial value⟩ TO ⟨final value⟩ BY ⟨increment⟩

or may include both forms, e.g., DO I=1 TO K WHILE (X<Y); . . .
END;. In addition, the test may be entirely omitted, in which case
the DO; . . . END; syntax serves only to create a single *compound
statement* out of the statements in the ⟨statement sequence⟩. The
order of evaluation of the expressions in the DO statement head is
clearly specified: The ⟨initial value⟩, ⟨final value⟩, and ⟨increment⟩
expressions are evaluated only once before the iteration begins, and
the test for termination is always made before the initial execution
of the ⟨statement sequence⟩ as well as after each iteration.

GOTOs and Labels. PL/I includes a GOTO-label structure of
intermediate run-time complexity: labels may not be computed
during execution, but label parameters, label variables, and label
arrays are allowed. A GOTO statement may transfer control to a
local label in the usual way but may also transfer control to a nonlocal label or to the label value of a variable or array element of type
LABEL. In each of the latter cases the label must be treated at run
time as an *environment pointer—code pointer* pair, and the proper
referencing environment must be reinstated whenever a transfer to
the label is made, as discussed in Section 6-9.

Assignment of values to variables or array elements of type
LABEL is restricted so that labels cannot be computed. An ordinary
assignment statement may be used, but the right-hand-side expression must either be a statement label or a simple reference to another
variable or array element of type LABEL. Alternatively, the
INITIAL attribute may be used in the declaration of a LABEL
variable to assign a particular statement label as its value, as, for
example,

DECLARE LAB1 LABEL INITIAL(STMT17)

Yet a third option is available in the case of label arrays: A reference
to an element of the array may be substituted for a statement label
within the program body. The designated label array element is thus
implicitly initialized to have a label value which designates the
statement to which the array reference was attached, for example,

DECLARE A(10) LABEL;

.

.

.

A(1): ⟨statement⟩

.

.

.

A(3): ⟨statement⟩

.

.

.

A(2): ⟨statement⟩

.

.

.

Subprogram Sequence Control

The ordinary CALL-RETURN subprogram control structure is basic. Recursive calls are allowed only when a subprogram has been explicitly declared RECURSIVE in its definition. The use of the explicit RECURSIVE attribute allows the compiler to produce more efficient code for procedure entry and exit in the normal non-recursive case, without restricting the programmer to nonrecursive routines.

Tasks and Parallel Execution. The operating environment of PL/I is assumed to include facilities for scheduling and parallel execution of subprograms. Basically a PL/I program may at any point during execution specify that some subprogram which it calls is to be executed in parallel. An activation of a subprogram to be executed in parallel is termed a *task*. The basic structure of these facilities in PL/I is discussed in Section 5-4. Tasks are initiated through an ordinary subprogram CALL statement which includes one of the TASK, PRIORITY, or EVENT options. The TASK and PRIORITY options are used to control the relative priority given execution of the newly created task by the underlying system scheduler if true parallel execution of the original and newly created tasks cannot be accomplished. More basic is the EVENT option which is used to synchronize the two tasks. The statement

CALL SUB2 (*parameter list*) EVENT(X)

appearing in subprogram SUB1 specifies that SUB2 is to be called as a separate task with the designated parameters. The variable X (of type EVENT) is to serve as a simple binary flag specifying whether execution of SUB2 is complete. Event variable X is set to 0 (incomplete) at the time the CALL statement is executed. When execution of SUB2 is complete X is set to 1 (complete). Ordinarily SUB1, at some later point in its execution, must pause to determine whether execution of SUB2 is complete; e.g., SUB2 may compute a value needed by SUB1. This synchronization is achieved by execution of the statement

WAIT(X)

in SUB1, which suspends execution of SUB1 until the value of X is changed to 1 by the completion of SUB2. Subtasks terminate by execution of an ordinary RETURN statement.

Commonly it is desirable to have other points at which SUB1 and SUB2 may be synchronized besides simply the point of completion of SUB2. The programmer may achieve such synchronization by declaring additional variables of type EVENT which are accessible to both SUB1 and SUB2. A special built-in primitive function COMPLETION may be used to access or set the values of event variables and the WAIT statement may be used to suspend execution of a task to await the "completion" of any event variable or set of event variables.

Whenever a PL/I task completes its execution and terminates, all the subtasks it has generated are terminated *abnormally* if they have not already been completed. The programmer is thus responsible to synchronize execution of generated tasks so that no task terminates before testing (with a WAIT statement) to be sure that all the subtasks it has initiated are complete.

Certain input-output operations also provide an option which allows a specified event variable to be set *incomplete* when the operation is initiated and *complete* when it is finished. Execution of the program itself may then proceed in parallel with the input-output operation, and the WAIT statement may be used to determine when the operation has been completed.

Interrupts. PL/I provides an extensive interrupt system for checking and handling various conditions which may arise during program execution. The interrupt conditions for which run-time checking may be enabled fall into three main categories:

1. *Computational conditions*, e.g., test for overflow or underflow on arithmetic operations, division by zero, an illegal character in a

string being converted to a number or bit string, or truncation of significant leading digits of a number during an assignment.

2. *Input-output conditions*, e.g., test for end-of-file on input, end-of-page on output, or data transmission hardware errors.

3. *Program testing conditions*, e.g., test for a subscript outside of the declared range, assignment of a new value to a variable, or transfer of control to a label.

In general, checking is automatically enabled for computational and input-output conditions and disabled for program testing conditions. However, the programmer may control explicitly the enabling and disabling of all but input-output conditions through explicit *prefixes* attached to statements, blocks, or subprograms within his program. Each interrupt condition is assigned a key word, e.g., OVERFLOW, SUBSCRIPTRANGE, and ZERODIVIDE. By writing the appropriate key word in parentheses preceding a statement, block, or subprogram, checking for the corresponding condition is enabled throughout execution of that program segment. A condition is disabled by writing NOOVERFLOW, NOZERO-DIVIDE, etc., as a prefix. For example, the programmer may wish to have subscript ranges checked in a given block during program testing but not within an enclosed sublock. This may be accomplished by writing

(SUBSCRIPTRANGE):   BEGIN

.

.

.

(NOSUBSCRIPTRANGE):   BEGIN

.

.

.

END;

.

.

.

END;

For each interrupt condition there is an implementation-defined system interrupt routine which is executed automatically when the associated interrupt occurs during program execution. The system action may be to print out an appropriate message and then either continue execution or, more commonly, terminate the program. The programmer, however, may explicitly specify his own interrupt routine in place of the system routine through use of the ON statement:

ON ⟨condition keyword⟩ ⟨statement or block⟩;

The ⟨statement or block⟩ is treated as a simple parameterless subprogram. ON statements may be inserted anywhere within a program. When executed, the ON statement does nothing more than to substitute the programmer-defined statement or block in place of the system routine (or previously specified programmer routine) as the code to be executed should the specified interrupt occur. The effect of an ON statement is local to the block within which it is executed.

13-7. DATA CONTROL

PL/I provides a variety of techniques for data control.

Referencing Environments

On entry to a BEGIN block or procedure a local referencing environment is established, which includes explicitly declared local variable and data structure names, formal parameters (in procedures), statement labels, and simple variables declared implicitly by use. For simple variables and data structures the programmer controls whether associations are created on entry and destroyed on exit or whether they are retained between calls by attaching the AUTO-MATIC or STATIC storage attribute to the declaration. AUTO-MATIC is assumed by default, so that, in general, local environments are recreated on each entry, using a run-time stack.

Nonlocal referencing is ordinarily based on the static block structure of the program. However, the programmer has an alternative: By attaching the EXTERNAL attribute to the declaration of an identifier, that identifier and its association may be entered into a global referencing environment. Any number of subprograms may have declarations for the same EXTERNAL identifier (and the declarations must then be identical). At run time all references to this identifier in any of the subprograms retrieve the same global association. The major use of the EXTERNAL attribute is in sharing data between separately compiled subprograms, in which case it serves essentially the same function as the COMMON statement in FORTRAN. For identifiers declared EXTERNAL the global refer-

encing environment may be created at load time before program
execution begins.

Parameter Transmission

Subprogram parameters are ordinarily transmitted by reference
(or value-result in some implementations). Actual parameters may be
any of the types discussed in Section 6-9, including statement labels
and subprograms. Full declarations (with the exception of array
subscript ranges and string lengths) must be specified in each
subprogram for each formal parameter.

Because PL/I subprograms may be separately compiled, it is not
possible for the compiler to check whether actual and formal
parameters in subprogram calls are declared identically. In general,
no run-time descriptors and type checking are provided, and thus the
programmer is responsible for ensuring correct correspondence
between actual and formal parameters. As a rule the actual parameter
provided at the point of call must be of an appropriate type to match
the formal parameter. However, the programmer may specify an
actual parameter of a different type and have the actual parameter
converted to the appropriate type at the time of call during
execution, provided that he tells the compiler what conversion will
be required so that the appropriate conversion can be compiled into
the executable code without run-time type checking being necessary.
Such an automatic conversion is specified by giving a separate
declaration in the *calling program* of the parameter types of the
called program. For example, if subprogram SUB is declared to have
a single real number as argument,

<pre>
          SUB: PROCEDURE(X);
                 DECLARE X FLOAT;

                              .
                              .
                              .

          END SUB;
</pre>

then in another subprogram in which SUB is called, the added
declaration

<pre>
          DECLARE SUB ENTRY (FLOAT);
</pre>

allows SUB to be called with an actual parameter of any type which
can be converted to FLOAT form. The compiler will match the
declared parameter type with the actual parameter type and compile

appropriate code for the run-time type conversion. A similar structure provides for declaration of the type of value returned by a function subprogram. Function values are restricted to elementary data items.

Generic Subprograms

Often it is desirable to be able to call a single subprogram with various types of actual parameters. The parameter type declaration discussed above provides a means to get all actual parameters converted to the appropriate type automatically before transmission to the subprogram. An alternative is to define the subprogram as a *generic subprogram*—a subprogram capable of accepting parameters of differing types at different calls. Generic primitive operations are commonplace, e.g., + often represents *real addition, integer addition,* etc., depending on the type of its operands. PL/I provides a facility for the programmer to define his own generic subprograms.

A generic subprogram is actually a set of subprograms defined in the ordinary way, each with a different set of declarations for its formal parameters. For example, suppose that we have the declarations

```
SUB1:  PROCEDURE (X,Y)          SUB2:  PROCEDURE (W,Z)
         DECLARE X FIXED,                DECLARE W FLOAT,
               Y FLOAT;                        Z FLOAT;
             .                                .
             .                                .
             .                                .
       END SUB1;                        END SUB2;
```

and we wish to use SUB1 and SUB2 as the two alternatives for a generic subprogram named SUB—a call to SUB with a FIXED first argument is to be treated as a call to SUB1, and with a FLOAT first argument as a call to SUB2. Then in the calling program where we wish to use the generic subprogram SUB the declaration

DECLARE SUB GENERIC (SUB1(FIXED,FLOAT),SUB2(FLOAT,FLOAT))

is added. Within this routine the statement

CALL SUB(U,V)

will be compiled into a call to either SUB1 or SUB2 depending on the declared type of U.

Data Control in Tasks and Interrupt Routines

In Section 6-8 some of the referencing difficulties are discussed which arise with the task and interrupt control structures. PL/I provides no special constructs for referencing within interrupt routines outside of some built-in functions which access data related to the cause of the interrupt. An interrupt routine cannot have parameters, and nonlocal referencing follows the same rules as for ordinary subprograms. Tasking and parallel execution present more complex problems. A PL/I task is always defined as a subprogram, and referencing follows the same rules as for ordinary subprograms. However, at run time the initiation of execution of a subprogram as a task causes a *fork* in the run-time stack of activation records. Subsequently, both the original task and the newly created subtask may proceed in parallel, both adding new activation records to the existing stack and both referencing identifiers back down the stack in their common nonlocal referencing environment. Of course the original task cannot reference identifiers within the subtask, but the subtask can reference (and modify) data within the original task. Because both original task and subtask may modify the same data items at different points during execution, it is sometimes necessary to temporarily synchronize access to a common piece of data. The programmer must provide for this synchronization through use of EVENT variables and WAIT statements.

13-8.   OPERATING ENVIRONMENT

PL/I is designed for a batch-processing environment. A central feature is the assumption of an environment in which parallel execution of subprograms is possible, as described in the preceding sections. The other major components of the operating environment are the external data files used for input-output. The language provides extensive declarations of the properties of external files and their modes of access, as discussed in Sections 13-4 and 13-5.

13-9.   SYNTAX AND TRANSLATION

The syntax of PL/I is designed to restrict the programmer as little as possible without leading to ambiguity. As a result, statements and declarations usually may be written in a number of equivalent forms, with the burden falling on the compiler to collect the appropriate information necessary to compile efficient executable code. The complex syntax of the language together with the desire for efficient executable code make compilation extremely difficult. In addition, the language provides a compile-time macro structure which allows the programmer to control the compilation sequence and to introduce string-valued variables and functions which are to be evaluated and the resulting string values substituted during compilation. These features are usually handled in an initial *prepass* during compilation.

Syntax

PL/I programs are written in a free format (with line boundaries ignored) without reserved words. Each statement or declaration ordinarily takes the form of a key word followed by some required information, followed by a choice of *attributes*, each of which consists of an additional key word possibly followed by further specifications in parentheses. For example, a full declaration for a simple integer variable might take the form

DECLARE X FIXED DECIMAL REAL (7) STATIC EXTERNAL

In this declaration only the key word DECLARE and the identifier X are required. The remaining attributes—FIXED, DECIMAL, REAL, STATIC, EXTERNAL, and precision 7—are entirely optional and may occur in any order. If any are omitted, default attributes are assumed by the compiler.

Where two or more identifiers share the same attributes, *factoring* of attributes is allowed. For example, the declaration

DECLARE (X,Y,Z) FIXED DECIMAL (7)

declares a common set of attributes for each of the identifiers X, Y, and Z. As an additional convenience certain key words may be abbreviated, as in the equivalent

DCL (X,Y,Z) FIXED DEC (7)

Most PL/I control statements are structured, so that other statement sequences may be nested within them. In addition, an ALGOL-like block structure dominates the overall program organization.

In general, PL/I attempts to balance readability and writeability—

statement forms use meaningful key words, but abbreviations and default options may be used to reduce the amount which must be coded. However, the requirement of full declarations for all variables and data structures (except where the default declarations are applicable) usually means that a substantial amount of program text is required for all but the simplest programs.

The Compile-Time Facilities

PL/I provides a number of special features which allow modification of a program *during compilation*, in a special prepass before ordinary compilation begins. These *compile-time facilities*, as they are termed, allow the programmer to specify the replacement of certain identifiers with arbitrary strings, the inclusion of program text taken from an external library, the repeated translation of a program segment, or deletion of part of the program text from compilation.

A statement to be *executed at compile-time* is designated by an initial % character on the statement. Only a few statement types may be used at compile time, e.g., assignment, GOTO, IF, DO, and END. Special compile-time variables and functions may be declared using DECLARE and PROCEDURE declarations, but only integer and character data types are allowed. Text from an external file is entered into the program text by a %INCLUDE statement. In addition, %ACTIVATE and %DEACTIVATE statements allow the compile-time associations for declared identifiers to be activated and deactivated at arbitrary points.

The compile-time facilities may be used by the programmer to speed up execution of his program by moving certain computations to compile time which ordinarily would be performed at run time. For example, suppose that the program contains a simple loop:

```
DO I = 1 TO 5;
A(I) = 2 * B(I);
END;
```

The sequence of statements

```
A(1) = 2 * B(1);
A(2) = 2 * B(2);
A(3) = 2 * B(3);
A(4) = 2 * B(4);
A(5) = 2 * B(5);
```

is equivalent and faster to execute but tedious to write (and the compiled code probably takes more storage: see below). If the programmer writes instead

%DECLARE I FIXED;
%DO I = 1 TO 5;
A(I) = 2 * B(I);
%END;
%DEACTIVATE I;

then the result is that the statements written are actually replaced by the simple five-statement sequence above before the main stage of compilation begins. This replacement occurs as follows. The %DECLARE statement sets up I as a compile-time integer variable. The %DO statement acts as an ordinary DO statement in the manner in which I is initialized and incremented through the values 1, 2, 3, 4, 5. The body of the *compile-time DO* is treated differently, however. Instead of being executed, it is treated as a character string to be scanned. On the initial pass through the loop each occurrence of identifier I in the statement is replaced by the current value of compile-time variable I (converted to a character string). Thus the result on the first iteration is the string A(1) = 2 * B(1);. Each subsequent iteration through the loop produces another copy of the body with the appropriate substitution for I made. After five iterations the resulting program text is the simple sequence above. The %DEACTIVATE I statement allows I to be used in subsequent program statements without a substitution occurring.

The result of the initial pass during compilation in which compile-time statements are executed is simply another PL/I program in which the original compile-time statements have been deleted and the designated substitutions in other parts of the program made. These features can be a useful aid to the programmer in avoiding tedious coding without introducing any additional execution cost. However, there is also a danger, as the example above illustrates: use of the compile-time facilities may cause a large increase in the size of the compiled program for only a small decrease in execution time. Thus the programmer must be careful in his application of these features.

13-10. STRUCTURE OF A PL/I VIRTUAL COMPUTER

PL/I programs are compiled into executable machine code, but a substantial amount of run-time software support is required for simulation of many PL/I features, e.g., input-output, tasks, interrupts, and data type conversions. In general, hardware data representations are used and run-time data descriptors are not required, except in the case of variable-size arrays, variable-length character strings, and array cross sections. Most of the primitive operations, outside of the basic arithmetic, relational, and Boolean operations, require software simulation. The large number of data types and primitive operations provided in the language make the number of necessary run-time support routines correspondingly large. However, this entire library need not be present during execution of every program; the compiler instead determines the exact set of run-time support routines needed for the execution of each program.

PL/I run-time storage management is rather complex. A large static area is required to store the compiled code for the executable program, the run-time support routines, STATIC data structures and variables, and various pieces of system-defined data. A central stack is used for subprogram and block activation records. Each activation record in general contains a static chain pointer, return point, storage areas for AUTOMATIC variables and data structures, system-defined data concerning interrupt enabling and interrupt routines defined by ON statements, and various other pieces of system data. Ordinarily the central stack is used for most run-time storage allocation.

A heap is necessary only when a program uses BASED or CONTROLLED variables or data structures, which can be created and destroyed anytime during program execution within the block or subprogram in which they are declared. Because of the relatively restricted use of the heap, it need not be particularly large. Management of storage in the heap is simple. Storage is allocated and freed only upon explicit use of ALLOCATE and FREE statements, and no attempt is made to avoid the generation of garbage and dangling references. Free storage in the heap is allocated in variable-size blocks. A typical storage management technique is to maintain a free space list linking together all the free blocks in the heap in order of increasing memory address. Storage is allocated from the free space list on a *first-fit* or *best-fit* basis, and returned blocks are linked back into the list at the appropriate point, after first performing a partial compaction to coalesce adjacent blocks. The techniques are discussed in Section 7-8.

13-11. REFERENCES AND SUGGESTIONS FOR FURTHER READING

Numerous introductory texts on PL/I exist, as well as the usual implementation manuals. A more thorough semantic description of the language is provided in an excellent article by Beech [1970].

Elson [1973], Wegner [1968], and Harrison [1973] also treat various aspects of PL/I in depth. Lawson [1967] describes the use of BASED variables in list processing. Sammet [1969] provides details of the history of PL/I; see also articles in Rosen [1967].

The most precise definition of the semantics and syntax of the language is found in the formal PL/I definition produced by the IBM Vienna Laboratory and described in a lengthy series of reports. The paper by Lucas and Walk [1969] provides an overview of this formal definition; see also Bandat [1968]. Two PL/I implementations are described briefly by Conway and Wilcox [1973] and Freiburghouse [1969].

13-12. PROBLEMS

13-1. Determine whether subprogram parameters are transmitted by *reference* or by *value-result* in your local PL/I implementation by experimenting with some test programs. *Hint:* A main program and a subprogram are needed. Viewed from the main program both transmission techniques should appear indistinguishable, but in the subprogram there are some subtle differences which appear when parameter transmission is coupled with nonlocal referencing.

13-2. Consider the program segment

```
          DECLARE 1 NODE BASED (P),
                   2 CAR POINTER,
                   2 CDR POINTER;
          DECLARE (Q,Z) POINTER;
          ALLOCATE NODE SET(Q);
                        .
                        .
                        .
 (1)               Q - > CDR = Z;
                        .
                        .
                        .
```

In line (1) an assignment is made to the CDR field of the structure of type NODE pointed to by Q. Unfortunately Q may not point to a structure of type NODE at the time of the assignment. For example, if another BASED structure type, TAB, has also been declared, line (1) might be preceded by a statement ALLOCATE TAB SET(Q) and then the assignment to the CDR field of Q would be nonsense. In PL/I implementations the programmer usually has no protection against such errors. *Problem:* Design two *safe* PL/I systems that will not allow an access or an assignment to a field of a BASED structure through an incorrect pointer:

a. *System 1.* This system utilizes *dynamic* (run-time) *type checking* to protect against such errors. Specify the run-time mechanisms and data necessary to make use of BASED variables safe.

b. *System 2.* This system utilizes *static* (compile-time) *type checking* but requires some slight restriction and modification of the language. Specify how the language needs to be modified to make this possible.

Do not concern yourself with problems of BASED and POINTER variables transmitted as parameters but only with local structures and variables. *Hint:* Hoare [1968] provides some useful suggestions.

14 LISP 1.5

14-1. INTRODUCTION

The LISP language was first designed and implemented by John McCarthy and a group at the Massachusetts Institute of Technology around 1960. The language has become widely used for research, most prominently in the area of artificial intelligence (game playing, theorem proving, robots, natural language processing, etc.). The basic definition of LISP is found in the M.I.T. manual (McCarthy et al. [1965]). However, almost every implementation extends that basic definition in various ways. The language described in this chapter is the basic LISP 1.5.

LISP is different from most other languages in a number of aspects. Most striking is the equivalence of form between programs and data in the language, which allows data structures to be executed as programs and programs to be modified as data. Another striking feature is the heavy reliance on recursion as a control structure, rather than the iteration (looping) which is common in most programming languages. A third key feature is the use of linked lists as the basic data structure together with operations for general list modification. List processing is the basis of most LISP algorithms, although numbers and characters may also be manipulated to a limited extent. The important storage management technique of *garbage collection* was also first introduced in LISP.

14-2. BRIEF OVERVIEW OF THE LANGUAGE

A LISP main program has the relatively trivial form of a sequence of function subprogram definitions followed by a sequence of calls on these functions with particular arguments. Each function subprogram is defined separately. There is no block structure or other complex syntactic organization. The only interactions between different functions occur through calls during execution.

LISP functions are defined entirely as expressions. Each operator is a function which returns a value, and subprograms are written as single (often very complex) expressions. Various special constructs have been added to the language to make this pure expression syntax appear somewhat like the ordinary *sequence of statements* syntax, but the expression form remains basic.

Data in LISP are rather restricted. Atoms (symbols) and numbers are the basic elementary types. Linked lists and property lists (represented as a special case of linked lists) form the basic data structures. All descriptor processing is done during execution, and no declarations of any sort are necessary.

LISP provides a wide variety of primitives for the creation, destruction, and modification of lists (including property lists). Basic primitives for arithmetic are provided. Run-time program translation and execution are also provided as primitives, and programs may be created and executed dynamically.

LISP control structures are relatively simple. The expressions used to construct programs are written in strict *Cambridge Polish* form and may include conditional branching. The *PROG feature* provides a simple structure for writing expressions in a sequence with provision for labels and **goto**s. Generator primitives (called *functionals*) are also provided for generating elements of lists in sequence. Recursive subprogram calls are heavily emphasized in most LISP programming.

LISP referencing is primarily based on the *most recent association* rule for nonlocal referencing, implemented using a simple linked list of current associations, the *A-list*, which is searched for the current association each time an identifier is referenced. A number of twists are provided, however, to allow this simple but slow technique to be replaced by faster methods. The most important allows any identifier to be given a global association called an APVAL, which takes priority over any other association for the identifier.

Subprogram parameters are transmitted either all by value or all by name depending on the classification of the subprogram, with transmission by value being the usual case except for some special primitive functions.

LISP is most easily implemented with a software interpreter and software simulation for all primitives. Most implementations also provide a compiler which can be used to compile selected subprogram definitions into machine code. These compiled functions are then executable by the hardware interpreter (but still require software simulation for many operations). LISP is rather poorly suited for compilation because most bindings are not made until execution. A complex storage management structure based on a garbage-collected heap is used as the primary storage for data and programs.

14-3. AN ANNOTATED EXAMPLE: BUILDING A LIST OF THE ATOMS ON A GIVEN LIST

Figure 14-1 shows a LISP function subprogram and a main program. The function, named LISTATOMS, is given a LISP list

```
Line

 1    DEFINE((
 2     (LISTATOMS(LAMBDA(X)
 3      (PROG(RES)
 4        LOOP (COND ((NULLX) RETURN RES))
 5              ((ATOM (CAR X))  (SETQ RES (CONS (CAR X) RES)))
 6              (T (SETQ RES (APPEND (LISTATOMS (CAR X)) RES))))
 7            (SETQ X (CDR X))
 8            (GO LOOP)
 9        )))
10      ))
11    LISTATOMS((A (B C) D E))
12    LISTATOMS(( ))
13    LISTATOMS(((A B) (((C)) D) E))
14    FIN
```

Fig. 14-1. Example LISP program.

structure as argument. The list structure is a tree containing LISP atoms (symbols) at its leaves. LISTATOMS constructs a new linear list containing only the atoms of the original list. For example, if the input to LISTATOMS is the list structure

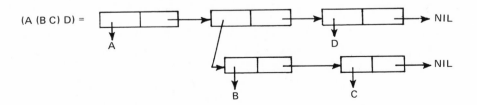

$(A (B C) D) =$ ... NIL ... A ... D ... NIL ... B ... C

then the result of LISTATOMS is the list

(D C B A) =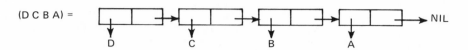

The main program simply defines the subprogram and then calls it three times with particular test list structures.

LISTATOMS operates by scanning the elements of the input list in sequence. Each element is either an atom or a sublist. If an atom, the atom is added to the output list being constructed. If a sublist, then LISTATOMS is called recursively to create a list of the atoms on the sublist, and this list is then concatenated onto the list being constructed for output. The annotations below refer to the line numbers to the left of the program listing, which are not a part of the listing itself.

Line 1. Beginning of the main program, which consists of a sequence of function calls with parameter lists. We wish to define the subprogram LISTATOMS, so the primitive function DEFINE is called first with the definition of LISTATOMS as its argument. The argument list for DEFINE begins on this line and continues to line 10. Since DEFINE is a function of one argument, which consists of a list of function subprogram definitions, the two parentheses are required.

Line 2. Beginning of the definition of LISTATOMS. The function name is given, followed by its body, which extends to line 9. The body begins with a formal parameter list, (X), preceded by LAMBDA, the primitive which causes actual and formal parameters to be paired and added to the local referencing environment. The form of this line is standard, (fn-name (LAMBDA (formal-parameter-list), and serves the same purpose as the usual subprogram definition header of other languages.

Line 3. Beginning of the subprogram body. The body is to be in PROG form—appearing as a sequence of "statements" (the alternative is a body which is an expression). One local variable, RES, is declared. RES is automatically initialized to have the null value NIL.

Line 4. A conditional branching statement begins here with COND and continues through line 6. The statement is preceded by a statement label, LOOP. The conditional consists of a sequence of tests. Each test is followed by a statement to be executed if the test is satisfied. The first test here is (NULL X), which tests if the list structure X is empty. If so, then (RETURN RES) is executed, which causes an exit from the subprogram with the value of RES as the result.

Line 5. The second test is (ATOM (CAR X)). CAR is a primitive which accesses the first element of its argument. Since the (NULL X) test of the previous line was not satisfied, we know X must have at least one element, which is retrieved by (CAR X). The element retrieved must be either a pointer to an atom or a pointer to another list. The primitive ATOM tests for a pointer to an atom. Thus the expression (ATOM (CAR X)) evaluates to true if the first element of list X is an atom. If this test is satisfied, then the remainder of the line specifies an assignment to be made. The assignment operator is SETQ. Its first argument is the variable whose value is to be changed, and its second argument is an expression giving the value to be assigned. RES is the local variable whose value is a pointer to the list of atoms found to this point. Since the test established that an atom begins list X now, we wish to add that atom to the list RES. This is done by the CONS primitive. The arguments to CONS are defined by (CAR X), which retrieves the atom to be added, and RES, which is the list to be extended. CONS adds the atom to the list RES and returns as its value a pointer to the modified list. SETQ then assigns this pointer back as the new value of RES.

Line 6. The last line of the conditional begun on line 4. The test here is the trivial T (true) which indicates that the associated statement is always to be executed if the preceding tests have all failed. Control can reach this line only if the first element of list X is a pointer to a sublist. The assignment beginning with SETQ specifies that a list of the atoms on this sublist is to be constructed (using LISTATOMS recursively) and then concatenated with the current list RES. The concatenation is done by the primitive APPEND, which is given two lists as arguments and returns a list composed of the two original lists concatenated to form one long list. Note that the recursive call to LISTATOMS uses exactly the same syntax as any other function call.

Line 7. The first element of list X is deleted since we have finished processing it. The CDR primitive, given a pointer to a list as argument, returns a pointer to the list with the first element deleted.

Line 8. Control is transferred back to line 4.

Line 9. End of the definition of LISTATOMS.

Line 10. End of the call to DEFINE.

Line 11. The newly defined subprogram LISTATOMS is called with the test list (A (B C) D E). It should return the list (E D C B A) as its value. The arguments and results of main program function calls are printed automatically by the LISP system, so no explicit PRINT command is necessary.

Line 12. LISTATOMS is tested with the null list ( ) as parameter. The null list could also have been written NIL.

Line 13. LISTATOMS is tested with a more complex list structure. The result should again be (E D C B A).

Line 14. End of the main program.

The function LISTATOMS could (and often would) be written without PROG, using only conditional branching and recursion to accomplish the same result. This definition might then appear as

```
(LISTATOMS (LAMBDA (X)
    (COND ((NULL X)        NIL)
          ((ATOM (CAR X))(CONS (CAR X)(LISTATOMS (CDR X))))
          (T (APPEND (LISTATOMS (CAR X))(LISTATOMS (CDR X))))
    )))
```

14-4. DATA

Atoms (symbols), numbers, and lists are the basic data types in LISP. Programs (function definitions) and property lists are special categories of lists of particular importance. All data items carry run-time descriptors.

Atoms

A LISP atom is the basic elementary data item. Syntactically an atom is just an identifier—a string of letters and digits beginning with a letter. Within LISP function definitions, atoms serve the usual purposes of identifiers; they are used as function names, formal parameters, local variables, statement labels, etc. In LISP data structures they serve as symbols—atomic data items on which no operations other than the test for identity are defined.

An atom is represented by a pointer during execution. The location pointed to contains a special *atom* data type designator and a pointer to a property list, which contains the various *properties* associated with the atom. One of the properties on this list is the *print name* (PNAME) of the atom, the character string representing

(1) Symbolic atom representation

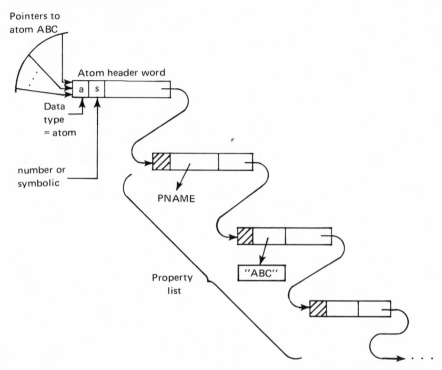

(2) Number representation

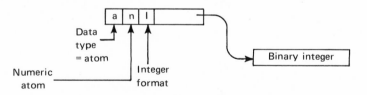

Fig. 14-2. LISP atoms and numbers.

the atom for input and output. Other properties may include the function named by the atom, the value of the atom if used as a variable name, etc. Figure 14-2 illustrates the structure of a LISP atom.

Numbers

Numbers in integer or floating-point format may be used. The hardware representation is used, but a run-time descriptor is also required, so each number uses two words. However, this representation coordinates well with that used for atoms; a number is an atom with a special type designator and a pointer to the bit string representing the number instead of a pointer to a property list, as shown in Fig. 14-2.

Lists

LISP lists are simple singly linked structures, as shown in Fig. 14-3. Each list element contains a pointer to a data item and a pointer to the following list element. The last list element points to the special atom NIL as its successor. The two pointers in a list element are termed the CAR pointer and the CDR pointer. The CDR pointer points to the successor of the list element. The CAR pointer points to the data item. (The terms CAR and CDR originated from the hardware organization of the first computer on which LISP was implemented but became such a basic part of the LISP jargon that their use has continued.)

A list element may contain (have as its CAR pointer) a pointer to an atom, a pointer to a number, or a pointer to another list. Each case is distinguished by a data type flag stored in the location pointed to. Since a list element may contain a pointer to another list, it is possible to build up list structures of arbitrary complexity. Ordinarily these are tree structures, but it is possible to have shared sublists, to build circular structures, and the like. Figure 14-4 illustrates a typical list with sublists.

Syntactically a list is represented by writing its elements in sequence with the whole enclosed in parentheses. Atoms are written using their print names, and numbers are written in the usual number syntax. Lists which share sublists or which are circular cannot be

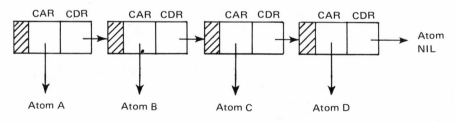

List syntax: (A B C D)

(hashed area contains system-defined data)

Fig. 14-3. Simple list representation.

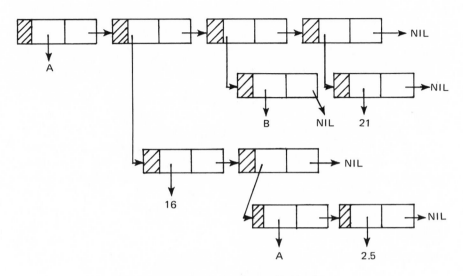

List syntax: (A (16 (A 2.5)) (B) (21))

Fig. 14-4.   List with sublists.

written down, but every other list may be so represented. Figures 14-3 and 14-4 illustrate the syntax for lists.

Property Lists

Each atom has an associated property list, accessible through a pointer stored in the memory location representing the atom. A property list is simply an ordinary LISP list, differing only in that its elements are logically paired into an alternating *property name— property value* sequence. Every atom's property list contains at least the property PNAME whose associated value is a pointer to a list containing the print name of the atom in character string form. If an atom is a function name, its property list contains the property name EXPR and a pointer to the list representing the function definition. Other properties may be added by the programmer as desired, and certain primitives also add properties. In much LISP programming the property lists of atoms are the central structures where much of the data are stored.

Programs

Programmer-defined functions are written in the form of lists for input, as seen in Fig. 14-1. The LISP input routines make no distinction between program and data lists but simply translate all lists into the internal linked list representation. Each atom encountered is looked up in a run-time symbol table called the *Ob-list* and the pointer to the atom retrieved if it already exists or a new atom created if not. All the LISP primitive operations are named by atoms which are system-defined at the beginning of execution but which otherwise are like any other atoms. This simple organization makes it possible to translate both programs and data into the same internal list form. Figure 14-5 shows a simple LISP function definition and its corresponding internal linked list form. As noted in the introduction, this common internal representation for programs and data structures allows LISP programs to be created dynamically by other programs during execution and later executed. Thus a *data list* may turn into a *program list*, and conversely, as required.

14-5. OPERATIONS

All operations in LISP are defined as functions.

List Manipulation

The central primitives are those for list manipulation.

CAR and CDR. The primitives CAR and CDR retrieve the CAR pointer and CDR pointer of a given list element, respectively. Effectively, given a list L as operand, (CAR L) returns a pointer to the first list element, and (CDR L) returns a pointer to the list with the first element deleted.

CONS. The CONS primitive takes two pointers as operands, allocates a new list element memory word, stores the two pointers in the CAR and CDR fields of the word, and returns a pointer to the new word. Where the second operand is a list the effect is to add the first element to the head of this list and return a pointer to the extended list.

CAR, CDR, and CONS are the basic operations for processing and constructing lists. By using CONS any list may be constructed element by element. For example, (CONS A (CONS B (CONS C NIL))) constructs a list of the three elements referenced by A, B, and C. Similarly, if L = (A B C) is a list, then (CAR L) is A, (CAR (CDR L)) is B, and (CAR (CDR (CDR L))) is C. By using CAR, CDR, and CONS appropriately any list may be broken down into its constituent elements, and new lists may be constructed from these or other elements.

Program list: (LAMBDA (X)(COND ((NULL X) X)

             (T (CAR (CDR X)))))

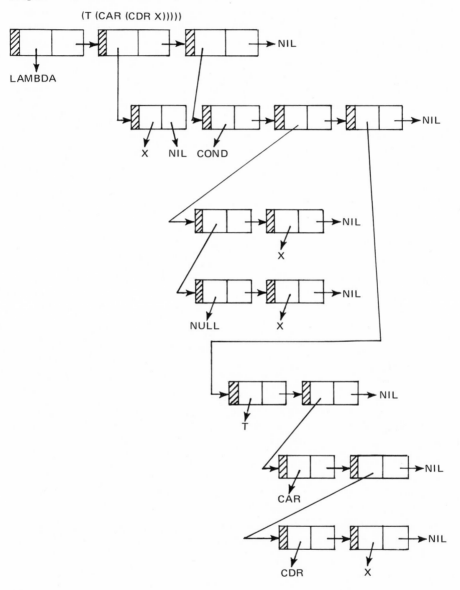

Fig. 14-5. Executable form (list structure) of LISP program.

LIST and QUOTE. The primitive LIST may be used to replace a long sequence of CONS operations. LIST takes any number of arguments and constructs a list of its arguments, returning a pointer to the resulting list. QUOTE allows any list or atom to be written as a literal in a program. For example, if L = (B C) is a list, then (CONS (QUOTE A) L) produces the list (A B C).

Other List Manipulation Primitives. APPEND may be used to concatenate two lists, COPY copies a list, EFFACE deletes a list element, and SUBST may be used to substitute one list element for another. Most LISP implementations extend this basic set to include other common list manipulation operations as well.

Arithmetic

LISP contains the basic arithmetic primitives: PLUS, DIFFER-ENCE, TIMES, and DIVIDE, and a few others. The syntax is the same as for other LISP operations; thus A + B * C is written (PLUS A (TIMES B C)). All arithmetic operations are generic operations, accepting arguments of either real or integer data type and making type conversions as necessary.

Relational, Logical, and Other Predicates

The basic logical primitives AND, OR, and NOT are provided, together with the arithmetic predicates LESSP (less-than), GREATERP (greater-than), ZEROP (equal-to-zero), and MINUSP (negative).

Two important predicates distinguish the data type of a data item: ATOM returns true (the atom T) if its argument is an atom (including a number); NUMBERP returns true if its argument is a number (real or integer). The predicate NULL returns true only if its argument is the special atom NIL (NIL also represents the *empty list,* and thus (NULL L) is used to test if list L is *empty*).

EQ and EQUAL are used to test equality. EQ applies only to atoms (not including numbers), while EQUAL applies to arbitrary list structures (including atoms and numbers). MEMBER tests if a given argument is an element of a given list.

Property List Manipulation

Basic functions are provided for insertion, deletion, and accessing on property lists. ATTRIB and DEFLIST are used to add property name/property value pairs to property lists; GET returns the current value associated with a given property name; and REMPROP deletes a property name/property value pair from a property list. For example, to add the name-value pair AGE,25 to the property list of atom JOE, one writes

(DEFLIST (((QUOTE JOE) 25)) (QUOTE AGE))

Later in the program the AGE property of atom JOE may be retrieved through the function call

(GET (QUOTE JOE) (QUOTE AGE))

Deletion of the AGE of JOE is accomplished by the call

(REMPROP (QUOTE JOE) (QUOTE AGE))

The primitives DEFINE, CSET, and CSETQ also modify property lists for special property names (see below).

Assignment

Direct assignment does not play as central a role in LISP programming as it does in other languages. Many LISP programs are written entirely without assignment operations, using recursion and parameter transmission to get somewhat the same effect indirectly. However, assignment is used within PROG segments, where the LISP program takes on the ordinary sequence-of-statements form. The basic assignment operator is SETQ. The expression (SETQ X VAL) assigns the value of VAL as the new value of variable X; the result of the expression is the value of VAL (thus SETQ is a function, but its value is usually ignored). The variable name (X above) must be explicitly given in a call to SETQ. The primitive SET is identical to SETQ except that the variable (which is just an atom) to which assignment is made may be computed. For example, (SET (CAR L) VAL) is equivalent to (SETQ X VAL) if atom X happens to be the first element of list L. SETQ and SET are used for changing the values of variables in the current referencing environment. Global variables are assigned values using the primitives CSETQ and CSET (see the next section). Two other primitives, RPLACA and RPLACD, allow assignment to the CAR and CDR fields, respectively, of any list element. For example, (RPLACA L VAL) assigns the value of VAL as the new first element of list L, replacing the current first element.

Input-Output

Most LISP output is automatic. For each function call in the main program the system automatically prints out the function name, its arguments, and the value returned by the function. A TRACE primitive allows any other function (programmer- or system-defined) to be tagged for similar treatment. When such a tagged function is entered during execution its name and parameters are printed out, and when it is exited its value is printed. Because there is little need in many LISP applications for specially formatted output, these simple automatic output features often suffice.

Input data may be included directly in the form of actual parameters in the main program function calls, as seen in Fig. 14-1. Thus many LISP programs run entirely without any explicit input-output commands.

Simple primitives are also provided for reading and writing sequential external files. READ reads in the next list, list structure, or atom from an input file; PRINT prints a list; and PRINTPROP prints a property list. Another set of functions allows the input file to be read character by character and an output line to be built up element by element under programmer control.

Translation and Execution of Programs

A LISP function definition takes the form of a list structure. As a result a function definition may be read in and translated into internal linked list form by READ just as any other list structure. The resulting list structure may then be manipulated as data, or it may be executed by the primitive APPLY. APPLY accepts as arguments (1) a function definition (beginning with LAMBDA and a list of formal parameters), (2) a list of actual parameters, and (3) an A-list to be used in resolving nonlocal references during execution of the function (see the next section). APPLY operates by first evaluating the actual parameters, then pairing the values with the formal parameters of the function, and finally adding the pairs to the top of the A-list in sequence. APPLY then calls a second primitive, EVAL, to evaluate the body of the function definition (which is always an expression in list structure form), using the modified A-list as a referencing environment.

Subprograms

Subprograms in LISP are always defined as functions. The syntax at first appears complex because of the use of the standard LISP list structure syntax. No special syntactic constructs are provided for function definitions. A function definition has the form

(*fn-name* (LAMBDA (*list-of-formal-parameters*) (*body*)))

The *body* is an arbitrary expression.

As actual parameters, functions may be given arbitrary data structures, and likewise any function may return any data structure as its value. Thus LISP functions are essentially unrestricted in their ability to create, destroy, or modify data structures. Since these data structures may be subprogram definitions, it is possible to write LISP programs which create or modify other LISP programs.

Subprograms may be defined at any point during program execution. Definition of a subprogram is quite simple. First the list structure defining the subprogram must be created or input, and then this list structure must be put on the property list of the atom which is to serve as the function name, associated with the property name EXPR. The primitive DEFINE allows this association to be set up easily. DEFINE takes a function definition (of the form given above) and stores the definition, paired with EXPR, on the property list of the atom which is to serve as the function name. Subprograms defined using DEFINE become globally callable. If it is desirable to name a subprogram only temporarily, in the local referencing environment, the primitive LABEL may be used instead of DEFINE.

14-6. SEQUENCE CONTROL

A LISP main program is composed of a simple sequence of function calls, each consisting of a function name followed by a list of actual parameters. These *top-level* function calls are executed in sequence until the atom FIN is reached.

Each function subprogram definition takes a quite different form. The body of a subprogram is not composed of statements but only of a single expression. Thus in LISP the expression structure is the key element in sequence control. The special PROG expression allows use of a syntax which roughly resembles an ordinary sequence of statements.

Expressions

LISP expressions are written in strict Cambridge Polish notation (function name followed by sequence of actual parameters) with full parenthesization. This makes the syntax quite simple and regular, but the parentheses often make the resulting structure difficult to follow. Each primitive operation is given a symbolic name, using some LISP atom, e.g., PLUS, CONS. Similarly, each programmer-defined function also is given an atom as its name. Expressions may be built most simply by use of nested function calls, e.g., (CONS (CAR L) (CAR (CDR L))). In such expressions the usual sequence of evaluation applies: The arguments are first evaluated, and then the function is applied to the result. However, certain special functions are applied without evaluating their arguments (see below). Careful attention is paid in the LISP definition to specification of the order of evaluation in expressions: Actual parameters are evaluated from left to right, and otherwise the nesting of parentheses completely determines evaluation order.

The COND primitive allows branching within expressions. Like all LISP primitives COND is written as a function with a list of parameters, but COND invokes a special evaluation rule which gives the effect of a branching control structure. The form is

$$
\begin{array}{ll}
(\text{COND} & (\textit{test-1} \quad \textit{result-expr-1}) \\
& (\textit{test-2} \quad \textit{result-expr-2}) \\
& (\textit{test-3} \quad \textit{result-expr-3}) \\
& \quad \cdot \\
& \quad \cdot \\
& \quad \cdot \\
& (\textit{test-k} \quad \textit{result-expr-k}))
\end{array}
$$

Each *test* is an expression which must evaluate to true or false. The test expressions are evaluated in sequence, and when one evaluates to true the corresponding result-expression is evaluated and the value returned as the value of the COND expression. The test result false is represented by the atom NIL; any other result is considered true.

Statements and the PROG Feature

Any LISP program may be written using only simple expressions, conditionals, and recursive function calls. However, for many algorithms which ordinarily would be coded using a loop such noniterative coding requires heavy reliance on recursion to give the effect of looping. The *PROG feature* allows a loop to be coded directly. The necessity to keep within the usual expression syntax makes the syntax for PROGs somewhat odd. A PROG takes the form

$$
\begin{array}{l}
(\text{PROG} \ (\textit{list of-local-variables}) \\
\quad (\textit{expr-1}) \\
\quad (\textit{expr-2}) \\
\quad \quad \cdot \\
\quad \quad \cdot \\
\quad \quad \cdot \\
\quad (\textit{expr-n}))
\end{array}
$$

An atom may be put between any pair of expressions in a PROG to serve as a label for the following expression. A **goto** is provided in the form (GO *label*), which transfers control to the expression following the designated *label*.

The expressions in a PROG are evaluated in sequence, skipping over atoms representing labels, with the GO transferring control in the usual way. A PROG may be exited either by completing evaluation of the last expression (in which case the PROG as a whole has the value NIL) or by a call to the primitive RETURN. The argument to RETURN is the value to be returned as the value of the PROG. An example of PROG was given in Section 14-3.

Generators for List Elements

A simple set of list *generators* is provided; these generators are called *functionals* in LISP terminology. The functional MAPCAR is typical. The function call (MAPCAR *list fn-name*) applies the function *fn-name* to each element of the list *list* in sequence. The value of MAPCAR is the list composed of the values produced by *fn-name* during this processing. MAPCAR may be used to replace the use of an explicit loop or recursion for the sequential processing of a list. Most LISP implementations provide a variety of other generators (functionals) for processing lists in various ways. In addition the programmer may easily write his own.

14-7. DATA CONTROL

In most language implementations the referencing environment is maintained as a system-defined data structure hidden from the programmer. LISP is unique in making the referencing environment an explicit data structure which is both visible and accessible to the programmer. The exact representation of referencing environments varies widely among LISP implementations. Compiler-based implementations tend to use rather complex representations which allow efficient referencing. However, the simplest and most general technique is that using an explicit association list, the A-list. We shall describe this technique here; articles in Berkeley and Bobrow [1964] describe other more efficient methods.

A-Lists and Referencing Environments

An A-list (association list) represents a referencing environment. The A-list is an ordinary LISP list, each of whose elements is a

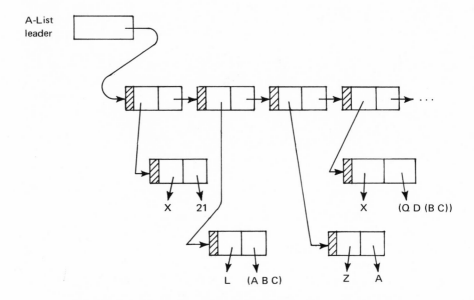

(Atoms, numbers, and lists serving as identifiers and values are themselves
linked lists, although this structure is not diagrammed)

Fig. 14-6. An A-list for a referencing environment containing associations for L, Z, and two
occurences of X.

pointer to a word representing an identifier (atom) and its current
association. These association pairs are list words whose CAR points
to the atom and whose CDR points to the value (list, atom, or
number) associated with the atom. Figure 14-6 illustrates this A-list
structure.

Referencing in LISP is strictly according to the most recent
association rule, which is implemented by a simple search of the
A-list from beginning (most recent associations) to end (oldest
associations) until an appropriate association is found. Thus to find
the current value of X, for example, the A-list is searched until an
entry is found whose CAR is the atom X. The CDR of that entry is
then the current value of X.

The A-list is modified during program execution in three basic
ways. When a function call occurs to a programmer-defined function,
the LISP interpreter (actually the function LAMBDA) pairs the atoms
representing formal parameters with their corresponding actual
parameter values and adds the resulting pairs to the beginning of the
A-list. A similar thing happens when a PROG is entered. The atoms

listed as local variable names for the PROG are each paired with the value NIL and added to the beginning of the A-list. When a function or PROG execution is completed, the associations added on entry are deleted. The programmer may directly modify the most recent association for an atom on the A-list by using SETQ (or SET). The effect of (SETQ X VAL) is to replace the current value of X on the A-list by the value of VAL. X may occur on the A-list more than once, but SETQ affects only the most recent entry. A function name may also be placed on the A-list and associated with its (list structure) definition through use of the primitive LABEL.

Global Referencing

LISP is unique in providing a facility for any atom to be given a *global association*, which is used in *preference* to an association on the A-list if it is present. An atom has a global association when the property name APVAL appears on its property list. The value associated with APVAL is the global value of the atom. The primitives CSETQ and CSET (corresponding to SETQ and SET) may be used to give an atom a global association. For example, (CSETQ PI 3.1416) sets the global value of the atom PI to 3.1416 by inserting the property name APVAL and the property value 3.1416 on the property list of PI. Whenever PI is referenced in any following part of program execution the value 3.1416 will be retrieved (regardless of whether or not PI appears on the A-list). The complete referencing rule for atoms used as variables is then as follows: Search the atom's property list for an APVAL first, and then search the A-list from the beginning. The first association found in this search is the one used.

When an atom is used as a function name a slightly different referencing technique is used. Instead of a search for an APVAL, the property list of the atom is searched for one of the special property names EXPR, SUBR, FEXPR, or FSUBR. The value associated with one of these properties is a function definition, differentiated as to method of parameter transmission and form of definition as follows:

EXPR. The function definition is in the form of a LISP list structure, and parameters are to be transmitted by value (evaluated before the function is executed).

SUBR. Like EXPR except the function is a system primitive coded in machine language or a compiled programmer-defined function.

FEXPR. Like EXPR except parameters are to be transmitted by name (unevaluated).

FSUBR. Like SUBR except parameters are to be transmitted unevaluated.

If a function name does not have such a property name on its property list, then the A-list is searched in the usual way, and the function definition found is treated as an EXPR.

Parameter Transmission

As indicated above, parameter transmission may be either by value or by name. Transmission by value is standard; DEFINE, for example, always defines a function as an EXPR. Transmission by name is done without transmitting the referencing environment of the point of call, so that local variables in the called function may interfere with proper evaluation of the actual parameters. For this reason transmission by name in LISP is usually not appropriate for programmer-defined functions.

Special provision is made for transmitting the referencing environment along with a function name (when the function is transmitted as an actual parameter to a subprogram) by using the primitive FUNCTION. The referencing environment at the point of transmission is represented by a pointer to the current top of the A-list. For example, to call a function SUB with another function NUB as actual parameter, the expression (SUB (FUNCTION NUB) *other-params*) is used. The atom NUB is then transmitted together with a pointer to the beginning of the current A-list, and whenever NUB is executed through a reference in SUB to the corresponding formal parameter, the transmitted A-list pointer is taken as the beginning of the A-list to be used as referencing environment during execution of NUB.

14-8. OPERATING ENVIRONMENT

LISP is designed for a batch-processing environment. Sequential files may be accessed through the I/O primitives. There is little provision for a more complex file-handling structure, although the original LISP system included a *monitor* which allowed copies of the entire memory to be written on and retrieved from external storage between processing of main program segments. These facilities tend to vary widely between implementations, however, with many LISP implementations having provision for program libraries, list storage on external files, special editors, etc.

14-9. SYNTAX AND TRANSLATION

Syntax

The key points of LISP syntax have already been mentioned in the preceding sections: the main program form as a sequence of function calls and the function definitions as list structures using fully parenthesized Cambridge Polish notation. Both programs and data share the same syntax. Even the primitive operations are named with the same atoms used for data.

The regularity and simplicity of the LISP syntax is both a virtue and a vice. The basic rules of LISP syntax may be learned in a few minutes by the beginner, and then writing programs is mainly a matter (syntactically) of getting the right arguments listed for each function call. The problem with this simple syntax lies in the parentheses. Every expression is fully parenthesized, and since each function body is a gigantic expression, the parentheses in a function definition often pile up 10 or 15 levels deep. The result may be extremely difficult to read and debug, and a parenthesis out of place is perhaps the most common LISP syntax error. Unfortunately a parenthesis out of place in many cases does not lead to a syntax error (i.e., it cannot be caught during translation) and instead the expression is often still "meaningful"—it just means something different from what was intended. This type of logical error is difficult to find in the best of circumstances, but the poor readability of LISP function definitions makes it doubly difficult here. Most LISP systems include an automatic parentheses counter which, when used, outputs integers beneath parentheses in the program listing to indicate parenthesis pairings.

Translation

A LISP main program is translated into a single *doublet list* by the LISP system. The doublet list contains the *function name—actual parameter list* pairs of the main program as elements. Each function name is usually an atom, and each parameter list is an ordinary LISP list structure. A parameter list may contain function definitions (if the function name is DEFINE) or data lists on which the defined functions are to operate. This translation is essentially trivial—the lists being translated are scanned element by element and the internal list structure representation built up. During the translation numbers are translated into their binary equivalents, with a descriptor in a separate word. The only difficult aspect concerns the handling of atoms.

During translation each reference to the same atom must be translated into an identical pointer, pointing to the beginning of the atom's property list. The translator must keep a symbol table in which each input atom may be looked up and its internal pointer representation retrieved. This table is the *Ob-list* and ordinarily is organized as a hash-coded table with *buckets* to handle collisions. Because lists containing the same atoms may also be read in during program execution, the Ob-list must remain in memory throughout execution.

Most LISP implementations also include a compiler which may be used as a primitive operation. Given a list of function names, the compiler translates each function definition into machine code. Most systems allow compiled functions to be interspersed with ordinary functions—each type is able to call the other—so that no flexibility is lost. The resulting LISP programs are essentially identical with those described here but with greatly speeded execution.

14-10. STRUCTURE OF A LISP VIRTUAL COMPUTER

The run-time memory organization in a typical LISP implementation was briefly described in Section 7-6. Figure 7-3 illustrates the pattern of memory usage. The major memory area is the heap, which contains both data list structures and list structures representing function definitions. Property lists are stored in the heap, and some of the system-defined lists, such as the A-list and the doublet list, may also use part of this storage. The heap is managed in fixed-size one-word units, utilizing a free space list and garbage collector. One part of the heap block is restricted to *full-word* data items—numbers and character strings—and requires a special garbage collection scheme.

Other memory areas include a statically allocated area for system programs, including the translator, interpreter, compiler (if used), primitive operations, and storage management routines. A third area is allocated for a stack of activation records for subprogram calls. Each activation record contains a return point and temporaries for the subprogram during its execution.

Execution of a LISP program by the LISP interpreter is straightforward. The translator has produced the doublet list containing the function name—parameter list pairs to be executed. The interpreter takes each doublet in sequence, deletes it from the doublet list, and applies the named function to the associated parameter list. When each doublet has been executed the program has been run. Execution of each individual function is done through a call to APPLY. APPLY and EVAL then call each other recursively until the list structure defining the program has been completely executed. At the base level are the machine-coded primitives like CAR and CDR which are tagged as SUBRs and executed by direct calls from EVAL during program execution.

During execution, subprogram calls are strictly nested so that the last subprogram entered is always the first one exited, and thus it is possible to use the usual activation record stack for system-defined data related to subprogram calls. The separate A-list linked stack is used to maintain the referencing environment.

The most significant features of the LISP run-time structure is the amount of simulation necessary. Almost no hardware features can be used directly on a conventional computer; instead everything must be software-simulated. Each primitive is represented by a software routine, PROG and recursion—the central control structures—are simulated, and even arithmetic must be simulated to the extent of doing run-time type checking (and possibly type conversion) for each arithmetic operation. The LISP virtual computer structure is almost completely at odds with conventional computer design.

14-11. SPECIAL TOPICS

In many ways LISP is the most unconventional language described in this book. Some of these aspects have been mentioned in the preceding sections: linked lists as the central data structure, recursion as the central control structure, the A-list representation of referencing environments, and the equivalence in run-time representations of programs and data. Garbage collection as a storage management procedure, at the time of the first LISP implementations, was a decidedly unconventional storage management technique, although it has been widely copied since then. Two important topics about LISP have not yet been mentioned.

Pure LISP

Pure LISP is the simple subset of LISP composed of (1) the basic primitives CAR, CDR, CONS, EQ, and ATOM; (2) the control structures using COND, recursion, and functional composition; (3) list structures containing only atoms and sublists, without numbers or property lists; and (4) LABEL and LAMBDA for subprogram definition. With this subset most of the usual LISP list processing may be done. In fact, pure LISP is a *universal language*, in a sense which we shall describe more completely in Chapter 17.

Pure LISP has been the basis for many theoretical studies of programs. It is particularly amenable to study because programs written in this subset have an exceedingly simple, regular, recursive structure, which simplifies formal analysis.

The LISP Definition

The LISP manual (McCarthy et al. [1965]) is one of the few programming language manuals that provides a fairly clear description of the run-time structures on which the language implementation is built. The center of this description is a complete definition of the *interpreter* which executes LISP programs, given in the form of LISP programs for the two primitives EVAL and APPLY. The interpreter mechanisms are so straightforward that the entire definition takes less than two pages. (The fact that the definitions take the form of LISP programs is of interest but not central—EVAL and APPLY are of course represented by machine language primitives in an actual implementation.)

There is more to the LISP definition of run-time structures than just the EVAL and APPLY definitions. The A-list as a mechanism for representation of referencing environments; the use of property lists to associate function names with their definitions; the descriptions of run-time representations for lists, atoms, property lists, and numbers; and the description of the garbage collection mechanisms all contribute to provide a picture of the run-time structure which is easy to understand.

This clarity of definition has been important for both the LISP programmer and the LISP implementor because it provides a common point of reference. Programmers use the definition to answer subtle questions of language semantics, and implementors use it as an implementation guide showing how particular constructs are supposed to work (although each implementation may modify the implementation details considerably from those described). This LISP definition is perhaps the most widely known *virtual computer* definition of a language. Unfortunately few other language definitions have followed this pattern.

14-12. REFERENCES AND SUGGESTIONS FOR
FURTHER READING

The basic LISP description is found in McCarthy et al. [1965].
Weissman [1967] and Friedman [1974] provide more elementary
introductions. Berkeley and Bobrow [1964] contains a collection of
articles on various aspects of LISP, including some applications of
the language. Most of the research described in Minsky [1968] was
also programmed in LISP. LISP has become such a central tool in
artificial intelligence research that knowledge of the language is
almost a necessity for a student planning to work in that area.

Harrison [1973] treats LISP and an extension of LISP called
BALM in the context of more general programming language
questions. Bobrow and Murphy [1967] discuss implementation
issues, especially storage management. Moses [1970] descirbes the
problems of transmission of functions as parameters to and results of
other LISP functions.

14-13. PROBLEMS

14-1.   Trace the operation of the pure recursive version of LISTATOMS given at
        the end of Section 14-3 when applied to the argument list (((A B)(((C))
        D) E)); i.e., give the argument and result of each recursive activation of
        LISTATOMS. The recursive version produces a result list which is the
        reverse of the list produced by the LISTATOMS of Fig. 14-1. Can you
        rewrite the pure recursive LISTATOMS so it produces a result identical to
        that of the original LISTATOMS?

14-2.   In the property list examples of Section 14-5, explain why the atoms
        AGE and JOE must be QUOTE'd in each call to DEFLIST, GET, and
        REMPROP.

14-3.   In the syntactic representation of a list in the usual *list notation* (as a
        sequence of elements in parentheses), the terminating CDR pointer to
        NIL is implicit, e.g.,

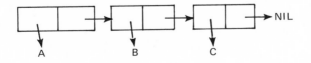

is written (A B C). Occasionally it is desirable to allow the last element of a list to have a CDR pointer to an atom other than NIL. In this case an alternative notation, the *dot notation*, may be used. In dot notation each list element is written as a pair of subelements representing the CAR and CDR of the element. The subelements are enclosed in parentheses and separated by a dot. For example,

is written (A . NIL), (A B) is written (A .(B . NIL)), and, ((A B) C) is written ((A .(B . NIL)) . (C . NIL)). Now the element

which cannot be written in list notation can be written (A . B) in dot notation. Write in dot notation

a. (A (B C)).
b. (((A)) B (C D)).
c. The program list of Fig. 14-5.
d. The A-list of Fig. 14.6. Note that this list cannot be written in list notation.

14-4. Property lists of atoms which contain properties other than the print name (PNAME) of the atom can never be garbage-collected, even if they are entirely inaccessible from any active list structure at the time of garbage collection. Explain why.

14-5. *The self-reproducing function.* The equivalence of program and data representations in LISP makes it possible to write many subtle programs easily that would be much more difficult in other languages. Some of these have the status of *classical LISP problems*, of which the *self-reproducing function* problem is typical: *Write a LISP function SRF whose value is its own definition.* SRF has no inputs. If SRF is defined as (SRF (LAMBDA () (... *body* ...))), then the result of the call (SRF) is the list structure (SRF (LAMBDA () ... *body* ...))). SRF must construct its result list piecemeal—it cannot access the property list of atom SRF to obtain its definition list.

15 SNOBOL4

15-1. INTRODUCTION

SNOBOL4 is the last and most widely implemented of a series of character-string-processing languages developed at Bell Telephone Laboratories during the 1960s. Its major application is to problems in which substantial amounts of character string data must be processed in complex ways, e.g., in processing natural language text. However, the language includes many features of general applicability to other types of data, and thus the language has become widely used in a variety of other areas. An excellent text, written by the language designers (Griswold et al. [1971]), describes the language. The original SNOBOL4 implementation design (on which this chapter is partially based) is described by Griswold [1972].

SNOBOL4 is different from the other languages described in this book in a number of important aspects. Most obvious is the emphasis on character string data and the associated pattern-matching operation (described briefly in Section 4-6). In addition, the language includes *extensible data structures*—facilities for adding new programmer-defined data types. SNOBOL4 shares with LISP the ability to translate and execute at run time programs which have been either constructed or read in as data. It is also similar to LISP in its overall emphasis on generality and flexibility at the expense of execution efficiency—SNOBOL4 implementation requires extensive software simulation on most computers.

15-2. BRIEF OVERVIEW OF THE LANGUAGE

SNOBOL4 data structures are the most extensive of any language described in this part, perhaps excepting PL/I. Simple variables and multidimensional heterogeneous arrays allow element types to vary at run time. Property lists, called *tables*, are also provided. Most interestingly, patterns to be used in pattern matching are treated as an independent data type. Patterns may be constructed and stored as the values of variables or array elements until needed. New data types may be defined by the programmer dynamically, and the SNOBOL4 system automatically generates the appropriate functions for creating structures of the new type and for accessing elements of such structures.

The central SNOBOL4 primitive operation is pattern matching. A large collection of primitives is provided for the creation of patterns. The basic arithmetic, logical, and relational primitives are provided as well. Data structure creation operations are extremely flexible. At any point during program execution a new simple variable, array, or structure of a programmer-defined type may be created. Structures are not destroyed explicitly but become garbage as all pointers to them are lost. Input-output operations are restricted to transmission of character strings to and from sequential files.

Sequence control in SNOBOL4 is rather simple. Expressions defining strings, numbers, and patterns are used extensively. Statements may be labeled, and each statement contains a *success-failure* **goto** field through which the successor to a statement may be explicitly specified. Each statement may succeed or fail for a variety of reasons—most commonly dependent on the success or failure of a pattern-matching operation. A simple call-return mechanism with recursion allows transfer of control to subprograms. Referencing is based on the *most recent association* rule, using a central referencing environment table.

The most common SNOBOL4 implementation (the *macro implementation* described by Griswold [1972]) is based on complete software simulation of the SNOBOL4 virtual computer. Programs are translated only into an internal Polish prefix executable *code string*, which is then decoded and executed by a software interpreter. The run-time memory organization centers around a central table of character strings, which contains a unique entry for each string currently existing at each point during execution, including variable names, statement labels, and other identifiers, as well as strings used as values of variables and array elements. As character strings are created during execution they are entered into this table if they do not already exist. The table values are stored in a heap storage area along with arrays, patterns, executable code strings for program statements, and programmer-defined data structures. The heap is managed using garbage collection and full compaction, as described in Section 7-8.

A compiler-based implementation of the language is an attractive alternative because of the cost of the software simulation, and a number of such implementations have been constructed (see, e.g., Dewar [1971]). However, the extensive run-time variability allowed by the language makes compilation difficult. This chapter is based on the simpler software-interpreted implementation, but where a compiler-based implementation is available, substantial savings in program execution speeds may be possible (usually with some slight restrictions on the language).

15-3. AN ANNOTATED EXAMPLE: REVERSING A STRING OF ELEMENTS

Figure 15-1 illustrates a simple SNOBOL4 subprogram and main program. The subprogram REVERSE reverses the elements of a given argument character string. The string consists of some arbitrary sequence of elements (words, numbers, etc.) separated by spaces. REVERSE picks off the elements of the string one by one and concatenates them in turn onto the front of a new string, which is built up and returned as the value of the function. The main program reads in a sequence of test strings and tests REVERSE on each in

Line Number		SNOBOL4 Program	
1		DEFINE ('REVERSE (X)Y','REV')	:(MAIN)
2	REV	X POS(O) SPAN(' ') =	
3	LOOP	X BREAK(' ') . Y SPAN(' ') =	:F(LAST)
4		REVERSE = Y ' ' REVERSE	:(LOOP)
5	LAST	IDENT(X,' ')	:S(RETURN)
6		REVERSE = X ' ' REVERSE	:(RETURN)
7	MAIN	A = INPUT	:F(END)
8		OUTPUT = 'INPUT IS:' A	
9		OUTPUT = 'INPUT REVERSED: REVERSE(A)	:(MAIN)
10	END		

Fig. 15-1. Example SNOBOL4 program.

turn. The annotations below are keyed to the line numbers on the left of the figure, which are not a part of the listing.

Line 1. The main program begins with a call to the DEFINE function to set up a subprogram definition. DEFINE simply enters the appropriate information in a run-time table of defined subprogram names. The arguments to DEFINE are (1) the subprogram name REVERSE, (2) the formal parameter name X, (3) the local variable name Y, and (4) the label REV of the statement which begins the body of the subprogram. After the call to DEFINE is completed, control is transferred to the statement labeled MAIN. This **goto** is required because otherwise control would transfer to the next statement in sequence, which happens to be the first statement in the body of REVERSE. As an alternative the body of REVERSE might have been put after the main program, immediately before the END, thus avoiding the necessity of transferring control around the subprogram body.

Line 2. Because this statement is labeled REV, it is the first statement of the body of REVERSE. When REVERSE is called, the formal parameter X is set to the value of the actual parameter, local variable Y and the variable REVERSE (used for the function value to be returned) are initialized to have null string values, and control transfers to this statement. This is a pattern-matching statement which is used to delete leading blanks from the argument string X. The pattern is defined by POS(0) SPAN(' '), which may be read "starting at the beginning of the subject string (position zero), match a sequence of blank characters of maximum length. The subject string X is named before the pattern. The following = designates that the string matched in X (if any) is to be replaced by the string which follows the =. Since nothing follows the =, the null string is to be used; i.e., the matched substring is to be deleted from X.

Line 3. This statement, labeled LOOP, is the main pattern-matching statement of REVERSE. This statement picks off the first element remaining in string X, assigns it to the local variable Y, and deletes the element and any following blank characters from X. Again X is the subject string in the pattern matching. The pattern is BREAK(' ') . Y SPAN(' '). The first part of the pattern, BREAK(' '), matches the first part of string X up to the leftmost blank character. The following .Y indicates that the substring matched by BREAK is to be assigned as the value of Y. The final portion of the pattern, SPAN(' '), again matches a sequence of blanks, as in line 2. The following = indicates that the entire matched substring is to be deleted from X. The **goto** field of the statement, following the :, specifies a transfer of control to statement LAST if the pattern matching *fails*; control otherwise continues to the next statement in sequence. Pattern matching in this case fails when string X has been reduced to at most a single element followed by no trailing blanks or, alternatively (if the original string had trailing blanks), to the null string.

Line 4. Control reaches this statement if the preceding pattern matching did in fact pick off an element from X and assign it to local variable Y. In this statement the value of Y is concatenated (together with an intervening blank character) onto the beginning of the string being built up for output as the value of REVERSE, and the resulting string is assigned as the new value of REVERSE. The subprogram name REVERSE is used here as a local variable. Concatenation of strings is specified by a blank character. Thus the expression on the right of the assignment operator = specifies two concatenations: concatenation of the value of Y and the literal string " " (a single blank) and concatenation of the result and the value of local variable REVERSE. Control is transferred from this statement back to the preceding statement LOOP, where another element is retrieved from X and the process repeated.

Line 5. When the string X has been exhausted, except for possibly one terminating element, control is transferred here. This statement tests whether X has been reduced to the null string by an identity test between X and the null string (represented by 2 single quotes ' '). If the test *succeeds*, control is returned to the calling program; otherwise, control passes to the next statement in sequence. The final value of the variable REVERSE becomes the function value returned.

Line 6. Final statement of the body of REVERSE. At this point X contains one final element, which is simply concatenated onto the beginning of the result string and control returned to the calling program.

Line 7. Second line of the main program. Control is transferred here directly from line 1. This statement reads the next input string from the standard input file and assigns the string read to variable A. The input occurs automatically whenever the special variable INPUT is referenced. The value of a reference to INPUT is always the next input string. If the input file is empty because all the input data have been read, then the reference to INPUT fails. In this case control is transferred to the statement labeled END.

Line 8. The newly input string is output immediately to the standard output file, but first the literal string INPUT IS: is concatenated onto the beginning. Output is specified by an assignment to the special variable OUTPUT. Whenever the value of OUTPUT is changed the new value is automatically output.

Line 9. REVERSE is tested on the input string A. The result of REVERSE is output, preceded by the string INPUT REVERSED:. Control is transferred back to the statement labeled MAIN for another input-test loop.

Line 10. End of the main program.

15-4. DATA

An extensive and flexible set of data structure types are found in SNOBOL4 All data items include a run-time descriptor. The basic data-structuring technique is that of representing each data item by a pointer to a block of sequential storage containing the descriptor and values for the data item.

Strings and Simple Variables

Character strings are the central data type in SNOBOL4. Each string is represented as a sequential block containing the appropriate sequence of character codes, together with a descriptor specifying the length of the string.

The concepts of character string data items and simple variables are combined as follows: *Every character string which exists at any point during program execution is also potentially the name of a simple variable.* Thus any string may have a value assigned to it. This interesting structure is clarified by considering the manner of its implementation in the usual SNOBOL4 system. A *central strings table* is maintained, which contains a unique entry for each string that has occurred in the program as an identifier (simple variable name, statement label, subprogram name, etc.) or which has been computed or input by the program during its execution. A string is always represented by a pointer to its entry in the central strings table. Thus if X is a simple variable whose value is the string ABY, then the value of X is actually a pointer to the entry for ABY in the central table. But moreover, since X is a string, it also occurs as an entry in the central table. If Y is another variable whose value is the string X, then the value of Y is a pointer to the entry for X in the central table.

Each entry in the central strings table contains a string and a pointer to the *value* of the string. Whenever a new string is created during program execution, the central table is searched to determine if the string has already been entered in the table. If so, a pointer to this entry is used. This simple scheme allows new variables to be created at will during program execution and is the source of much flexibility in the language. The disadvantage lies in the cost of the table search each time a new string is created. Since many SNOBOL4 statements create new strings, the table search occurs frequently. The table is usually represented as a hash-coded table with buckets to handle collisions.

Numbers

Real and integer numbers are provided. Each carries a run-time type descriptor in addition to the bit string hardware representation of the number itself.

Arrays

SNOBOL4 heterogeneous arrays are created dynamically by a primitive operation (function) ARRAY, which may be called at any point during program execution. Types of elements may vary during the lifetime of the array, but the array may not change in length once created. The fixed size allows an array representation as a sequential block of storage with attached descriptor. Each entry in this block contains a pointer to the value of an array element, except in the case of numeric values which are usually stored directly. Arrays in SNOBOL4 are not named; instead an array is represented by a pointer to the block of storage containing the descriptor and values. If an array pointer is assigned as the value of some string (in the central strings table), then that string serves temporarily as the name of the array. Array elements may be accessed individually by subscripting this temporary name. For example, the statement

$$X = ARRAY(10)$$

creates an array of ten elements (through the call on the ARRAY primitive). The pointer to this array returned by the ARRAY function is immediately assigned as the value of the variable X, stored in the central strings table. A later reference to $X < 3 >$ accesses the third element of this array in the usual way. However, the assignment

$$Y = X$$

causes a copy of the same pointer to be assigned as the value of Y. Now the array has two temporary names, and both X < 3 > and Y < 3 > access the same element of the array. The array may become lost altogether (i.e., may be made garbage) if subsequent assignments change both the values of X and Y.

Arrays may have arbitrary numbers of dimensions and subscript ranges. The values of array elements may be numbers or strings, but they also may be of other data types: patterns, tables, or other arrays. Thus it is possible to construct arrays of arrays, where each element of one array contains as its value a pointer to another array.

Tables

A SNOBOL4 *table* is a heterogeneous linear array of variable size accessed through subscripts which are arbitrary strings rather than integers. Thus a table is a type of *property list*. Each table entry consists of a *subscript*, which is a pointer to a string in the central strings table, and a *value*, which is either a number or a pointer to a string, array, or other data item. A table is created by use of a primitive function, TABLE, with arguments specifying an initial size and an increment size for the table. For example, the statement

$$T = TABLE(50,30)$$

causes creation of a block of storage for a table of 50 subscript-value pairs plus descriptor. The function TABLE returns a pointer to this block, which is then assigned to the variable T. T serves as the temporary name for the table. Reference to table elements and creation of new table elements is done by subscripting the variable T. For example, T⟨'AGE'⟩ = 25 causes a table search for the subscript AGE. If found, its associated value is changed to 25. If AGE is not found, then a new entry of the pair AGE-25 is made. Entries in a table may not be deleted. When 50 entries have been made in the table a new block of storage for 30 (the second parameter in the initial call of TABLE) pairs is allocated and linked to the original block via a pointer. Ultimately then the table appears in storage as a linked list of blocks of storage, each of the same length except the first.

Patterns

Patterns are a data type of importance in SNOBOL4 because of the use of pattern matching as the central operation. Each pattern-matching operation is controlled by a pattern data structure.

The pattern matcher decodes and interprets the pattern structure while simultaneously searching the subject character string for the specified pattern. The details of pattern elements are discussed in the next section when we take up the pattern-matching operation itself. The presence of patterns as an explicit data structure type means that patterns are legitimate values for variables, array elements, and table elements. A pattern is represented during execution in an internal form suitable for efficient interpretation by the pattern matcher; commonly this form is a linked set of storage areas forming a tree structure, which reflects the natural structure of the pattern as a set of alternatives and concatenated subpatterns.

Labels and Subprogram Names

The presence of all identifiers in the central strings table during program execution allows a simple direct use of statement labels and subprogram names as data items. The central table is augmented by two auxiliary tables. The *labels table* contains pairs consisting of a pointer to a string used as a statement label and a pointer to the corresponding code position in the executable program structure. The *subprograms table* consists of similar pairs of *pointer to string/pointer to subprogram definition* (an entry in yet another auxiliary table). The presence of these run-time tables allows any string to be read in or computed and then subsequently used as a statement label in a **goto** or as a subprogram name in a subprogram call. The string is simply looked up in the appropriate table at the time of **goto** or call, and an appropriate transfer of control is made. If the string has not been used as a statement label or subprogram name, then a run-time error message results and execution terminates.

Programmer-Defined Data Types

SNOBOL4 provides some simple but flexible features which allow a programmer to define and use data structures of new types. Basically a data type definition specifies a class of heterogeneous fixed-length linear arrays whose elements are referenced by character string subscripts. The definition of the data type itself defines only the name of the type, the length of each array of that type, and the subscripts of the elements of each array of that type. Data type definition is done with a call to the primitive function DATA. For example,

DATA('EMP-REC(NAME,AGE,ADDRESS)')

defines a data type called EMP-REC. Each data structure of this type, when created, will consist of a linear array of three elements, accessible by the subscripts NAME, AGE, and ADDRESS, respectively. The primitive DATA acts to create and enter into run-time tables a descriptor for the data type EMP-REC, which specifies the length of an element and the subscripts. In addition, a *pseudosubprogram* is entered into the run-time subprograms table under each of the names EMP-REC, NAME, AGE, and ADDRESS. The EMP-REC subprogram represents a *creation primitive* for arrays of type EMP-REC. Whenever it is called, it allocates space for a new array of type EMP-REC and initializes the values of the array elements. For example, the statement

$$X = EMP\text{-}REC('KING',29,'1708\ HALIFAX')$$

creates a three-element array of type EMP-REC and initializes the values of the array elements to the string KING, the number 29, and the string 1708 HALIFAX, respectively. The value returned by the function EMP-REC is a pointer to this new array, which is assigned as the value of X. A later reference to an element of this new array is made using one of the functions NAME, AGE, or ADDRESS. For example, the statements

$$Y = AGE(X)$$
$$AGE(X) = 30$$

have the effect of retrieving the value of the second array element and assigning it the new value 30, respectively.

Using these basic facilities for the creation and use of programmer-defined data types the programmer may construct arbitrary linked structures by letting the value of an element in one structure be a pointer to another structure. Thus linked lists, trees, and general directed graphs may be created and processed.

Programs as Data

Program execution in the usual SNOBOL4 implementation is done by a software interpreter. Programs are represented at run time in a special internal form which is a variant of a Polish prefix representation. We shall term this program representation a *code string*. A program to be executed is immediately translated into a code string before execution begins. During execution, additional program segments may be translated and later executed as though they had been part of the original program. This translation is initiated by a call on a primitive function CODE. The argument to

CODE is a character string representing a valid SNOBOL4 program segment (with statements separated by semicolons), and the result returned is a pointer to the new code string representing the translated program. Code strings are a separate data type, and as with other data types in SNOBOL4, code strings may be saved as the value of variables, array elements, etc. A code string may be executed beginning at its first statement, or any **goto** may lead into a labeled statement in a code string.

Keywords

Access to various items of system-defined data is provided by a set of *keywords*. A keyword is actually just a simple variable whose name begins with the symbol &. Keyword variables may be *protected*, in which case their values may be accessed but not modified, or *unprotected*, in which case their values may be both accessed and modified. Protected keywords usually contain system-defined data items which may occasionally be of value to the programmer. For example, the number of statements which have been executed is accessible as the value of the keyword &STCOUNT, the number of the statement currently being executed is the value of &STNO, the number of the last statement executed is accessed through &LASTNO, the current depth of subprogram calls is found through &FNCLEVEL, etc. Unprotected keywords serve as *flags*, which may be set by the programmer to modify execution parameters. For example, tracing output is produced if the value of &TRACE is nonzero, and execution terminates if the number of statements executed exceeds the value of &STLIMIT.

15-5. OPERATIONS

Because SNOBOL4 is designed for problems involving character string processing, the language contains an extensive set of primitives for string manipulation, including the central operations of pattern creation and pattern matching. The language also contains many operations for the creation and accessing of data structures, as described in the previous section. Arithmetic, relational, assignment, and input-output primitives appear in lesser roles.

Simple String Manipulation Primitives

Concatenation of two character strings is the most basic string manipulation primitive. A blank symbol appearing between two string-valued expressions indicates concatenation. For example, in

'LAUGHING' 'LIONS'

the blank between the two strings LAUGHING and LIONS indicates concatenation; the result is the string LAUGHINGLIONS.

Other primitive functions may be used to find the length of a string (SIZE), to substitute characters within a string (REPLACE), and to duplicate a given string an arbitrary number of times (DUPL). In general, however, more complex string manipulations are performed using the pattern-matching operation.

Pattern Matching

In Section 4-6, the basic structure of pattern matching in SNOBOL4 is discussed. While illustrating the pattern-matching concept, that rather cursory introduction barely begins to show the power and complexity of the SNOBOL4 pattern-matching operation. Griswold [1972] notes that patterns and pattern matching form almost a sublanguage of the whole language. Patterns serve essentially as *programs* for the pattern-matching operation.

The pattern-matching operation is specified in a SNOBOL4 program through use of the special *pattern-matching* or *pattern-matching and replacement* statement. The former has the syntax

⟨subject string⟩ ⟨pattern⟩

where ⟨subject string⟩ is a string-valued expression whose value is the string that is to be searched for a substring matching the pattern that is the value of the expression ⟨pattern⟩. The pattern-matching and replacement statement has the form

⟨subject string⟩ ⟨pattern⟩ = ⟨replacement string⟩

where ⟨subject string⟩ and ⟨pattern⟩ are as above, and ⟨replacement string⟩ is a string-valued expression whose value is to replace the matched substring of the subject string if pattern matching succeeds.

A pattern-matching operation, if it succeeds, always results in the identification of some contiguous substring of the subject string. The pattern-matching and replacement statement allows another string to be designated to replace the matched substring within the subject string (thus permanently altering the subject string). In the simple pattern-matching statement, the subject string is left unaltered, with the pattern matching serving only as a test for the presence of an appropriate substring. In either case the *success* or *failure* output of the pattern matching may be used to control a program branch. Besides these explicit results, a pattern-matching operation may also produce side effects through assignments of substrings to variables during matching. Often these side effects are as important as the explicit results of the matching. Although the matching operation itself always searches for a contiguous substring, these side effects during matching allow all or part of the subject string to be broken down into any number of substrings and reconstructed from the same or other pieces during the course of a single pattern match.

The pattern-matching operation for a given subject string STR and pattern PAT is most easily understood in terms of three pointers:

1. The left end pointer, LEFT, which points to the character in STR which represents the left end of the substring being matched at any point during matching.

2. The right end pointer, CURSOR, which marks the rightmost matched character within STR at any point during matching.

3. The NEEDLE, a pointer to the element of PAT which is currently the pattern element being matched.

Pattern matching proceeds left to right through the subject string STR. LEFT and CURSOR initially point to the leftmost character in STR, and NEEDLE points to the first alternative in PAT. NEEDLE is advanced through the pattern structure, which basically has the form of a tree of alternatives. Simultaneously, CURSOR moves right through the subject string. The various alternatives specified by PAT are tried exhaustively until either a complete match is found (if NEEDLE traverses PAT to a terminal point) or no match is found (if all alternatives are exhausted). If a complete match is found, then the pattern-matching operation succeeds and the final positions of LEFT and CURSOR delimit the substring of STR which has been matched. If the statement causing the pattern match was a pattern-matching and replacement statement, then this substring is replaced by the designated replacement string; otherwise the subject string is left unmodified.

The action taken on failure of pattern matching when the pointer LEFT is positioned at the left end of STR depends on the pattern-matching *mode*. In *anchored mode* LEFT must remain positioned at the left end of STR, and thus the entire pattern-matching operation fails if no match is found with LEFT in its initial position. In *unanchored mode*, however, pattern matching continues after initial failure: LEFT is advanced one character position to the right in STR, and again CURSOR and NEEDLE are used to exhaustively test for an appropriate substring beginning at the new position of LEFT. In unanchored mode, pattern matching ultimately fails only when LEFT has advanced to the right end of STR without an appropriate substring being matched.

The exhaustive search required for this pattern-matching operation is obviously extremely time-consuming if STR is very long or PAT is very complex. In general, it is only the success or failure of pattern matching which is of concern to the SNOBOL4 programmer, and thus it is desirable to avoid searching "blind alleys" insofar as possible. SNOBOL4 implementations typically utilize a number of heuristic rules to avoid useless searching. Occasionally a special situation arises where the full exhaustive search is desirable, an option which the programmer may choose when needed. Other than the anchored/unanchored mode designation and the heuristics/no heuristics choice, the remainder of the pattern-matching operation is controlled through the manner in which the programmer constructs the pattern PAT used in the matching operation.

Patterns and Pattern Creation

A pattern is a data structure. Patterns are created by the evaluation of pattern-valued expressions. Once created, the elements of a pattern cannot be accessed or modified; the only use of a pattern is as an argument for a pattern-matching operation. In the simplest case the pattern-valued expression defining a pattern is inserted directly into the pattern-matching statement in which the pattern is to be used. For example,

$$\text{STR 'AND' | 'OR'}$$

is a pattern-matching statement containing the pattern-valued expression 'AND' | 'OR' which defines a pattern that matches either the string AND or the string OR. Alternatively, the pattern may be created using a separate assignment statement:

$$\text{PAT = 'AND' | 'OR'}$$

and the created pattern later used in the pattern-matching statement

$$\text{STR PAT}$$

The advantage of the latter alternative is that the pattern data structure need be created only once even though it may be later used repeatedly in pattern matching. In the former case the identical pattern structure is created and then immediately discarded each time the pattern-matching statement is executed, causing a considerable waste of storage and execution time.

A pattern is constructed from various primitive pattern elements, which we shall now consider individually. Each primitive element may be viewed as defining a valid way in which the CURSOR may be advanced from its current position during pattern matching.

Strings as Patterns. The simplest pattern element is a single character string, e.g., AND or 2. A pattern consisting only of such a string may be used to search the subject string for that substring. For example, the pattern-matching statement

STR 'AND'

causes the subject string which is the value of STR to be searched for the leftmost occurrence of AND. The details of this search clarify the use of more complex pattern structures (for this example we ignore the obvious heuristics that would ordinarily be used to speed the search). In the search, LEFT and CURSOR initially point to the first character of STR. The pattern 'AND' allows CURSOR to be advanced from its current position only if the next three characters in the string are A, N, and D in that sequence. Assuming that the value of STR is the string GREEN EGGS AND HAM, the attempt to advance CURSOR from its initial position at the left end of the string will fail. Because there are no other alternatives in the pattern, both LEFT and CURSOR are advanced to the point to the second character position in the subject string. Again, CURSOR cannot be advanced, and both LEFT and CURSOR move to the third character position in the subject string. Eventually both LEFT and CURSOR are positioned at the first A in GREEN EGGS AND HAM and CURSOR may then be advanced to the blank character following the D. Since there are no other following pattern elements, the matching operation is complete and matching succeeds, with the final positions of LEFT and CURSOR designating the matched substring.

Pattern-Valued Functions. Pattern-valued functions are built-in primitives which produce pattern structures as values. SNOBOL4 contains a large set of such primitives, the most important of which are

LEN. The function LEN, given a positive integer k as argument, produces a pattern structure which matches any string of k characters. Thus, for example, LEN(5) in a pattern expression specifies that CURSOR is to be advanced five character positions from its current position in the subject string.

ANY. The argument to ANY is a single character string composed of a set of distinct characters. The value of ANY is a pattern structure which matches any occurrence of one of those characters. Thus, for example, ANY('012') in a pattern expression specifies that CURSOR may be advanced one character position provided that the character passed over is one of 0, 1, or 2.

SPAN. SPAN is like ANY except that CURSOR is advanced as far to the right as possible until a character is found that is *not* a character in the argument string. For example, SPAN('012') matches any string composed entirely of zeros, ones, and twos that is followed by the end of the subject string or by a symbol other than 0, 1, or 2.

NOTANY. NOTANY is like ANY except that CURSOR is advanced one character position only if the character involved is *not* a character in the argument string.

BREAK. BREAK is like SPAN except that CURSOR is advanced as far as possible until a character is found which *is* in the argument string.

REM. The value of REM is a pattern which matches the entire remainder of the subject string; i.e., REM specifies that CURSOR is to be advanced to the right end of the subject string.

TAB and RTAB. Given a positive integer k as argument, TAB produces a pattern which allows CURSOR to be advanced to the kth character position in the subject string, provided its current position is to the left of the kth position. RTAB is the same except that CURSOR advances to the kth position from the right end of the subject string.

ARB. The value of ARB is a pattern that matches any string of zero or more characters beginning at the current CURSOR position.

BAL. The value of BAL is a pattern that matches any string of zero or more characters beginning at the current position of CURSOR which contains no unpaired parentheses.

POS and RPOS. Given an integer k as argument, POS produces a pattern which matches only if CURSOR is positioned at the kth character of the subject string, and otherwise has no effect. RPOS is similar but uses the kth character position from the right end of the subject string.

Concatenation and Alternation. Complex pattern structures may be built up from explicit strings and pattern-valued functions using the operations of concatenation and alternation. If P and Q are two patterns, then the concatenation of P and Q, written P Q, is a new pattern that matches any string which begins with a string matched by P and whose remainder is matched by Q. The alternation of P and Q, written P | Q, is a pattern which matches any string matched by P or by Q. In such composite pattern structures the order of matching often becomes critical. The rule for matching in an alternation P | Q is as follows: Try all the alternatives for P first at the current CURSOR position, and then try the alternatives for Q. For the concatenation P Q the sequence is as follows: Match one alternative for P at the current CURSOR position, advance CURSOR to the end of the matched substring, and then try to match the pattern Q beginning at the new CURSOR position. If no match for Q is found, back up CURSOR to its original position and try to find another substring which matches P. If one is found, advance CURSOR and try Q again; if none is found, then the match of the concatenated pattern fails.

Assignment During Pattern Matching. A successful pattern-matching operation identifies a substring of the subject string which is matched by the entire pattern structure used. Often it is desirable to also identify sub-sub-strings of this substring which were matched by subelements of the overall pattern. For example, the pattern

$$SPAN(`\ ')\ BREAK(`\ ')\ SPAN(`\ ')$$

matches the leftmost substring of the subject string which begins and ends with blanks and which has at least one nonblank character. Ordinarily it would be desirable to obtain the nonnull part of the substring matched, the component matched by BREAK(' '). A copy of such a substring may be obtained by specifying a *conditional value assignment* (operator .) in the pattern. For example,

$$SPAN(`\ ')\ BREAK(`\ ')\ .\ WD\ SPAN(`\ ')$$

specifies that after a successful match of the pattern a copy of the substring matched by the BREAK(' ') part of the pattern is to be assigned to the variable WD. Using conditional value assignment a copy of any part of a matched string may be obtained. A less frequently used alternative is *immediate value assignment* (operator $) which allows assignment during a pattern match even though the matching operation ultimately fails. The most common use for immediate value assignment is during program testing—an immediate value assignment to variable OUTPUT may be used to print a trace of the steps during pattern matching.

Parameters in Patterns (Unevaluated Expressions). Ordinarily the structure of a pattern is fixed at the time of evaluation of the pattern-valued expression which creates the pattern. In particular, every variable in the pattern expression is evaluated and its current value copied into the pattern structure being created. Sometimes it is desirable to leave certain variables or expressions as parameters in the pattern and evaluate them only at the time during pattern matching when their values are actually required. The * operator before a variable name (or any subexpression) in a pattern indicates that the variable is to be left unevaluated until the time of use of the pattern in pattern matching. For example, the assignment

$$PAT = LEN(*N)$$

creates a pattern structure with parameter N, whose value may vary each time the pattern PAT is used. Unevaluated expressions in patterns also allow recursive patterns to be used. For example, the pattern

$$P = 'A' \mid *P \; 'A'$$

matches any sequence of As.

Assignment

The specialized *conditional value assignment* and *immediate value assignment* operations used during pattern matching have been described in the preceding paragraphs. The ordinary assignment operator, = , has also appeared in many of the preceding examples. SNOBOL4 assignment statements are rather novel in that the expression on the right-hand side may create any type of data structure. Thus the value assigned may be a pointer to an array, table, pattern, or programmer-defined data structure, as well as a string or a number. In general, the right-hand-side expression evaluates to a pointer, and assignment simply involves making a copy of this pointer, which is assigned as the new value of the variable designated by the left-hand expression of the assignment. This left-hand expression may also be arbitrarily complex as long as the result produced is a variable name, array element, or other data storage location to which an assignment can reasonably be made.

Arithmetic, Relational, and Boolean Operations

The basic arithmetic operations (including exponentiation) on integers and reals are provided, as well as the usual relational primitives (represented by the functions EQ, NE, LT, GT, LE, GE). Run-time type checking and type conversion are necessary. Character strings may be compared for equality using the primitive IDENT; e.g., IDENT(X,Y) succeeds if the values of X and Y are identical strings.

No Boolean operations are included directly except *not* (syntax ¬). Boolean values are treated in a novel way. There are no explicit Boolean values in SNOBOL4. Instead an operator such as EQ (= on numbers) either succeeds or fails, and this result may be tested in the **goto** field of the statement. When an operator fails, the entire statement immediately fails. When an operator succeeds, execution of the statement continues without interruption. One result of this approach is that relational and other tests may be inserted in the middle of expressions. When the expression is evaluated, if the test succeeds, nothing is changed, but if the test fails, then evaluation is immediately terminated and the entire statement containing the expression fails. For example, the assignment

$$N = EQ(N,0) \ N - 1 \qquad :S(LOOP)F(NEXT)$$

causes the value of N to be decremented by 1 and control transferred to the statement labeled LOOP, provided that the initial value of N is not already zero. If zero, the value of N is not modified and control is transferred to statement NEXT.

Input-Output

The SNOBOL4 input-output system is based on the direct transmission of character strings between central memory and external sequential files. Using the pattern-matching operation and the other string manipulation primitives, input strings may be broken down into components and output strings formatted easily. As a result the input-output operations need transmit only character strings.

Input and output operations utilize an interrupt scheme. Certain variables are tagged as *input variables* and others are tagged as *output variables*. Each tagged variable is associated with a particular external file. Whenever the value of an input variable is referenced during execution, execution is interrupted and a new record (character

string) is read in from the associated external file. This character
string becomes the new value of the input variable, and execution
proceeds. If the file is empty (i.e., if all the data have been read),
then the reference to the variable fails, causing the statement being
executed to fail. Similarly, when a new value (which must be a string
or number) is assigned to an output variable, execution is interrupted
and the new character string value is copied to the external file. The
variables INPUT and OUTPUT are predefined as input and output
variables, respectively, but other input and output variables may be
designated by the programmer at any point during execution. Use of
INPUT and OUTPUT is illustrated in the example of Section 15-3.

Subprograms

SNOBOL4 subprograms have a number of novel aspects. Subprogram definition is strictly a run-time operation. During translation
a main program and a set of subprograms are simply a long list of
statements, with no syntactic distinction among the elements of the
different routines. Execution begins with no subprograms defined
other than system-defined primitives. Before a subprogram may be
called it must first be defined by means of a call to the DEFINE
primitive:

DEFINE('⟨subprog-name⟩(⟨formal-params⟩)⟨local-vars⟩',
      '⟨label of first statement in body⟩')

The DEFINE primitive enters into a run-time table of *defined
subprograms* the subprogram name, the number and names of its
formal parameters, the number and names of its local variables, and
the label of the first statement in its body. The label of the first
statement may be omitted, in which case the subprogram name is
also taken to be the label of the first statement. Subprogram
definition and calling structure is taken up in more detail in
Section 15-7.

The statements forming the body of a subprogram have no
necessary syntactic relation with the DEFINE call which defines the
subprogram. They may be placed anywhere, but the programmer is
responsible to see that control does not inadvertently flow into a
subprogram body during execution of the main program or another
subprogram. The statements in a subprogram body need not even
exist when the subprogram is defined—they may be read in or
constructed as strings and then later translated into executable form
by the primitive CODE before the subprogram is called.

A subprogram may be defined at any point during program execution prior to the first call on it. A later DEFINE may redefine a previously DEFINE'd subprogram name (because only run-time table entries need to be modified). The names of system primitives such as LEN and SIZE as well as infix or prefix operator symbols may also be redefined to name programmer-defined subprograms, but the special system function OPSYN must be used instead of DEFINE. For example, the statement

$$OPSYN('+','ADD',2)$$

causes any subsequent use of + as a binary operator to be executed as a call of the subprogram ADD; thus the statement Z = X + Y is made equivalent to Z = ADD(X,Y).

15-6. SEQUENCE CONTROL

SNOBOL4 sequence control mechanisms are rather simple. The most complex control structures arise in the control of pattern matching; these are described in the preceding section.

Expressions

SNOBOL4 expressions produce values which are either strings, numbers, or patterns. Expressions are constructed from a mixture of infix binary operators, Polish prefix operators, and ordinary mathematical prefix operators. The usual precedence order and associativity rules for arithmetic operations are extended to include the operations of concatenation, alternation, and conditional and immediate value assignment. Parentheses may be used for explicit control as needed.

Statement Sequence Control

Only one construct for controlling statement execution sequence is provided. Each statement execution may succeed or fail. For example, a statement involving pattern matching may fail because the pattern was not found, a statement referencing INPUT may fail if the input file is empty, or a statement involving a call to a programmer-defined subprogram may fail because the subprogram returns via FRETURN (see below). Each statement may contain an optional **goto** *field* which specifies either an unconditional transfer of control to a designated successor statement, a transfer only if the statement execution succeeds, a transfer if execution fails, or transfers on both conditions. Omission of part of the **goto** field specifies an implicit transfer of control to the next physical statement in sequence. Statements may be labeled by identifiers.

This basic **goto**—*statement label* structure is made more flexible by allowing any label to be computed. The **goto** field of a statement may specify an arbitrary string-valued expression to be used to compute the string representing the statement label to which control is to be transferred. Implementation requires maintenance of a run-time table of statement labels and their associated code positions. The computed string is looked up in the table when the **goto** is reached during execution, and a transfer to the associated code position is made.

Subprogram Sequence Control

The usual subprogram call is provided, with unlimited recursion. The control flow through a subprogram is rather novel, however. When a subprogram is called, control is transferred to the first statement of the subprogram (this statement's label is given in the DEFINE statement defining the subprogram). From there control may pass to any other statement in the whole program, including statements in the main program or other subprograms. Return from a subprogram occurs only when a **goto** to one of the labels RETURN, NRETURN, or FRETURN is specified, and such a **goto** causes a return only from the last subprogram entered (as designated by the activation record on the top of the run-time stack). RETURN and NRETURN cause an ordinary return; FRETURN causes the statement to which return is made to fail.

A set of tracing features provides an alternative subprogram calling structure based on interrupts. Statement execution may be interrupted on one of six conditions: change in value of a designated variable; transfer of control to a designated label; call, return, or call and return from a designated subprogram; or change in the value of certain key words. For each type of interrupt the programmer may specify a subprogram to be executed whenever the interrupt occurs or a default system-defined action may be used. This interrupt structure is most useful for tracing during program debugging but may also be used to advantage in other situations; for example, pattern matching may be interrupted for execution of a programmer-defined subprogram by setting an interrupt to occur upon conditional or immediate value assignment to a variable within a pattern.

15-7. DATA CONTROL

The current referencing environment of a SNOBOL4 program is closely tied to the *central strings table* used for character string storage. Because each string which is currently in use is treated also as the name of a simple variable, every string in the central strings table may have an association and may be referenced. Of course the program text itself contains only certain variable identifiers which were known when the program was written. However, any string created during program execution may be referenced as a variable using the *indirect reference operator*, $. The operator $ applied to any string retrieves the value associated with that string in the central strings table. For example, if the variable X has as its value the string ABC, then the value of the variable ABC may be obtained by the expression $X. If the value of ABC is the string QRS, then $$X retrieves the value of QRS, etc.

The assumption that every string is automatically a usable variable, and thus is part of the current referencing environment, allows the central strings table to serve also as a central referencing environment table. Each table entry is augmented by a *value pointer* which points to the data item that serves as the value of the associated string. When a new string is created it is entered into the table with a null value (the *null string*). Subsequent references may assign it a nonnull value, or retrieve its value. Ultimately strings which are in the table but are not accessible from any other point, and which have a null value, may be garbage-collected and the storage reused. New strings are always entered in the central table as global variables, and thus their existence is not affected by subsequent subprogram entries or exits.

Local variables are designated when a subprogram is defined through a call of the primitive function DEFINE. For example, execution of the statement

DEFINE('SUB(X,Y),U,V')

defines a subprogram named SUB by entering the name SUB into a run-time table of subprogram names. Part of this same entry is a list of formal parameter names and local variables. In the example X and Y serve as formal parameter names and U and V serve as local variable names. The name of the subprogram, SUB, also serves as a local variable whose value is returned as the value of the subprogram. When subprogram SUB is called during program execution, the central strings table is modified to reflect the appropriate referencing environment for execution of SUB. First the existing values of the strings SUB, X, Y, and U, and V in the central table must be saved. These are saved (along with the return point and other system-defined data) as an activation record on a *hidden* stack. Then new values for each of the strings are entered into the central table. SUB, U, and V receive null values. X and Y are initialized to the values passed as the values of the corresponding actual parameters in the call. Once this updating of the central table is complete, control is passed to the first statement of the subprogram (the statement labeled SUB in this case) just as in an ordinary **goto**. The subsequent execution of a **goto** to one of the special labels RETURN, NRETURN, or FRETURN signals the end of execution of the subprogram body. The top activation record on the hidden stack is accessed to provide a return point and to indicate the appropriate string-value pairs in the central table whose values must be restored. After the values are restored control is returned to the point of call, with the last value of the subprogram name SUB becoming the value of the subprogram (function) call.

The effect of using the central strings table as the referencing environment is basically to make nonlocal referencing follow the most recent association rule. On subprogram entry the current associations for all local identifiers are deactivated and on exit they are restored, but all other identifiers retain their existing (and thus most recent) associations.

Parameter Transmission and Value Return

Parameters to programmer-defined subprograms are transmitted uniformly by value. The actual parameter is evaluated to obtain a pointer to a data item, which may be a string, number, pattern, array, etc. The pointer is transmitted to the subprogram and becomes the initial value of the corresponding formal parameter (stored in the central strings table). Neither subprogram names nor statement labels may be transmitted directly as parameters; instead the *string* representing the name or label is transmitted. Within the subprogram the string may be used as the object of a **goto** or subprogram call by referencing the associated formal parameter (using $ or the primitive APPLY as appropriate). This technique ignores the problems of referencing environment transmission usually associated with subprogram name and label parameters—the only referencing environment modifications made automatically are those prescribed by the DEFINE statement for a subprogram.

Although parameter transmission is strictly by value in SNOBOL4, some of the effects of transmission by reference and by name may be obtained without difficulty. For example, to transmit variable Q to SUB by reference, the string Q is transmitted. If the corresponding formal parameter within SUB is X, then $X references Q as a variable within SUB. The value of Q may be modified or accessed through such indirect references. Similarly, an expression such as A * B * C may be transmitted *unevaluated* by transmitting the string A * B * C as an actual parameter. The primitive function EVAL may then be used to evaluate the string as an expression. Both these techniques, however, suffer from the defect that the referencing environment is not updated before evaluation of either $X or A * B * C, and thus the local referencing environment may interfere with evaluation (see Problem 15-3).

A subprogram may return any data item as its value, including strings, patterns, arrays, tables, and numbers. The last value assigned to the subprogram name within the subprogram is returned as the value of the subprogram call. If the result is to be used immediately as the object of an assignment, then the return must be by a **goto** the special label NRETURN; otherwise the label RETURN is used. In both these cases the call of the subprogram is said to succeed, and evaluation of the expression containing the subprogram call is resumed, using the value returned. An alternative is that of returning through a **goto** the label FRETURN. Such a return causes the subprogram call to fail. In this case no value is returned, and instead the execution of the calling statement is terminated immediately and the failure branch of the calling statement is taken.

15-8. OPERATING ENVIRONMENT

SNOBOL4 is designed for a batch-processing environment. Input-output of character strings to external sequential data files is the major means provided for access to the environment. In addition, access to an external library of precompiled programs (written originally in FORTRAN or assembly language) is provided at run time through a LOAD primitive. For example, the statement LOAD('SUB(REAL,INTEGER)REAL') causes run-time loading of a subprogram SUB and entry of the subprogram name and the types of its parameters and result into the run-time subprogram names table.

The newly loaded subprogram may subsequently be called just as any ordinary subprogram defined using DEFINE. An UNLOAD primitive may be used to reverse the process—deleting the subprogram name from the subprogram names table so that it is no longer callable and freeing the storage allocated for the subprogram code when loaded.

15-9. SYNTAX AND TRANSLATION

The most striking aspect of the syntax of SNOBOL4 is the complete *lack* of any syntactic distinction among the bodies of subprograms and the main program. A program consists basically of a list of statements. There is no way to determine syntactically whether a particular statement is part of the main program or of any particular subprogram. In fact, a single statement may be part of both the main program and any number of subprograms simultaneously.

This rather chaotic program structure allows new program segments and subprograms, translated into executable form at run time, to be easily integrated with existing program elements. In many cases, however, the structure leads to errors because omission of an explicit **goto** on a statement may cause control to flow into or out of a subprogram body inadvertently.

Statements. Individual statements have a common syntactic base—the pattern-matching and replacement statement. The basic syntax is

⟨*label*⟩ ⟨*subject string*⟩ ⟨*pattern*⟩ = ⟨*replacement string*⟩ :⟨*goto*⟩

The ⟨*label*⟩ is a single identifier beginning in the first character position. The ⟨*subject string*⟩ and ⟨*replacement string*⟩ are defined by string-valued expressions. The ⟨*pattern*⟩ is defined by a pattern-valued expression. The ⟨*goto*⟩ may specify an unconditional branch or alternatives for success and failure of the statement. Labels and **goto**s are optional in any statement.

Assignment statements follow the above syntax with the ⟨*pattern*⟩ field omitted. Simple pattern matching without replacement is specified by omission of the = ⟨*replacement string*⟩. A subprogram call may be specified by omission of both ⟨*pattern*⟩ and ⟨*replacement string*⟩ fields. For an unconditional **goto** alone all except the ⟨*goto*⟩ field may be omitted. SNOBOL4 provides no structured statements of any form.

Translation. In the usual implementation of SNOBOL4, programs are translated into an executable form which is decoded and executed by a software interpreter. The syntactic structure of SNOBOL4 programs makes translation relatively trivial. Because there are no subprogram boundaries, declarations, or structured statements, each statement in a program may be translated without regard for the context in which it appears. Thus translation may proceed essentially line by line. The late binding time of most elements of SNOBOL4 statements also simplifies translation because so little of the interpretation of a statement is fixed at translation time. For example, in translating the expression X + Y none of the properties of the variables X and Y are known to the translator, and the symbol + may not even represent addition when the expression is evaluated during execution (because the meaning of + may be changed by the primitive OPSYN). The translator is thus reduced to making simple syntactic checks and translating each statement into a block of executable *code* which is largely just a direct encoding of the original statement in a somewhat more convenient form for execution. In the usual SNOBOL4 implementation these code blocks take the form of a sequence of prefix instructions, each composed of an operator symbol and list of operands. The operands may themselves be prefix form instructions to be evaluated, so the overall form is similar to a tree structure of operator-operand combinations.

15-10. STRUCTURE OF A SNOBOL4 VIRTUAL COMPUTER

The run-time structure of a SNOBOL4 implementation is made complex by the large amount of run-time variability that the language allows. Considerable software simulation is required regardless of whether a software interpreter with a simple translator or the hardware interpreter with a compiler is used as the basis for the implementation. The software-interpreter-based system is the simplest and thus is the one which has been used in this chapter.

Storage Management

A tripartite memory organization is required: a static area for storage of system routines (including the translator) and various fixed-size tables, a stack for storage of subprogram activation records, and a heap for storage of translated user programs, user data structures, variable-size system tables, and other system data. The heap is allocated in variable-size blocks, and garbage collection and full compaction occur when free space is exhausted, as explained in detail in Section 7-8.

The static area and stack require little comment. Subprogram activation records in the stack contain the deactivated values for formal parameters, local variables, and the subprogram name identifiers, because the central referencing environment table method is used to maintain the current referencing environment. Thus the stack serves as a hiddden stack and plays no direct role in referencing.

The heap is the central storage area. SNOBOL4 allows a programmer to create strings, arrays, tables, and programmer-defined data structures at arbitrary points during program execution, and as a result all programmer-defined data (each with full run-time descriptor) are allocated space in the heap. In addition, the translator may be called at any point during execution to translate a character string representing a set of SNOBOL4 statements into executable form. Such run-time-translated programs also require storage allocation in the heap. These aspects of the language have been discussed in previous sections.

Run-Time System Data

Almost every aspect of program and data structure in SNOBOL4 is subject to change at unpredictable points during program execution. As a result a large amount of run-time data must be maintained by the run-time system and continuously accessed and modified as execution proceeds. Most of these data are the sort which in other languages would be generated and used by the translator in creating the executable program form and then discarded before execution. It is most convenient to characterize this run-time system data in terms of a set of tables, although different implementations may store these system data in different ways. The run-time tables which must be maintained during execution of a SNOBOL4 program include

1. *Central strings table (referencing environment).* The central run-time table in which character strings and their associated values are stored has been discussed in the preceding sections. Each entry in the central table consists of a character string and a pointer to its current value. Ordinarily, because the table must be accessed frequently, it is structured as a hash-coded table of fixed size in which each entry is a bucket consisting of a linked list of all the entries with the same hash index. The value of a string in the table

may be a pointer to another string in the table, a number, or a pointer to an array, table (property list), pattern, or data structure of programmer-defined type. Strings and their values are stored in the heap, but the basic fixed-size hash table (with pointers to the buckets in the heap) is stored in the static area.

2. *Statement labels table.* The label designated in the **goto** field of a statement may be an arbitrary computed string. This structure requires a run-time table of statement labels and pointers to their associated code positions in the executable code. Because strings are always entered into the central strings table, this labels table need only contain a pointer to the entry for the string and a pointer to the code position for each label. The possibility of translating new program statements containing labels into executable form during program execution means that the labels table may grow unpredictably during program execution and thus must be allocated storage in the heap.

3. *Subprogram and operator names.* A new subprogram name is defined whenever the DEFINE function is called during program execution. In addition, the OPSYN primitive allows any operator symbol (e.g., +) to be associated with a programmer-defined subprogram. This run-time variability requires a run-time table of associations between subprogram names and subprogram definitions and between operator symbols and operator definitions which may be modified by DEFINE and OPSYN and accessed whenever an operator is invoked or a subprogram called. The operator symbols and subprogram calls appearing in a program when it is translated may be translated into direct pointers to the appropriate table entries. However, the language also includes an indirect subprogram call (the APPLY function) which allows any computed string to be used as the subprogram name, thus requiring a search of the subprogram names table at run time.

4. *Input, output, and trace associations.* The input, output and trace features of SNOBOL4 are activated by interrupts which occur whenever tagged identifiers are referenced in certain contexts. For example, an output interrupt occurs whenever an assignment to a tagged *output variable* is made, a label trace interrupt occurs whenever control is transferred to a tagged label, etc. Such tagged identifiers may be created at any point during program execution through execution of one of the primitives functions TRACE, INPUT, or OUTPUT. A run-time table is required to specify the associations which are current for each tagged variable, which may include association with an input file, with an output file, or with

tracing when used as a label, subprogram name, or when its value is modified. In addition to the run-time table (or tables) of associations, each reference to an identifier requires run-time checking for an appropriate interrupt tag because the interrupt system is unlikely to be supported by hardware and thus must be software-simulated.

5. *Data types and fields.* Programmer-defined data types may be created at arbitrary points during execution. Each component (field) of such a data element receives an identifier as its name, and the same field name may be used in many different data types. A run-time table must be maintained specifying for each *data type—field name* pair, the position of that field within a data element of that data type. In addition, a run-time table of data type tags and their associated type names must be maintained because the programmer may request the type of the value of a variable at any point during execution using the primitive DATATYPE.

It should be clear from this discussion that the maintenance of the run-time system data in a SNOBOL4 implementation is a substantial part of the run-time virtual computer structure. The storage and execution time required for this system data handling represents a substantial part of the cost of program execution.

15-11. REFERENCES AND SUGGESTIONS FOR FURTHER READING

The basic description of the SNOBOL4 language is found in the text by Griswold et al. [1971]. A "primer" by Griswold and Griswold [1973] provides a more elementary introduction to the language.

The standard implementation of SNOBOL4 is described in a book by Griswold [1972], which contains excellent discussions of many of the issues which arise during implementation. Recent papers by Gimpel [1973] and Tennent [1973] provide formal definitions of much of the semantics of the language.

15-12. PROBLEMS

15.1. Consider the program segment

```
X = 'GREEN EGGS AND HAM'
Y = X
X 'AND' = 'PLUS'
```

The final value of X is the string GREEN EGGS PLUS HAM.

a. What is the final value of Y?

b. Explain the run-time changes that occur in the central strings table (including the values of X and Y) as a result of execution of each of these statements.

15-2. Explain why strings in the central table to which no path exists may be garbage-collected only if they have a *null value*.

15-3. The indirect referencing operator $ makes it possible to get some of the effects of parameter transmission by reference (or by name) even though SNOBOL4 parameters are always transmitted by value. A simple example is the subprogram ADD1, which when called with a simple integer-valued variable as argument will add 1 to the value of the variable. In FORTRAN the program would be

```
SUBROUTINE ADD1(I)
I = I + 1
RETURN
END
```

In SNOBOL4 ADD1 would be written as

```
        DEFINE('ADD1(I)')        :(NEXT)
ADD1    $I = $I + 1              :(RETURN)
```

The calling sequence in FORTRAN

```
K = 2
CALL ADD1(K)
```

(which results in K being given the value 3), is written in SNOBOL 4 as

```
K = 2
ADD1('K')
```

Unfortunately, while this sequence results in K being given the value 3, the sequence

```
I = 2
ADD1('I')
```

results in a run-time error diagnostic because an argument given to + is not a number. *Problem:*

a. Explain why ADD1('K') works, while ADD1('I') fails.

b. Suppose that your SNOBOL4 subprogram SUB is defined to have formal parameters P1, P2, . . . , Pm, local variables L1, L2, . . . Ln, and the first actual parameter is expected to be a string representing a variable name (as in ADD1) which will be referenced indirectly as $P1 in SUB (i.e., you wish to use P1 as a *by reference* parameter). To make SUB available as a useful SNOBOL4 subprogram, what restrictions must be placed on the string (identifier) transmitted as the first actual parameter to SUB to ensure that SUB will work correctly?

15-4. In the SNOBOL4 implementation described in this chapter, strings are entered in the central strings table at the time of their *creation*. An alternative would be to enter strings into the central table only when they are used as identifiers (i.e., when they are given an association as a subprogram name or label or when they are given a value). Strings with no association would be saved in temporary storage only until they became garbage and could be destroyed. Discuss the advantages and disadvantages of this alternative representation.

16 APL

16-1. INTRODUCTION

The original APL programming language was defined in a book by Kenneth Iverson, *A Programming Language*, published in 1962. The acronym APL is derived from the title of the book. Iverson's original intent was not to develop a conventional programming language that might be implemented on a computer as much as to develop a *notation* adequate to express concisely many important algorithms in mathematics. As a result the original APL utilized a myriad of special notational conventions and symbols, including subscripts, super-scripts, and a two-dimensional program syntax with arrows desig-nating flow of control that made the notation difficult if not impossible to directly implement on a computer. The original APL proved to be a useful conceptual tool for the precise statement of algorithms, which might then be translated by hand into conven-tional programming languages. Applications of this original APL included a concise and complete formal description of the IBM 360 computer hardware (Falkoff et al. [1964]).

A modified version of the original APL, termed APL\360, was implemented in the late 1960s by Iverson, Falkoff, and a group at IBM. Since then many other APL implementations have appeared, all based largely on the APL\360 design. It is this implemented version of APL that is described in this chapter. APL has two distinguishing characteristics that set it apart from the other languages described in this part:

1. *Interactive language.* APL is the only language of those described here that is expressly designed to be *interactive*. By

interactive we mean a language designed to be used by a programmer sitting at a computer terminal who is building, testing, modifying, and using programs dynamically. APL includes a number of special features designed expressly for an interactive environment, including immediate execution of expressions entered at the terminal and facilities for subprogram creation, editing, and storage.

2. *Direct processing of entire data structures.* In APL the primitive operations accept whole arrays as arguments and produce whole arrays as results. Thus in APL the basic unit of data tends to be an entire array rather than a single array element as is the case in languages such as FORTRAN and ALGOL. This emphasis on array processing gives programming in APL a unique "style" quite different from other languages.

APL has attracted a devoted group of users and evoked much controversy in its relatively brief period of use. Iverson's original notation is remarkable in its conciseness, power, and elegance, and most of this has been carried over into the implemented APL, even to the extent of insisting on a character set for APL users which provides a greatly expanded set of special characters. The power and conciseness of the language make it well suited to the interactive environment, because a line of only a few characters typed in at a terminal can accomplish a surprising amount of computation. The interactive features added to the original APL notation have also been nicely designed to enhance the convenience of using the language. The resulting APL language is particularly attractive to the programmer who wishes to get on the computer at a terminal, do some computing, obtain the desired results, and get off in a minimum amount of time. The language is much less suitable for construction of large programs which will be used repeatedly for production computing. In addition, the restriction to homogeneous array data structures in the language makes it difficult to apply to problem areas where flexible data structuring is a prime consideration, such as work in business data processing or artificial intelligence.

16-2. BRIEF OVERVIEW OF THE LANGUAGE

APL is based on simple homogeneous array data structures of type number or character. Typing is strictly dynamic and of no direct concern to the programmer (except that certain operators apply only to arrays of numbers). A large class of primitive operators are built-in, including many which create, destroy, and modify arrays. Every APL primitive is defined as a function which returns a value. From these primitives extremely powerful expressions may be constructed. APL control structures are quite simple. Within expressions there is no hierarchy of operations, and right-to-left associativity is used in place of the more usual left-to-right technique. Between statements and subprograms all that is provided is a simple **goto**, which allows a computed statement number, and recursive subprogram calls. Additionally, various kinds of interrupts may be set to interrupt program execution and return control to the programmer at his terminal, allowing him to enter new data, modify old data values, or modify the program before restarting the interrupted program at a designated statement.

Subprograms are restricted to at most two arguments, transmitted by value, and a single result. However, the ability to accept array arguments and return array results in any subprogram makes these restrictions relatively minor. Subprograms have the form of a simple sequence of statements, each of which has a system-generated *line number* and which may, in addition, have a programmer-supplied label. **Goto** statements may designate their object either by a line number or statement label. A subprogram may have a designated set of local identifiers. Existing associations for these identifiers are deactivated on subprogram entry and reactivated on subprogram exit. Nonlocal referencing obeys the *most recent association* rule.

There is no concept of main program in APL. Subprogram execution is initiated either by a call from another subprogram or by the programmer at his terminal through entry and execution of an expression containing a function call. In the latter case control returns to the programmer at the terminal after subprogram execution is complete. In a sense the programmer creates and executes the main program line by line during a session at the terminal.

APL has perhaps the most extensively specified operating environment of any language described in this book. This environment, of course, includes the programmer at his terminal. Control may be passed back and forth between an executing program and the programmer as necessary. For external storage, programs and data are grouped into *workspaces*; these may be saved from session to session by the programmer. Each workspace may contain various program and data structures, including partially written programs and programs that have been partially executed and then interrupted. *System commands* are provided to allow workspaces to be brought into central memory from external storage and stored back again after being updated. In addition, subprogram definitions and data structures may be transferred individually by name between a stored workspace and the currently active one.

A typical APL implementation is based on purely software-interpreted program execution. Programs are stored essentially as entered, with only slight translation done. Two static storage areas are allocated, one for system routines and one for the workspace currently in use by the programmer. The system routines are ordinarily shared between several users, each with his own workspace area. The workspace area contains some static storage for system data and three dynamic storage areas: a stack for subprogram activation records (local referencing environments and return points), a heap for array storage and storage of the bodies of defined subprograms, and a table of global identifier associations. Garbage collection and full compaction are used when necessary. Arrays are stored with full run-time descriptors in the usual sequential simulation.

16-3. AN ANNOTATED EXAMPLE TERMINAL SESSION: A PROGRAM TO COMPUTE THE FIRST N PRIMES

Figure 16-1 contains the listing of a partial APL terminal session in which the programmer enters, tests, corrects, and saves a function subprogram that computes a vector containing the first N prime numbers, for a given input parameter N. The programmer is assumed to already have gained access to the APL system and to have completed any earlier work. The annotations below refer to the line numbers to the left of the example listing, which are not a part of the program.

Line 1. The programmer clears his workspace of previous work. All subprogram and data structure definitions entered previously and not explicitly saved in the workspace library are destroyed.

Line 2. The programmer enters *definition mode* by typing the ∇ and follows with a subprogram header. The subprogram is defined in lines 3—9 following. The header declares the subprogram name, PRIMES, the name of its formal parameter, N, and two local variables, RES and T. The final value of RES is to be returned as the value of the function.

Line

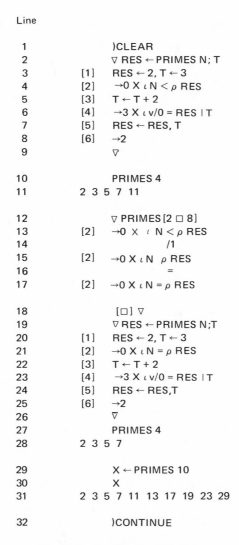

```
1                       )CLEAR
2                       ∇ RES ← PRIMES N; T
3               [1]     RES ← 2, T ← 3
4               [2]     →0 X ι N < ρ RES
5               [3]     T ← T + 2
6               [4]     →3 X ι v/0 = RES | T
7               [5]     RES ← RES, T
8               [6]     →2
9                       ∇

10                      PRIMES 4
11              2 3 5 7 11

12                      ∇ PRIMES [2 □ 8]
13              [2]     →0 X  ι N < ρ RES
14                              /1
15              [2]     →0 X ι N  ρ RES
16                              =
17              [2]     →0 X ι N = ρ RES

18                      [□] ∇
19                      ∇ RES ← PRIMES N;T
20              [1]     RES ← 2, T ← 3
21              [2]     →0 X ι N = ρ RES
22              [3]     T ← T + 2
23              [4]     →3 X ι v/0 = RES | T
24              [5]     RES ← RES,T
25              [6]     →2
26                      ∇
27                      PRIMES 4
28              2 3 5 7

29                      X ← PRIMES 10
30                      X
31              2 3 5 7 11 13 17 19 23 29

32                      )CONTINUE
```

Fig. 16-1. An APL terminal session.

Line 3. Initial values are assigned to RES and T. The ← indicates assignment, and the "," indicates concatenation. The expression is evaluated from *right to left* as follows: (1) T is assigned the value 3, and 3 becomes the value of the expression T ← 3 (thus assignment is a function returning the value assigned as its value); (2) the value 3 is concatenated with the value 2 to form a vector of two elements; and (3) the two-element vector is assigned as the value of the variable RES. Note that the statement created a two-element vector during its execution. The right-to-left evaluation of expressions is standard throughout APL.

Line 4. This statement indicates a transfer of control because it begins with →. Control is returned to the calling program if the length of the vector that is the value of RES is greater than the value of N input. If not, then control passes to the next statement. In other words, the routine terminates here if N + 1 primes have been computed (an error which is corrected below). In detail the statement is evaluated from right to left as follows: (1) The operator ρ returns the length of a vector argument, so ρ RES gives the length of the vector named by RES; (2) the operator < compares the value of N and the length of RES, returning 1 for true and 0 for false; (3) the operator ι, for an integer argument *k*, produces a vector of the first *k* integers, or the *null vector* if *k* is zero, which in this case (argument either 1 or 0) gives either the vector containing only 1 or the null vector as result; (4) the operator × represents multiplication, in this case multiplication of zero times the result of step (3), giving either the null vector or the vector containing only a single zero; and finally (5) the branch operator → does nothing if its operand is the null vector and otherwise it transfers control to the statement whose number is the value of the first element of its vector argument, which in this case would be a branch to the statement numbered zero; no statement has the number zero, and such a branch is by definition a subprogram return. This structure seems inordinately complicated at first, but the trick of reading the expression → 0 × ι as "branch to 0 if the following expression is true, and otherwise continue to the next statement" simplifies things somewhat.

Line 5. The value of T is increased to the next odd integer.

Line 6. Another *test and* **goto**, this time to the statement numbered 3 (line 5) if the expression ∨/0 = RES | T returns true. This expression is evaluated from right to left as follows: (1) T contains the next number to be tested for primeness, while RES contains a vector of the primes found to this point; the operator | returns the remainder (residue) of division of its two arguments; thus the expression RES | T produces a vector of the remainders obtained by dividing each element of the vector RES into the value of T; (2) each element of the vector resulting from step (1) is compared to zero, giving a vector of Boolean values (1s and 0s) depending on whether the remainder in the original vector was zero or nonzero, respectively; and finally (3) the operator ∨ is applied *between* each two adjacent elements of the Boolean vector resulting from step (2), giving a result of 1 (true) if the vector produced in step (2) contains any 1s and a result of 0 (false) if the vector is all zeros. Since the vector contains a 1 in some position only if the corresponding prime in RES exactly divides the test integer T, a vector of all zeros indicates that the test number is a prime.

Line 7. If the value of T is a prime, the value is concatenated (operator,) onto the vector RES, giving a new vector, and the new vector is assigned as the new value of RES.

Line 8. Direct **goto** to statement number 2 (line 4).

Line 9. End of subprogram definition. The definition is automatically stored in the programmer's active workspace as the association for the identifier PRIMES. The terminal is returned to *immediate execution* mode, where any APL expression entered is immediately executed.

Line 10. First test of the new subprogram PRIMES. PRIMES is called with the argument 4. It should return as its value a vector of the first four primes. The result of the function call is printed automatically unless it is assigned as the value of a variable.

Line 11. Program bug detected. PRIMES returned the first five primes.

Lines 12–17. The subprogram definition is edited to correct the error, which is due to the $<$ comparison in statement [2].

Line 12. The programmer reenters definition mode (with ∇) and specifies listing of statement [2] of subprogram PRIMES, set for editing to begin on character 8 of the line.

Lines 13–14. Statement [2] is displayed and the terminal carriage is positioned on the next line beneath the eighth character. The programmer then spaces over or back to the exact position to be modified and enters /1, with the slash beneath the character to be deleted and the 1 indicating that the deleted character is to be replaced by one new character.

Lines 15–16. Statement [2] is redisplayed with the character deleted and the carriage positioned beneath the empty space. The programmer types the character to be inserted.

Line 17. The corrected statement is displayed again.

Line 18. The programmer requests display of the entire corrected function definition before leaving *definition mode*.

Lines 19–26. The function definition is listed.

Lines 27—28. The function is tested again and this time returns correct results.

Line 29. A vector of the first ten primes is computed and assigned as the value of the variable X. Since X has not been referenced previously, it is created automatically before the assignment is made.

Lines 30—31. The programmer requests and gets a printout of the value of X.

Line 32. The programmer ends the terminal session. The active workspace , containing the definition of subprogram PRIMES and the vector X of the first ten primes, is saved in the programmer's workspace library under the name CONTINUE. When the programmer signs on for his next terminal session this workspace will be automatically loaded as his initial active workspace.

16-4. DATA

APL is quite restricted in its data-structuring facilities. Numbers and single characters are the elementary data types. Data structures are restricted to homogeneous multidimensional arrays containing elements of one of these two types. The arrays may have an arbitrary number of dimensions. The lower bound on subscript ranges is implicitly 1 but may be set at 0 by a special system command. Arrays are stored sequentially with a full run-time descriptor. Characters are stored in their hardware representation. Numbers are stored in fixed- or floating-point formats and are automatically converted as the need arises during execution; the programmer has no control over the internal storage representation of numbers.

No declarations for data are used in APL. Identifiers are not declared explicitly unless they are formal parameters or local identifiers in a subprogram in which case the declaration serves only to indicate a scope of definition. An identifier may name a simple variable, an array, or a subprogram at different points during a terminal session. Full run-time descriptors are carried for all data items.

Syntax. The usual syntactic representation is provided for numbers and characters. Vectors of numbers may be written directly as a sequence of numbers separated by spaces. Character vectors are written as a character string. Arrays of higher dimension may be easily created from vectors using built-in operators (see the next section).

16-5. OPERATIONS

The APL primitive operation set is the most powerful and elegant of any language described here. Primitives are provided for a wide variety of simple and complex manipulations on arrays. In general, each primitive operation takes arrays as operands and produces an array as a result. The primitives themselves are powerful, but equally importantly they may be combined into expressions in very complex ways, allowing a single expression to compute results which would require a lengthy program in other languages. It is this powerful expression capability that leads to the APL phenomenon of *one-liners*—entire complex computations written as one-line programs composed of single expressions.

A complete description of the entire set of APL primitives is unnecessary. Detailed definitions of the various operators may be found in the reference manuals, e.g., Pakin [1972]. We shall classify the various operators into categories to give an idea of the diversity and power of the operations.

Arithmetic Operations. The usual arithmetic operations— addition, subtraction, multiplication, division, negation, and exponentiation—are provided, but many others also appear as primitives: absolute value, reciprocal, logarithm, square root, sine, cosine and other trignometric functions, maximum, minimum, factorial, and random number generation. These operations may be applied to single numbers (or pairs of numbers) in the usual way, but more importantly they may be applied to any array of numbers (or pairs of arrays of the same shape and size). When applied to arrays the operations are applied to each element of the array (or each pair of elements), and the result of the operation is a new array of the same size. For example, if A and B are arrays of the same shape and size, then the expression A + B produces a new array by adding corresponding elements of A and B. Similarly, A ⌈ B produces a new array whose components are the maximum of corresponding pairs of components in A and B.

Relational and Logical Operations. In APL the Boolean values are represented by the numbers 1 (true) and 0 (false). Thus the relational and logical operations are special cases of arithmetic operations. This representation is useful because it allows arithmetic, relational, and logical operations to be interspersed without type conflicts. The logical and relational operations may be applied to arrays in the same manner as the arithmetic operations. The primitive relational operations are the usual *equal, not-equal, less-than, greater-than, less-than-or-equal,* and *greater-than-or-equal.* Logical operations include *not, and, or, nand,* and *nor.*

Accessing and Assignment. In keeping with the basic APL design philosophy that every primitive should be generalized as far as possible, the basic operations of accessing and assignment appear in a much more general form than usually seen. Any variable may have an array as value (or a single number or character). The entire array is retrieved just by referencing the variable in the usual way. However, individual array elements may also be accessed by subscripting; e.g., A[2;3] designates the element in the second row and the third column of the array which is the value of A. Subscripting is extended to allow arbitrary subarrays of an array to be accessed. For example, A[;3] accesses the third column of the matrix value of A; similarly, A[2;] gives the second row. But also A[1 2;] gives a matrix composed of the first two rows of A; A[1 2; 2 4] gives a 2 by 2 matrix composed of $A_{1, 2}$, $A_{2, 2}$, $A_{1, 4}$, and $A_{2, 4}$.

Assignment (symbol ←) is performed differently depending on whether the variable on the left is subscripted or not. If a simple variable appears, then the value being assigned replaces the current value of the variable in the usual way, except that the value assigned may be an array. For example, if A and B are arrays of the same shape and size, then

$$C \leftarrow A + B$$

assigns the sum array as the new value of C, destroying the old value of C, which may also have been an array. It is not appropriate in APL to think of A, B, or C as the names of particular arrays, in the way one would in FORTRAN or ALGOL. Because assignment may associate any of these identifiers with a new array at any time, it is best to think of A, B, and C as simple variables whose *values* happen to be arrays.

Assignment to a subscripted variable works differently. Subscripting indicates that the array which is the current value of the variable is to be retained (rather than destroyed) and only the values of selected elements of the array are to be modified. Thus A[2;3] ← 7 assigns 7 as the new value of A[2;3] as expected. The assignment, however, is not restricted to a single element of A. For example,

$$A[2;] \leftarrow 7$$

assigns 7 as the new value of each element in the second row of A. The assignment

$$A[1\ 2;2\ 4] \leftarrow 7$$

sets the elements $A_{1\ 2}$, $A_{1\ 4}$, $A_{2\ 2}$, and $A_{2\ 4}$ each to 7. Assignment is extended further to allow any array to be assigned to a subarray of another array of the same shape and size. For example, if B is a 2×2 matrix, then the assignment $A[1\ 2;2\ 4] \leftarrow B$ changes the value of each specified element of A to the value of the corresponding element of B.

Array Modification. A variety of other operators that modify arrays in various ways, without changing values of array elements, is provided. A basic operator, ρ, allows access to the descriptor of an array, returning a vector of upper bounds on each subscript of the array. For example, if A is a 3×4 matrix, then ρA returns the two-element vector (3 4) as its value. A double application of ρ produces the number of dimensions of an array, e.g., $\rho\rho A = 2$. Thus a program may always determine dynamically the size and shape of any array.

An array of any number of dimensions may be turned into a vector using the operator ",". The array elements are taken in row-major order. An array of any number of dimensions may be formed from a vector or another array using the operator ρ as a binary operation. For example, if A is the vector (2 3 4 5 6 7), then the expression $2\ 3\ \rho\ A$ produces the 2×3 matrix

$$2\quad 3\quad 4$$
$$5\quad 6\quad 7$$

as its value.

Two vectors or arrays may be concatenated to form a new array. A vector may be modified by deletion of leading or trailing elements. A matrix transpose primitive and a rotation operator which rotates the elements of a vector (or rows or columns of a matrix) end-around are also provided. Expansion and compression operators allow arbitrary insertions and deletions of elements within an array. Moreover, each of these primitives applies to arrays of higher dimension as well, with a choice of which dimension is to be used, (where such extension is appropriate).

Much of the power of APL lies in this set of primitives for structural modification of arrays. In general, given a set of arrays, these primitives allow the arrays to be taken apart, restructured, and the pieces recombined in almost any desired manner. In the process, of course, the array element values may also be modified using the arithmetic, logical, and relational operations.

Generators. Three built-in *generator* operations play a central role in much APL programming. Each accepts one or two other primitives and one or two arrays as arguments and applies the primitives to the elements of the arrays in a fixed sequence. The most basic of these is the *reduction* operation (symbol /), which accepts a vector (or an array) and one of the basic binary arithmetic, relational, or logical primitives as arguments. The primitive is applied to the last two elements of the vector, then to the result of that operation and the third from the last vector element, etc. The effect is as though the elements of the vector were written out in sequence with the primitive between each adjacent pair and then the resulting expression executed from right to left in the usual APL manner. For example, if A has as its value the vector (2 3 4 5 6 7), then +/A evaluates to the sum of the elements of A, -/A gives the value $(2-(3-(4-(5-(6-7)))))$ or $2-3+4-5+6-7$. Reduction may be applied to arrays of higher dimension by designating the dimension along which the reduction is to be made. For example, if B is a matrix, then +/[1] B produces a vector of the sums of the columns of B, and +/[2] B produces a vector of the row sums.

The other two generator primitives are *inner product* (symbol .) and *outer product* (symbol °.). The *inner product* primitive takes two binary primitive operations and two arrays (of conformable shapes) as arguments. The second primitive is applied to corresponding pairs of elements of the two arrays, and then the first primitive is applied to reduce the result. More specifically, the expression A+.× B, where A and B are vectors of the same length, is equivalent to the expression +/(A × B), i.e., corresponding elements of A and B are multiplied to produce a new vector of the same length, and then this new vector is summed to produce a single number. If A and B are matrices, then A+.× B is ordinary matrix multiplication. Other uses for the inner product primitive abound; for example, two vectors may be tested for component-by-component equality by the expression A+.≠B, which evaluates to zero only if A and B are identical.

The third generator primitive, *outer product*, takes two arrays and a binary primitive as arguments and applies the primitive to each pair of elements of the two arrays, generating a new array with number of dimensions equal to the sum of the number of dimensions of the two original arrays. Thus the outer product of two vectors results in creation of a matrix, the outer product of a vector and a matrix gives an array of three dimensions, etc.

A number of other more specialized array manipulation primitives are provided, including matrix division, matrix inverse, and sorting primitives.

Creation and destruction of arrays is an implicit aspect of almost every APL primitive. Unlike other languages there are no special creation and destruction operations.

Input-Output. APL input-output operations are restricted to simple input and output of numbers, character strings, and arrays to the programmer's terminal. No access to external data files is ordinarily provided (although some recent APL implementations include such features). The input operation symbol is □. The occurrence of □ as a variable in an expression being evaluated causes evaluation to be interrupted and a request for input sent to the programmer's terminal. After he has entered a number, vector of numbers, or character string, evaluation of the expression is resumed. Output is handled similarly: The appearance of □ as the object of an assignment within an expression specifies that the value is to be printed at the programmer's terminal. In addition, automatic output of the value of an expression occurs when the expression has been input by the programmer for immediate evaluation.

16-6. SEQUENCE CONTROL

APL is rather weak in sequence control mechanisms, particularly in statement sequence control. However, much of the sequence control structure ordinarily needed for array processing in languages like FORTRAN and ALGOL is made unnecessary by the powerful APL primitives, and thus this weakness is not as significant as it might appear. Note for example, that the summation of the elements of a vector, which would require a set of statements including a loop in FORTRAN or ALGOL, may be written in APL as

$$\text{SUM} \leftarrow +/V$$

No statement sequence control is required.

Expressions. APL operations appear only in two forms, regardless of whether they are primitives or programmer-defined subprograms:

1. Binary operations (operations with two operands) are written in infix notation, e.g., A−B or A?B.

2. Unary operations (operations with one operand) are written in Polish prefix notation (without parentheses), e.g., $-$C or ?C.

The only exception to this rule is the *subscripting operation*, which is represented by enclosing the subscript in a pair of brackets, e.g., D[2].

The simple syntax for expressions allows an equally simple evaluation rule, the *right-to-left* rule: An APL expression is always evaluated from right to left with the operands of an operation evaluated before the operation is applied. Parentheses may be used in the usual way to control the order of evaluation. For example,

$$A-B-C-D \text{ is evaluated as } A-(B-(C-D)).$$
$$A\times B+C\times D \text{ is evaluated as } A\times(B+(C\times D)).$$

Note that the right-to-left rule applies to programmer-defined function subprograms as well as built-in primitives. Since no special syntax is provided for function subprogram calls, they also appear as infix operations; for example, A FUN B represents the function call FUN(A,B). The expression A$-$B FUN C$\div$D is evaluated as A$-$(B FUN (C$\div$D)) or in the more common function notation as A$-$FUN(B,C$\div$D).

The right-to-left rule leaves open the question of the order of evaluation of the two operands of a binary operation; e.g., in (A$-$B) + (C$-$D) both (A$-$B) and (C$-$D) must be evaluated before the + operation is applied, but the order of evaluation of (A$-$B) and (C$-$D) is not defined. The order makes no difference except where side effects occur, but then it may be crucial. APL function subprograms may have side effects; moreover, because assignment is defined as a function, direct side effects through assignments embedded in expressions may occur. For example, the result of the expression

$$A-(B\leftarrow C)-B$$

is dependent on the order of evaluation of the assignment to B and the reference to B, and this order is not defined by the right-to-left rule. Similarly, if FUN has the side effect of changing the value of B, then the result of (A FUN C)$-$B is undefined. The result of evaluation in such cases is implementation-dependent.

Implementation of expression evaluation is made complex by a number of language features. Intermediate results of evaluation may be arbitrarily large arrays, for which temporary storage must be allocated in the programmer data area. In addition, any expression may include the $\square$ operation specifying a request for input from the programmer's terminal. This requires an interruption of evaluation, during which the active workspace is ordinarily copied to external storage by the APL system, to be brought back into central memory when the programmer has entered his data. Evaluation of a function call in an expression may be interrupted by an error, during which the programmer is given control. The programmer may attempt to modify the statement containing the partially evaluated expression by editing the original function definition. Careful monitoring of such editing attempts is necessary to ensure that execution can still be continued.

Statement Sequence Control

Each statement in a function definition receives a line number automatically upon input. In addition, statements may be labeled by preceding the statement by ⟨*label*⟩:. Statements are executed in sequence in the usual way. The **goto** operator (symbol →) may be used to modify this sequence. A **goto** statement must begin with → followed by an arbitrary expression. The value of the expression must be either an integer or a statement label. The → operator transfers control to the statement with this line number or label in the usual way.

This simple computed **goto** command is made more flexible by a number of conventions. First it should be noted that since a single APL expression may perform a complex computation which includes testing conditions of various sorts and varying the computation accordingly, the basic **goto** command can be used either as a simple **goto**, as in →3, which transfers control unconditionally to statement 3, or as a two-way or multiway branch by using more complex expressions. This basic structure is extended by the following conventions:

1. If the expression evaluates to a vector, the first element of the vector is taken as the integer line number for the **goto**,

2. If the expression evaluates to the special null vector (the vector of no elements), then no transfer occurs and control passes to the next statement in sequence.

The same **goto** may also be used as a subprogram return or halt (see below).

Subprogram Sequence Control

Subprogram execution is controlled by the ordinary call and return structure, with unrestricted recursive calls allowed. Return from a subprogram is done by a **goto** to a nonexistent statement number, usually statement number zero, e.g., →0. Return from an entire subprogram calling chain back to the top level, where the programmer is again free to enter commands directly, may be accomplished by a statement consisting only of the **goto** arrow without an operand, →.

Besides the subprogram call and return it is also possible to interrupt subprogram execution, leaving the subprogram in a *suspended state*. Execution is interrupted automatically if an error occurs during execution. The interrupted subprogram is placed in a suspended state, and control returns to the programmer at his terminal. Programs may be left in the suspended state indefinitely while other subprograms are executed. In fact, any number of subprograms may be in the suspended state simultaneously. Interruption of subprogram execution also may be specified to occur when particular lines of the subprogram are reached during execution. This is done by setting up a *stop vector*—a vector of line numbers at which execution is to be suspended. For example, if subprogram SUB is to be interrupted prior to execution of lines 6 and 17, the statement

$$S\Delta SUB \leftarrow 6\ 17$$

entered at the terminal will tag the appropriate statements in SUB for interruption when SUB is executed.

When subprogram execution is interrupted and the subprogram put into the suspended state, control returns to the programmer at the terminal, who may now proceed to modify the suspended subprogram, write new subprograms, etc. The only real restriction on his activity is that he must be careful not to modify subprograms which are partially executed in certain ways, for the obvious reason that then return of control might be made impossible.

The interrupt features of APL are useful in allowing very flexible program testing schemes. For example, a partially written subprogram may be tested by setting interrupts for statements leading into missing program segments. Or execution may be interrupted just prior to a call on a subprogram which has not yet been written.

16-7. DATA CONTROL

The first line of a subprogram definition is used to declare the identifiers local to that subprogram, including formal parameters and a result parameter used as a local variable to designate the result returned (if the subprogram is a function). For example, a subprogram definition might begin

$$\nabla \quad R \leftarrow A \ SUB \ B; \ L;M;N$$

This statement identifies the subprogram name as SUB, the formal parameters as A and B, the result parameter as R, and the local variables as L, M, and N. Parameter transmission is always by value, so that A and B are treated identically with L, M, and N during execution, the only difference being that A and B are assigned initial values (the values of the actual parameters) while the initial values of L, M, and N are undefined. The result parameter R also acts as a local variable, except that on termination of execution the value of R is transferred back to the calling program as the value of SUB. Subprograms are restricted to at most two parameters. The result parameter may be omitted if the subprogram returns no value and is not to be used as a function. The formal parameters, result parameter, and local variables make up the local referencing environment of a subprogram.

Global identifiers may be defined in two ways. Subprogram names automatically become global identifiers when a subprogram is defined. Global variables may be defined implicitly by an assignment to an identifier which has not previously been used (or declared as local). Such assignments may be entered directly by the programmer for immediate execution or may occur in subprograms being executed. This structure allows identifiers to be added to the global referencing environment at any time. Identifiers may be deleted from the global environment by the ERASE command. For example,

)ERASE SUB X Y

deletes the identifiers SUB, X, and Y from the global environment (and frees the space taken up by their values, whether arrays or function definitions).

Nonlocal referencing in subprograms is controlled by the most recent association rule, but with a twist. Recall that using the most recent association rule, if the subprogram being executed references identifier X and X is not a local variable, then the association used for X is found by simply searching back down the calling chain to a subprogram having an association for X. This is the basic nonlocal referencing technique in APL. Should there *fail* to be an association for X in the calling chain, however, the search continues back through the subprograms and their calling chains which are in *suspended execution* because of an interrupt. This search is made in the reverse order of suspension, so that the most recently suspended subprogram and its calling chain is searched first, then the next previously suspended subprogram, etc. If no association for X is found in this search (which covers all the local identifiers which have any current association), then the global association for X is used. If X has no global association, then a referencing error is signaled.

APL provides facilities for programmer access to the current referencing environment and subprogram calling chains at any point during execution. The list of subprograms which are in the calling chain of the subprogram currently being executed and of subprograms whose execution has been suspended by an interrupt (and their calling chains) is termed the *state indicator list* and may be printed by executing the command)SI. For example, the state indicator list during execution of the third statement of a subprogram SUB might be

$$SUB[3] \quad *$$
$$Q[5]$$
$$P[17]$$
$$SUB1[3] \quad *$$
$$R[5]$$

The asterisks indicate subprograms interrupted during execution and placed in the suspended state. In this example, SUB was called from the fifth line of subprogram Q, which was called in turn from the seventeenth line of subprogram P, which was called directly by the programmer in an expression entered for immediate execution. Prior to entry of that expression, subprogram SUB1 had been interrupted at line 3 and placed in the suspended state. SUB1 had been called from the fifth line of subprogram R, which was directly invoked by the programmer.

To obtain a complete list of all local identifiers for each subprogram in the state indicator list the command)SIV is executed. The listing then also includes on each line a list of the local identifiers declared in the subprogram header. The programmer thus at any time may interrupt execution of a subprogram and ask for a listing of its referencing environment.

16-8. OPERATING ENVIRONMENT

One of the most elegant aspects of the APL design is its interactive operating environment. A brief overview is given in

Section 8-4. The key components of the APL operating environment are (1) the *programmer* at his terminal; (2) the *active workspace*, which serves as temporary storage for programs and data during a terminal session; and (3) the *workspace* library, which serves as permanent storage for workspaces between sessions. Workspaces and libraries are manipulated through four subsystems of the APL virtual computer: an *active workspace manager*, which manipulates the active workspace; a *library manager*, which provides access to private and public libraries of workspaces; an *editor*, which manipulates individual subprogram definitions within the active workspace; and an *interpreter*, which executes APL programs. The programmer directs these subsystems through various *system commands*, which he enters at his terminal for immediate execution.

A terminal session begins when the APL programmer signs on to an APL terminal. Immediately an active workspace is set up for him, and he is put in contact with his private workspace library through the library manager. The initial active workspace is empty unless the programmer has left a workspace named CONTINUE in his library from a previous session, in which case a copy of this workspace becomes the initial active workspace.

Workspace and Library Structure and Manipulation

The workspace is organized around a table of identifiers, called the *symbol table*. Each identifier in the symbol table is usually the name of either a subprogram, a simple variable, or an array, and in these cases the table entry contains a pointer to the subprogram or data structure which is stored in another part of the workspace. Some identifiers in the symbol table may be *group names*—names for groups of subprogram and variable names. Also some may be identifiers without a current definition, representing, for example, subprograms which have been referenced but not yet defined.

Initially the symbol table of a workspace is empty. The programmer may add entries to the symbol table in a number of ways. Subprogram names are added when the programmer enters the special character ∇ at his terminal, followed by a subprogram definition and a terminating ∇. The body of the subprogram is then stored in the workspace, and the subprogram name is entered into the symbol table with a pointer to the stored body. Similarly, assignment of an array to an identifier causes the array to be stored in the workspace and the identifier to be entered into the symbol table with an associated pointer to the array. Eventually the programmer builds up a collection of subprogram and data structure definitions in his workspace, each accessible through a name in the symbol table. At some point it may be convenient to collect some of these into a *group* so that the collection may be referenced by a single name. This is done using the system command)*GROUP group-name list-of-names*, which enters the *group-name* into the symbol table together with a pointer to the *list-of-names*, which designates the identifiers in the group. Some of these identifiers may not yet have been used, in which case they are entered in the symbol table with a null pointer.

Once having set up these various symbol table entries the programmer may now access the symbol table to obtain listings of the various identifiers using the system commands:

)FNS: gives a list of subprogram names
)VARS: gives a list of variable names
)GRPS: gives a list of group names
)GRP *group name:*   gives a list of the identifiers in the specified group

Any individual subprogram definition or variable value may be listed also. Symbol table entries may be deleted using the command)ERASE *list-of-names*, or the entire symbol table (and thus the entire workspace) may be cleared by the command)CLEAR.

The *workspace library* serves as permanent storage for the workspaces which the programmer constructs. Whenever the programmer wishes to permanently save the contents of the current active workspace he first provides a name for the workspace, using the command)WSID *name*, and then enters a copy into his workspace library using the command)SAVE. A saved workspace may later be retrieved by the command)LOAD *name*, which replaces the current active workspace with a copy of the named workspace from the library. A listing of the names of all library workspaces may be obtained with the command)LIB; deletion of library workspaces is accomplished through)DROP *name*. Selected subprogram definitions or data structures may be copied from a library workspace to the currently active workspace using the command)COPY *wksp-name list-of-names*. These facilities combine to make access to workspace libraries simple. Besides the programmer's *private library* of workspaces, other *public libraries* and the private libraries of other programmers may be accessed through special library numbers.

Entering and Editing Subprogram Definitions

Another component of the operating environment in APL is an *editor*, which the programmer may use to enter or modify subprogram definitions. Note that system commands which communicate with the active workspace or library managers always begin with a). To gain contact with the editor the programmer enters a line beginning with the symbol ∇. His communication is then with the editor until another ∇ is entered. An example of initial subprogram entry and editing is given in Section 16-3.

16-9. SYNTAX AND TRANSLATION

The syntactic structure of APL is the simplest of any language discussed here, with the possible exception of LISP. Each subprogram definition is entirely separate from the others. The only interaction between subprograms comes when one calls another during execution. Each subprogram definition is composed of a simple sequence of lines, each with an attached line number. Each line is composed of a single expression. Each expression is a combination of numbers, character strings, variables, and prefix and infix operators. The entire syntactic structure is so simple and regular that it can be mastered easily even by beginning programmers.

The most problematic feature of the APL syntax is the use of a large set of special characters to represent operators. The APL character set includes the following special characters, many of which must be produced by backspacing the terminal typewriter and overstriking:

$$< \ > \ = \ \neq \ \leq \ \geq \ \vee \ \wedge \ \sim \ \barwedge \ \veebar \ + \ - \ \times \ \div \ * \ ? \ \in$$
$$\uparrow \ \iota \ \phi \ \circledast \ \lceil \ \bar{\nabla} \ ! \ \perp \ | \ / \ . \ \circ \ \circ \ \boxminus \ \rho \ \downarrow \ \llcorner \ \mⴰ$$
$$[\ ] \ (\ ) \ \top \ \bot \ , \ \backslash \ \Box \ \boxed{|} \ ' \ \leftarrow \ \rightarrow \ \mⴰ \ \nabla \ \Delta \ ; \ :$$

The special characters for operators have an obvious advantage: Programs are shorter because fewer characters need be used. However, they have what is probably a more serious disadvantage: Programs are so compact that they are difficult to read. This extreme conciseness is a particular problem because of the power of the individual operations, which allow rather large computations to often be compressed into a single expression. For example, an expression such as (from a program by Greiner [1972] in the APL newsletter *Quote-Quad*)

$$\rightarrow \times \ \rho,M[\times\rho M;] \ \leftarrow D \times \ M[\times\rho M \leftarrow 1 \ 1 \ \downarrow M\text{-}M[;1]^\circ.\times M[1;1] \div D\leftarrow 1\rho M;]$$

may take many minutes, or even hours, to decode. Programming languages specialist Daniel McCracken [1970] notes that it once took him *four hours* to decode a *four-line* APL program.

Related to the overly concise expression syntax is the almost total lack of redundancy in APL expressions. Each operator symbol usually represents not just one powerful operation but two, one when used as a prefix operator with one operand and a different one when used as an infix operator with two operands. For example, X ÷ Y represents division, but ÷Y alone represents the reciprocal. When ar. expression is input the omission of an operand like the X in the first expression above results in another expression which looks very similar to the correct one. Unfortunately the incorrect expression is probably still executable, but it computes something quite different from the intended result. Such errors are difficult to track down in a complex expression.

Translation

The usual APL implementation executes APL programs with a software interpreter. Only a trivial translation of each program line into an internal form is made when a program line is input. These translated lines are then stored as the executable program form to be interpreted by the software interpreter. During the translation to internal form numbers are converted into their hardware representation (with descriptor attached), identifiers are converted into pointers to symbol table entries, and operator symbols are left as character codes. This trivial translation makes reconversion of the program to its original input form easy. Since this reconversion must be done frequently, e.g., for listings, editing, and error messages, simple reconversion is of value. Also since APL programs tend to be relatively short, the cost of line-by-line software interpretation, while high, is not so expensive as might otherwise be the case.

16-10. STRUCTURE OF AN APL VIRTUAL COMPUTER

A typical APL implementation is structured around two memory areas: an active workspace area and an APL system area. The *system area* contains the programs which simulate the APL virtual computer and cannot be modified by the programmer. The system area is usually shared by all the APL programmers who are using APL at any one time—each may use the various routines in the system area. The system area also contains the monitor which supervises interactions with the various APL terminals. Each APL programmer who is at a terminal also has an *active workspace* area which contains his private programs, data, and system-defined status indicators and data items.

The active workspace may be viewed as organized into four major parts, as shown in Fig. 16-2. The contents of these parts are

1. *Programmer data area.* This heap storage area contains definitions of programmer-defined subprograms and programmer-created data structures (arrays). Space is used beginning at the bottom of the heap block and is allocated toward the middle as needed. No free space list is maintained as storage is freed. Instead a garbage collection and compaction is initiated when all available storage has been exhausted.

2. *Global referencing environment table.* This area is of fixed size (typically 256 table entries) and contains one entry for each identifier which the programmer uses at his terminal which is not a local variable in a subprogram. Entries are made as the programmer introduces new identifiers in expressions entered at his terminal.

3. *Subprogram activation record stack.* A stack of subprogram activation records is maintained during subprogram execution. Subprograms may be recursive, so the stack is allowed to grow as necessary. The stack is allocated sequentially and maintained at the opposite end of the heap block from the programmer data area. The stack and programmer data area grow toward each other, with garbage collection and compaction of the programmer data area taking place when the two areas meet.

4. *System-defined data area.* A small statically allocated area is reserved for special system data items. Some, such as the length of a print line and the number of significant digits printed for numbers, may be modified by the programmer; others represent hidden system status indicators and the like.

The APL virtual computer is almost entirely software-simulated. The key simulation routines, which reside in the system area, are (1) the *expression interpreter*, which decodes and executes single APL expressions when entered directly by the programmer, or when called by (2) the *subprogram interpreter*, which executes APL subprograms, setting up activation records, calling the expression interpreter to execute each line of the subprogram as appropriate, and deleting activation records; (3) the *primitive operations*, each of

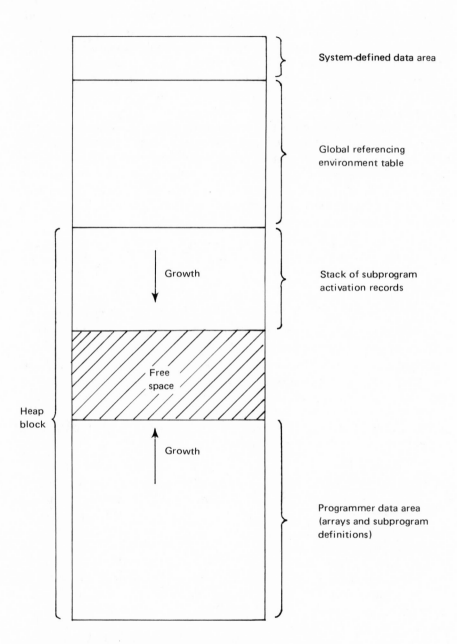

Fig. 16-2. Organization of an APL active work space.

which is simulated by a routine in the system area; and (4) the *storage manager*, which manages allocation, recovery, and compaction in the heap storage area and also allocation and recovery in the symbol table and stack.

Data representations for arrays, numbers, and characters are based on hardware representations. Arrays, in particular, are stored sequentially in a block of memory. However, all APL data must carry a run-time descriptor because no data properties are fixed by declarations. Thus numbers and characters must be tagged as to data type, and arrays must be accompanied by *dope vectors* giving number of dimensions, type, subscript bounds, etc.

16-11. REFERENCES AND SUGGESTIONS FOR FURTHER READING

The original definition of APL is found in Iverson [1962]. Pakin [1972] describes the implemented version of APL on the IBM 360. A number of introductory texts on the language also exist. Harrison [1973] discusses APL and a related language SETL. A useful concise overview of the language is provided by Falkoff and Iverson [1968].

Breed and Lathwell [1968] provide an overview of the APL\360 implementation. A firmware realization of APL on a microprogrammed computer is described by Hassitt et al. [1973]. The APL newsletter *Quote-Quad*, which appears periodically in *SIGPLAN Notices*, provides information on current issues in APL design, implementation, and application.

16-12. PROBLEMS

16-1. Right-to-left associativity (with all operators of equal precedence) is the usual evaluation rule when Polish prefix notation is used in expressions, but it is quite surprising to find it coupled with *infix* operators in APL. Give two advantages and two disadvantages of the use of this expression evaluation rule in APL.

16-2. Give a BNF grammar for APL statements, using the basic syntactic categories ⟨infix operator⟩, ⟨prefix operator⟩, ⟨identifier⟩, and ⟨number⟩. There are only two classes of APL statements, a ⟨GOTO statement⟩ and a ⟨simple statement⟩ (actually just an ⟨expression⟩).

17 EPILOGUE: THE TURING LANGUAGE AND LANGUAGE UNIVERSALITY

Before leaving this survey of programming languages one last question might be posed. The languages described in this part differ radically among themselves in almost every aspect: data structures, primitives, control structures, etc. Yet clearly there are many problems whose solution could be coded in any one of them, and other problems which could not be coded easily in any of them. Had we expanded our survey to include 10, or 100, other languages, nothing would really be different. Some new language structures would appear, but at some point we would certainly stop to ask the question: What more can be done with this new language that cannot be done without it? Is there any real increase in the power to solve problems from the introduction of another programming language?

A FORTRAN programmer of my acquaintance was somewhat more direct when he asked, Why should I spend the time and energy to learn another programming language—I can do anything I want in FORTRAN! In a sense he was entirely right—FORTRAN is a *universal language*. Any algorithm which can be coded in any programming language has an equivalent in FORTRAN. The concept of universal language and its relation to programming languages is the subject of this chapter.

17-1. UNIVERSAL LANGUAGES

A more precise definition of universal language may be made as follows. Consider that any program, regardless of the language, is a

500

function mapping an input character string into an output character string. The input to the program must always be written down in order to be input. And when written it may be considered as a character string, because even if we think of it as a sequence of numbers, or bits, or as a set of separate inputs, the numbers are strings of digits, the bits are the characters 0 and 1, and the separate inputs may be considered as pieces of one long input string. The output of a program similarly may be considered as a single character string, because an output listing necessarily takes such a form. Thus, although we may not ordinarily view a program as a mapping from a set of input character strings to a set of output character strings, it certainly is possible to do so.

Given this simplistic view, a *program* is any precise specification of a procedure for mapping one set of input character strings into another set of output character strings. Two programs are *equivalent* if they define the same mapping from input character strings to output character strings. Finally a programming language is *universal* if for any given program an equivalent program may be written in the language. Note that two equivalent programs need not operate in a similar manner so long as they both produce the same output for the same input. Simply stated, in a universal language we can always find some way to write a program to perform any desired computation.

In considering whether a language is universal we want to ignore minor questions such as output formatting. More importantly we assume no limits on data storage space, program length, or execution time. Obviously no language implemented on a particular actual computer with a fixed memory size (and without unlimited external storage) could be universal, because there will always be some computations which take more memory space than is available (or could be provided) or which take longer than the physical lifetime of the computer itself to run, etc. Thus our concept of universal language is an abstract one—language X is universal because we could code and execute any computation in it that we wished, given enough space and time.

17-2.   TURING MACHINES AND THE TURING LANGUAGE

Before answering the question of whether the languages described in this book are universal, let us look more closely at the amount of *machinery* necessary to achieve universality. Clearly some languages are not universal, for example, the "programming language" of inputs to a desk calculator, and others, such as FORTRAN, are universal. Where is the dividing line?

Surprisingly this question was posed, and answered, before the advent of computers, although not in exactly this form. The question originally was: How much machinery is necessary to be able to compute anything which is computable? *Computable* here means computable by some precisely specified algorithm. A number of answers were given to this question in the 1930s and 1940s by proposing simple abstract computers or programming languages which seemed to suffice. Later most of these languages and computers were proved equivalent in the sense that anything computable with one could also be computed with any of the others. Of course there can never be any *proof* of the universality of a language in an absolute sense, because the meaning of *universal* can be made precise only by defining some other language or computer which we believe to be universal, and then proving that anything computable in the new language was also computable in the old.

A very simple universal language may be constructed around the classical *Turing machine*, a simple abstract computer defined by A. M. Turing in 1936. A Turing machine has only a single data structure—a variable-length linear array T called the *tape*. Each element of the tape always contains a single character. There also exists a simple variable H, called the *read head*, which always contains a pointer to some element of T. This pointer may be represented by an integer subscript, and thus H may be considered a simple integer variable. This structure is illustrated in Fig. 17-1.

The Turing machine can only perform a few simple operations:

1. It can access the value of T[H], compare the value against some known character, and branch depending on whether the characters are the same or not.

2. It can assign a new character as the value of T[H].

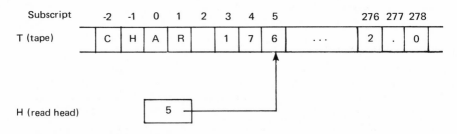

Fig. 17-1. Turing machine data structures.

3. It can increase or decrease the value of H by 1, causing the subscript to advance to point to the next tape element or to back up to the preceding one. Should this operation advance H so that it points beyond the end of the tape at either end, then the tape is extended in that direction by the addition of a new element containing the special character #. The subscript of this new element, of course, is that of the current value of H.

4. It can halt.

These basic operations are combined into simple programs as follows. Each program begins with a single READ statement which reads in an input character string of some arbitrary length, n. The vector T of the same length is created and the input string stored in $T[1]$ through $T[n]$. The variable H is also initialized to the value 1. The main part of the program now begins, consisting of a sequence of operations in which the tape vector T is scanned, extended, and modified, using the read head H as the only point of access. When execution is complete the program ends with a single WRITE operation, which prints out the final contents of the tape T as a character string.

It is convenient to have a syntax for the Turing language so that we may write programs in it. Let us assume that the character set consists of the letters, digits, and the usual special characters, e.g. $(,), =, +, -, *,$ (the exact set makes no difference). Programs have the fixed form

READ

.

.

.

sequence of statements

.

.

.

WRITE.

Statements must be one of the following:

1. IF T[H] = ⟨*character*⟩ GO TO ⟨*label*⟩, where ⟨*character*⟩ is any single character in the character set and ⟨*label*⟩ is some statement label.

2. T[H] := ⟨*character*⟩.

3. H := H+1.

4. H := H-1.

5. GO TO ⟨label⟩.

Statements (other than READ) may be labeled by writing *label:* preceding the statement. Execution terminates when the WRITE statement is reached.

Let us try a simple example program. Because the Turing language is such a low-level language, we must pick a really trivial problem. A good one would be the following: Write a Turing language program to add 1 to a positive binary integer. The READ operation beginning the program reads into T a string of 0s and 1s, and the read head H is initialized to 1, which means it is pointing to the leftmost digit of the input number. The algorithm to be coded is the obvious: Scan down T to the rightmost digit, add 1, and then propagate the carry to the left as necessary. The program is

```
            READ
LOOP:       H := H+1              find right end of tape T
            IF T[H] = "#" GO TO KICK
            GO TO LOOP
KICK:       H := H-1
            IF T[H] = "1" GO TO CARRY    no carry required
            T[H] := "1"
            GO TO END
CARRY:      T[H] := "0"
            GO TO KICK            carry required
END:        WRITE.
```

A program to add two binary numbers is a little more complicated. Assume that the input numbers are separated by a +. The *beginning* of a program which writes the answer to the *left* of the input numbers, followed by an =, is the following:

```
            READ
            H := H-1              put = at left end of
                                  tape
            T[H] := "="
            H := H-1              initialize carry bit to 0
            T[H] := "0"

LOOP1:      H := H+1
            IF T[H] = "+" GO TO L-NUM     find rightmost digit of
            GO TO LOOP1           first number
```

L-NUM:	H := H−1	
	IF T[H] = "=" GO TO L-DONE	no unprocessed digits left in first number
	IF T[H] = "1" GO TO L-ONE	rightmost unprocessed digit is a 1
	T[H] := "+"	replace zero by + to indicate processed digit
LOOP2:	H := H+1	
	IF T[H] = "+" GO TO LOOP2	begin search for digit of second number, skip over +s
	IF T[H] = "#" GO TO R-DONE	no unprocessed digits in second number
LOOP3:	H := H+1	
	IF T[H] = "+" GO TO R-NUM	find rightmost unprocessed digit in second number
	IF T[H] = "#" GO TO R-NUM	
	GO TO LOOP3	
R-NUM:	H := H−,1	
	IF T[H] = "1" GO TO SUM01	
SUM00:	T[H] := "+"	if execution reaches this point, the digits to be added are both zero
LOOP4:	H := H−1;	
	IF T[H] = "#" GO TO CARRY00	find left end of tape
	GO TO LOOP4	
CARRY00:	T[H] := 0	write 0 as new carry bit, leave old carry bit in place, and loop to begin new cycle
	GO TO LOOP1	
	.	
	.	
	.	

The program continues with code for the cases where the digits to be added are 0-1, 1-0, 1-1, and in each case there are two subcases depending on the value of the carry bit. The terminating cases must also be coded. The program is complex in part because we do not have any handy temporary storage for the digits; instead digits must be "remembered" by using program branching—for example, if execution reaches statement SUM00, then the two digits to be added must be both zeros.

The problem of addition of two binary numbers is rather simple. If the Turing language is truly universal, then it must be possible to code any program in it, including such things as a FORTRAN compiler, the SNOBOL4 interpreter and pattern matcher, and a generalized matrix inversion program. Is it really possible to code such complex algorithms in the Turing language?

Coding a complex program in the Turing language would be terribly painful. A program for even the simple calculation of the first N primes (done in *seven* APL statements) would easily run to thousands or tens of thousands of statements, judging from the fact that addition of two binary numbers takes 50 to 100 statements. Rather than writing such a program out, however, you want to convince yourself that it *could* be done in this simple language without actually doing it.

Consider the problem of computing the first N primes by a program in the Turing language. Assume that the READ statement reads in a decimal integer N and stores it one digit per element in T. The final contents of T should be the first N primes, in sequence, separated by blanks, and stored one digit per element in T. In coding this program one central problem is storage. The Turing language provides no data structures except the tape T. Thus in computing the primes not only does T contain the input at the beginning and the output at the end, but it must also serve as temporary storage during each step of the calculation. Essentially we treat various segments of the tape as separate variables or data structures, always being careful to delimit the different segments by a special character (e.g., $). Once we have the tape organized for temporary storage the remainder of the program is straightforward but extremely laborious to write. For example, we will need to perform an integer division, but since the Turing language has no arithmetic operations we must write a program segment for division. This program segment must first cause the read head to run down to the segment of the tape containing the proper digit of the numerator, remember it by branching to an appropriate code segment, move the read head to the proper digit of the denominator, remember it, move the read head to the segment of the tape in which the quotient is being stored, write a digit of the quotient there, etc.

The program organization required is extremely complex. Most of execution is spent running the read head back and forth on the tape, copying information, writing new data down, or reading old stored data. Large amounts of branching are necessary to "remember" the data during these traversals of the tape. For example to remember one decimal digit in order to transfer it to another part of the tape requires a ten-way branch and ten separate program segments, each of which does approximately the same thing.

We shall not continue further with this rather ridiculous program. No one would want to write such a program. The point here is just to show that it could be done, even with these most trivial operations and control structures—provided that there are no restrictions on length of the tape vector T, on length of the program, or on execution time. We can always find *some way* to represent the data as characters in vector T and the algorithm in terms of a sequence of the primitive Turing operations, so that an appropriate Turing language program can be written.

If you can accept this leap from the Turing language program which adds two numbers to the Turing language program which computes the first N primes, then it is not much further to the argument which we really wish to make: *The Turing language is universal.* That is, given any algorithm to be coded, we can always find some way, no matter how grotesque, to code that algorithm in the Turing language, given enough time and space. Of course there is no way to prove this; we can only argue as we did above—showing roughly how some complex algorithm might be coded and leaving it to your intuition as to how this might be extended to other cases. Suffice it to say that the hypothesis of the universality of the Turing language has been considered in great depth by many mathematicians and programmers and has been generally accepted.

Any program can be coded in the Turing language. In other words we really have no essential need for FORTRAN, ALGOL, LISP, PL/I, or any of the other programming languages in existence, because (paraphrasing the FORTRAN programmer mentioned earlier) "we can do anything we want in the Turing language." And we might even go further and argue that the Turing language is very nice because it can be so efficiently compiled into simple machine code on almost any computer (except for the growing vector T, which may require some software storage management to store the vector on external storage as it grows too large to fit in main memory). Regardless, both translation and execution of Turing language programs can be made very efficient without great difficulty.

17-3. THE DIFFERENCES AMONG PROGRAMMING LANGUAGES

Having accepted the universality of the Turing language, should we now move to use this simple, easy-to-learn, and "efficient" language for all our programming? Clearly not. In fact the problem with the Turing language is that while any program can be written in it, no program can be written *easily* in it. The simplest algorithms require lengthy Turing language programs, and any algorithm of even a modicum of complexity cannot be coded without writing a program which is completely unmanageable in size and structure. The Turing language is clearly not the answer to our programming difficulties.

The central fact that the Turing language illustrates is this: *It takes almost no machinery to achieve universality, other than some sort of unlimited storage capacity.* Many other simple universal languages and machines are known which illustrate this fact as well. For example the *pure LISP* subset of LISP mentioned in Chapter 14 is universal. Another example is a *two-counter* language, a language which provides only two simple integer variables and operations which add 1, subtract 1, and test for zero on the values of these variables. The book *Computation: Finite and Infinite Machines* by Marvin Minsky [1967] gives many other examples of simple universal abstract machines and languages.

All this leads back to the comment of the programmer who felt that FORTRAN was all he needed because he "could do anything in FORTRAN." He was right, of course, because FORTRAN clearly supplies far more than the minimum necessary to achieve universality. But the argument is really no argument at all, because every programming language which anyone would want to suggest using is universal if bounds on time and memory are ignored. The differences among programming languages are not quantitative differences in what can be done but only qualitative differences in how elegantly, easily, and effectively things can be done.

All programming languages are equivalent in what might be termed "raw problem-solving power," because of their universality, and we are left to consider more subtle differences, differences in "effective problem-solving power." These comparisons must necessarily be made in the context of particular problems or classes of problems. LISP is preferable to ALGOL for a class of problems which involve symbolic data and data structures which grow and shrink dynamically and irregularly; APL is preferable to FORTRAN for a class of problems which involve common types of numeric array manipulation; FORTRAN is preferable to ALGOL for another class of problems, etc. We have come full circle back to the same questions with which we were confronted in Chapter 1. What makes a good language? Clarity of semantic and syntactic structure, natural representations for problem data and algorithms, ease of extension, and efficiency are all important. And the appropriateness of a given language must always be thought through anew with each new problem. The programmer's task remains that of finding the most appropriate language for a given problem and then extending it until his problem is naturally and effectively coded.

17-4. REFERENCES AND SUGGESTIONS FOR FURTHER READING

This chapter has only touched on one of the many fascinating results of the study of simple abstract languages and machines. These *automata*, as they are usually termed, are discussed in a number of books, e.g., Minsky [1967] and Arbib [1969].

17-5. PROBLEM

17.1. Code the following in the Turing language:
  a. A program to add 1 to any input decimal number.
  b. A program to add two numbers in unary notation (where the number k is represented by a sequence of k 1s). The numbers are input separated by a +.
  c. A program which copies its input. The output should be the input and its copy, separated by a $. Assume that the input contains only the letters a, b, and c.
  d. A program which searches an input string for a given substring. The input consists of the string to be searched followed by the substring, separated by $. The output should be the string "yes" or "no", depending on the result of the search.

REFERENCES

ACM [1964] "FORTRAN vs. Basic FORTRAN," *Comm. ACM*, 7, 10, 591—625.

[1972] "Proceedings ACM Conference on Proving Assertions About Programs," *SIGPLAN Notices*, 7, 1 and *SIGACT News*, No. 14.

AHO, A., and J. ULLMAN [1972] *The Theory of Parsing, Translation and Compiling*, Prentice-Hall, Englewood Cliffs, N. J.

ANSI [1966] *American National Standard FORTRAN (ANS X3.9—1966)*, American National Standards Institute, New York.

[1968] *American National Standard COBOL (ANS X3.23—1968)*, American National Standards Institute, New York.

[1971] "Clarification of FORTRAN standards—second report," *Comm. ACM*, 14, 10, 628—642.

[1972] *Draft Proposed Revised X3.23 American National Standard Specifications for COBOL*, American National Standards Institute, New York.

ARBIB, M. [1969] *Theories of Abstract Automata*, Prentice-Hall, Englewood Cliffs, N. J.

ASA [1963] "Suggestions on ALGOL 60 (Rome) Issues," *Comm. ACM*, 6, 1, 20—23.

BACKUS, J. [1960] "The Syntax and Semantics of the Proposed International Algebraic Language of the Zurich ACM-GAMM Conference," *Information Processing*, UNESCO, Paris, 125—132.

BACKUS, J., et al. [1957] "The FORTRAN Automatic Coding System," *Proc. Western Jt. Comp. Conf.*, AIEE (now IEEE), Los Angeles, 188—198. Reprinted in Rosen [1967].

BAECKER, H. [1972] "Garbage Collection for Virtual Memory Computer Systems," *Comm. ACM*, 15, 11, 981—986.

BANDAT, K. [1968] "On the Formal Definition of PL/I," *Proc. Spring Jt. Comp. Conf.*, Thompson, Wash. D. C., 363—373.

BARRON, D. [1968] *Recursive Techniques in Programming*, American Elsevier, New York.

[1969] *Assemblers and Loaders*, American Elsevier, New York.

BEECH, D. [1970] "A Structural View of PL/I," *Computing Surveys*, 2, 1, 33—64.

BELL, C. G., and A. NEWELL [1971] *Computer Structures: Readings and Examples*, McGraw-Hill, New York.

BEMER, R. [1969] "A Politico-Social History of ALGOL," *Ann. Rev. Auto. Prog.*, 5, 151—231.

BERKELEY, E., and D. BOBROW (eds.). [1964] *The Programming Language LISP: Its Operation and Applications*, M.I.T. Press, Cambridge, Mass.

BERZTISS, A. [1971] *Data Structures: Theory and Practice*, Academic Press, New York.

BOBROW, D. [1972] "Requirements for Advanced Programming Systems for List Processing," *Comm. ACM*, 15, 7, 618—627.

BOBROW, D., and D. MURPHY [1967] "Structure of a LISP System Using Two-level Storage," *Comm. ACM*, 10, 3, 155—159.

BOBROW, D., and B. WEGBREIT [1973] "A Model and Stack Implementation of Multiple Environments," *Comm. Acm*, 16, 10, 591—602.

BOYLE, J. and A. GRAU [1970] , "An Algorithmic Semantics for ALGOL 60 Identifier Declaration," *J. ACM*, 17, 2, 361—382.

BRANQUART, P., J. LEWI, M. SINTZOFF, and P. WODON [1971] "The Composition of Semantics in ALGOL 68," *Comm. ACM*, 14, 11, 697—708.

BREED, L., and R. LATHWELL [1968] "The implementation of APL\360." In Klerer and Reinfelds [1968].

BROWN, P. [1969] "A Survey of Macro Processors,"*Ann. Rev. Auto. Prog.*, 6, 2, 37—88.

BURKHARDT, W. [1965] "Metalanguage and Syntax Specification," *Comm. ACM*, 8, 5, 304—305.

CHEATHAM, T. [1971] "The Recent Evolution of Programming Languages," *Proc. IFIP Cong. 1971*, C. V. Freiman, (ed.), North-Holland, Amsterdam, 118—134.

CHESLEY, G., and W. SMITH [1971] "The Hardware-Implemented High-Level Machine Language for SYMBOL," *Proc. AFIPS 1971 SJCC* Vol. 39, AFIPS Press, Montvale, N. J., 563—573 (and related papers in the same volume).

CHOMSKY, N. [1959] "On Certain Formal Properties of Grammars," *Info. Control*, 2, 137—167.

CONWAY, M. [1963] "Design of a Separable Transition-Diagram Compiler," *Comm. ACM* 6, 7, 396—408.

CONWAY, R., and T. WILCOX [1973] "Design and Implementation of a Diagnostic Compiler for PL/I," *Comm. ACM*, 16, 3, 169—179.

DAHL, O. [1968] "Discrete Event Simulation Languages." In Genuys [1968], 349—395.

DAHL, O., and C. A. R. HOARE [1972] "Hierarchical Program Structures." In Dahl et al. [1972], 175—220.

DAHL, O., and K. NYGAARD [1966] "SIMULA—an ALGOL-Based Simulation Language," *Comm. ACM*, 9, 9, 671—678.

DAHL, O., E. DIJKSTRA, and C. A. R. HOARE [1972] *Structured Programming*, Academic Press, New York.

DAVIES, P. [1972] "Readings in Microprogramming," *IBM Syst. J.*, 11, 1, 16—40.

de BAKKER, J. [1969] "Semantics of Programming Languages," *Advan. Info. Systems Science* Vol. 2, J. T. Tou (ed.), Plenum, New York, 173—227.

DENNING, P. [1970] "Virtual memory," *Computing Surveys*, 2, 3, 153—190.

[1971] "Third Generation Computer Systems," *Computing Surveys*, 3, 4, 175—216.

DEWAR, R. [1971] "SPITBOL Version 2.0," *SNOBOL4 Project Rept. S4D23*, Illinois Institute of Technology, Chicago.

DIJKSTRA, E. [1968a] "Go to Statement Considered Harmful," *Comm. ACM*, 11, 3, 147—148.

[1968b] "Co-operating Sequential Processes." In Genuys [1968], 43—112.

[1972a] "Notes on Structured Programming." In Dahl et al. [1972], 1—82.

[1972b] "The Humble Programmer," *Comm. ACM*, 15, 10, 859—866.

D'IMPERIO, M. [1969] "Data Structures and Their Representation in Storage," *Ann. Rev. Auto. Prog.*, 5, 1—75.

DONOVAN, J. [1972] *Systems Programming*, McGraw-Hill, New York.

ELSON, M. [1973] *Concepts of Programming Languages*, Science Research Associates, Chicago.

ENGELER, E. (ed.) [1971] *Symposium on Semantics of Algorithmic Languages*, Springer, Berlin.

FALKOFF, A., and K. IVERSON [1968] "The APL\360 Terminal System." In Klerer and Reinfelds [1968].

FALKOFF, A., K. IVERSON, and E. SUSSENGUTH [1964] "A Formal Description of SYSTEM/360," *IBM Syst. J.*, 3, 3, 198–263.

FELDMAN, J., and D. GRIES [1968] "Translator Writing Systems," *Comm. ACM*, 11, 2, 77–113.

FEUSTAL, E. [1973] "On the Advantages of Tagged Architecture," *IEEE Trans. Comps.*, C-22, 7, 644–656.

FISHER, D. [1972] "A Survey of Control Structures in Programming Languages." In Leavenworth [1972].

FLOYD, R. [1967] "Nondeterministic Algorithms," *J. ACM*, 14, 4, 636–644.

FOSTER, J. [1967] *List Processing*, American Elsevier, New York.

FREIBURGHOUSE, R. [1969] "The Multics PL/I Compiler," *Proc. AFIPS Fall Jt. Comp. Conf.*, 35, 187–199.

FRIEDMAN, D. [1974] *The Little Lisper*, Science Research Associates, Chicago.

GALLER, B. and A. PERLIS [1970] *A View of Programming Languages*, Addison-Wesley, Reading, Mass.

GENUYS, F. (ed.) [1968] *Programming Languages*, Academic Press, New York.

GIMPEL, J. [1973] "A Theory of Discrete Patterns and Their Implementation in SNOBOL4," *Comm. ACM*, 16, 2, 91–100.

GRAU, A., U. HILL, and H. LANGMAACK [1967] *Translation of ALGOL 60*, Springer-Verlag, New York, Inc., New York.

GREINER, W. [1972] "Algorithm 81: Determinant," *Quote-Quad*, III, 4, in *SIGPLAN Notices*, 7, 4, 33.

GRIES, D. [1971] *Compiler Construction for Digital Computers*, Wiley, New York.

GRISWOLD, R. [1972] *The Macro Implementation of SNOBOL4*, W. H. Freeman, San Francisco.

GRISWOLD, R., and M. GRISWOLD [1973] *A SNOBOL4 Primer*, Prentice-Hall, Englewood Cliffs, N. J.

GRISWOLD, R., J. POAGE, and I. POLONSKY [1971] *The SNOBOL4 Programming Language*, 2nd ed., Prentice-Hall, Englewood Cliffs, N. J.

HANSEN, W. [1969] "Compact List Representation: Definition, Garbage Collection and System Implementation," *Comm. ACM*, 12, 9, 499—507.

HARRISON, M. [1973] *Data Structures and Programming*, Scott, Foresman, Glenview, Ill.

HASSITT, A., J. LAGESCHULTE, and L. LYON [1973] "Implementation of a High Level Language Machine," *Comm. ACM*, 16, 4, 199—212.

HETZEL, W. (ed.) [1973] *Program Test Methods*, Prentice-Hall, Englewood Cliffs, N. J.

HIGMAN, B. [1967] *A Comparative Study of Programming Languages*, American Elsevier, New York.

HOARE, C. A. R. [1968] "Record Handling." In Genuys [1968], 291—348.

[1972] "Notes on Data Structuring." In Dahl et al. [1972], 83—174.

HOPGOOD, F. R. A. [1969] *Compiling Techniques*, American Elsevier, New York.

HUSSON, S. [1970] *Microprogramming Principles and Practices*, Prentice-Hall, Englewood Cliffs, N. J.

IFIP [1964] "Report on Input-Output Procedures for ALGOL 60," *Comm. ACM*, 7, 10, 628—630.

INGERMAN, P. [1961] "Thunks," *Comm. ACM*, 4, 1, 55—58.

IVERSON, K. [1962] *A Programming Language*, Wiley, New York.

JOHNSTON, J. [1971] "The Contour Model of Block Structured Processes." In Tou and Wegner [1971], 55—82.

KIVIAT, P., R. VILLANUEVA, and H. MARKOWITZ [1969] *The SIMSCRIPT II Programming Language*, Prentice-Hall, Englewood Cliffs, N. J.

KLERER, M., and J. REINFELDS [1968] *Interactive Systems for Experimental Applied Mathematics*, Academic Press, New York.

KNUTH, D. [1967] "The Remaining Trouble Spots in ALGOL 60," *Comm. ACM*, 10, 10, 611—617.

[1968] *The Art of Computer Programming*, Vol. 1: Fundamental Algorithms, Addison-Wesley, Reading, Mass.

[1969] *The Art of Computer Programming*, Vol. 2: Seminumerical Algorithms, Addison-Wesley, Reading, Mass.

[1973] *The Art of Computer Programming*, Vol. 3: Sorting and Searching, Addison-Wesley, Reading, Mass.

KNUTH, D., and R. FLOYD [1971] "Notes on Avoiding Go To Statements," *Info. Proc. Letters*, 1, 1, 23—32.

KNUTH, D. and J. MCNELEY [1964] "SOL—A Symbolic Language for General Purpose Systems Simulation," *IEEE Trans. Elec. Computers*, Aug., 401—408.

KNUTH, D., et al. [1964] "A Proposal for Input-Output Conventions in ALGOL 60," *Comm. ACM*, 7, 5, 273—283.

LAWSON, H. [1967] "PL/I List Processing," *Comm. ACM*, 10, 6, 358—367.

LEAVENWORTH, B. (ed.) [1972] *SIGPLAN Notices—Control Structures in Programming Languages*, 7, 11.

LEDGARD, H. [1971] "Ten Mini-Languages: A Study of Topical Issues in Programming Languages," *Computing Surveys*, 3, 3, 115—146.

LEE, J. [1972] *Computer Semantics*, Van Nostrand Reinhold, New York.

LINDSEY, C., and S. VAN DER MEULEN [1971] *Informal Introduction to ALGOL 68*, North-Holland, Amsterdam.

LUCAS, P., and K. WALK [1969] "On the Formal Description of PL/I," *Ann. Rev. Auto. Prog.*, 6, 3, 105—182.

MAISEL, H., and G. GNUGNOLI [1972] *Simulation of Discrete Stochastic Systems*, Science Research Associates, Chicago.

McCARTHY, J., et al. [1965] *LISP 1.5 Programmer's Manual*, 2nd ed., M.I.T. Press, Cambridge, Mass.

McCLURE, R. [1972] "An Appraisal of Compiler Technology," *AFIPS Spring Jt. Comp. Conf.*, 40, 1—9.

McCRACKEN, D. [1970] "Whither APL;" *Datamation*, Sept. 15, 53—57.

McKEEMAN, W., J. HORNING, and D. WORTMAN [1970] *A Compiler Generator*, Prentice-Hall, Englewood Cliffs, N. J.

MINSKY, M. [1967] *Computation: Finite and Infinite Machines*, Prentice-Hall, Englewood Cliffs, N. J.

(ed.) [1968] *Semantic Information Processing*, M.I.T. Press, Cambridge, Mass.

MOSES, J. [1970] "The Function of FUNCTION in LISP," *SIGSAM Bull.*, July, 13—27.

NAUR, P. (ed.) [1963] "Revised Report on the Algorithmic Language ALGOL 60," *Comm. ACM*, 6, 1, 1—17.

NEWELL, A. (ed.) [1964] *Information Processing Language V Manual*, Prentice-Hall, Englewood Cliffs, N. J.

ORGANICK, E., and J. CLEARY [1971] "A Data Structure Model of the B6700 Computer System." In Tou and Wegner [1971], 83—145.

PAKIN, S. [1972] *APL\360 Reference Manual*, 2nd ed., Science Research Associates, Chicago.

PETERSON, W., T. KASAMI, and N. TOKURA [1973] "On the Capabilities of While, Repeat and Exit Statements," *Comm. ACM*, 16, 8, 503—512.

PRENNER, C., J. SPITZEN, and B. WEGBREIT [1972] "An Implementation of Backtracking for Programming Languages." In Leavenworth [1972].

PRESSER, L., and J. WHITE [1972] "Linkers and Loaders," *Computing Surveys*, 4, 3, 149—168.

RANDELL, B., and L. RUSSELL [1964] *ALGOL 60 Implementation*, Academic Press, New York.

REYNOLDS, J. [1970] "GEDANKEN—A Simple Typeless Language Based on the Principle of Completeness and the Reference Concept," *Comm. ACM*, 13, 5, 308—319.

ROSEN, S. [1967] *Programming Systems and Languages*, McGraw-Hill, New York.

   [1972] "Programming Systems and Languages 1965—1975," *Comm. ACM*, 15, 7, 591—600.

ROSIN, R. [1969] "Contemporary Concepts of Microprogramming and Emulation," *Computing Surveys*, 1, 4, 197—212.

ROSS, D. [1967] "The AED Free Storage Package," *Comm. ACM*, 10, 8, 481—491.

RUSTIN, R. (ed.) [1972a] *Design and Optimization of Compilers*, Prentice-Hall, Englewood Cliffs, N. J.

   (ed.) [1972b] *Formal Semantics of Programming Languages*, Prentice-Hall, Englewood Cliffs, N. J.

RUTISHAUSER, H. [1967] *Description of ALGOL 60*, Springer-Verlag, New York, Inc., New York.

SAMMET, J. [1969] *Programming Languages: History and Fundamentals*, Prentice-Hall, Englewood Cliffs, N. J.

   [1972] "Programming Languages: History and Future," *Comm. ACM*, 15, 7, 601—610.

SAYRE, D. [1969] "Is Automatic Folding of Programs Efficient Enough to Displace Manual?" *Comm. ACM*, 12, 12, 656—660.

SCHAEFER, M. [1973] *Mathematical Theory of Global Code Optimization*, Prentice-Hall, Englewood Cliffs, N. J.

SCHORR, H., and W. WAITE [1967] "An Efficient Machine Independent Procedure for Garbage Collection in Various List Structures," *Comm. ACM*, 10, 8, 501–506.

SCHUMAN, S. (ed.) [1971] *SIGPLAN Notices—Proc. Inter. Symp. Extensible Languages*, 6, 12.

SILBERG, B. (ed.) [1971] *SIGPLAN Notices—Special Issue on Decision Tables*, 6, 8.

STANDISH, T. [1967] A Data Definition Facility for Programming Languages," Ph.D. Thesis, Carnegie-Mellon University, Pittsburgh.

STONE, H. [1972] *Introduction to Computer Organization and Data Structures*, McGraw-Hill, New York.

TEITELMAN, W. [1969] "Toward a Programming Laboratory," *Proc. Inter. Jt. Conf. Artif. Intel.*, Washington, D. C.

TENNENT, R. [1973] "Mathematical Semantics of SNOBOL4," *Acm Symp. Principles Prog. Langs.*, ACM, Boston, 95–108.

TOU, J. and P. WEGNER (eds.) [1971] *SIGPLAN Notices—Proc. Symp. Data Structures Prog. Lang.*, 6, 2.

TURING, A. [1936] "On Computable Numbers, with an Application to the Entscheidungs-Problem," *Proc. London Math. Soc.*, 42, 230–265.

VAN WIJNGAARDEN, A. (ed.), B. MAILLOUX, J. PECK, and C. KOSTER [1969] "Report on the Algorithmic Language ALGOL 68," *Numerische Mathematik*, 14, 2, 79–218.

WATSON, R. [1970] *Timesharing System Design Concepts*, McGraw-Hill, New York.

WEBER, H. [1967] "A Microprogrammed Implementation of EULER on the IBM 360/30," *Comm. ACM*, 10, 9, 549–558.

WEGBREIT, B. [1970] "Studies in Extensible Programming Languages," Ph.D. Thesis, Harvard University, Cambridge, Mass.

WEGNER, P. [1968] *Programming Languages, Information Structures and Machine Organization*, McGraw-Hill, New York.

[1971] "Data Structure Models for Programming Languages. In Tou and Wegner [1971], 1–54.

[1972] "The Vienna Definition Language," *Computing Surveys*, 4, 1, 5–63.

WEISSMAN, C. [1967] *LISP 1.5 Primer*, Dickenson Publishing Company, Inc., Encino, Calif.

WEIZENBAUM, J. [1963] "Symmetric List Processor," *Comm. ACM*, 6, 9, 524—544.

WIRTH, N. [1969] "On Multiprogramming, Machine Coding and Computer Organization," *Comm. ACM*, 12, 9, 489—498.

[1971a] "Program Development by Stepwise Refinement," *Comm. ACM*, 14, 4, 221—227.

[1971b] "The Programming Language PASCAL," *Acta Informatica*, 1, 1, 35—63.

INDEX